DAILY LIFE IN GREECE
AT THE TIME OF PERICLES

Robert Flacelière was born in Paris in 1904 and educated at the *College Sainte-Barbe*, the *Lycée Henri IV* and the *Ecole Normale Supérieure*. From 1925–1930 he was a member of the French School in Athens and from 1932–48 he was Professor of the Faculty of Letters at Lyons. Robert Flacelière was then appointed to the Chair of Greek Language and Literature at the University of Paris, a post he held until 1973 when he became Director of the *Ecole Normale Supérieure*. He wrote a number of books including *L'Amour en Grèce* and *Histoire littéraire de la Grèce*, and was also a *Chevalier* of the Legion of Honour. Robert Flacelière died in 1982.

DAILY LIFE IN GREECE AT THE TIME OF PERICLES

Robert Flacelière

Translated from the French by Peter Green

PHOENIX

5 UPPER SAINT MARTIN'S LANE
LONDON
WC2H 9EA

A PHOENIX PRESS PAPERBACK

Originally published in France in 1959 under the title
La Vie quotidienne en Grèce au temps de Périclès
First published in Great Britain
by Weidenfeld & Nicolson in 1965
This paperback edition published in 2002
by Phoenix Press,
a division of The Orion Publishing Group Ltd,
Orion House, 5 Upper St Martin's Lane,
London WC2H 9EA

Second impression December 2002

A CIP catalogue record for this book is available
from the British Library.

Printed and bound in Italy by
Grafica Veneta S.p.A.

ISBN 1 84212 507 9

CONTENTS

ILLUSTRATIONS

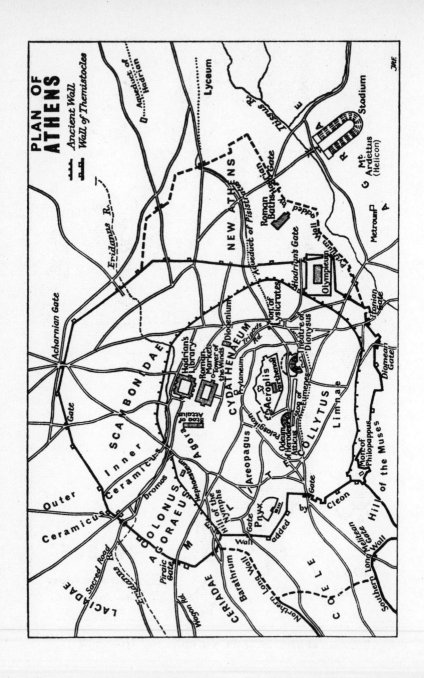

PLAN OF ATHENS

Ancient Wall
Wall of Themistocles

Aqueduct of Hadrian

Eridanus R.

Lyceum

Acharnian Gate

NEW ATHENS

Roman Baths

Aqueduct of Pisistratus

Diochares Gate

Hadrian's Gate

Olympeum

Ilissus R.

Stadium

Mt. Ardettus (Helicon)

Metroum

added

Outer Ceramicus

Inner Ceramicus

Gate

SCAMBONIDAE

Hadrian's Library

Roman Market

Tower of the Winds

CYDATHENAEUM

Prytaneum

Diogeneum

Mon. of Lysicrates

Tripods Rd.

Theatre of Dionysus

Ardettus

Ionian Gate

Diomean Gate

Ceramicus

LACIADAE

Sacred Road

Eleusinian

Dromos

COLONUS AGORAEUS

Melphotron

Agora

Stoa of Attalus

Areopagus

the Acropolis

Odeum of Herodes Atticus

Pelasgicum

Stoa of Eumenes

OLLYTUS

Limnae

Wagon Rd.

Piraic Gate

CERIADAE

Barathrum

Long Wall

Wall

Hill of the Nymphs

Gate

Pnyx

added

Melitean Gate

Gate

by Cleon

COELE

Mon. of Philopappus

Hill of the Muses

Northern Long Wall

Southern Long Wall

JRF.

Greece at the time of the war with Persia (500–479 BC)

TRANSLATOR'S NOTE

A work of this nature presents the translator with certain problems which, in the normal way of things, he is unlikely to have to face. Perhaps the most awkward stumbling-block is the presence of numerous quotations from ancient authors, both poets and prose writers, which are often a paragraph long or more. The prevailing practice is to replace these already-translated extracts with similar existing versions in the new language. But apart from creating awkward problems of copyright, such a procedure makes for lack of unity in the text; and I have therefore, after much thought, preferred to translate all extracts myself, from the original Greek.

Since M Flacelière is using the passages he cites primarily for social illustration, it seemed better to translate them into prose throughout, and not attempt any verse equivalent in the case of poetry. I have also always had his chosen French translation beside me in each case, since many passages in classical authors are either textually dubious, or admit of more than one interpretation; and my business is to convey the meaning M Flacelière attaches to the extracts he quotes, not those which I myself may find there. By the same token, it must not be supposed that I necessarily agree with all M Flacelière's findings; it would be very surprising (classical scholars being what they are) if I did.

At one or two points I have added notes of my own, but these are always clearly distinguished from the author's text or references; and in one instance only I have made a one-word modification to the text itself (see Chapter Eight, p. 225, and note 84 *ad loc.*). Otherwise I have been at considerable pains to present M Flacelière's stimulating essay unchanged in its new English dress. The bibliography, however, has been largely revised for the benefit of English-speaking readers who will not want to be directed to those general works so judiciously selected by M Flacelière for the French student or lay reader.

I cannot pretend to have been wholly consistent in the matter of spelling and transliteration. In the end I have adopted a compromise solution. All Greek words which need to be transliterated direct are printed in italics: the following conventions may be noted – *chi* is represented by ch, *kappa* by k, *upsilon* by y, *omega* by ô, *eta* by é. In all other cases there is an obvious and direct equivalent letter. However, in the general matter of proper names, whether of persons or places, I have adhered to the traditional anglicization of consonants, vowels and diphthongs, on the grounds that many names are familiar enough in this guise to make their respelling irksome rather than helpful. I see no point in printing Aischylos rather than Aeschylus, or dressing up Plutarch as Ploutarchos. Since the French are equally inconsistent in this respect (they turn Statius into 'Stace', and pronounce Pythagoras as though he were some bloodthirsty character called Peter Gore) I am sure M Flacelière will forgive me.

PETER GREEN

PREFACE

The Greeks – not only the inhabitants of the Balkan peninsula, but also those settled in Asia Minor, Sicily, and places as remote as Marseilles or the cities round the Euxine (Black Sea) – all recognized their common racial kinship, and felt bound by a deep-rooted unity of language (despite various local dialects), religion, and *mores* in contradistinction to the world they termed 'barbarian' – that is to say, all those nations that spoke languages other than Greek. Yet the name of Greece – or rather, Hellas – never had any true political significance in antiquity; Greece, properly speaking, never formed a single 'state' until subjugated first by Macedonia and latterly by Rome. Though three cities with more strength and ambition than the rest – Athens, Sparta, and Thebes – did in fact sway the country's destiny through their successive hegemonies, the confederations which they formed were of short duration, and, most important, did not absorb by any means every city in Greece. Each city, however small its territory, was determined to remain absolutely independent, and possessed its own political, religious, and legal institutions; very often, indeed, it also had its own coinage and system of weights and measures.

In the midst of such diversity, and confronted with such a scatter of sovereign states, how can one set about describing daily life 'in Greece'? The existence of the Spartan, enrolled for pre-military training at the age of seven, and kept under a most rigorous discipline of life till he reached sixty, differed radically from that of the Athenian, whose upbringing was more liberal, and whose obligations, in consequence, less exacting. We therefore have no option but to select – though our selection is to a great extent dictated by what literary and archaeological evidence remains available. Almost all the authors from the classical period whose works we still possess were Athenians; and obviously the bulk of the information they provide us with will concern their fellow-countrymen. As for the ruins that have been brought to light by the spade of the archaeologist, they confirm Thucydides' prediction (1.10.2) as to the relative impressiveness of the two cities in after ages; here, too, Athens is much luckier than most other Greek cities, Sparta in particular. It is true that as far as private houses are concerned, the site of Olynthus, in the Chalcidic peninsula, is far richer than that of Athens: but except for the ground-plans of their homes, what do we know about the daily life of the Olynthians?

So it is primarily Athens, and the Athenians, that I shall be discussing in the present volume, though this will not prevent me from glancing at other cities intermittently by way of comparison. Besides, even in antiquity, Athens was already regarded as the Greek city *par excellence*.

As for the period to be covered, I have found it impracticable to restrict myself to the years of Pericles' administration (from about 450 to 429 BC): too many crucial documents in my chosen field are of earlier – or, more often, later – date than this brief epoch. Even if we extend it to take in the fifty years – Thucydides' *pentekontaetia* – from the Battle of Plataea (479) to the death of Pericles (429), we should still have to exclude the vital testimony of Aristophanes and the fourth-century orators. I have at times even cited authors from the third century; but my general rule is to use the 'Periclean Age', in its widest interpretation, as my chronological framework, defining it (conveniently if arbitrarily) as beginning *circa* 450 BC, after the major crisis of the Persian Wars, and ending a century later (350) before the Battle of Chaeronea in 338. Chaeronea ushered in the era of Macedonian domination, and was thus the prelude to those numerous radical changes, both political and social, which characterized what we now call the Hellenistic or Alexandrian Age.

CHAPTER ONE

THE BACKGROUND: TOWN AND COUNTRY

The Greek Landscape – The site of Athens – Roads and districts – Architecture and appearance – Housing – The Suburb – The Countryside

THE GREEK LANDSCAPE

Any traveller flying in to Athens from the west will – the moment he passes over the Gulf of Corinth – perceive the two basic features of the Greek landscape: a predominance of mountains, which cover no less than four-fifths of the entire land-mass, and the deep interpretation of land and sea, the latter thanks to a broken and deeply indented coastline.

These mountains are not particularly high. The loftiest peak of Northern Greece, Olympus, regarded in antiquity as the abode of the gods, is rather less than 9000 feet; Parnassus, in the Central Greek state of Phocis, reaches a bare 7500 feet; the mountains of Attica – Parnes, Pentelicus, Hymettus – range between 3000 and 4500 feet, while in the Peloponnese only Taygetus, Cyllene and Erymanthus overtop the 6000-foot mark. Such mountains are by no means impassable; but ancient Greece never possessed any equivalent of the later Roman highways. Her roads were very poor, dirt tracks for the most part, and seldom wide enough to allow two chariots to pass without difficulty.

As a result the Greeks generally preferred to travel by sea if their journey was of above-average length. Only a hero such as Theseus would prefer the long, dangerous overland route from Troezen in the Argolid to Athens[1] – especially when the journey was so easy by sea. There is no part of Greece more than about sixty miles from the coast. To the Greeks 'the sea' meant, above all, the Aegean, which formed the very hub and centre of Hellas with its numerous scattered islands, stepping-stones between

Europe and Asia. Squalls are frequent in the Aegean, and navigation can be a tricky business except during the summer months;
but few Greeks put to sea at other times of the year.

Throughout history earthquakes have occurred frequently in
Greece. In 464 BC so great a shock struck Laconia that the Helots
took advantage of the general chaos and confusion to launch a
rebellion. In 426 it was the cities of Locris which suffered. In
373 the Achaean towns of Helice and Bura were destroyed by a
combined earthquake and tidal wave. It is well known that in the
present century a succession of seismic shocks have done serious
damage to Heraklion (1926), Corinth (1928), and, most recently,
the Ionian Isles and Santorini. Terrible is the wrath of Poseidon,
the sea-god who wields the trident. It was to him, the 'earth-
shaking' deity as Homer calls him, that the ancients attributed
earthquakes, just as they held Zeus, the 'cloud-gatherer', the god
of sky and air, responsible for storms.

This much-tormented Greek landscape is not, taken by and
large, particularly fertile. True, there is no lack of sunshine,
since Greece lies in what geographers call the 'warm-temperate'
zone. The luminous clarity of the air, especially in Attica, is
quite extraordinary, and we know how often this clarity was
referred to by the Greek poets, who saw it as a perfect token and
symbol of the happy life. But there is a price to be paid for this
wonderful light: drought. Rain is infrequent and scanty, with the
exception of certain storms so sudden and torrential that they are
liable to produce nation-wide disasters. Water-courses, such as
those of the Athenian Ilissus and Cephisus, are most often bone-
dry, but can suddenly become transformed into raging torrents.
Rivers (such as the Peneus in Thessaly, the Acheloüs in Acarnania,
and the Alpheus in the Peloponnese) which maintain their flow
all the year round are very rare. It is easy to understand why, in
so parched a country, rivers and springs assumed such vital
importance that they soon came to be regarded as sacred. Every
river and brook was a divinity, since its water was necessary for
the survival of crops, herds, and human beings alike. Every
spring was a nymph.

The vegetation is that common to all Mediterranean countries,
conditioned by the fierceness of the sun and the minute degree
of humidity in the atmosphere. The forests – far more widespread than at the present time – covered the greater part of the

mountainous areas. They included numerous planes, oaks, and a variety of other species. On the open uplands the trees were replaced by arborescent shrubs and bushes. Those wild beasts – such as the Nemean lion – which had haunted the forests in heroic times were already dying out during the classical period; wolves and bears, on the other hand, are still quite frequent up in the mountains. Over the vast stretches of shrub-clad *maquis*, where myrtle, arbutus, heather and buckthorn grew in rank profusion, abundant game was still to be had – hares, partridges, thrushes, quails, larks; but bigger game, such as the stag and the boar, could now only be found in the mountains; it was here too, up on the high pastures, that cattle were mostly grazed.

Human activity was, and remains, concentrated on the lowest foothills and in the plains, since it is only there that fertile soil, suitable for the cultivation of cereals, is to be found. The vast spaces of the Thessalian Plain made horse-breeding possible, while the Boeotian Plain yielded abundant quantities of corn and barley. Attica was less well endowed, and ancient writers criticized her dry, stony soil. The plains of Marathon and Eleusis were somewhat unhealthy, being in part marshland. Between Mount Hymettus and Laurium lay the Mesogeia, or 'interior', the most fertile and intensely cultivated part of Attica: it was here in particular, among a sprinkling of cypresses, that the region's dwarf vines and olive trees flourished, the former sacred to Dionysus, the latter to Athena, and both a staple element in Attica's economy. Indeed, she had practically no agricultural exports of any kind apart from oil and wine. These were dispatched in clay jars, and help to explain the importance which the potter's art – ceramics – was to assume in Attica. The area's only mineral resources were the argentiferous lead deposits at Laurium; these are being exploited again today, and the yield now includes other metals besides.

THE SITE OF ATHENS

The historian Thucydides knew that all Greeks had, in former times, inhabited miserable little villages. The unification of several neighbouring villages might provide the nucleus for a town. This is what happened in the open seaward plain contained by the mountains of Parnes, Pentelicus, and Hymettus, ultimately producing an urban agglomeration with the Acropolis as its centre. According to legend it was Theseus who united all the townships of Attica by the process known as *synoikismos*, so that their inhabitants became, without distinction, Athenian citizens. But the central agglomeration was itself made up of several villages – a fact that explains why its name always remained plural: *Athenai* literally means 'the Athenses'.

In the fifth century BC the Acropolis had become a vast plinth on which nothing stood save the temples of the gods. It had not always been so. Once again, Thucydides is our informant: 'Before Theseus' time,' he wrote, 'the present Acropolis was the town, together with the low-lying region beneath it, particularly to the south.'² Of the whole urban area in the plain it is, in point of fact, the part immediately south of the Acropolis which appears to have been inhabited longest: in the swampy region known as the Marsh, not far from the Ilissus, several extremely archaic cult-centres have been located.

Athens, then – like most cities both ancient and modern apart from colonies and special foundations – was conceived without any deliberate plan; and there was certainly nothing rational about its subsequent development. The ground-plan reflects the vaguely organic growth of the Attic people within their allotted orbit – the immediate environs of the Acropolis, the knoll of Colonus Agoraeus, the Hill of the Nymphs, the Pnyx, the Museum, Mount Lycabettus and Mount Ardettus: Athens too could justifiably be called the 'city built upon seven hills'.

It was primarily round the focal point of the Acropolis, and its southern annexe the Marsh, or Limnae, that urban life developed: from the end of the seventh century BC it expanded towards the north-west, forming the workers' quarter known as the Ceramicus, a name sufficiently explained by the large numbers of potteries and kilns found there. It was in this quarter that Athens' public place of assembly, the *agora* of the Ceramicus, was situated: a centre that combined religious, political and economic functions. Here, on the *orchéstra* or dancing-floor, were held the earliest dramatic representations, in honour of Dionysus, god of the theatre. Here too the assemblies of the people took place, in an area originally marked off with ropes stretched across it, the so-called *perischoinisma*. The *agora* was also used as a market for agricultural produce and industrial goods. But the market, and the passers-by cluttered the place up so much that very soon it became highly inconvenient to hold political assemblies or dramatic festivals in so overcrowded a spot. As a result the former were transferred to the Pnyx (to the west of the Areopagus and the Acropolis) and the latter to the sanctuary of Dionysus Eleutherus (on the southern slopes of the Acropolis). Only the market remained *in situ* at the *agora*; though the members of the Council and the *prytaneis* used it as their meeting-place, and a Citizen Assembly could always be held there if occasion demanded.

Athens' first city-wall was constructed in the sixth century BC, during the reign of the tyrant Pisistratus and his sons, who brought Athens to a high peak of prosperity and power. The wall was enlarged and fortified by Themistocles at the time of the Persian Wars, in the years immediately following the Battle of Salamis (480). These new ramparts had a more or less oval perimeter, some four miles long and fifteen hundred yards across. The Acropolis was not quite in the middle, but slightly to the south of centre, as a result of the growing importance of the Ceramicus and its *agora*. This wall was linked, on its south-west side, to the Long Walls, and embraced several other quarters, each corresponding to an urban deme (an administrative division created by Cleisthenes in 508 BC, at the same time as the ten tribes). On the northern side there was the vast residential quarter of the Scambonidae, with access to the country through the Phyle and Acharnian Gates. To the south-west, between the Ceramicus and the Marsh, were the lower-class quarters of Collytus and Melité. On the eastern side, beyond the ramparts, stretched a pleasant ex-urban area known as Agryle, which, many centuries later, was to be incorporated in the city by the Emperor Hadrian, under the name of 'New Athens'.

The Long Walls linked Athens to its port, the Piraeus. North wall and south wall were each nearly five miles long: they enclosed a military highway a stade broad – that is, something like a hundred and fifty yards. (In peacetime, however, easily the most frequented road between Athens and the Piraeus ran outside the Long Walls, on the northern side.) The effect of these walls was to turn city and port into a single fortress, which was easy to defend, and made it possible for the Athenians to bring in supplies even during wartime, since the bulk of their traffic was seaborne. Thus according to Pericles' master-plan, so long as

Athens kept the mastery of the sea, she would remain safe from any Peloponnesian attack. The Lacedaemonians and their allies might ravage Attica, cutting down the vines and olives, but Athens continued to be revictualled from the Piraeus, and her fleet of warships inflicted some nasty defeats on the enemy.

The Piraeus, like the city-wall of Athens, was first put on an organized footing by Themistocles. We read that when the Athenians decided to develop it they called in Hippodamus of Miletus, a philosopher with a special interest in geometry, who has some claim to be called the father of the axial-grid town-planning system – in which all the streets cut one another at right angles, breaking up the town into square or rectangular 'islands'. In point of fact, such ruins as survive from the ancient Piraeus do not suggest that the plan was all that regular; but it does betray signs of genuine town-planning. The area allotted to public buildings is clearly defined, so as to allow for a controlled development of every sort of port installation, ranging from offices to temples, from dockyards to warehouses.

ROADS AND DISTRICTS

Unlike the Piraeus, the town of Athens was born and grew without any plan at all, as though by pure accident. In the fifth century its religious centre was still the Acropolis, where Pericles was to rebuild, in so magnificent a fashion, the temples that had been destroyed by Xerxes' army. Here – in sharp contrast to the city sprawling beneath it – everything was magnificently planned. It has been suggested that 'at Athens rational, planned aesthetics could only triumph on the Acropolis, since there the Persians had made a *tabula rasa* of the past'.[3] But Athenians' social and economic life, and a large proportion of their political and legal activities beside, took place in the Agora of the Ceramicus, which – thanks to American archaeologists – we are beginning to know fairly well.

Some distance from the still partially preserved Dipylon Gate, where the roads from the Academy and Eleusis – the Sacred Way – debouched, and not far from the cemetery of the Outer Ceramicus, the *Dromos*, or main road, which ran beside the river Eridanus, now divided into two: one branch, known as the Panathenaic Way, lay diagonally across the Agora, and reached

the Acropolis from its south-east side, while the other branched
off right to the south, and linked up with the Street of the Tripods,
where the fine monument of Lysicrates may still be seen to this
day. To the right of this last road, immediately after it forked off,
stood the Agora's most ancient public buildings, sandwiched
between it and the knoll of Colonus Agoraeus. On this last there
stood (it is still largely intact) the temple known as the Hepha-
esteum, and also as the Theseum. Starting at the north end,
there were the King's Portico (or Portico of Zeus: it seems very
probable that these two titles designate the same monument);
the temple of Apollo Patröus; the Metröun, or sanctuary of the
Mother of the Gods (Cybele) in which the public archives were
lodged; the *Bouleutérion*, where the Council of Five Hundred met,
and the *Tholos*, a circular building in which the fifty *Prytaneis*,
or permanent committee of the Council, met in session and took
their meals. On the other side of the same road, at some little
distance from it, stood the altar of the Twelve Olympian Gods
(regarded as the city's official centre), the temple of Ares, and the
monument of the eponymous heroes who had given their names
to Cleisthenes' ten tribes. We do not know the exact site of the
famous Painted Colonnade (*Stoa poikilé*), built under Cimon's
administration; nor that of the Sanctuary of Theseus, dating
from the same period, to which in 475 were brought the bones of
the hero himself, discovered by Cimon on the island of Scyros.
Only the bodies of heroes could be buried within the city limits:
cemeteries, such as that of the Ceramicus, were always situated
extra muros.

In the second century BC the south and east sides of the Agora
were enclosed by two vast colonnades; but in the fifth century
– though further excavation on the site may possibly modify
this conclusion – it looks as though only the west side had a
truly monumental appearance. This would not, doubtless, match
up to the majestic town squares of the Hellenistic period, which
were entirely surrounded by the most sumptuous colonnades;
but it must have been very impressive none the less.

When we try to get an idea of what the east side of the Agora
was like, the part which served as the market proper, we have to
turn to the written word for guidance: there is no other available
evidence.

There were a number of plane trees in the Agora, planted by

7

Cimon.[4] Every foot of space available was crammed with innumerable booths and workshops, since custom was greatest in the Agora, and it was here that shopkeepers and craftsmen did their best business. The 'invalid' for whom Lysias wrote a defence speech had this to say in the course of his plea for justice before an Athenian court:

> My accuser claims that my shop is used as a meeting-place by a parcel of ne'er-do-wells, who have run through their own fortunes, and attack anyone doing his best to build up a little capital. But please note that such charges are no more applicable to me than to any other shopkeeper; nor is there a penny to choose between my customers and theirs. You all like to stroll round and drop in somewhere – at the barber's or the cobbler's or the perfumer's, whichever happens to suit you; and you nearly always pick a shop near the Agora rather than one on the outskirts.[5]

Many of these shops were, quite certainly, very flimsy affairs, like modern fairground booths, mere clapboard huts roofed with skins or wattles. Demosthenes tells us how, during the panic which followed the news of Philip's occupation of Elatea in 339 BC, all these market-booths were set on fire – partly to clear space for an immediate meeting of the Assembly, and partly as a signal to bring in the country-folk from the districts around Athens.[6]

Despite their higgledy-piggledy lack of order (which must in itself have been rather picturesque: one can get some idea of it from an Oriental *souk*) these stalls appear to have been roughly grouped according to the particular merchandise they were offering for sale. One corner of the Agora was reserved for the booksellers, another for the sellers of pots and other household utensils. Here you could buy vegetables and wine, and there women's cosmetics, or myrtle-wreaths for funerals. Resident Athenians were not the only people to patronize the market or the barbers' shops; country-folk came swarming in as well, not only to make purchases but also to sell their own produce. Sometimes – especially at the time of the Great Dionysia, towards the end of March – many strangers would be in town, visitors from tributary Greek townships taking a look at the great imperial city to which they owed allegiance.

ARCHITECTURE AND APPEARANCE

The monuments on the Acropolis and, to a lesser degree, those of the Agora, as well as the suburban parks where the various *gymnasia* were located – the Academy on the west side, Cynosarges to the south, the Lyceum away to the east – always excited the admiration of visitors. On the other hand the streets of Athens – apart from the Dromos and the Street of the Tripods – were narrow, tortuous, and lined with what were for the most part extremely shabby houses. In this respect a sharp distinction must be made between the various quarters: between, for example, that of the Scambonidae, which was a wealthy citizen's first choice, and those such as Collytus, Melité, or the Ceramicus, which were both popular and populous in every sense. Here various crafts and trades would be found grouped in districts or streets, rather like the stalls in the Agora. The very name 'Ceramicus' reminds us that potters abounded there. Besides the potters there were carpenters and leatherworkers, butchers, fishmongers, and many others. These traditions were preserved down the ages; even today, in modern Athens, the lower-class quarters round the foot of the Acropolis (not far from the site of the ancient Agora) still have the Street of the Slipper-Makers, the Street of the Coppersmiths, and the Street of the Blacksmiths.

On the whole, the lower part of the town was not much to look at. A traveller in the third century BC wrote: 'The city of Athens is very drought-ridden: its water-supplies are inadequate, and being so ancient a town it is badly planned. A stranger, coming on it unawares, might well doubt whether this could be the city of the Athenians.'[7] It seems very probable that between the fifth and third centuries the general appearance of Athens had been considerably improved: and therefore this judgment applies, *a fortiori*, to its condition during the Periclean Age.

If anyone finds this a surprising statement, he should bear two important facts in mind. Firstly, in all Mediterranean countries men spend a great part of their time out of doors, often only returning home to sleep; and during the summer, even so, they frequently sleep out on the terrace, to keep a little cooler. It is true that Athens can get very cold in winter, but such periods of low temperature are normally brief, and as soon as the sun comes out again the weather improves. The second point is this. All people in antiquity – not the Greeks alone – were imbued with a

9

naturally religious spirit, and were much more concerned to build sumptuous dwelling-places for their gods than to guarantee themselves a minimum degree of comfort.

In this respect the contrast between the magnificent order of the Acropolis and the random chaos of the lower town is highly significant. National pride was fostered by the sight of the temples Pericles erected on the Acropolis, and also, no doubt, by the colonnades and municipal buildings of the Agora; but to build over-sumptuous habitations for the use of mere mortals would have seemed sacrilegious. The Delphic motto 'Nothing in excess' found – here as elsewhere – an apt application.

Perhaps the tyrants of the sixth century had demanded more for their personal satisfaction; but in the democratic, egalitarian Athens of the succeeding centuries, private luxury was always regarded as something scandalous. Observe the way in which Demosthenes attacks certain politicians of his day, who used what he regarded as their ill-gotten wealth to embellish their private houses:

(Statesmen in the old days) led circumspect private lives, and their behaviour conformed to the traditions of our city: so much so that (as any of you who knows them can see for yourselves) the houses of men such as Aristides or Miltiades or any other famous citizen of those times was in no way more distinguished than its neighbours. The reason is clear: politicians did not then enter public service to line their own pockets, but because each felt it his duty to serve the common good of his city. They dealt faithfully by their fellow-Greeks abroad; they showed piety towards the gods; they acted with democratic impartiality over the city's domestic affairs. Not surprisingly, they won us a great measure of prosperity . . . Today, I am told, our public life may be somewhat in decline, but our civic amenities are vastly improved. What proof of such an assertion have we? Trumpery details such as repointed parapets on the city-walls, or repairs to fountains, or newly surfaced roads. Take a good look at the men who implement this kind of policy. Some have jumped from poverty to affluence, others from obscurity to the highest public honours. Some have built themselves houses that outshine our public edifices; and indeed their fortunes have risen in proportion as those of the city have declined.[8]

Such arguments, though they undoubtedly smack of demagoguery, do nevertheless reflect the opinion of a majority of Athenians; and it seems a plain inference that those who wanted to play an active part in the city's political life avoided too ostentatious a display of luxury, such as might excite envious feelings among their fellows.

This passage from Demosthenes also shows us that there was a programme for the renovation of walls, roads and public fountains being carried out in his day. Responsibility for public finances originally devolved on the Council of the Areopagus, composed of ex-*archons*, which met on the Hill of Ares (*Areoupagos*) close to the Acropolis. After Ephialtes and Pericles reduced the powers of this aristocratic council, public finances were taken on by the Council of Five Hundred. But to help the Council in its task, it soon became necessary to create several 'colleges', or administrative sub-echelons, of civil officers with various specialized functions. There were the ten *astynomoi* (five for Athens and five for the Piraeus) whose responsibility it was to provide a city police force and maintain public works. Control and supervision of the markets was undertaken by ten *agoranomoi*, similarly divided between the upper town and the port. The duties of the *astynomoi* covered a remarkably wide field. They were responsible for public morality, which meant keeping an eye on flute-girls, dancers, and courtesans. They were also responsible for the upkeep of the roads, which involved them in such tasks as rubbish-disposal, sanitary inspection, and ensuring that private property-owners did not encroach on the public highway. They supervised building and organized festivals. They were particularly to ensure that dung-collectors (*koprologoi*) did not discharge their loads less than ten stades from the city-wall.[9] The *agoranomoi* enforced the regulations governing price-controls and the leasing of space in the markets: for checking weights and measures they had the assistance of ten inspectors called *metronomoi*. There is a passage in Xenophon where someone congratulates the handsome young Charmides on having, by a well-balanced course of physical exercise, developed his arms as well as his legs; he goes on, jokingly: 'You seem to me so proportionately developed in all your limbs that if you cut yourself in two, and weighed the top and bottom halves of your body before the *agoranomoi*, like a couple of loaves, I'm sure you wouldn't find yourself liable for a fine.'[10]

We also find the *astynomoi* assisted by a body of subordinate officials known as *hodopoioi*, or road-surveyors, who in this capacity had a pool of public slave-labour at their disposal. Finally, Athens had an official architect-in-chief, though this person seems to have enjoyed strictly limited powers, at least as far as the lower part of the city was concerned. Doubtless his sole responsibility was the maintenance of temples and other public buildings.

In a town as dry as Athens, the water-supply was the most important problem of all. The sixth-century tyrants had been much concerned by it, and had – as a result of major public works – provided Athens with several fountains, of which the *Enneakrounos*, or 'fountain with nine mouths', was the most famous. In the fourth century the water-supply was in charge of a special official, whose importance was such that instead of being picked by lot, like the majority of his fellow-officials, he was appointed by election. He had to enjoy sufficient private means to contribute to the expenses of his office. An Athenian decree of the year 333 BC honours the 'Supervisor of Fountains', one Pytheas of the deme Alopéce, 'for having zealously acquitted himself in the performance of all his duties; and in particular for having completed the new fountain beside the Sanctuary of Ammon, and having built the fountain of the Sanctuary of Amphiaraus, where he has ensured constant water and adequate drainage'. In recompense Pytheas was to receive a golden crown valued at a thousand drachmas.[11] It is clear that this official's duties were not restricted to the fountains of Athens itself, but included those throughout Attica, since he had provided a new fountain for the Sanctuary of Amphiaraus, which was situated quite close to the Boeotian frontier.

All these officials, however, however seriously they took their responsibilities, could not make all that much difference to what was, by definition, a pretty hopeless state of affairs. The streets of Athens scarcely ever ran in a straight line, but rather followed the natural contours between the hills; frequently, far from maintaining a constant width, they would become even narrower as they progressed. The houses were badly placed, some being set far back from the road, some projecting over it. Rain-water (such of it as was not collected in private cisterns) and dirty slops all went out into the street, emptied through doors or out of windows. By the fourth century, however, the open gutter down the middle of the street had in many cases been replaced by underground drains and sewers. The streets were not paved; the water pouring down them turned them into a sea of rutted mud, and during periods of bad weather they soon became veritable middens. Such conditions show a fundamental ignorance of common hygiene, let alone of urban development, and it is easy to see how epidemics – such as the Great Plague of Athens in 429, which carried off Pericles – could spread so rapidly in such a town. (The situation was further exacerbated in 429 by the rural population being packed inside the city limits; this produced quite abnormal crowding.) Naturally the streets were not lit at night, as is shown by the following anecdote, which Plutarch tells to illustrate Pericles' lofty self-control:

> One day, in the Agora, Pericles was abused and reviled continually, from morning till night, by some idle lout; he put up with this individual's attentions uncomplainingly, though he had a great deal of urgent business to get through at the time. When evening came, he walked home unperturbed, though the man followed at his heels, still shouting the most unpleasant insults at him. As Pericles went indoors – it now being dark – he told one of the house-slaves to take a torch and escort his tormentor to his own home.[12]

The 'heliasts' (roughly equivalent to empanelled jurymen) in *The Wasps*, dragged out of bed while it is still dark to go and try a case, avoid the mud-holes as best they can, aided by the lamps which young slave-boys carry ahead of them to light their path.[13]

HOUSING

The same third-century traveller who expressed disappointment at the general appearance of Athens[14] added: 'The majority of the houses are extremely shabby, and only one or two reach a decent standard of comfort.'

Some poorer dwelling-places were hewn out of the rock-face, for example, in the quarter known as Coële ('The Hollow'), at the point where the Long Walls met the city ramparts. One of these artificial caves consists of three rooms, plus a lean-to entrance passage, and is known, erroneously, as 'the prison of Socrates': in point of fact it was a rock-dwelling, which later, during the Roman occupation, served as a tomb. Other houses were simply built against a squared-off rock wall, or else set on small levelled ledges. Near these troglodyte dwellings cisterns have been found hollowed out of the rock.

In the lower-class quarters, most of the houses were extremely small, built on one floor only and containing only two or three cramped little rooms. When they did possess an upper storey, with one or two bedrooms, access to this was often by an external wooden staircase. These garrets might be let to poor country people or non-Athenians who wanted a *pied-à-terre* in town. 'There was an upper floor in our house,' one litigant observes, 'which Philoneus occupied when he was residing in the city.'[15]

The walls of these houses were made either of wood, baked brick, or stonework held together by a mortar which was largely mud. They were so easy to knock holes in that burglars never bothered about forcing doors or windows: they much preferred to go directly through some skimpy party-wall. So universal was this practice that burglars in Athens were known as *toichorhychoi*, or 'wall-piercers'. One Athenian, well known for his house-breaking activities, was surnamed Chalcous, or 'man of bronze'. On a certain occasion he was jeering at Demosthenes in the Assembly, for being so industrious and conscientious as to spend half the night working on his speeches. The orator replied: 'I am well aware that my late-burning lamp must be an embarrassment to you, Chalcous; and as for you, men of Athens, can you wonder that robbery is so rife, when thieves are brazen, and walls mere mud?'[16] Such walls were normally common to adjacent houses, and the Athenians could have done what the Plataeans did in 431, after a surprise assault by the Thebans: 'In order to assemble secretly, without being observed on the streets, they dug through the party-walls of their houses.'[17]

Any houses of which traces survive in Athens are always built on a very tiny scale. Their doors, Plutarch tells us, always opened outwards, and before going out people used to rap on them as a warning, to spare passers-by the disagreeable experience of walking into a too-suddenly opened door. Roofs were flat, and windows – when they existed at all – had to be very diminutive, little more than skylights, since the use of transparent glass was unknown in antiquity. If one wanted to block windows up in bad weather, the only way to do it was with some opaque material

When such houses were rented out the landlord was liable to take extremely energetic action if he did not receive regular payment when it fell due. He would remove the front door, or strip off the roof-tiles, or, as a last resort, refuse the tenant access to the well. Such penniless tenants would be thrown out to join the other homeless vagrants – and in Athens there was a substantial number of them.

Amongst those whom we could categorize as down-and-outs, several distinct groups must be taken into account. There were respectable people who had fallen on hard times, succumbing to the implacability of fate, or of their fellow-men, or both. There were also the 'voluntary poor', those philosophers who were to become a common phenomenon during the Hellenistic Age, whose proud boast it was that they despised not only wealth, but even the most basic necessities of life. We have not yet reached the epoch of Diogenes and his barrel; but Antisthenes, the founder of the Cynic School, was a disciple of Socrates. As Teles noted in the third century:

> If the Cynic philosopher feels the need to rub himself with oil, he goes to the public baths and rubs himself with the oily leavings [that the bathers have removed from their bodies by means of the *strigil*]. He will take his handful of small fish and grill them over the fire in some blacksmith's forge: pour a little oil over them, sit down, and so take his repast. In summer he sleeps in temple sanctuaries, and during the winter, in the public baths. He lacks for nothing, since he is content with what he has.[18]

We know that as early as the Periclean Age poor folk used to seek refuge in the baths when the weather turned cold, to get a little warmth; sometimes they huddled up too near the furnace, and burnt themselves. In Aristophanes' *Plutus*, Chremylus asks Poverty: 'What good can *you* bring us except burns from the baths?'[19]

More often than not food had to be cooked in the open air, on a brazier, as it still is today in many a Greek village. Indeed, prior to the fourth century houses do not appear to have been equipped with kitchens; and even where a kitchen existed, there was not, as far as we can tell, any permanent range. The fire was kindled outside, and only brought indoors when the wood or charcoal was red-hot, and therefore producing less smoke. But the problem of how to get rid of smoke still arose in winter, nevertheless, since then people needed to keep themselves warm. The simplest method (still to be found in use today in some peasant houses) consisted in removing a tile or its equivalent from the roof when the fire was lit: this could be done from inside, with a pole. These air-holes (*opai*) – not to be confused with the windows (*thyrides*) – might also be located in the upper part of the wall, under the cornice.[20] But the ancient texts also mention 'smoke-conduits' (*kapnodoké*)[21] made of baked clay, a fact which proves that something less rudimentary than the air-hole technique was also in use. Such chimneys are mostly found in more civilized houses than those we have so far been considering: the homes of the rich – or at least comfortably off – middle classes.

Of the ten thousand houses which Xenophon, at a rough estimate, reckoned to the Athens of his day,[22] most must have resembled the poorer sort of dwelling discussed above; but some at least, especially in residential quarters such as those of the Scambonidae, were, it is clear, more comfortable – at any rate by the fourth century, since they aroused the envy of Demosthenes' contemporaries. At Vouliagméni in Attica there has been unearthed, near the sanctuary of Apollo Zôstér, a peristyle-type building which appears to date from the sixth century; another large mansion, also with colonnades, and of the same period, has been found in the Athenian Agora[23] – but are these in fact private houses? It seems highly unlikely: they were more probably municipal buildings of a residential nature, designed to accommodate some body of officials.

We know that, at least as early as the fourth century, there existed in Athens certain large buildings leased out to numerous tenants, rather on the lines of our modern apartment blocks, as we learn from the orator Aeschines:

Synoikia is the name by which we call a residence shared among a number of tenants, while the simple term *oikia* denotes a house occupied by one family only. If a doctor sets up in one of the small shop-premises that line our streets, it becomes known as a surgery. If the doctor leaves and a blacksmith takes over from him, the place is then labelled a smithy. The same thing applies if the incoming tenant is a fuller or a

> carpenter ... When prostitutes arrive there with their procurer, the house promptly turns into a house of ill-fame.[24]

No large, wealthy houses that are incontestably private residences have so far been discovered in Attica. To get a picture of what such places were like, we must turn to the remarkable remains excavated at Olynthus, in Northern Greece, on the Chalcidic peninsula; and those on the island of Delos, in the Aegean.[25] The houses discovered at Olynthus date from the fourth century. The best-preserved display an almost completely four-square ground-plan. All the rooms open, not on to the street, but on an inner colonnade (*pastas*), leading to a courtyard (*aulé*) approached by way of a lobby (*prothyron*). This arrangement already foreshadows the interior-peristyle houses of the Hellenistic and Roman periods. The *pastas* is normally orientated so as to face due south, in accordance with the advice given by Socrates in the pages of Xenophon: 'When a house faces south, the sun penetrates its rooms in winter, while in summer it shines high overhead, above the roof, and leaves us in the shade.'[26] The front door might be set either on the south or the east side of the house without it making any difference to the positioning of the *pastas*. Similarly, the mosaic-decorated salon where banquets were held, the *andrôn*, could be either at the north-east or south-east corner, whereas the vast living-room (*diaitétérion*) was invariably situated on the north side, behind the *pastas*, through which it got its light. Lastly, the ordinary dining-room (*oikos*) was located between the bathroom and the kitchen. A store-room and a work-room completed the tally of ground-floor apartments. The upper floor was used for bedrooms only: the conjugal chamber (*thalamos*), the women's apartments (*gynaikeia*), and garrets under the eaves where the slaves slept.[27] It is interesting to note the habitual juxtaposition of kitchen and bathroom, the reason for which is not far to seek: the kitchen could pass on some of its warmth next door. In *The Wasps* of Aristophanes Bdélycléon is holding his father Philocléon prisoner in his own house, against the old lunatic's determination to get out and join his fellow-jurymen. Bdélycléon, hearing his father crashing about, says to one of his servants: 'The old boy's got into the kitchen now; he's scratching around the furnace like a mouse. Go and make sure he doesn't slip away through the hole in the bath-tub.'[28] It has recently been suggested that what we translate as 'the hole in the bath-tub' was really the hot-air pipe pierced through the wall separating the two rooms[29] – but in that case how could Philocléon have got out once he was in the bathroom? The joke is a fairly laboured one – the idea of Philocléon being small enough to squeeze down the waste-pipe – but those who know their Aristophanes will not hesitate to credit him with it. In the event Philocléon emerges through the chimney, and says, triumphantly [v. 144]: 'I'm smoke escaping.' In the ruins of Olynthus a roof-tile was discovered pierced with an elliptic hole 47 cms long by 23 cms broad, through which a man could easily have wriggled up on to the roof. By using this archaeological evidence in conjunction with Aristophanes' text, we may infer that houses of such a type were in existence in Athens from the latter part of the fifth century. Another passage, from Demosthenes this time, adds confirmatory evidence: an insolvent debtor, just as the authorities are arriving to arrest him, conceives the idea of escaping by way of the tiles, and slipping away across the rooftops to some friendly neighbours of his.[30]

The houses on Delos were no longer restricted to the single arcade of the *pastas*; they had colonnades round several sides of the inner court, and on occasion ran to a full peristyle, which closed it in completely. But these houses date from the Hellenistic period, and there is no proof that such a pattern was already established in Athens during the fourth century.

What is certain is that many private residences had at least one upper floor. In one of Lysias' speeches we find a middle-class Athenian describing his domestic arrangements as follows:

I must tell you, to begin with (these details are very relevant) that my small house has an upper floor: the layout is the same both upstairs and down, with the women's quarters on one floor and the men's on the other. Then came the birth of our child, which my wife decided to nurse herself. Every time she wanted to bath it, she had to come downstairs, and risk falling on the staircase; that is why I decided to move up to the first floor myself, and put the women down below. I soon got used to the new arrangement, and my wife was thus enabled to sleep with the baby on frequent occasions, to give it the breast and stop it crying.

He adds: 'In my naïvety, I thought my wife the most respectable woman throughout the entire city.'³¹ Alas for innocence: she very soon took advantage of this reallocation of sleeping-space to entertain her lover in great comfort on the ground floor, while her husband was snoring away upstairs.

Very often the upper storey projected over the street, though the civic authorities regarded these balconies as an illegal encroachment. Hippias, the son of Pisistratus and tyrant of Athens, had already 'offered for sale such houses as encroached upon the public highway in any manner, eg with staircases, balconies, and outward-opening doors'.³² Iphicrates, in the fourth century, proposed that the Athenians should tax every such projecting edifice, as a way of improving the city's impoverished public finances.³³ The upper-storey balconies, as we know from fourth-century vase-paintings, might be adorned with balustrades and pillars.

Originally the internal decoration of houses was restricted to a plain coat of plaster over the walls. By the fourth century we find mosaics, such as those uncovered at Olynthus, adorning the *andron* or the courtyard enclosed by the peristyle. Phocion's house in the Melité quarter 'was decorated with bronze plaques, but otherwise simple and bare'.³⁴ It is doubtful whether the line in Bacchylides which says that 'the houses were resplendent with gold and ivory'³⁵ should be taken at its face value. The walls of wealthier citizens' houses were hung with tapestries and embroidered cloth, and sometimes their ceilings were panelled and decorated. Alcibiades was said to have shut the painter Agatharchus up in his house for three months on end while he completed a series of frescoes under duress.³⁶ Yet the much-vaunted luxury of Alcibiades' house was a decidedly relative affair:

The catalogue of his property, sold at public auction in consequence of the sentence pronounced upon him after his trial for complicity in two notorious affairs – those of the mutilated Herms and the profanation of the Mysteries – does not suggest a very high or spendthrift degree of affluence. Two *himatia* which *may* have been the 'purple cloaks' that Plutarch mentions; a list of furniture, itemized in minute detail, of which the most luxurious lot was a dining-room suite consisting of four tables and a dozen couches, the latter of 'Milesian workmanship', and totalling no more than a hundred and twenty drachmas in value – such, it appears, when one gets down to facts, were the wardrobe and furnishings of a man whose private luxury outstripped the more modest way of life practised by normal Athenians in the fifth century BC.[37]

Apart from beds, tables, chairs and stools, the main items of furniture were the chests and caskets used for storing clothes and jewelry in. It seems probable, too, that many painted vases, the signed work of famous artists, were not used for any practical domestic purpose, but were kept as ornaments in certain rooms of the house, like those decorated wall-plaques or rare vases which we find in the apartments of the well-to-do today. The house of the rich Athenian Callias (described by Plato in his *Protagoras*) was, we may suppose, very like this. Under the *prostôon* (the colonnade nearest the entrance) the famous sophist would stroll up and down, in conversation with a group of friends and disciples: it was here – after a little bother in persuading the doorkeeper, a eunuch, to admit them – that Socrates and the young Hippocrates found them, a company whose wisdom of discourse was matched only by the harmony of their movements.[38]

But such houses were a rarity in Periclean Athens. Many bore a closer resemblance to hovels, and hardly any of them were large enough to allow the luxury of sanitary installations. As a result the *amis*, or chamber-pot, was in common use,[39] even among garrison troops, who sometimes employed it for coarse practical jokes.[40]

At night the Athenian removed his cloak and tunic-girdle, but kept the tunic itself on in lieu of a nightshirt. From a very saucy passage in Aristophanes we learn that the beds were wooden frames criss-crossed with webbing, on which the *psiathos* (a thin mat woven from reeds or osiers) was placed as a kind of mattress. Pillows and blankets were in use, but sheets were unknown. In summer people preferred to sleep out on the flat roofs of their houses, so as to enjoy the cool night air to the full. On such occasions they rolled themselves up in blankets, only to have their slumbers disturbed, more often than not, by the attentions of fleas and lice: it was the bites of such creatures that drove poor old Strepsiades out of his bed.[41]

With living conditions such as these, hygiene was bound to

remain fairly rudimentary. We shall have more to say in Chapter
Six about personal cleanliness, which, it is clear, varied a good
deal according to the individual's social class and standard of
living. Rats, flies and mosquitoes spread every kind of disease,
and epidemics were by no means rare. The filth and stench which
predominate today in many Eastern cities were assuredly not
absent from Athens during the classical period.

THE SUBURB

If one left Athens by the Dipylon Gate, on the north-west side
of the city, one found oneself almost immediately in the main
cemetery, which lay on either side of the road to the Academy.
This necropolis dates back at least to the eighth century, since
excavations there have revealed examples of those large geometric-
style funerary urns known as 'Dipylon vases'. It was here, at a
later date, that the Athenian State was to erect a common tomb
for soldiers killed on active service, and here that their memory
was celebrated by some officially nominated speaker – a Pericles,
a Demosthenes, a Hyperides.

The avenue of tombs revealed by the excavator's spade forms
a secondary road, to the south of the main highway leading to the
Academy, near the banks of the Eridanus: there are qualities
about it which make one think of the Alyscamps at Arles, or the
Roman Via Appia. Its sides are flanked by terraces, divided by
low walls into a series of little plots, each belonging to an Athenian
family, whether of citizens or resident aliens, and each containing
the tombs, not only of members of the family, but also of their
slaves. The funerary monuments consist, for the most part, of
slabs of dressed marble (*stelai*) decorated with bas-reliefs; but
full-scale shrines have also come to light, complete with ornamental façades. Some tombs were surmounted by marble urns,
in particular *lecythoi* (oil-flasks) and *loutrophoroi* (black water-
jars), both these types being elongated vases with one or two
handles, used to denote the graves of unmarried persons. Slaves
had to make do with plain round cippi (truncated columns) that
bore their names and nothing else. We find representations of
symbolic animals – bulls, lions, dogs, Sphinx or Sirens – either
on tall plinths or set up in the corners of the plots. The sculptured
stelai generally portray scenes that symbolize farewells or reunions; we also find a young lady called Hegeso at her toilet, and

a twenty-year-old Athenian knight, Dexileus, striking down an enemy before perishing himself.

If one continued westward away from Athens, beyond the grounds of the Ceramicus cemetery, one came to the deme of Colonus, where the poet Sophocles was born, and finally reached the Academy – that is to say, the Park of Académos, a name that may denote either the former proprietor of the land, or else a local hero who had his rustic shrine there. The Academy was a large sacred grove, which had been walled round by Hippias, Pisistratus' son. It was dedicated to Athena, and here one could see the goddess' twelve sacred olive-trees (*Moriai*), which were said to have been grown from a slip of the olive tree in the Erechtheum: these trees provided the oil that was given as a prize to the victors in the Panathenaic Games. Various other gods and heroes had altars there: notably Hermes, the tutelary deity of all *gymnasia*, and Eros, the God of Love. The Athenians were fond of strolling through the grounds of the Academy. Cimon, who 'turned the hitherto parched and waterless Academy into a well-watered garden with shady avenues', also established a *gymnasion* there;[42] its running-tracks were used by the *ephéboi* (youths of eighteen entering upon military service), who also paraded before the Council there. Recent excavations have enabled us to locate the site of this *gymnasion*, together with the ruins of a *palaistra* (wrestling-school), some sections of the enclosing wall, and a small temple.

Aristophanes gives a very pleasant picture of this *gymnasion* in *The Clouds*, while describing the ideal at which the old-time system of education aimed:

Flower-fresh, oil-smooth, you will spend your time in the *gymnasion*, instead of carrying on as young folk do today – taking part in thorny, ill-tempered, hair-splitting debates in the Agora, or getting caught up with some mimsy, pettifogging, dishonest lawsuit. You will go down to the Academy, and there, under the sacred olives, crowned with a wreath of green reed, you will run a course against some decently-behaved young man of your own age, redolent of woodbine, and happy unconcern, and deciduous white poplar, rejoicing in springtime, when plane and elm whisper together. If you follow these precepts of mine, and stick to them, you will always have a robust chest, a clear complexion, and broad shoulders . . .[43]

But if the Academy has become famous, so famous that it has given its name to all our 'academies' today, the credit must go to Plato; for it was there, in 387, that he established a regular school. Since nothing like our universities existed in ancient Greece, during the period of the 'sophists', ie professional scholars and philosophers, the *gymnasia* became a recognized meeting-place for well-defined intellectual groups whom we should call 'schools'. It has been well said that 'the *gymnasia* are the exact equivalent of those "cultural centres" in which our contemporary urban architects plan to house all activities concerned with our physical or intellectual well-being'.[44] The *gymnasia* had to be supplied with water for the athletes to wash in, and it is certainly no accident that the Academy was situated close to the Cephisus.

Similarly the Lyceum, on the east side of Athens, which was to house the later school of Aristotle, stood near the source of the Eridanus, and Cynosarges in the south, where the Cynic Antisthenes taught, was not far from the Ilissus – doubtless within reach of that charming spot so memorably described by Plato in the *Phaedrus*, the words being put into Socrates' mouth for the occasion:

> By Hera, it is a delightful place to rest in. Here we have this tall, wide-spreading plane-tree; and see how high and shady the willow grows – it is in full blossom, too, so that the whole place smells sweetly of it. The spring looks most charming as it flows beneath the plane-tree; and – having dipped my foot in it – I should say its water was very cool. To judge from the figurines and statuettes dotted about the place, it looks as though it is a shrine of the Nymphs and the river-god Achelous. Then again, observe what a pleasant, gentle breeze pervades it, and hark to that shrill summer chorus of cicadas in the air! But the most pleasant thing of all is the turf growing here on this gentle slope, just thick enough to be comfortable when you lean your head back on it.

Phaedrus expresses surprise at this enthusiasm, coming as it does from a man 'who never leaves Athens – indeed, who never so much as sticks his nose outside the city-walls, let alone thinks of crossing the frontier'. To which Socrates (who did in fact, as we know, frequent the Lyceum, and occasionally the Academy too) made the following reply: 'The countryside and the trees refuse to teach me anything, whereas the men I meet in Athens teach me a great deal.'[45] Nevertheless this passage does indicate a genuine love of nature on Plato's part. The third-century *Idylls* of Theocritus mark a completely new development in literary awareness as regards man's attitude to nature; but these two passages from Aristophanes and Plato I have quoted are sufficient demonstration that the Greeks were no less susceptible than we are to fresh green meadows, beautiful trees, or the peaceful atmosphere of the countryside – a fact confirmed by the sites they chose for their *gymnasia*.

THE COUNTRYSIDE

Doubtless many rich middle-class Athenians had a country residence outside the walls, in the fashionable suburb of Agrylé or elsewhere. But the roads were appalling. Apart from the Sacred Way to Eleusis, along which the religious procession of the Mysteries passed, and the two highways, one civil, one military, linking Athens to the port of Piraeus – where traffic must have been heavy and constant – there were practically no communications except dirt roads or mere tracks, which one travelled by mule or donkey or on foot: a light two-wheeled chariot would make very heavy weather of them.

Furthermore, the moment it was dark these roads became even less safe than the dark, twisting alleys in Athens itself, where thieves and cutpurses lurked. In Aristophanes' play *The Birds* the Athenian Euelpides gives the following account of such a misadventure that befell him:

> I was unlucky enough to lose a good cloak of Phrygian wool, and all because of a cock crowing. I had been invited to some child's name-feast, on the tenth day after the birth. Well, I had a drink or two in town first, and snoozed for a bit; and then, some time before the other guests went off to dinner, this cock started up. I thought it was morning, and started straight off to Halimus [a village close to the Piraeus]. But hardly had I got outside the walls before some footpad gave me a great clout from behind with a cudgel. Down I went, but before I could open my mouth to roar for help, he'd whipped my cloak and made off.[46]

Naturally there were inns along the roads to entertain travellers and offer them bed and board. Once again it is Aristophanes who provides the evidence for their existence – though at the same time casting serious doubts on their cleanliness. Consider this passage from *The Frogs*: Dionysus is enquiring of Heracles as to the best route to follow to Hades:

> Tell me, in case I need them, the names of those who befriended and entertained you when *you* went down there after Cerberus; give me a list of them – not to mention the best harbours, bakers' shops, brothels, snack-bars, lodging-houses, fountains, roads, towns, turn-ins, and the landladies who had fewest bugs on the premises . . .[47]

For many years rural Attica had contained a number of large country estates, owned by the 'Eupatridae', or aristocrats. In Solon's day the top class of citizen (from whose ranks alone the office of archon could be filled) comprised those Athenians whose annual income reached or exceeded five hundred *medimnoi* of grain. [The *medimnos* in Attica was about 51.8 litres: the nearest English equivalent is the bushel, at 36.3 litres.] These were the class known as the *pentakosiomedimnoi*, and they must have harvested, each, some six hundred bushels *per annum*. Even in the fifth century Miltiades' son Cimon was rich enough to boost his popularity by the most extraordinary acts of largesse:

> He turned his house into a public *prytaneion* for all citizens [that is, he gave free meals to all who demanded them, just as great benefactors of the State were entertained free in the *prytaneion*, or city hall] and allowed strangers to wander through his grounds, eating or carrying away fruit and other seasonal produce just as they pleased.[48]

Pericles, too, possessed land and country houses in Attica; these he swore he would hand over to the State if the Spartans (who were then invading the country) deliberately refrained from ravaging them so as to render him suspect amongst his fellow-citizens.[49] Attica's economy still rested basically on agriculture and cattle-raising, with trade as a sideline. Some big houses have been found out in the rural demes, but their remains are so scanty that we can glean little information from them, and nothing for certain.

We will do better, then, to consult the description given by

Xenophon the Athenian of his estate at Scillous, a part of Elis in the Peloponnese:

> The land is watered by the Selinous river . . . which abounds both in fish and shellfish; there are also good hunting districts on the estate. Xenophon erected an altar and temple to Artemis there . . . Game such as boar, deer, and stags was taken either in the sacred enclosure itself, or else in the neighbouring territory of Pholoé. The estate lies on the road from Sparta to Olympia, about twenty stades beyond the temple of Zeus. In the sacred enclosure there is meadowland, and low tree-clad hills suitable for the raising of pigs, goats, cattle, and indeed horses . . . The temple is set in an orchard planted with fruit-trees, which bear exceedingly well in due season.[50]

But it is above all in the *Oeconomica* that Xenophon gives us most information concerning the life of a country gentleman. He pens a most glowing tribute to agriculture there, regarding it as the source of all the virtues. This idyllic picture is without doubt linked with his own personal experience, and we shall return to it again later.

Meanwhile the growth of democracy in Athens demanded crippling sacrifices from her wealthier citizens, in the shape of *leitourgiai* (public services such as the *trierarchia* or *chorégia*, the former requiring one to equip a trireme for public use, and the latter a chorus for performance at a dramatic festival). Such impositions, and – an even more serious matter – the constant breaking up of property amongst numerous heirs, soon diminished the number and importance of the big estates. In the fifth century Attica was mostly cultivated by smallholders, who worked their little plot of land themselves, assisted by a few slaves and farm-labourers. This middle class of small landowners, a hard and stubborn breed, formed the backbone of Athens during the Persian Wars, and from their ranks, beyond any doubt, came the bulk of the men who fought at Marathon – those *Marathanomachoi* whose glorious memory Aristophanes and other Athenian writers took such delight in extolling.

Up in the hills life was hard. The principal means of livelihood there were the breeding of livestock (mainly pigs, sheep, and goats), the collection of honey from the hives on Mount Hymettus, and charcoal-burning – this last flourishing on the wooded slopes of Mount Parnes, where the large country village of Acharnae also stood. Aristophanes' comedy *The Acharnians* paints us a very realistic picture of these rough, stubborn hill-dwellers.

Down in the plain there was little cultivation of cereal crops, and Athens had to import a large proportion of the wheat she consumed; but bumper harvests were obtained from vineyards and fruit orchards, with figs and olives giving an especially good yield. Strepsiades in *The Clouds*, Dicaeopolis in *The Acharnians*, and Trygaeus in *The Peace* are among the most representative portraits of these Attic peasants, whose land – in the happy days of peace – provided them with a decent livelihood. Here is Strepsiades, who has moved into the city, mourning the un-trammelled, ample life he led in the country, before his disastrous marriage:

I led the most enjoyable kind of rustic existence – one of the Great Unwashed, never bothered by bugs, lying around any old how, my world full of bees and sheep and olives. And then I went and married a regular city belle: Megacles' niece, no less, a stuck-up, prinking, expensive bit, typical of *that* family – me, a common country bumpkin! Still, I wed her, and when we got in the bridal bed together, there was I stinking of wine-lees, drying figs, and greasy wool-bales, while *she* was redolent of myrrh and saffron and deep tongue-kisses, rich food, long bills, and those two great goddesses, Copulation and Childbirth.[51]

Dicaeopolis in *The Acharnians* tells a similar story:

I gaze out towards the country, yearning for peace, sick of the town, missing my own old village, where you never heard the word 'buy', it just wasn't known, for charcoal, vinegar, oil, or anything else; our land yielded everything for us, no 'buy' there.[52]

Lastly Trygaeus, in *The Peace*:

I long myself to be off to the country, and to hoe my little plot once more. Remember, gentlemen, the old life you once led, which Peace made possible for you – the figs both fresh and dried, the myrtle and the sweet wine, violets blowing beside the well, the olives we miss so much![53]

This picture is doubtless embellished somewhat for the sake of the argument, since Aristophanes is out to make his audience hate war by emphasizing the rewards of peace, and we may well wonder whether he himself ever tilled the soil or worked in a vineyard. Nevertheless it seems clear that many peasants in Attica, despite the rough and primitive conditions which they endured, lived well contented with their lot.

CHAPTER TWO

POPULATION: CITIZENS, RESIDENT ALIENS, SLAVES

The concept of a city – Civic life – The City Assembly – Bouleutai, Prytaneis *and Magistrates – Metics – Slaves – Numerical proportions of the classes*

THE CONCEPT OF A CITY

A city, in ancient Greece, can be identified with the men who occupy it rather than the territory over which it extends. Inter-State frontiers, unless determined by the course of a river, remain vague and imprecise, being normally located in what were known as *eschatiai* – mountainous border regions, high pasture-lands where lean herds crop the all too scanty grass. What determines the *polis* is its population. Official documents never refer to 'Athens', but always to 'the Athenians', or 'the people', or 'the city of the Athenians'. The classical *polis* has been well defined as 'a community of citizens, wholly independent, with sovereign power over the individual citizens who compose it, bound by cults and regulated by laws'.[1]

'Wholly independent' – it is true that, though members of a city might know themselves part of a far larger ethnic and cultural unity, nevertheless that city would never acknowledge itself politically subordinate to any other power. It was to preserve their precious autonomy that several city-states, Athens and Sparta at their head, threw back the barbarian hordes first of Darius and afterwards of Xerxes. This fierce passion for independence, a fundamental characteristic of ancient Greece as a whole, did nothing but good, since it prevented any permanent federation of the various Greek states into a unified political entity. Each city dreaded, more than anything else, the thought of subjugation by a rival, while at the same time doing her best to dominate her own immediate neighbours. So it came about that Athens, Sparta and Thebes all, at various times, created alliances (*symmachiai*), in which the member cities – described as 'allies' to soothe their delicate susceptibilities – were virtual subject states; but the overriding urge towards autonomy always rendered such alliances precarious and of brief duration.

'With sovereign power over the individual citizens who compose it' – the ancient city was an end in itself, an absolute which left none of its members any great measure of liberty, and severely restricted all individual activities. In this sense, it was a basically totalitarian concept, which is obvious enough when we look at Sparta. In Athens, however, the more liberal aspects of the Athenian character may tend to mask this profound truth, though they cannot ever eradicate it. Freedom of speech and opinion, especially in the religious sphere, simply do not exist – as the 'impiety trials' and the death of Socrates testify. We should note, too, that it was not under the oligarchic régime of the Thirty Tyrants that the hemlock was administered to Socrates; that act was left to the restored democracy which succeeded them.[2] A citizen could be ostracized, in the technical sense, without any specific charge having been laid against him.

'Bound by cults' – the ancients made no distinction between matters spiritual and temporal. Athens was Athena's city, and the priests of Athena, like those of the other gods, were city officials. Religion – the official religion, at least – was one with the State; even certain mystery cults, such as the Eleusinian Mysteries, were under State control and patronage. It is this which explains why the State was *inevitably* intolerant: the bond uniting all its citizens was not merely political and social, but also sacral.

'Regulated by laws' – these were the *nomoi* which regulated every citizen's life from the cradle to the grave, even in Athens, though there such subjugation was enforced with less inflexible rigour than at Sparta. Doubtless these laws had been passed by the citizens themselves or their forefathers (ancestral tradition and unwritten law were no less binding than constitutional legislature by decree of the Assembly), and it was this fact that made them feel themselves free men and Greeks when confronted with barbarians – men subjected to a master who might be unjust or arbitrary. But this freedom, in fact, operated within severely fixed limits. Demaratus told Xerxes: 'If the Spartans are free men, yet they are not wholly free: they have a master, the Law, whom they fear far more deeply than your subjects fear you.'³ Plato personifies these laws in the *Crito*:

> Look at it this way [says Socrates]. Suppose we were on the point of escaping from this prison, or whatever it should be called, and the Laws and the Commonwealth were to come before us and say: 'Tell me, Socrates, what is it you intend to do? Is it not your purpose, in undertaking your present course of action, to destroy us, the Laws, and the whole city insofar as you are able? Or do you believe a state can survive, and not be brought to ruin, in which the courts lack power to enforce their verdicts, and see them made null and void by the whim of some private individual?'⁴

CIVIC LIFE

Athens was a direct democracy, where every citizen could, by way of the Assembly (*ecclésia*), have some share in the government of the State. Though the ancients were not altogether ignorant of representative government as practised in modern societies (the constitution of the Boeotian Federation, as it was functioning between 447 and 386, appears – as far as we can tell – to have been a typical case of representative government⁵) nevertheless the majority of ancient cities were directly governed by their citizens in general assembly, and the Assembly as such was the source of all authority, legislative, executive, and judiciary. Obviously such a form of government is only practicable in states of extremely limited size; the only place today where we can get some idea of what the *ecclésia* in an ancient city-state must have been like is the Local Assembly of a Swiss canton.

In order to qualify for citizenship, and the right to a place in the People's Assembly, two preliminary conditions had to be fulfilled. Firstly, one's father – and after Pericles' law in 451, one's mother too – must be Athenian-born. Secondly, one must have attained one's majority. This took place on the candidate's eighteenth birthday; but as he then did two years' military service, he did not reach the Assembly until he was twenty. The Athenians could, if they so wished, confer citizenship upon a non-Athenian by special decree; they could also deprive a person of citizenship by condemning him to *atimia* – loss of civic rights.

An Athenian citizen's daily life was dominated by his concern with affairs of state: in principle at least, since it is obvious that country-folk from the rural corners of Attica – people such as Strepsiades, Dicaeopolis and Trygaeus before their compulsory move into the city – could not be constantly leaving their farms and the work on the land, especially at the times of ploughing and harvest, in order to come and sit in council on the Pnyx. This explains why, with an approximate total of some 40,000 Athenian citizens, a quorum of 6000 voters sufficed to deal with even the most serious decisions.[6] But such absenteeism, though inevitable, was kept down as far as possible; and no doubt this was the reason why every meeting of the Assembly, together with its agenda (*programma*), had to be published four days in advance, so that country members might have adequate warning.

Public opinion was very hard upon anyone who appeared not to concern himself with affairs of state, and it was not till the end of the fourth century BC, after Athens' loss of independence at Chaeronea (338), that a philosophical school, that of Epicurus, dared to suggest that the wise man should occupy himself exclusively with his own personal affairs, and the pursuit of his own happiness. In the days of the 'Marathon warriors' no one ever dreamed that the individual's happiness could be considered in dissociation from the prosperity of the State. The institution of a fee for those citizens present at meetings of the Assembly (*misthos ecclésiastikos*), which took place after the Peloponnesian War, was not a mere demagogic measure, as has so often been asserted: without such an indemnity how could the *thétes* (that is, the Athenian wage-earners or proletariat) possibly have attended sessions which sometimes lasted all day, and took place four times a month at least, often much more frequently?

If we were describing the daily life of a twentieth-century European, there would be no need to include any account of his electoral obligations, since he only has to fulfil them at infrequent intervals. But a citizen of Athens not only took part in these regular meetings of the Assembly: he was also liable to be nominated, for a year, as a magistrate or judge or member of the Council of Five Hundred (*bouleutés*), and in such a capacity he would certainly find the great majority of his time occupied by affairs of state. It is essential, therefore, before we go any further, to give at least an outline of how the Athenian political and admin strative system worked. The organization of justice will be dealt with in Chapter Nine.

The Assembly on the Pnyx was not the only one which a free-born Athenian citizen was obliged to attend. There were also the assemblies of the phratries, the demes, and the tribes, which dealt with matters of local government. In 508 Cleisthenes had abolished the ancient divisions of Attica, rather in the same way as the French Revolution was later to replace provinces by *départements*, and had reallocated the citizens in ten tribes (*phylai*), each of which had a hero of Attica as its patron, and bore his name: Erechtheis after Erechtheus, Aegeis after Aegeus, Theseus' father, Pandionis after Pandion, and so on. Each tribe possessed land, and elected officers to administer its property. The same was true of the demes, which formed a sub-division of the tribe. (To begin with there were a hundred demes, ten to a tribe: but the number afterwards increased.) The Ceramicus, Collytus, Melité and Scambonidae were urban demes; Acharnae, Marathon and Decelea were rural demes. Every Athenian citizen was officially designated by three names: his own, his father's, and that of his deme, eg Pericles, son of Xanthippus, of the deme Cholargus, or Alcibiades son of Cleinias, of the deme Scambonidae, or Demosthenes, son of Demosthenes, of the deme Paeania. The *demarchos*, or chief official in the deme, had duties roughly comparable to those of a modern mayor. He kept the nominal roll of citizens belonging to his deme, which formed a sort of parish register or electoral list; and he was elected for a year's term of office by his fellow-parishioners.

Finally we come to the phratry, a sub-division of the deme, about the organization of which we know nothing. Its name suggests a group of families linked by blood-relationship, since the word certainly derives from the same source as the Latin *frater*. These assemblies of tribe, deme and phratry hedged the Athenian citizen about with a whole network of obligations and rights; but they met less often than the City Assembly.

THE CITY ASSEMBLY

The first scene of Aristophanes' comedy *The Acharnians*, produced in 425 BC, shows us the Assembly in session. It is, of course, a caricature rather than a realistic portrait, but if we make the necessary allowances and corrections, we can nevertheless take

Aristophanes as a reliable guide. He may be rather less complete and exact than Aristotle, but he is a good deal more entertaining. We can supplement the picture with details from another of his plays, the *Ecclesiazusae*, or *Women in Parliament*, the very title of which contains a joke: since women in antiquity enjoyed no political rights they could not take part in an Assembly, and therefore the feminine participle of the verb *ecclésiazô* ('to take part in a meeting of the *ecclésia*') was never employed – except here by Aristophanes.

We have already met the hero of *The Acharnians*, Dicaeopolis.[7] When the play opens he is all alone on the Pnyx (ie the place where people are 'packed together', or 'squeezed close') which was the regular meeting-place for the Assembly during the fifth century. (Earlier it had been held in the Agora, and later, in the fourth century, it moved across to the more comfortable seats in the Theatre of Dionysis.) The hill on which the Pnyx was situated stands south-west of the Areopagus, opposite the main approach to the Acropolis. The remains of the Pnyx itself are still visible to this day, on the rocky outcrop facing the Areopagus and the Propylaea; a vast semi-circular esplanade, some hundred and twenty yards in diameter, built above a massive retaining wall and capable of holding up to twenty thousand people. The *bema*, or speaker's rostrum, was carved out of the solid rock and still survives – a square block of stone with three steps leading up to it, flanked by two other small stepped approaches on either side, and a bench and some small seats behind. From here a speaker could see – and make his audience look at – both the Propylaea and the Parthenon. The seats and benches were for official clerks. The square cube of stone itself may perhaps have been the altar of Zeus Agoraeus, on which a sacrifice was offered up at the beginning of every debate. Behind and above this platform there are traces of two stepped seats, carved in the rock, and doubtless reserved for the Presidents of the Assembly. The latter originally consisted of the fifty *prytaneis* of any one tribe, members of the Council (*boulé*) who formed a permanent committee for one tenth of the year, ie for about thirty-five or thirty-six days, this period being known as a *prytaneia*. In the fifth century the President of the Assembly was a chairman appointed daily by lot from among the *prytaneis*, and known by the title of *epistatés*.

Dicaeopolis, all alone on the Pnyx, is bored and impatient:

nothing he has ever suffered in the past, he declares, can compare with what he feels now 'at seeing the Pnyx deserted when a regular Assembly (*kyria ecclésia*) has been summoned to meet at dawn' [vv. 19–20]. There were four such Assemblies held monthly, each under a different set of *prytaneis*, and sessions began at daybreak. The sign of a debate in progress was the *semeion*, some sort of emblem or banner raised above the Pnyx.[8]

But though a little later [v. 40] Dicaeopolis asserts, with obvious exaggeration, that it is already nearly noon, the Athenians have not yet left the Agora in the Ceramicus: 'They're down in the Agora gossiping, keeping well clear of the red-painted rope' [vv. 21–2]. The Agora was, in fact, a favourite resort for every idle layabout in town: and Athens had many such. Demosthenes was to taunt them a century later with the words: 'You are always strolling about asking each other "What's new?" '[9] and the author of *Acts* echoes him: 'No townsman of Athens, or stranger visiting it, has time for anything else than saying something new, or hearing it said.'[10] How could such loungers be made to turn up on the Pnyx? The police – a body of public slaves –barricaded the roads leading to the Agora, and herded citizens in the right direction by means of a rope smeared in wet red paint, which they carried stretched across the road. Being smeared with red paint was quite unpleasant enough in itself, and I see no reason to suppose that Athenians to whom this happened were *also* compelled to pay a fine, or found themselves docked of their *misthos ecclésiastikos*.

Dicaeopolis goes on: 'Even the *prytaneis* haven't put in an appearance yet. They'll turn up hours late, pouring in all together, each trying to elbow his way into a front seat . . .' [vv. 23–6] and goes on a little later: 'What did I tell you? Here come our noonday *prytaneis*, and just look at the way they're scrambling for the best places!' [vv. 40–2]. As has been said already, the fifty *prytaneis* presided over the Assembly, under the chairmanship of their *epistatés*.

The town crier now called on the citizens to come forward and take their place 'within the *katharma*' – that is, the consecrated enclosure [vv. 43–4]. This term reminds us that at the beginning of every session certain priests known as the *peristiarchoi* sacrificed pigs on the altar, and traced a sacred circle right round the Assembly with the blood of the victims; after which the town crier addressed a prayer to the gods, and called down curses upon any person who might attempt to deceive the people.

However, as is only to be assumed, Aristophanes has here shortened and simplified the procedure drastically for the sake of dramatic effectiveness. In actual fact the President ordered the town crier to read the report of the Council (*boulé*) on the agenda for the day (this report, drafted as a bill for the Assembly's ratification, was known as a *probouleuma*); he then asked the Assembly to signify by a show of hands whether they accepted the bill as it stood, or wanted to debate it. It was only in the latter case that the crier pronounced the ritual formula which we find at line 45 of *The Acharnians*: 'Who wishes to take the floor?' The citizen who got up would then come forward to the speaker's platform, and place a myrtle-wreath on his head, which gave him a sacred and privileged status.[11]

On this occasion the speaker is one Amphitheus, who claims that the gods have charged him with the task of going and negotiating a peace with Sparta, and complains that the *prytaneis* refuse to grant him travelling expenses (*ephodia*) for his mission. At once, on a sign from the President, the crier summons 'the archers' [v. 54] to seize Amphitheus and expel him from the Assembly. These were the Scythian archers who acted as a police force, and stood guard over the Assembly.[12]

Dicaeopolis protests at this, but the crier silences him [vv. 55–9] and brings in the ambassadors whom Athens had sent to the King of Persia, obviously with the aim of soliciting his aid against the Peloponnesians, since the Greeks' internecine quarrels more and more tending to leave the Great King as arbiter of the situation. Such embassies did, in fact, report on their mission, first to the Council and latterly before the Assembly, as we learn (for example) from the two fourth-century speeches of Demosthenes and Aeschines concerning Athens' embassy to Philip of Macedon. As we might expect, this particular embassy's report is an exaggerated caricature. Aristophanes uses it to express the jealousy felt by the Athenian man in the street for politicians and orators who got disgustingly well paid (two drachmas a day, v. 66) for going on pleasant trips at the State's expense, trips which they made last as long as possible. The ambassadors have brought back with them a so-called Persian envoy, the 'King's Eye', accompanied by two eunuchs: all three are unmasked as Athenians by Dicaeopolis. Yet despite this, the 'King's Eye' is invited by the Council to the Prytaneum, or City Hall [vv. 123-4] ie to an official state reception. This practice is confirmed by numerous decrees that have been preserved, declaring that 'the people's will is that the ambassadors shall be entertained tomorrow in the Prytaneum as guests of the State'.

Next the crier introduces yet another ambassador, just back from the court of Sitalces, King of Thrace, one of Athens' allies. The ambassador presents some Odomantian warriors, an earnest of the relief army which Sitalces, he says, is shortly sending to help the Athenians. Nevertheless, these foreigners contrive to surreptitiously filch Dicaeopolis' bag of garlic; at which he exclaims, in outraged tones: 'How *can* you let me be treated like this, *prytaneis* – in my own city, and by a mob of barbarians to boot? You're not going to debate the question of paying the Thracians, I'll put a stop to *that* right now. I declare a sign from heaven: I felt a spot of rain.' [vv. 167-71] The crier at once proclaims: 'The Thracians are to leave, and come back the day after tomorrow. The *prytaneis* have adjourned the Assembly' [vv. 172-3]. A mere raindrop may not have been enough to halt the Assembly's deliberations, but it is certainly true that a storm, an earthquake or an eclipse could do so – providing the *exegetai* decided they were a sign of Zeus' will, an unfavourable omen. This is why, in another of Aristophanes' plays, the personified Clouds tell the Athenians:

We render the City more service than any of the gods; yet to us alone, who guard and protect you, you offer neither sacrifice nor libation. If some scheme is stupidly concocted, at once we thunder, or send down torrents of rain. When you were planning to elect Cleon general – that Paphlagonian tanner, the gods' pet abomination – we knit our brows and frowned horribly, and heavens! what a crash and flash of thunder and lightning we raised! The Moon went into eclipse, and the Sun's wick shrank right inside him – he said he wouldn't give you light any more if you elected Cleon.[13]

The Assembly could reject the Council's report, or modify it with such amendments as they thought fit. Xenophon has preserved us an account of two especially dramatic sessions of the Assembly, during which the commanders who had fought and won the naval battle of the Arginusae Islands (406 BC) were charged with failing to pick up the crews of sunk ships. The debate could not be finished in a single meeting of the Assembly 'since it was now late and the show of hands could not have been counted' as they were raised for the vote (*cheirotonia*).[14] So we see that a session which began at daybreak could go on till dusk. In such circumstances we can understand why many Athenians, like Dicaeopolis, brought a bag of provisions along with them.

BOULEUTAI, PRYTANEIS AND MAGISTRATES

The *prytaneis* who presided over the Assembly were drawn from the Council, or Boulé. This Council, which in certain respects foreshadows the representative system adopted by modern parliaments, consisted of five hundred members, fifty from each tribe; the fifty *bouleutai* of a tribe acted as *prytaneis*, or Presidents of the Council, for one tenth of the year, or, roughly, thirty-six days.

The *bouleutai* were drawn by lot from such members of the deme over thirty as chose to put themselves up for candidature. Selection by lot was supposed to indicate the will of the gods. In one urn were placed a number of tablets bearing the candidates' names; in another, a corresponding number of beans, some black, some white, the latter equal to the number of *bouleutai* that had to be elected. A name and a bean were drawn simultaneously: if the bean was white, the candidate whose name had been taken from the second urn was declared a *bouleutés*.

These candidates were not as numerous as one might suppose, ncsie the office involved spending an entire year in the service of the State, with corresponding neglect of one's private affairs. The remuneration was no more than five obols a day, and a drachma (that is, six obols) for the *prytaneis*: since we know that a good worker could make two drachmas a day, this scale of fees cannot be called exactly extravagant. Legally an Athenian could not act as a *bouleutés* more than twice in his life. Since five hundred *bouleutai* were required *per annum*, and the total number of citizens was about 40,000, it is clear that every Athenian, if he so desired, had a good chance of serving on the Council.

The *bouleutai*-elect now had to go before the Council in office at the time and undergo a form of examination (*dokimasia*). If the results of this proved favourable, they were then sworn in.

Their meetings were held in the Bouleutérion, which stood in the Agora of the Ceramicus. Throughout their year of office they remained exempt from military service and had special seats in the theatre. Their sessions were convoked by the *prytaneis*.

The latter were accommodated in the Skias or Tholos, a circular building near the Bouleutérion, but not to be confused with the Prytaneum – the city's public banqueting hall, to which were invited those, either Athenians or foreigners, whom the State wished to honour: ambassadors, for instance. At least one third of the *prytaneis* were always in residence there, day and night. Their *epistatés*, drawn by lot every day, and holding office for twenty-four hours from sunset, was in fact the Athenian Head of State, though his authority remained extremely brief. He had the state seal in his custody, together with the keys to those temples where public funds were stored; he also presided over the Council and the Assembly. A citizen could only be appointed to the office of *epistatés* once, which meant that out of fifty *prytaneis* thirty-six at least undertook the Presidency (in years with an intercalated month there were *prytaneiai* lasting longer than thirty-six days), so that the average Athenian, with a fair chance of serving on the Council if he wanted to, had almost as good a prospect of spending one day in his life as President of the Republic.[15]

The *prytaneis* were the supreme officers of state; but there were many other public officials, always organized in groups or 'colleges', and nearly always in a college of ten members, one from each tribe. We have already referred to the *astynomoi*, the *agoranomoi* and the *metronomoi*.[16] There were also various financial officials: *pôletai* (public works contractors), *praktores* (tax-collectors), *apodektai* (receivers), *kolakretai* and Treasurers of Athena (the last two named being responsible for the safe-guarding and administration of public funds), and *Hellenotamiai*, or 'treasurers of the Greeks', who levied tribute from allied cities and other similar sources.

On the civil side the most important office was that of *archon*; on the military, that of *stratégos*. There were nine archons; this uneven number is explained by the fact that the office was older than any other, long pre-dating Cleisthenes and his division of Attica into ten tribes. However, the college also had a secretary, thus bringing the total number of members up to ten, so that the archons – and their secretary – could each be responsible for one particular tribe, during the allocation of heliasts between the various courts, for instance, a highly complicated process described by Aristotle.[17] They also had widely differentiated individual functions. The 'eponymous' archon, who gave his name to the year in which he held office, was responsible for family lawsuits (particularly those to do with inheritance) and also for certain religious festivals such as the Greater Dionysia. The 'king-archon' had inherited the religious and judicial functions once exercised by the king. The *polemarchos* was, primarily, commander-in-chief; but he also supervised trials involving foreigners or resident aliens, and organized the public funerals held for citizens killed in battle. Lastly there were the six *thesmothetai*, the 'guardians of the laws'.

The archons, like most other public officials, were chosen by lot, the process being similar to that described above for the election of *bouleutai*. But the ten *stratégoi* were elected by the Assembly, one to every tribe, and could be re-elected an indefinite number of times. Their duties, indeed, called for so high a degree of competence that to choose them by lot was quite out of the question; and those of proven ability must, in the interests of the State, be allowed to continue in office. They were, broadly speaking, responsible for national defence, and during a campaign commanded Athens' armies and fleets. They negotiated treaties on behalf of the State, and could formally request the *prytaneis* to convene the Assembly. Pericles, as we know, governed Athens year after year without bothering to hold any greater office than that of *stratégos*.

The suspicion felt by the Athenian democracy towards any individual it entrusted with even the slightest degree of power was quite extraordinary. The large number of officers of state – always collected in colleges – was one major safeguard. Like the *bouleutai*, too, they could not take office until they had undergone a very searching scrutiny, the *dokimasia*, which investigated not only their competence but also their personal morality. Every official was sworn in, and could always be stripped of his office by a vote of the *ecclésia* – even condemned to death, as were the *stratégoi* who won the Battle of Arginusae in 406. At the end of their year they were further liable to a most rigorous inspection of their accounts (*euthyna*). In the last resort, any politician whose behaviour in office suggested an over-ambitious nature could be 'ostracized', ie exiled for ten years by vote of the Assembly, without any specific charges having been brought against him.

METICS

The ability of the Athenians to devote so large a proportion of their time to the city's political affairs was due to the fact that many of them were freed from all domestic activities by the other two classes in their society: resident aliens, and slaves. The city-state of antiquity, as I said at the beginning of this chapter, was totalitarian by nature: totalitarian in its curtailment of individual liberty among citizens, and even more totalitarian in all its dealings with foreigners, whom it regarded, *a priori*, as enemies. Any foreigner living in a Greek city was more often than not a prisoner-of-war, a slave. At Sparta there took place a periodical expulsion of foreigners, known as a *xenelasia*. Athens was more liberal in her attitude, and allowed numerous non-Athenian Greeks to reside within her boundaries – even to enjoy quite appreciable rights there. These domiciled foreigners were known as 'metics' (those who 'live with'): it is hardly surprising that this word, like that other Greek term 'barbarian', used to designate all non-Greeks, has kept its pejorative sense down the centuries. The intense national pride felt by each individual city-state is more than enough to explain it. Most Athenian metics were Greek by birth, though Phoenicians, Phrygians, Egyptians, and even Arabs were sometimes found amongst them.

Metics formed a very considerable proportion of the total Athenian population during the fifth century: there were about 20,000 of them, or something like half the total number of citizens. They were liable to nearly all an ordinary citizen's financial obligations, including the bulk of the *leitourgiai* (public services); for instance, the *chorégia* associated with the Lenaean Festival. Those chosen by the archon were required to maintain and rehearse a dramatic chorus for this festival, at their own expense. On the other hand, they were exempt from the *trierarchia*, since this involved the command of a warship. Metics also paid a special tax – a very light one, it must be admitted – called the *metoikion*: twelve drachmas per annum for men, and six for women, or the equivalent of six and three days' work respectively. Metics were debarred from ephebic training, but they were allowed to use the public *gymnasia* (from which slaves were excluded); they served in the Athenian army as hoplites or light infantry, and above all in the fleet, as rowers; their main military function was to help in the territorial defence of Attica. Marriages between citizens and metics were, doubtless, sanctioned by law; but from 451 BC onwards even the child of an Athenian father and a resident alien mother did not qualify for citizenship, much less one born of an Athenian woman who had married a metic. They could acquire household chattels and own slaves, but were not permitted to buy houses or property, unless granted this right of acquisition (*enktesis*) as a very exceptional favour. In such cases it was generally accompanied by another privilege, *isotelia*, which, from the financial viewpoint, put them on exactly the same footing as any ordinary citizen.

Legally they could be put to the torture, though this provision was seldom enforced. If they appeared in court they were represented by a citizen who acted as their *prostatés*, or patron. A man who murdered a metic could be punished by exile, but not executed, as he was liable to be for the murder of a citizen: it follows that the law did not regard a citizen's and a metic's life as of exactly equal value. Their possessions, however, were safeguarded by the *polemarchos*, whose word was final in all lawsuits where metics were involved. Resident aliens were entirely at liberty to celebrate the cults of their own country, and for this purpose could form religious associations known as *thiasoi*. Such foreign deities as the Thracian goddess Bendis or the Great Mother of Phrygia won numerous converts amongst the Athenians themselves. A special place was found for metics in the celebration of certain official festivals, such as the Hephaesteia or the Panathenaic Games, where they appeared side by side with the allies and cleruchies (that is, groups of citizens resident in an Athenian colony). We may conclude, then, that metics were treated fairly liberally in Athens – at least as compared with the attitude taken towards them by Sparta and many other Greek cities – and we can more readily understand the claim that Pericles makes in the pages of Thucydides: 'Our city is open to all men: we have no law that requires the expulsion of the stranger in our midst, or debars him from such education or entertainment as he may find among us.'[18]

The metic population was distributed through the demes, and

thus incorporated, for administrative purposes, with the main citizen body; but, needless to say, metics possessed no political rights. They were allowed to perform certain strictly subordinate public duties, such as those of town crier, public medical officer, tax farmer, or public works contractor; but most of them were in business or industry, or else practised what we nowadays call the liberal professions.

They were often to be found in industrial crafts, particularly weaving, tanning, pottery-making and metal-working. In the last-named field, indeed, they appear to have enjoyed a virtual monopoly. Cephalus the Syracusan, drawn for us by Plato, in the first few pages of *The Republic* as an extremely likeable old man whose wealth is only equalled by his wisdom, owned an arms factory in Athens: he was, incidentally, the orator Lysias' father.

Metics also took first place in trade, both retail and wholesale. They dealt extensively in textiles, grain, and vegetable products themselves: they also acted as middlemen and import-export agents. It was a metic, nearly always, who organized the cargoes which reached Athens: timber from Macedonia, gold-leaf from the Orient, wheat and salted fish from the Black Sea. The largest salt-curing business in Athens was that owned by Chaerephilus and his sons: Chaerephilus himself was to win Athenian citizen-ship, and make an ex-voto offering at Delphi afterwards with this inscription: 'In fulfilment of a vow, Chaerephilus, son of Pheidias, an Athenian, has set up this offering to Pythian Apollo.' But we know, from other evidence, that he was not Athenian by birth.[19] The biggest bankers (*trapezitai*) in Athens were either metics or ex-slaves, who acquired metic status on enfranchisement.

Many metics, having thus by their business activities earned themselves a comfortable sufficiency (or even, at times, consider-able wealth) were able to give their sons a first-class education, so that afterwards they shone in one of the professions, as artist. doctor, or public speaker. For instance, the Syracusan arms manufacturer Cephalus, already mentioned above, had his son Lysias educated with the best families in Athens, and in due course the boy became a well-known orator. But there were also many gifted men, men who had already acquired fame in their own country, who came to Athens, drawn by the city's incompar-able brilliance and the certain fulfilment it offered to their talents. Often they settled there for good. Among such we may note three great painters: Polygnotus of Thasos, Zeuxis of Heraclea, and Parrhasius of Ephesus. Hippocrates of Cos, the Father of Medicine, enjoyed a great success in Athens; and the Father of History, Herodotus of Halicarnassus, gave public readings (or, as we would say, lectures) there, spending long years as a resident before he finally took ship to Southern Italy, as one of the pan-Hellenic colonists of Thurii – a project approved by Pericles and under Athenian organization.

To judge from Pericles' law of 451, aimed at restricting any extension of the citizenship, he might well have had xenophobic tendencies; but in fact he surrounded himself with metics, including his teacher, Anaxagoras of Clazomenae, and his mistress, Aspasia of Miletus. The architect of the Piraeus, Hippodamus (also a Milesian), and Phaeinus the astronomer, Meton's teacher, were likewise metics. As for the 'Sophists', itinerant scholars or instructors in the art of rhetoric who stopped off at Athens and sometimes stayed for good, we learn about them from their enemy, Plato. There was Protagoras, from Abdera in Thrace; Gorgias, from Sicilian Leontini; Prodicus, from the island of Ceos; Hippias, from Elis. The list of what were considered the ten greatest Athenian orators included three metics: Isaeus of Chalcis, Deinarchus of Corinth, and Lysias, the son of the Syracusan Cephalus. Thanks to his wealth, Lysias was also to play some part in the restoration of the democracy in 403, and came very close at this point to winning his citizenship, just as Chaerephilus did. He surely deserved the honour, considering the fact that his speeches are regarded as the best example of pure Attic in existence.

There can be no doubt whatsoever that the metics contributed largely to Athens' economic strength no less than to her intellectual and artistic prestige. Plato, however, remained suspicious of them, and wanted to see their activities severely curtailed: one can only suppose that this attitude was inspired by his admiration for the constitution of Sparta – the xenophobic city *par excellence*. However, another, more realistically minded Athenian (also a great enthusiast for Spartan institutions) advised his fellow-citizens, in their own best interests, to extend even greater facilities to metics. This was Xenophon. He had lived as an expatriate for so long (even fighting against his own country on one occasion) that he strikes us rather as a precursor of the cosmopolitanism which characterizes the Alexandrian period. Despite their unswerving loyalty to the city of their adoption, the presence in Athens of so many intensely active resident aliens must have prepared people's minds for this universalizing trend. But such an attitude, as Plato knew very well, was in direct opposition to the Greek city-state's basic totalitarianism. The way in which the Athenians actually treated their metics was an honourable compromise between their traditional political principles and their would-be liberal character.

SLAVES

A metic who failed to pay the *metoikion*, or who made false claims to citizenship, was reduced to slavery – a fact which reminds us of the Greek city-states' first, and most instinctive, attitude to foreigners. But metics could not be all-sufficient in themselves; and we have already seen that many of them were, in fact, entrepreneurs, employers with a labour force working under them. This labour force was largely composed of slaves.

The great philosophers of the fourth century accepted slavery as a fact and made no kind of protest against the fundamental injustice which it represents. Plato, in *The Laws*, merely advised against the enslavement of Greeks, and exhorted masters to treat their slaves decently; and, as we shall see, when he wrote thus he was basing his argument on the humane attitude adopted by the great majority of his fellow-countrymen to their own servants. But Aristotle, in Book One of his *Politics*, chapters I and II, takes a much tougher line. He refers to those who claim that 'law alone lays down the distinction between the free man and the slave, and that nature plays no part in it; they assert, further, that this distinction is an unjust one, since it is violence – violence in battle particularly – which has brought it about'; but he, Aristotle, is very far from sharing such a view, which was already quite well known by his day: 'The human race,' he declares, 'contains certain individuals as inferior to the rest as the body is to the mind or brute beasts to men; these are the men who will respond best to the use of physical force. Such persons are destined by nature itself for enslavement, since there is nothing that suits them better than to obey.' He even goes so far as to state: 'Warfare is, in some sense, a legitimate method of acquiring slaves, since it allows for one's need to hunt, not wild beasts only, but also men, who are born to obey yet refuse to submit to the yoke.'

Slave-hunts were a living reality in Laconia, where they went by the name of *krypteia*. But Aristotle knew very well that the only justification for slavery was the necessity, since the entire economy of life in a Greek city-state rested upon slave labour:

> If every tool could, at the word of command, go to work by itself – if the looms wove untended, and the cithara played of its own accord – then employers would dispense with workers, and masters dismiss their slaves.

Homer had already pictured the abode of the Gods as equipped with marvellous 'robots' fashioned by Hephaestus, tripods which 'on wheels of gold move by themselves to the palace where the gods are assembled, and then return to their own place again'; and especially two handmaidens that he had wrought in gold, who attended him and supported his lame leg as he walked. The bellows of his forge, too, worked spontaneously at Hephaestus' command.[20] We may say, then, that the Greeks had foreseen the phenomenon which today we call 'automation', just as Icarus' wings were a foreshadowing of human flight; but the only energy they had at their disposal was provided by the arms of their slaves.

The main source of slave labour, as in Homeric times, was still warfare. The vanquished warrior whose life had been spared was enslaved by the man who had defeated him, and unless his relatives were able to pay an agreed sum in ransom, he remained in that man's service for good. When a town was captured, those of the inhabitants who were not killed found themselves reduced to slavery: such was the fate that befell Hecuba, Andromache and Cassandra. Piracy also ensured a good supply of slaves: Eumaeus, in the *Odyssey*, recounts how a band of Phoenician pirates, who doubled the roles of merchants and kidnappers, stole him away from his father's palace. By the fifth century Athenian thalassocracy had almost eliminated the pirates, but wars went on more or less non-stop. Thucydides, for instance, after reporting the tragic discussion between the Athenians and the inhabitants of the little island of Melos (the so-called 'Melian Dialogue'), whose only crime was their desire to remain neutral, gives a brief account of the capture of Melos by an Athenian squadron, and concludes: 'The Athenians killed every Melian of an age to bear arms, and reduced the women and children to slavery.'[21] The Melians, we should remember, were Greeks.

In time of peace the supply of slaves was still kept up from various sources. Among the barbarians and even in Greece (except in Attica after Solon's time) the head of a family had the right to sell his children. Dealers in 'human cattle' found their best areas for supplies were Thrace, Caria, and Phrygia: slaves with these countries of origin are particularly numerous. Even at Athens, a father who, whether because of poverty or mere selfishness, did not wish to rear a child had the right to 'expose' it at birth, ie to throw it out on a rubbish-heap. The infant either died, or, if rescued (like Oedipus and several other heroes) became a slave. An unemployed member of the proletariat, who was dying of hunger, could likewise sell himself as a slave to some master in return for bed and board. We even hear of a certain doctor, Menecrates of Syracuse, who only agreed to treat desperate cases on one condition: they were to sign a contract agreeing to become his slaves if they recovered.[22] An undischarged debtor – again, except in Athens after Solon's reforms – was sold into slavery, and the price he fetched paid to his creditor.

The philosopher Plato had a decidedly unpleasant adventure in 388 BC. He had gone to Sicily as a guest of Dionysius of Syracuse, and, having fallen out of favour with the tyrant, was shanghaied aboard a Lacedaemonian boat, the captain of which intended to sell him as a slave in Aegina. Luckily, he was bought up by a Cyrenaean, who sent him back home to his friends and his life of philosophy. Even in Attica, either out in the country or, sometimes, in the city itself, children and adolescents were 'snatched' by slave kidnappers (*andrapodistai*): we know this through the existence of a law in Athens providing for just such a contingency.

The main slave marts were those of Delos, Chios, Samos, Byzantium and Cyprus. There were two in Attica: one at Sunium, designed to keep the nearby mines of Laurium supplied with an adequate labour force, and the other in Athens itself, a monthly auction held in the Agora at the time of the new moon. The price of a slave varied considerably according to the period, and was also, obviously, conditioned by individual qualities and skills.

The ransom price of prisoners-of-war during the fifth century was about two minas, ie two hundred drachmas; by the end of the fourth century this price had risen to five minas. Unskilled labourers went for about two minas; women, as a rule, cost slightly more, and a skilled craftsman could fetch anything between three and six minas.

A distinction must be drawn between house-born and purchased slaves. It should not be supposed that masters encouraged unions between slaves (which did not count as true marriages or *gamoi*) for the purpose of acquiring more human livestock on the cheap, since this would involve them in supporting the children for long years before they showed any productive return on the investment. It was rather as a means of securing the loyalty of good slaves that they were, sometimes, permitted to start a family. In Xenophon's *Oeconomica* we find Ischomachus saying:

> I shall show my young wife the women's apartments, which are separated from those of the men by a locked door: thus no one can smuggle anything out improperly, and the slaves are unable to have children without our express permission. As a general rule we may say that if good slaves are allowed to have a family, their loyalty increases; whereas when bad ones do so, they merely have greater opportunity for trouble-making.[23]

In rural districts, except for the Laurium mining area, the slave population was relatively small, since small landowners (*autourgoi*) were not wealthy enough to maintain many dependants. But those in fairly comfortable circumstances, such as Ischomachus, had several slaves, under the direction of an overseer who was a slave himself. Smallholders could also hire out slaves for seasonal work, since many rich citizens and metics invested their capital in the purchase and maintenance of a slave-labour pool, which they then leased out as occasion demanded, for an agreed period.

It was industry, beyond any doubt, which absorbed the greatest number of slaves: the Laurium silver-mines, at the southern tip of the Attica peninsula, had a permanent labour force of over 10,000, which may at certain periods have risen to almost twice that figure. As Aymard writes:

> Their lack of technical knowledge meant that the work was done with rudimentary tools, in narrow galleries lit only by

the flames of smoky oil-lamps. Above ground, the smelting of the ore, which was strongly tainted with sulphur, produced poisonous fumes that destroyed vegetation and gave the surrounding countryside a grimly desolate appearance. It was here that the slaves were lodged, in squalid camp-sites, and without any families – this last provision being imposed to save the extra cost of feeding useless mouths.[24]

But such a concentration of labour seems to have been unique in Attica; as regards other industries, we hear of no industrialist who employed more than a hundred and twenty slaves – this being the number working in the arms factory of Lysias' father, the metic Cephalus.

Athenian commerce, in its healthily flourishing condition, also needed a large labour force, particularly at the Piraeus, for the loading and unloading of cargoes: these dockers, or the greater number of them at least, were undoubtedly slaves. From certain speeches by Demosthenes we learn of two slaves advanced to positions of trust in the banking world, who subsequently did extremely well for themselves. One Pasion, a bank employee, so distinguished himself by his diligence and sound head for business that his master enfranchised him; and later, having been able – thanks to the funds at his disposal – to do the State some service, Pasion actually acquired Athenian citizenship, an extremely rare honour for a man of servile extraction. When he died, in 370, he left a widow and two sons, one aged twenty-four, the other ten. As he had no great confidence in the older boy's financial abilities (he was a good deal better at spending money than making it) he laid down in his will that his trusty employee Phormio – an enfranchised slave like himself – should take over the direction of the bank, and that of a shield factory which he ran as a sideline. He further decided that Phormio was to marry his widow and act as the tutor of his younger son. As might be expected, this will was contested, on legal grounds, by Pasion's elder son.[25] Here we have a classic instance of how talented slaves could, on occasion, rise to most enviable positions in the world.

All domestic work in the city was, there can be little doubt, ordinarily performed by slaves. An extremely wealthy citizen, such as the statesman Nicias, owned more than a thousand house-slaves, many of which he rented out, since obviously he could not find employment for all of them himself. A comfortably off Athenian such as Plato would have an average of fifty. The ordinary middle-class citizen seems to have run to a dozen: a porter, a cook, the *paidagogos* who escorted his children to school and generally supervised them, and, lastly, the women who swept the house, fetched in water, ground corn in the mill, and spun and wove under their mistress' direction. Many poor Athenians, however, had no slaves at all. Such was the position of Lysias' 'Cripple', a barber or cobbler in all likelihood (we do not know his exact occupation), who declared: 'I have a trade, but it brings me in very little; I already find it a strain to keep going on my own, and I can't save enough to purchase a slave to do the work for me.'[26]

Finally the State itself owned slaves, as did the temple-sanctuaries, in the form of *hierodouloi*. Of the public slaves known to us we mention, first, the clerks, beadles, and other underlings who served the Ecclĕsia, the Boulé, the law-courts, or the offices of the various civil authorities: indispensable cogs in the administrative machine, and the nearest we get, in Athens, to any sort of permanent civil service. There were also such state employees as the public executioner (eg the minion of the Eleven who prepared and administered the hemlock to Socrates), the streetsweepers, the skilled workers in the Mint, who struck Athens' drachmas, and, lastly, the police force, those Scythian archers we have already seen in action. This corps was created in 476, and must not be confused with Athens' normal auxiliary troops, who were also armed with the bow. The Scythians were purchased directly by the State, and were responsible for policing the streets, the Agora, the Assembly, and the law-courts. There were about one thousand of them, and they had their barracks on the Areopagus, whence they had a convenient bird's-eye view of the Agora and the city generally.[27]

Slaves, whether public or private, had in theory no legal rights. They were regarded, in law, as *objects*, chattels, which could be sold, hired out, or pawned: in a juridical sense they did not exist as persons, and could not even give evidence in court. Yet a slave-owner, when involved in a trial, would frequently offer to have his slaves put to the torture, so that their testimony, given under such conditions, should add weight to his own statements. Slave unions had no legal status, and were authorized by the master of the house, to whom any resultant children belonged. A runaway slave was severely punished, and branded with a red-hot iron.

It is quite clear that the slaves at Sparta, known as 'helots', led a most miserable existence: in this connection the institution of the *Krypteia* and the story of the intoxicated helot are highly significant. The helots also took advantage of the great earthquake in 464 BC to stage a rebellion. In Athens, however, custom – and consequently the laws – gradually became less inhumane. The slave who escaped from a cruel master could seek refuge in a sanctuary, either that of Theseus or the Erinyes; he was then protected by the right of asylum, and his master had no option but to offer him for sale. Further, the law protected a slave, just as it did a free man, against outrage and violence (*diké hybréôs*): it even guaranteed the slave a *synégoros*, that is, a kind of advisory lawyer, to help in any contested points to do with his enfranchisement. The savings a slave was allowed to build up belonged in theory to his owner, but the latter most often let him enjoy the profits of his thrift undisturbed.

Young slaves born in the house did not, as a rule, receive any education. They could not frequent the *gymnasia*, which were reserved for free citizens and their children. But purchased slaves, when brought to Athens, were put through a ceremony which made them one of the family: they were made to sit by the hearth, and the mistress of the house then scattered figs, nuts, and sweets over their head.[28] At the same time they were given a name. This ritual was not dissimilar to those of marriage and adoption; no doubt it signified that the new arrival would henceforth be a stranger no longer, but a member of the family, sharing the same religion. So it came about that slaves participated in family prayers, and attended religious festivals; and this was also why slaves had to be buried in the family plot,[29] a practice we have already observed in the Ceramicus cemetery. Slaves of Greek origin could also be initiated into the Eleusinian Mysteries. The enfranchised slave was not freed of all obligations towards his former master's family: the ties of religion remained.

It seems, then, that the position of domestic slaves in Athens was, on the whole, quite tolerable. As for the slaves in public service, they led a life scarcely to be distinguished from that of any other *petit fonctionnaire*. They lived where they pleased (except for the Scythian archers), they received a salary, and were allowed to contract non-legal marriages. Similarly, many slaves in commerce and industry could live where they pleased and build up businesses on their own: though all the profits, legally, belonged to their master, the latter frequently found it highly advantageous to grant them an 'interest' in the venture, and let them keep a percentage of the profits. It was in this way that Pasion, and his successor Phormio, contrived to build up so solid a financial edifice.[30]

The theatre – especially the comic theatre – reflects the important part played by slaves in the affairs of everyday life. Xanthias, in Aristophanes' play *The Frogs*, is presented as a character endowed with all the qualities (notably courage and ingenuity) so signally lacking in his master, the god Dionysus. In the same author's *Plutus*, the slave called Cario figures prominently; and we know how the stock figure of the artful, tricksy, insolent slave (often called Daos) was to play an increasingly important part in the New Comedy, typified by Menander.

But there were at least two categories of slave whose condition remained grim in the extreme: those employed to grind corn in the mills, and the Laurium miners, whom we have already discussed above. Very often a dishonest or recalcitrant slave would be sent by his master, as a punishment, for a spell in the mills or the mines. During the Peloponnesian War, Spartan raids into Attica allowed slaves from Laurium to desert *en masse* and scatter through the countryside, where they proceeded to terrorize the inhabitants.

NUMERICAL PROPORTIONS OF THE CLASSES
Fifth-century Athens had a population of some 40,000 citizens and 20,000 metics. If we add the women and children to both categories, we arrive at a possible 'free' population of about 200,000. Now, though we have no means of estimating their number, even approximately, the slaves were at least as numerous, and may indeed have totalled 300,000, or even more.

So we see that out of a total population in Attica of some half a million souls, only two fifths were free citizens. The men who possessed full political rights and took part in the government of the city constituted no more than a fractional minority. In any discussion of Greek democracy, this fact should never be forgotten. We should remember, too, that the Greeks of the classical period had inherited from an earlier age considerable contempt for 'servile labour' – that is, for any work which made a man depend on another man for his food and income. Trade and commerce were particularly looked down on, and it was for this reason that the Athenians so readily abandoned such occupations to metics.[31] We know that in Lacedaemonia any kind of business activity was forbidden to Spartiates enjoying full civic rights, who lived off their inalienable estates, which were worked for them by helots. At Athens, it is true, there had been since Solon's time a law which made it illegal for citizens to have no occupation – the *diké argias*. Plutarch tells the following anecdote on the subject:

A certain Spartan, finding himself in Athens on a day when the courts were in session, heard that a citizen had been condemned on a charge of 'non-activity': this citizen had returned home in a greatly distressed condition, accompanied by his friends, who were all commiserating with him and sharing his unhappy burden. The Spartan thereupon asked those who were with him to point out this person – 'condemned merely for living as befits a free man'. So convinced were the Lacedaemonians that it befitted none but slaves to follow a trade or work for their living.[32]

The Lacedaemonians were by no means the only people to hold such an opinion, which was shared, even in Athens, by a great number of people – in defiance of Solon's laws.

The fact of the matter is that manual labour was regarded by the Greeks as a strictly banausic occupation, beneath the dignity of any free citizen. Plato and Aristotle considered the fabrication (*poiesis*) of any object, and even the creation of a work of art, as a strictly second-class activity; the wise man should follow no pursuits apart from *praxis* and *theôria*, that is, the business of politics and leadership on the one hand, and, on the other, the study of philosophy.[33] In the myth of the *Phaedrus*, Plato classes ways of life, according to their value, in nine groups: the labourer and the artisan are to be found in the seventh division, just above the demagogue and the tyrant, who are, in the philosopher's opinion, humanity's worst scourge, and the most contemptible of men.[34]

A democracy with such significant prejudices about manual labour and commerce; a democracy which only grants citizen rights to a small minority of the population – does not such a democracy bear an uncommon resemblance to an aristocratic régime?

CHAPTER THREE

WOMEN, MARRIAGE AND THE FAMILY

The status of women – Marriage – The gynaikeia *– Conjugal and family love – Marriage and children – Funerals*

THE STATUS OF WOMEN

In Athens, the wives of citizens enjoyed no more political or legal rights than did their slaves. Women had lost the important rôle they formerly played in Minoan society,[1] and which, as it seems, they had at least partially preserved during the Homeric period.[2] Yet though a married Athenian woman might be confined to her house, here at least she enjoyed absolute authority – subject always to the consent of her lord and master: to her slave-girls she was the *despoina*, the mistress. In any case, her husband was so busy with other matters – in the country, hunting or farming; in the city, his profession, and political or legal affairs of state – that he was compelled, more often than not, to leave his wife to run their home as she pleased.

The dependent and subordinate position of Athenian women can be deduced, first, from the life led by young girls, and the way in which they came to be married. There was no question of a girl being free to meet other young people, since she scarcely ever left the women's apartments, the *gynaikeion*. Whereas married women seldom crossed the thresholds of their own front door, adolescent girls were lucky if they were allowed as far as the inner courtyard, since they had to stay where they could not be seen – well away, even, from the male members of their own family. There is nothing in fifth-century Athens corresponding to the 'school' for well-connected girls which the poetess Sappho conducted, at the beginning of the sixth century, on the island of Lesbos. Nor do we find anything in Athens resembling the physical training given to young Spartan girls, in short tunics which 'exposed their thighs' (*phainomerides*),[3] and concerning which Euripides wrote:

> . . . Spartan maidens, allowed out of doors with the young men, running and wrestling in their company, with naked thighs and girt-up tunics . . .[4]

In this respect, and this alone, disciplinarian Sparta was more tolerant than Athens; and Euripides chooses just this aspect of Lacedaemonian *mores* to criticize as scandalous, for the simple reason that here he has a direct contrast with accepted Athenian custom.

Everything a young Athenian girl learnt – which meant, basically, domestic skills such as cooking, spinning, and weaving, with perhaps a little reading, music and arithmetic thrown in – she would be taught by her mother, or her grandmother, or some family slave-girl. The only occasions on which girls normally went out were during certain religious festivals, when they assisted at the sacrifice and took part in the procession, as we learn from the Panathenaic frieze on the Parthenon. Still, some of them must have been trained to sing and dance, in order to join the festival choir – though in such choirs boys and girls were always kept strictly apart.

In Xenophon's *Oeconomica* Ischomachus says of his young bride:

> What can she have known about life when I married her, my dear Socrates? She was not yet quite fifteen at the time she crossed my threshold; and till that moment she had lived under the most cramping restrictions, trained from childhood to see and hear as little as possible, and ask an absolute minimum of questions.[5]

This was, indeed, the ideal aimed at – *sôphrosyné* – when giving girls a good education.

Here is another statement on the subject by Ischomachus. This time it is his wife he is addressing:

> Do you now understand why it was I married you, and why your parents betrothed you to me? There would have been no difficulty in finding another girl to share my bed: I am quite

sure you realize *that*. No; the decision was only taken after a great deal of thought – both by me on my own account and by your parents on yours – as to the best helpmeet each of us could find for the care of our home and future children. Eventually I picked on you, just as your parents settled for me – probably after considering various other potential husbands.

It was, in fact, the girl's *kyrios* (that is, her father, or, failing him, a blood-brother, or a grandfather, or, in the last resort, her legal guardian) who chose a husband for her and decided when she was to be married. Doubtless in many cases her own wishes were ascertained; but we have no evidence to suggest this, and her consent was not in the slightest degree necessary. Herodotus, it is true, tells a very strange anecdote about one sixth-century Athenian: 'His treatment of his three daughters was as follows: when they reached marriageable age, he gave them the most magnificent dowry, and then let each of them choose – from the whole body of Athenian citizens – the man she desired for a husband; to whom, in due course, he married her off.'[6]

Herodotus, who was himself a product of the fifth century, appears to find this paterfamilias' behaviour admirable, and certainly quotes it in an approving manner. But he also makes it clear that it was the exception rather than the rule. The rule was that formulated in verse by a much later author: 'Girl, wed the man your parents wish you to.'[7]

An Athenian citizen married, primarily, to have children: he expected them not only to care for him in his old age, but also – more important – to bury him with the full appropriate rites and keep up the family cult after he was gone. The first and foremost reason for marriage was thus a religious one, and on this point the conclusions of Fustel de Coulanges, in his *Cité antique*, have lost none of their validity. A man married, above all, in order to have male children: one son at least, to perpetuate the line and guarantee him the cult-honours which he, the father, performed for *his* ancestors, and which were regarded as indispensable for the well-being of the dead in the nether world.

At Sparta, confirmed bachelors were liable to legal sanctions; there was no such law of enforcement in Athens, but the pressure of public opinion was strong, and any unmarried male found himself subjected to much scornful censure. Despite this, a man whose elder brother had married and produced children found it somewhat more socially permissible to remain single himself.

It looks very much as though the majority of Athenians married for religious and social convenience rather than from personal choice. According to the poet Menander, writing at the end of the fourth century, they regarded marriage as a 'necessary evil'.[8] At any rate, we have no evidence of love between the engaged couple prior to the New Comedy. Besides, how could an Athenian have conceived a passion for a girl whom, in most cases, he had never so much as set eyes on? We know that the Greeks of the fifth and fourth centuries used the word *erôs* (love) in the first instance to describe the passion linking an *erastés* with his *erômenos* – in other words, just that type of relationship which we mean when we talk of 'Greek love', and which I shall discuss further during the next chapter, in an educational context.

All this, of course, does not mean that love could not subsequently come about between husband and wife. Xenophon makes Socrates say, in his *Symposium*: 'Niceratus, from what I hear, is passionately in love with his wife, and she with him.'[9] The poet Euripides, though he was commonly regarded as a misogynist, made a play out of the sublime self-sacrifice and devotion of Alcestis, who gave up her own life for love of her husband; and even Plato, the theorist of ideal pederasty, once wrote: 'Only those who love can ever be willing to die for another's sake: and this applies to women no less than men.' He cites the instance of Alcestis, 'whose case impressed the gods so much that they allowed her to return from Hades and behold the light of heaven once more'.[10] The works of Aristotle, who had married the niece of his friend Hermias, and found his wife eminently satisfactory, are full of passages in which marriage is regarded, not as a mere alliance, the sole function of which is to perpetuate one's line, but as a relationship full of affection and mutual tenderness, capable of satisfying all the moral and emotional demands that life may make on it. Nevertheless, it was only through late Stoicism – probably under the influence of Roman *mores* – that conjugal love was to be finally rehabilitated in Greece. The philosophical tradition favouring all-male love was strong and persistent; even at the beginning of the second century AD Plutarch, before embarking on his apologia for marriage, feels constrained to demonstrate that young girls are just as capable of arousing the passions as young boys![11]

Incest was not legally forbidden in Athens, but unions between parent and child were regarded as an abomination that called down the wrath of the gods: Sophocles' *Oedipus Rex* is ample demonstration of this. The same religious taboo was extended to unions between brother and sister born of the same mother, but a half-brother could marry his sister if the common strain came through their father. For instance, a daughter of Themistocles named Mnesiptolema, born to the great statesman by his second wife, married her own brother Archeptolis, he being the child of a different mother.[12] Similarly we find a plaintiff referring to his grandfather's marriage – the old man wed his sister, but they had different mothers.[13] The principle of endogamy, that is to say marriage within a limited social group, results in unions between close relatives being not only tolerated but actively encouraged. We find one Athenian admitting, in the course of a lawsuit, that he married his daughter off to his nephew rather than to some stranger, so as to preserve and reinforce family ties. Marriages between first cousins, or even uncle and niece, are by no means rare: in the latter case the bridegroom's brother would also become his father-in-law. An *epiklēros*, that is, a daughter who inherited her defunct father's estate in the absence of any male heir, was obliged to marry her father's closest relative who would agree to the match. Here we have an unmistakable instance of the primitive urge to ensure the continuity of race and family cult alike.

Hesiod's advice was that a man should marry at about thirty, choosing for his wife a girl of sixteen.[14] There were no formal laws in Athens governing the minimum age of marriage (though philosophers in the fourth century wanted a ruling on the point); Hesiod's recommendation seems to have been adopted quite frequently. [It is still the general custom in rural Greece today. (Trs.)] Girls *could* be married off as soon as they attained the age of puberty, ie at about twelve or thirteen, but it seems that ordinarily their families waited another two or three years. Ischomachus' wife, as we have seen, was under fifteen on her wedding-day.[15] But at all events it is certain that girls were not married *before* they reached puberty, as happened in Rome.[16] Young men, it appears, never got married before they attained their majority, at eighteen; and they very often waited till they had finished their two years' *ephebia*, or military service, which they performed between the ages of eighteen and twenty. The age-gap between husband and wife was often considerable.[17]

MARRIAGE

Legal marriage between a citizen and the daughter of a citizen in Athens was characterized by the *engyésis* (literally, 'giving of a pledge into the hand') which was something more than a mere betrothal. It was, basically, a pact, an agreement none the less binding for being spoken only, between two persons: the suitor, and the young girl's *kyrios*, who, naturally, would be her father if he was still alive. The two men shook hands and exchanged some very simple ritual phrases: the following piece of dialogue by Menander probably reproduces them fairly faithfully:

PATAECUS: I give you this girl, that she may bring children into the world within the bond of wedlock.

POLEMON: I accept her.

PATAECUS: I agree to provide a dowry of three talents with her.

POLEMON: I accept that too – with pleasure.[18]

There must have been witnesses present at this ceremony, so that they could, should the need arise, testify that it had in fact taken place. Nothing was set down in writing.

Was the bride-to-be herself present at the *engyésis*? We cannot be certain about this. What *is* certain is that if she was there she played no active part in the proceedings, nor was her consent to them required. It should be remembered that originally the head of a family had the same absolute rights over his children as he did over his slaves: he could even sell them, a custom still prevalent in many places during the fifth century, though not in Attica. In the Homeric Age, moreover, it was the suitor who offered gifts to his prospective father-in-law (he was, in fact, buying the man's daughter); but the roles later became reversed. A girl *could* marry without a dowry in Athens, but this was an exception to the general rule; there are even grounds for supposing that the existence of a dowry was one factor that distinguished legal marriage from mere concubinage.

As soon as the husband-to-be attained his majority he was no longer obliged to let his father represent him, and would carry out the *engyésis* ceremony in person. It is probable, however, that in most cases he would have asked his father's consent before becoming engaged, and that very often he chose his bride in accordance with his father's advice. One plaintiff tells us: 'As I had reached my eighteenth birthday, my father insisted on my marrying Euphemus' daughter: he wanted to see me beget children. My own feeling was that I must, in duty bound, do anything to please him; I therefore bowed to his wishes, and it was thus that I came to be married.'[19] In such a case it is clear that the father would choose his son's wife (either from the family group or elsewhere) in accordance with his own plans for establishing or strengthening various personal relationships – the prime consideration being one of material self-interest.

The *engyésis*, then, was a promise of marriage, but an extremely binding one: it established strong links between the suitor and his future bride long before they were actually married. In order to understand it fully, we have to bear in mind the immense importance which the ancients attached to any solemnly pronounced statement or ritual gesture: such words and actions, even if no formal oath was involved, they regarded as fraught with most serious consequences, and one could not repudiate any engagement entered upon under conditions of this sort without exposing oneself to the possibility of divine retribution. It was not only a prayer or curse that possessed this unequivocally magical power: any formula by which one bound oneself in the presence of the gods had a similar efficacy, and there is reason to suppose that the ceremony of *engyésis* took place in front of the domestic altar. Nevertheless, we know of at least one case in the fourth century where *engyésis* was not followed by marriage. Demosthenes' father, before he died, betrothed his daughter (then only five years old) to a relative of his called Demophon. Demophon received the dowry immediately, but was not to cohabit with the girl 'until she was of suitable age, that is, in ten years' time' – which offers confirmatory evidence that fifteen was regarded as a normal age for girls to get married. This betrothal, however, remained inoperative: the wedding was never celebrated.[20]

On the details of the actual wedding ceremony (known as *ekdosis*, the 'giving away' of the bride to the bridegroom) our information is far from complete; but we can draw a fairly clear general picture of what went on. The marriage existed, legally speaking, from the day of the *engyésis*; but cohabitation between the partners remained, nevertheless, its ultimate avowed purpose, since it was contracted primarily for the begetting of children. It was this consummation of marriage, the *gamos*, which necessitated the transfer of the fiancée to her suitor's house; and the transfer itself formed the central element in the wedding. Ordinarily it was meant to take place very soon after the *engyésis*. However, various superstitions made the Greeks marry, for preference, at the time of the full moon,[21] and in winter rather than summer.[22] Weddings were especially frequent during the month Gamelion (January), the seventh month in the Athenian year, since this was sacred to Hera, goddess of marriage, and its very name means 'the wedding-month'.

The sequence of ceremonies began on the evening before the bride's change of abode. First, a sacrifice was offered up to those gods and goddesses who protected the marriage bed: Zeus, Hera, Artemis, Apollo, and Peitho, or Persuasion. The bride offered up her toys, and all other objects associated with her childhood, as we see from the following epigram: 'Timareta, being about to be married, has consecrated to thee, O Artemis of the Marshes, her tambourines, and the ball she was so fond of, and her hairnet (*kekryphalos*); her dolls, too, she has dedicated in a befitting manner, with her clothes – a virgin's offering to thee, O Virgin Goddess.' We possess a bronze cymbal that has been dedicated in this way – and to Artemis of the Marshes, as the inscription on it reveals.[23]

But the principal rite – a purificatory ceremony – was the bridal bath, for which a procession had to go and fetch water from a special fountain called Callirhoe. We find this procession illustrated in vase-paintings: a crowd of women holding torches, and amongst them a flute-player, marching ahead of one woman who bore a special-shaped receptacle, in which the water for the bath was to be brought back – a *loutrophoros* with ovoid belly and long slender neck, double-handled. (This particular scene is actually painted on a *loutrophoros* itself: but such vessels are also decorated with scenes of mourning, and, as we have seen, it was a *loutrophoros* that stood on the grave of an unmarried person.) The bridegroom, likewise, had to take a ritual bath.

On the day of the wedding (*gamos*), the houses of both bride and groom were decorated with garlands made from olive and laurel leaves,[24] and there was a sacrifice and a banquet at the house of the bride's father. The bride herself was present at this feast, veiled and wearing her finest clothes, with a wreath on her head: she had all her girl-friends around her, and at her side the *nympheutria*, a woman whose task it was to guide and help her throughout the marriage ceremony. Similarly, the bridegroom was accompanied throughout by his *parochos*, or best man. It hardly needs saying that in the banqueting chamber the men were seated apart from the women. This wedding-feast included certain traditional dishes, such as sesame cakes, a symbolic guarantee of fertility. A young boy with both parents living (*amphithalés*)[25] went round among the guests, offering them bread from a basket, and repeating a ritual phrase which recalls certain religious formulas in the mystery cults: 'I have eschewed the worse; I have found the better.' When the meal was over the bride received presents. Perhaps she also removed her veil at this point, but we cannot be certain. As one scholar remarks: 'If the purpose of the veil was to protect her against maleficent influences during the dangerous period when she was in the process of changing her status, it would be more plausible to suppose that the unveiling did not take place till she reached the threshold of her husband's house.'[26]

At last, towards evening, the procession formed up to convey the bride to her new home. Originally this change of abode had been carried out as though it were a forcible abduction, a custom still kept up at Sparta:

Marriage in Lacedaemonia was a matter of the man abducting his chosen bride. The young girl thus abducted was entrusted to the care of a woman called the *nympheutria*, who close-cropped her hair, dressed her up in a man's clothes and shoes, and bedded her on a straw palliasse, alone and without any light. Her bridegroom, who had dined in the common mess, with his companions as usual, now came in, untied her girdle and carried her to the bed. After spending a brief time with her he would go straight back to his communal dormitory for the rest of the night.[27]

In Athens bride and bridegroom were carried from one house to the other in some sort of vehicle, generally a waggon drawn by mules or oxen, with a friend of the bridegroom's to drive it. The bride carried a sieve and a gridiron, symbols of her future domestic activities. The waggon moved slowly along, with relatives and friends following behind on foot, lit by flaring torches: during the procession the marriage hymn was sung, to the accompaniment of flutes and lyres. The bride's mother carried a torch herself. When they reached the door of the bridegroom's house his father and mother were waiting there, the first wearing a myrtle wreath and the second holding a torch. Nuts and dried figs were showered on the bride – a ritual which was also, as we have seen, performed on the entry of a new slave into the household.[28] She was offered a part of the wedding-cake, made from sesame and honey, together with a quince or a date, both symbols of fecundity.

From here the couple proceeded straight to the bridal chamber (*thalamos*), and it may not have been till then that the bride removed her veil. The door was closed and guarded by one of the bridegroom's friends, known as the *thyrôros*, while the rest of the company sang some nuptial hymn at the tops of their voices, kicking up a tremendous din in order – or so it is believed – to scare away evil spirits. It goes without saying that the pomp and ceremonial of a wedding varied according to the financial resources of the families involved: the wedding-feast was sometimes so sumptuous that laws were passed on several occasions limiting the number of guests.

The day following the wedding there still remained one ceremony to perform: the bride's parents came in solemn array to the newly-wed couple's house, accompanied by flute-players, and bearing gifts (*epaulia*). It was doubtless at this point that the dowry promised during the *engyésis* was handed over. At some slightly later date the bridegroom offered a banquet, complete with sacrifice, to the members of his phratry. He did not introduce his wife to them; instead he chose this way of solemnly notifying them that he was now married – an important point for the future, since his male children would have to be enrolled in the phratry.

Of all the rites connected with the marriage that are known to us, not one appears intended to consecrate, in some visible and tangible fashion, the personal union of two betrothed individuals. Everything seems, rather, aimed at ensuring the prosperity of the *oikos* – the small socio-religious nucleus which the new home represented – and the procreation of children, through which the future of the *oikos* would be assured. For instance, when the bride was required to consume a piece of cake and a quince before her new husband's hearth, she did not – as we might expect – share them with him. In Sparta, we know that all legislation regarding the family, and relations between the sexes, was dominated by a concern for eugenics, which went so far that an elderly husband married to a young wife was allowed to let some young man sleep with her in order to produce healthy, vigorous children.[29] In Athens they did not go to quite such lengths; but it must be said that nothing, either in the preparations for marriage or the ritual which solemnized it, placed any stress on affection or mutual love between husband and wife.

Yet when Ischomachus is telling Socrates of the way he initiated his young bride into her new duties as mistress of the house, he says: 'But first of all I offered a sacrifice to the gods, asking them to grant that I should teach, and she should learn, all that might be most profitable for us both.'[30] It is clear that this sacrifice, by which the newly-weds solemnly inaugurated their new life together, involved the wife no less than her husband.

A man always retained the right to repudiate his wife, even though he might be able to adduce no valid cause for so doing. A wife's adultery, if established by the courts, in fact made such repudiation obligatory on the husband's part, and failure to put away a peccant wife might render him liable to *atimia*, or loss of civil rights. Barrenness was in all likelihood a frequent motive for repudiation: and indeed, since a man married primarily to ensure the survival of his family (and, indirectly, of his city), he was doing no more than his bounden religious and patriotic duty when he put away a barren wife. On the other hand, the fact that a wife was pregnant did not make her exempt from repudiation. However, any husband who sent his wife back home had to return her dowry too: this provision was the only check (a very effective one, doubtless, in many cases) on a rocketing divorce rate.

If divorce through the husband's decision was a quite informal process, the wife who sought a separation found herself in a very different position, since legally she was presumed incapable of managing her own affairs. The only course open to her was to approach the archon – the traditional protector of all such 'incapables' – and put before him a written statement, detailing the reasons for her application. The archon was sole judge of what weight should be attached to offences alleged by an appellant wife. It was unlikely that flagrant infidelity on her husband's part would be regarded, *per se*, as justifying a separation, since custom tolerated complete sexual liberty amongst Athenian married men. Violence, however, and indeed any sort of ill treatment, might be taken as valid reasons for seeking a separation if, on enquiry, such charges proved well-founded. Despite this, public opinion was against wives who obtained a separation from their husbands in this way. Medea – whom Euripides makes talk exactly as though she were a contemporary Athenian woman – is quite unequivocal on the point: 'To leave their husbands brings women into ill-repute, and to repudiate them they have no right.'[31]

THE *GYNAIKEIA*

Marriage did not put an end to the confined and sedentary existence that women led before it. In Athens, it is true, the *gynaikeia* were not locked up (except at night) and did not have barred windows; but customary usage sufficed to keep women within doors. This rule was strictly enforced, and gave rise to various categorical aphorisms such as: 'Respectable women should stay at home: the street is for worthless hussies.'[32] Even those who lingered on their doorsteps, out of sheer curiosity, were treated as suspect. It was husbands or slaves who normally went to market and did the daily shopping.

Nevertheless, it is important to distinguish, in this respect, between the various social classes. Poor Athenians, with nothing but cramped lodgings at their disposal, were more inclined to allow their wives out. In any case, the wives often had to take a job in order to make ends meet: we know, for instance, that many of them worked as stallkeepers in the market. Athenians of the middle class, on the other hand, and those with large incomes, seem to have been far more strict in the seclusion of their women; but then the wives of such citizens possessed a far more ample *gynaikeion*, often provided with an inner courtyard where they could take the air, safe from the inquisitive eyes of the multitude.

Still, every woman, even one from the ranks of the bourgeoisie, on occasion needed to do some essentially personal shopping, eg for clothes or shoes, which meant that she had to go out. On such occasions she was obliged to take one of her attendants with her – that is, one of her slaves. But the main occasions on which women were allowed away from their homes were during the various city festivals, or for special family events. Athens was remarkable in having one festival specially reserved for married women, the Thesmophoria.[33] We find a deceived husband, who has killed his wife's lover, telling the court: 'To begin with, my wife was a paragon of marital virtue – she ran the house efficiently and economically, in short she was a first-class domestic manager. But then I lost my mother, and her death was the cause of all my subsequent misfortune. You see, it was while walking in her funeral procession that my wife was first spotted by Eratosthenes, who managed, in course of time, to seduce her: he lay in wait for the slave-girl who did her shopping, used this girl as a go-between to make contact with her mistress, and finally achieved the latter's ruin.' The same plaintiff later reveals how he was tipped off about his wife's infidelity by the slave of yet another married woman who had succumbed to Eratosthenes' advances, and how, by means of threats, he made his own wife's maid tell him the whole truth: 'She told me how he had accosted her after the funeral . . . and finally how, at the time of the Thesmophoria, when I was away in the country, she had gone to the sanctuary with his mother.'[34]

Women were not even supposed to take any interest in what went on outside the house: that was strictly the men's business. Nor did they have much opportunity for talking at any great length to their own husbands, since the latter were nearly always out, and do not seem to have been in the habit of taking meals with their wives. 'Is there anyone of your acquaintance with whom you have less conversation than your wife?' Socrates asks Critobulus, and the latter replies: 'Hardly anyone, I think.'[35] When an Athenian invited friends to his home, his wife never appeared in the *andrôn*, the banqueting-chamber, except perhaps to supervise the slaves waiting at table; nor did she accompany her husband out when he was a guest in his turn. It was only at family festivals that men and women mingled.

Yet it was the wife who held supreme authority within the home, where she was responsible for everything: Xenophon's

Oeconomica acquaints us in detail with the duties that devolved on the mistress of the house. These instructions, laid down for his wife by Ischomachus, will suffice to give us some idea of her responsibilities:

> You are to stay in the house, and ensure that all those servants whose work takes them out of doors leave at the same time. You are also responsible for supervising those who remain, and who perform their duties in the house itself. You must personally take charge of all goods brought into the house, and issue what is needed for necessary outgoings – budgeting in advance for a reserve, and taking care not to squander in a month what should last a full year. When your slaves bring you spun wool, you must see to it that this wool is used to make clothes for those who need them. You must keep a constant eye on the grain in the store-room, and make sure it remains fit to eat . . . When a servant falls ill, you must always ensure that he is receiving proper care and attention.[36]

The wife did not bake bread herself except in the very poorest families. When Alexander's envoys accompanied the Athenian Phocion to his home, Plutarch tells us, 'they found his domestic arrangements austere indeed: his wife was busy kneading dough, and Phocion himself took a bucket off to the well to get water for washing his own and his guests' feet'.[37] Normally such tasks were performed by slaves, under the supervision of the *despoina* – as in Homeric times, when Eurycleia washed the feet of Odysseus.[38]

A wife's badge of authority consisted of the keys she carried about with her, in particular those to store-room and cellar. Theophrastus' picture of the Distrustful Man contains these words: 'When he is in bed he will ask his wife if she has locked up the big chest and the silver cabinet, and whether the back door is properly bolted.'[39] Gluttony, drunkenness, or prodigality in a wife might lead her husband to withdraw the keys from her.

It is hard to evaluate Aristophanes' evidence on the social life of women, since we can never be quite sure where realism ends and caricature begins. Yet the overall impression one gets from his comedies is that by the end of the fifth century the traditional seclusion of women was giving rise to numerous exceptions, and it is not hard to understand why. The Peloponnesian War meant that Athenian menfolk, whether serving in some expeditionary force or manning the ramparts of Attica, were absent from their homes for even longer periods than in peacetime. The chorus of women in the *Lysistrata* – free women, certainly, and Athenians – observe: 'At crack of dawn I went and filled my water-pot from the fountain – and what a business it was! All that crowd, and the noise, and jars banging against each other, and a mob of servants and branded slaves elbowing past you . . .'[40]

According to Aristophanes, women went not only to the fountain, but down to the market as well, to do their shopping and sell their own produce: like Euripides' mother, who was, it seems, some sort of greengrocer.[41] We also hear, in a plaintiff's brief, of one Athenian woman who was in turn a ribbon-seller and a paid nurse;[42] but whereas freeborn Athenian women only took jobs in the last resort, as a matter of extreme necessity, the wives of metics were often wool-weavers, shoemakers, dressmakers, and so on. Some of them seem to have been genuine 'businesswomen'.[43]

It also happened on occasion that some rather slow-witted Athenian – a country bumpkin as often as not – would find his authority usurped, willy-nilly, by a spirited and unscrupulous wife. The peasant Strepsiades, as we have seen, laments having married a stuck-up little city madam, who even stops him giving their son the name he has chosen: Strepsiades wants to call the boy Pheidonides ('the Thrifty' or 'the Parsimonious') after his own father, according to popular custom, but she insists it must be a name compounded from *hippos* ('horse'), because horsy people were a well-heeled, aristocratic group. [There is a reference here to the class of *hippeis*, or Knights – originally those who could afford to serve in the cavalry arm in time of war, latterly the second census-group, with an income of between 500 and 300 *medimnoi* of corn *per annum*. (Trs.)] Both of them stuck to their own idea, and in the end they compromised on the name Pheidippides ('He who spares his horse').[44] There may be some truth in the supposition that, at least as far as the Attic countryside was concerned, 'the woman of the house altogether lacked that humble and self-effacing character which the French peasant housewife was to preserve for so long in rural areas'.[45] It is certainly a fact, observable to this day in some parts of France, that when the head of the family invites guests to dinner, the mistress of the house waits at table, without herself joining the men.

Athenian housewives – always with one or more slave-girls in attendance – did, however, pay frequent visits on each other: ostensibly to borrow something for kitchen or sewing-room, but in fact using this as an excuse for a good gossip and exchange of news, as we can see from one fourth-century court speech.[46] *The Syracusan Women*, by Theocritus, takes us into the third century BC, and far away from Athens, to Alexandria; but it seems very likely that this vivid exchange between Gorgo and Praxinoa could just as easily have taken place in fourth-century Athens:

GORGO [*at the door*]: Is Praxinoa in?

PRAXINOA [*hurrying out*]: Darling Gorgo! Yes, here I am. *What* a time it's been since you were here – though I'm surprised you made it today, I must say. [*To her slave-girl*] Here, Eunoa, go and get a chair for Madam – and put a cushion on it.

GORGO: Oh, it's very comfortable as it is, thank you –

PRAXINOA: Do sit down.

GORGO [*sitting*]: Honestly, I am a silly – I hardly got here alive, Praxinoa, such a crowd there was, and all those chariots too: everywhere thick with hobnailed boots and full-dress uniforms. The road just went on for *ever* – you live further and further away –

PRAXINOA: Blame that halfwitted husband of mine. He comes out here to the back of beyond and then buys this *shack* instead of a decent house – out of pure spite, the mean bastard, just to stop us being neighbours. It's typical of him.

GORGO [*seeing the baby's astonished expression*]: Darling, you shouldn't say such things about poor Dino when the little one's there. Look how he's staring at you, woman! [*To the child*] Don't worry, Zopyrion, sweetie – she isn't talking about Daddy.

PRAXINOA: Heavens above, the child understands!

GORGO: *Nice* Daddy!

PRAXINOA: Yes, well, the other day – just the other day it was – I told *Daddy* to pop out to the stall and get me some washing-soda and ruddle – and back he came with a packet of *salt*, the great lump. Oh, he's *wonderful*.[47]

We see that even in Alexandria, as late as the third century, it was still the husband who did the shopping. Gorgo and Praxinoa continue to run down and abuse their better halves for a while; then they sally forth together, each with a slave-girl, to attend the Festival of Adonis. Fourth-century Athenians (as I have already pointed out) also went out most often on the occasion of some religious festival.

Theatrical presentations formed an integral part of the festival in honour of Dionysus, and women (whatever may have been said on this vexed topic) were quite certainly allowed to be present on such occasions. They doubtless exercised this right in respect of the tragedies, though the proceedings were wound up with a satyr-drama, which often contained much licentious matter. But did they attend Aristophanes' comedies, such as the *Lysistrata*, which showed scant respect for that virtuous modesty – *sôphrosyné* – regarded by Athenians as the prime requirement in their womenfolk? A passage in Plato's *Laws* suggests that well-bred Athenian ladies preferred tragedy, and therefore, doubtless, refrained from attending comedies.[48] Aristotle, during a discussion of the licentious ritual traditionally associated with so many Greek cults, exhorts husbands to attend these ceremonies alone, leaving their wives and children at home.[49] Doubtless those men with a special concern for their families' morals would do so; but, as one scholar remarks, 'it remains probable, despite everything, that such persons were in a minority, and that Aristophanes' audience included a number of lower-class women, as ready as anyone to enjoy – and laugh out loud at – the coarsest sort of obscenity.'[50]

CONJUGAL AND FAMILY LOVE

It seems fairly clear, then, that there was little intimacy, intellectual contact, or even real love between husband and wife in classical Athens. Men constantly met and entertained one another: in their homes, in the Agora or the law courts of the Assembly, about their business affairs. Women, by contrast, lived a wholly secluded life. The *gynaikeion* was always kept well away from the *andrôn*. Many Athenians must have held opinions on marriage such as Montaigne was later to express: 'In this discreete match, appetites are not commonly so fondling; but drowsie and more sluggish . . . A man doth not marry for himselfe, whatsoever he

aleageth; but as much or more for his posteritie and familie . . .
Nor is it other than a kinde of incest, in this reverent alliance and
sacred bond, to employ the efforts and extravagant humor of an
amorous licentiousnes . . . A good marriage (if any there be)
refuseth the company and conditions of love.'[51]

But these carnal or emotional needs that the Athenian did not
satisfy at home (since he saw his wife merely as the mistress of
his house and the mother of his children) he tended to find an
outlet for elsewhere, in the company of boys or courtesans.
Here we must make a distinction between the fifth and the fourth
centuries. The Athenian family, as a social unit, seems to have
stood firm throughout the greater part of the fifth century; but
the Peloponnesian War, a savagely fought conflict which lasted
for thirty long years, brought about fundamental changes in
Athenian *mores*. The terrible Plague of 430–429, which claimed
Pericles among its victims, was directly attributable to the
war, and Thucydides thus describes its effect upon public
morality:

> These sudden changes of fortune which people witnessed – the
> wealthy struck dead overnight, paupers inheriting their riches
> – made them the more willing to indulge openly in such
> pleasures as they would before have taken care to conceal.
> They sought quick returns for their money, and saw immediate
> self-gratification as the one reasonable pursuit in a world
> where they, and their wealth, were liable to perish at any
> moment.[52]

Many women acquired more free and easy habits, following the
example of Spartan wives, who lived a far less secluded life
than did their Athenian counterparts, and spent a good deal
more time in men's company. The resultant disorder led to the
appointment of a special magistrate, whose job it was to control
the behaviour and, in particular, the extravagance of women –
a problem to which Solon, too, had already bent his mind. This
magistrate was known as the *gynaikonomos*.[53] To read the *Lysistrata*, which dates from 411 BC, and the *Women in Parliament*,
performed as late as 392, one might be forgiven for inferring that
many Athenian women, having seen an exclusively masculine
government carry the city headlong to disaster, were convinced
that things might go a little better if *they* expressed their views

and gave their husbands advice, but these two plays by Aristophanes are wildly exaggerated fantasy-farces, which afford us no
evidence that there existed what today we would term a 'feminist
movement' – something quite inconceivable in ancient Athens.

Besides, Praxagora herself, disguised as a man and speaking
in that capacity, draws an interesting contrast between women's
placid traditionalism and the restless, never satisfied urge for
change and discovery which characterizes men (the speech is
taken from *Women in Parliament*):

> Women's methods are much better than ours, as I shall show
> you. To begin with, they invariably dye their wool by boiling
> it, in the good old-fashioned way; you won't catch *them* trying
> any new-fangled methods. And wouldn't it have been better
> for Athens if *she'd* let well alone, instead of messing about
> with a lot of novel ideas? Women roast their barley sitting,
> just as they always have; they carry loads on their heads,
> just as they always have; they keep the Thesmophoria, just
> as they always have; they bake cakes, just as they always have;
> they nag their husbands, just as they always have; they sneak
> their lovers into the house, just as they always have; they buy
> themselves little tit-bits, just as they always have; they prefer
> their wine unwatered, just as they always have; and they
> enjoy a good fuck – just as they always have.[54]

As for their husbands, this interminable war meant that they
were constantly away from their wives and homes, and therefore
also less hesitant about giving free vent to their appetites. It was
a plaintiff from the fourth, not the fifth, century who one day
declared in open court: 'We have courtesans for pleasure, concubines to perform our domestic chores, and wives to bear us
legitimate children and be the faithful guardians of our homes.'[55]

We do, indeed, find in the fifth century such an irregular
liaison as that between Pericles and Aspasia. At the time of his
first meeting with the beautiful Milesian he was already married
to a distant cousin of his, and the father of two sons. However, he
put away his wife in order to live with Aspasia. Divorce was
permissible in Athens, and Pericles could have married Aspasia
en secondes noces if she had been Athenian-born, or from a town
to which Athens had granted the right of *epigamia* (intermarriage
between states). But this right was not enjoyed by Aspasia's city

of origin, Miletus. So she became Pericles' mistress, and lived with him – on terms of great intimacy, it would seem – until his death. She was an intelligent and highly cultured woman, and Socrates (if we can trust Xenophon and Plato)[56] thought the world of her. The comic poets, on the other hand, attacked her with immense virulence, going so far as to portray her as a prostitute and a brothel-keeper.[57]

As Marie Delcourt wrote in her study of Pericles: 'No one would have thought the less of Pericles for making love to young boys, or for treating his first wife so shabbily; but they *were* shocked by his treating her successor like a human being – by the fact that he *lived* with her instead of relegating her to the *gynaikeion*, and included his friends' wives when he issued invitations to dinner. It was all too amazing to be proper; and Aspasia was so brilliant she could not possibly be respectable.'[58] There may be much truth in this; but my own feeling is that what people found it hard to forgive Pericles, the first citizen of Athens (and therefore one who should have set an example in his private conduct), was the way he put away an Athenian wife and replaced her by a foreigner.

In the fourth century, it would appear, many Athenians kept a concubine (*pallaké*) without considering this a reason to dismiss their legitimate wives. But did these concubines (who might equally well be Athenians, slaves, or freeborn foreigners) enjoy any legal, publicly recognized status? From the advocates' speeches in which allusions to them occur, we might well doubt it.[59] But custom, if not the law, looked on them with remarkable tolerance, and a large number of Athenians seem to have been, to all intents and purposes, bigamous. Socrates is supposed to have had a second wife called Myrto, as well as the acidulous Xanthippe; but this story may well be pure fiction. The misogynist streak which Euripides reveals in several of his plays was explained by the assertion that he, too, was bigamously married, and therefore had twice as much opportunity as most men to study feminine malice! Some authorities – late ones, it must be said – also inform us that during the Peloponnesian War, as a measure designed to counter the slump in population, every male Athenian was authorized to have another woman, over and above his legally married wife, to bear him children: the woman might be a foreigner, and all offspring of such a union were treated as legitimate.

But long before this we find the case of Themistocles, whose father, it is true, was an Athenian citizen but whose mother was a Thracian slave, one Abrotonon: his illegitimacy had proved no bar to a successful career. 'When one's legal wife becomes intolerable,' Plutarch wrote, 'is not the best solution to take a companion like Abrotonon of Thrace or Bacchis of Miletus, without any *engyésis* – just buy them outright, and scatter a few nuts over their head?'[60] But if the concubine was an Athenian, how could one make a distinction between her and one's legal wife, especially if the children she bore were likewise considered Athenian citizens? Isaeus informs us that 'even those parents who give their own daughters into concubinage negotiate a fixed sum, payable to the concubine'.[61] We may well suppose that some poor Athenians, who could not provide a dowry for their daughters, made them contract an alternative union of this nature instead, asking nothing on their behalf except some financial recompense in case of a separation. A legally married wife, on the other hand, normally brought her husband a dowry.

As for the *hetairai*, or courtesans, they were for the most part slaves. Many of them were content with the modest enough fee of one obol, though some – the top-grade *hetairai* – cost their lovers a pretty penny. During the Hellenistic epoch certain courtesans even managed to marry reigning princes, and thus become queens: 'Flute-girls, dancers from Samos, an Aristonica or an Agathocleia or an Oenanthe with her tambourine – all these have trodden a royal diadem underfoot.'[62] Even as early as the fourth century the celebrated Phryne, a Boeotian from Thespiae, had managed to make a really rich killing. Her actual name was Mnesarete, which means 'mindful of virtue'; 'Phryne' was a nickname, given her on account of her yellowish complexion (the word in fact means 'toad'; though this, apparently, did not make her any the less beautiful). It is well known what methods the orator Hyperides, himself one of her lovers, is supposed to have employed in order to secure her acquittal on an impiety charge that had been brought against her; but this anecdote is highly suspect.[63] [Hyperides is said to have made her bare her bosom before the court, an argument which proved irresistible. (Trs.)] She was also Praxiteles' mistress, and served as the model for several statues he made of Aphrodite. Her personal fortune was so immense that it enabled her to set up her own statue, in gold, in the sanctuary at Delphi, amongst those of generals and kings. Plutarch, himself a priest of Pythian Apollo, was to take great exception to this centuries later: he described the statue as 'a trophy won from the lechery of the Greeks'.[64]

Brothels had existed in Athens at least since Solon's day, in the Ceramicus and, particularly, the Piraeus;[65] a percentage of the profits had gone to build the temple of Aphrodite Pandemos.[66]

Were these courtesans (whether freelance or institutionalized) really, as is sometimes claimed, better educated and more culturally aware than respectable Athenian matrons? To judge from those whom we can observe in conflict with legitimate wives, during various court hearings, the matter is at least open to doubt. Consider Alcé the brothel-madam, who gobbled up poor old Euctémon,[67] or Neaera, who lived with Stephanus, or her daughter Phano, who managed to hook an Athenian holding the office of King-archon, and later took part with him in various highly sacred rituals:[68] none of these women would appear to have received a refined education. Neaera was reared by a procuress 'who was highly skilled in picking out future beauties on the strength of their appearance in infancy'; but her education seems to have consisted, first and foremost, in learning the secrets of dressing and make-up, and other aids to physical seduction. We hear that Phryne was beautiful; no one suggests that she was clever or cultivated, like Aspasia. It was by their compliant ways and willingness to please that these *hetairai* kept their lovers. As one comic poet put it: 'Is not a mistress always more loving than a wife? Indeed she is, and for a very good reason. However unpleasant your wife may be, you are legally bound to keep her. A mistress, on the other hand, knows that a lover can only be kept by constant attentiveness, failing which he will turn elsewhere.'[69]

It is quite likely, however, that many courtesans received a somewhat freer and wider education than the middle-class ladies of Athens, especially in such fields as music, singing, and dancing: numbers of them had been trained to perform on the flute (*aulos*), and were employed to play, sing, and dance at banquets.

MARRIAGE AND CHILDREN

Greek marriages were not over-productive of children: there were two reasons for this. Firstly, the husband could easily gratify his sexual instincts through extra-marital activities; and secondly, whether through poverty or mere selfishness, people dreaded having extra mouths to feed. There was also anxiety lest the family estates might have to be divided amongst too many heirs, thus reducing each person's share. Hesiod is already quite categorical about it: 'Try, if you can, to have an only son, to care for the family inheritance: that is the way wealth multiplies in one's halls.'[70] Plato echoes this view: 'The number of children regarded as adequate by law will be one boy and one girl.'[71] It is only in the case of the daughter left *epikléros* that Solon advises her eventual husband 'to have intercourse with her at least three times a month',[72] since here the production of a male heir at the earliest opportunity is vital to ensure the perpetuation of the *oikos*. When Plutarch says, in the *Amatorius*, that 'Solon's intention in promulgating this law was to ensure that the marriage should be, as it were, renewed and made fresh by the bestowal of such a mark of affection',[73] there can be no doubt that his own preconceptions about conjugal love blind him to the legislator's true intentions. The most common feeling on this topic in antiquity is formulated by Menander: 'There is no more unfortunate man alive than a father, unless it be another father with a larger family.'[74] Here, too, distinction must be made between sons and daughters. One comic poet remarks: 'Sons are always brought up somehow, even in the poorest family; girls are exposed, even by the well-off.'[75]

There were at least two ways of avoiding an over-numerous family, abortion and the exposure of newborn infants: both were generally regarded as legitimate. Abortion was not, in fact, illegal: the law only intervened to protect the rights of the child-to-be's 'master', ie its father. A mother could not undergo abortion without her husband's consent, nor a slave-girl without that of her owner. If a third party procured an abortion either for a free woman or a slave, he was thereby committing an offence against their *kyrios*, whether father or master. Religious scruples, at any rate, were rather more squeamish than the civil code: this is why Aristotle advised those practising abortion to do so 'before the foetus received life and feeling',[76] that is, before it was a true living creature. Similarly, an ancient religious law of Cyrene distinguished between a formed and an unformed embryo: when a miscarriage occurred, the defilement that fell upon the house was, in the first case, equivalent to that occasioned by a death, but in the second, no more than would follow an ordinary case of childbirth.[77] There is no suggestion here of a general principle recognizing the right of a child to life while still within its mother's womb: merely an instance of religious taboo.

The same taboo, or scruple, while forbidding the murder of a child once it had been born, did not object to its being left to die from lack of care and nourishment. It has been said – and I think with some justice – that 'infanticide was, by and large, very often regarded as a morally neutral act, since the infant had not yet begun to participate in the life of its social group. As long as it had not passed through those formal rites which gave it at least the beginnings of an individual personality – in particular, as long as it had not received a name – it had no real existence, and its disappearance would not distress what we call people's "natural feelings".'[78]

Creon, we recall, having condemned Antigone to death, did not execute her, but walled her up in a tomb to die of hunger and asphyxiation – the same punishment as was later to be meted out to Vestal Virgins who broke their vow of chastity. By a similarly hypocritical device, Athenians did not *kill* the child they were unwilling to bring up; they simply abandoned it outside, in a clay pot or jar that subsequently served as its tomb.[79] Naturally illegitimate children were exposed in far greater numbers than those born in wedlock: witness the tale of Ion, child of Creusa's seduction by Apollo when she was still a young girl. Even so, 'an overwhelming number' of legitimate children suffered the same fate. It is true that these newborn rejects could be rescued and brought up by foster-parents to a life of slavery; sometimes they even fulfilled the desires of barren wives, who duped their husbands by a simulated pregnancy, and finally produced an exposed infant to take the place of the son and heir they had so long coveted.

At Sparta, where they were much concerned with eugenics, each newborn infant had to be presented to the elders of the tribe: 'They examined the child: if it was well-formed and lusty, they allowed it to be reared, but if it was sickly or misshapen, they had it taken to the place called Apothetae, a high cliff near the Taygetus.'[80] Prior to this, the newborn child had undergone another preliminary ordeal: 'Spartan women did not wash their newborn children with water, but with wine, in order to test their temperament. It is alleged that infants subject to epilepsy, or of a basically sickly physique, will go into convulsions after contact with undiluted wine.'[81] Alternatively the children were tested with icy water, or even with urine.

Athenian wives had their children at home, with all the women of the house crowding round to lend a hand. The word *maia* can denote any woman above a certain age, any experienced servant capable of acting as an *omphalotomos* (literally, 'cutter of the navel-cord'). Nevertheless, in difficult cases recourse was had to a midwife, or even to a doctor.

Before the child's birth, the house was smeared with pitch – either to keep evil spirits at bay, or because pitch was regarded as a protection against ritual defilement.[82] It followed that any birth constituted a defilement not only for the mother, but for the entire household: this was why no *accouchement* could ever take place inside a sanctuary. The moment the child was born, the fact was notified by an emblem hung up over the front door – an olive-branch for a boy, a strip of woollen material for a girl. This was both a token of rejoicing, and a handy way of letting the neighbours know both when the child was born and what sex it was.

On the fifth or seventh day after the birth, the family festival known as the Amphidromia was held. This involved a purification ceremony for the mother and all those who had been in direct contact with her during labour, together with the ritual by which the child itself was admitted as a member of its social group: it was carried, at the run, all round the hearth (*amphidromia* means 'a running round'). All the members of the family were united for this occasion. From now on the child was an accepted member of the community: the decision to rear it had been irrevocably taken, and its father no longer had the right to get rid of it.

Finally, on the tenth day after the birth, the members of the family assembled once more for a sacrifice and a banquet.[83] It was now that the child received its name. In Athens the eldest son was normally given the name of his paternal grandfather; but the rule was not inflexible, and exceptions to it are known.[84] Relatives invited to this feast brought gifts with them, in particular amulets, for the child. It was on the tenth day, too, that the mother was regarded as 'purified', and could resume her normal occupations.[85]

FUNERALS

Respect for the old was particularly emphasized at Sparta, but it was general throughout ancient Greece. A son's first duty was to care for his parents in their declining years, and provide them with every necessity. A law promulgated in Delphi, and partially preserved as an inscription, begins: 'If any person shall omit to provide for his father and his mother, he shall, upon denunciation to the Council, be fettered and cast into prison until such time . . .' Here the inscription breaks off: the stone is broken.[86] Even temporary imprisonment was a very weighty sanction against a freeborn citizen, and not employed except in connection with what were considered particularly serious offences.

This obligation to assist one's aged parents was defined by terms coined especially for that purpose (*geroboskia, gerotrophia*), and those who neglected it, in Athens at any rate, found themselves liable to both a fine and partial deprivation of civil rights for having infringed a law established by Solon. But the most stringent obligations were those concerning burial: children had to bury their parents according to prescribed ritual, under pain of defaulting in their prime filial duty.

The closest relatives of the deceased person were responsible for laying him out for the funeral: they anointed the body with perfumed oils, and dressed it in clean garments, usually white. Then they wound it in cere-cloths and placed it in the coffin, leaving the face exposed. It was forbidden by law to bury a man in more than three garments.[87] Valuable articles such as rings, torques, and bracelets were buried with the dead person, and archaeologists exploring tombs have found such things in large quantities. At certain periods a coin was placed in the corpse's mouth, the obol which he would have to pay Charon the ferryman for his passage across the Styx. This practice becomes rather more comprehensible when we recall that the lower classes in Athens commonly used their mouths in lieu of a purse, as several passages from Aristophanes testify,[88] together with the following text from Theophrastus: '[The totally immoral man] pouches his ill-gotten takings in his cheek.'[89] Sometimes a honey-cake was placed beside the dead man, with which he could placate Cerberus, the watchdog of Hades.[90]

The body was now laid out on a bier (this process was called the *prothesis*) and left in the lobby of the house for a day or two, feet facing the door. The scene is depicted on a number of painted 'vases, most notably on those white-slip *lekythoi* that were placed beneath the funeral bier. The dead man's head, wreathed in flowers, rested on a pillow; around him were the women, with parasols and fans to protect him against the sun and the flies respectively; others, standing on either side of the bier, would scatter ashes in their hair, tear their cheeks with their nails, beat their breasts, or hold their right hand stretched out towards the deceased; and all would be giving noisy vent to those ritual shrieks and lamentations (*ololygé*) which various laws did their best to curtail.

Any men who presented themselves were allowed into the house, but the attendance of women was most strictly limited by legislative decree. At Iulis, for instance, in the island of Ceos, there was a regulation according to which 'no women shall enter the house of the deceased except those who are defiled (by contact with the dead person): that is, mother, wife, sisters, and daughters; and beyond this, no more than five women and two young girls from the kin of the deceased, to the degree of first cousin's child; none other shall be admitted'.[91]

Similarly at Athens, according to Solonic legislation, 'only those women related to the deceased within the degree of first cousin's child shall be allowed to enter the house of mourning, or follow the funeral procession to the tomb'.[92] Mourners wore the appropriate costume, which might be black, or grey, or even white on occasion; their hair was cropped as a token of their grief. Official mourners, both male and female, were often hired to chant the funeral lament (*thrénos*); but in this respect, too, the law placed firm limits on funereal luxury and ostentation. Outside the front door there was placed a jar (*ardanion*) filled with lustral water fetched from some neighbour's home, since that in the house of death itself was regarded as being contaminated: anyone coming out would sprinkle himself with this water, and the presence of the jar informed passers-by that there was a corpse in the house.

The funeral procession, or *ekphora*, normally took place on the day after the laying-out. Solon's law prescribed that 'the deceased shall be laid out at home, according to the wishes of the family; but it must be removed the following day before sunrise'.[93] At Athens, therefore, funerals took place at night, again because of religious scruples: it was feared that the corpse might defile the very rays of the sun. Before setting forth from the house, libations were poured in honour of the gods, and then the procession formed up. The body was carried on the same bier that had served for its laying-out: the bier itself was either borne on the shoulders of relatives or slaves, or else transported in a waggon drawn by horses or mules. At the head of the procession walked a woman holding a jar for libations; then came the male mourners, followed by the women (restricted to near relatives of the deceased) and, lastly, the flute-players. In the case of a person who had been murdered, a spear was borne immediately before the body, in token of the blood vengeance to be wrought upon the murderer.[94]

When the cortège reached the cemetery (which was always situated outside the walls of the town) the body was either buried, or burnt on a funeral pyre; in the latter case, the ashes and bones were gathered up in a cloth and consigned to a special urn. Then libations were poured to the deceased; the law of Iulis specified that no more than three *congii* of wine and one of oil were to be brought to the graveside (the *congius* was a measure containing just under six pints). A last farewell was taken of the dead person, and then the procession returned to the house of mourning, where lengthy and detailed purification ceremonies now took place. Defilement caused by contact with the dead was the worst possible sort of pollution,[95] and the relatives of the deceased had to wash all over before they could take part in the funeral feast. On the following day, according to the law of Iulis, the house itself was purified with sea water and hyssop. Further feasting and sacrifices took place on the third, ninth, and thirtieth days after the funeral, and subsequently on each anniversary. Such was the way in which the cult of the dead was inaugurated.

CHAPTER FOUR

CHILDREN AND EDUCATION

---

*The 'way of life' in Sparta – The 'way of life' in Athens –
The educational system in Athens – Elementary education –
Musical training – Physical training – Pederasty – The Sophists*

THE 'WAY OF LIFE' IN SPARTA

In the previous chapter all the emphasis was on Athenian women, the family and marriage as they existed in Athens. When we turn to education, however, we can no longer ignore Sparta, since it is in this sphere, beyond any doubt, that we find the most clear-cut distinction (and most diametrically opposed contrast) between the 'ways of life' practised by Athenians and Spartans respectively. In any case, even if one was exclusively concerned with education in Attica, it would still be important to know just how much influence the 'Spartan mirage'[1] had on it.

Spartan institutions appear to have been, so to speak, 'frozen' about the middle of the sixth century – the point at which an aristocratic *coup* put an abrupt stop to those democratizing tendencies that had appeared in Sparta, just as they had in many other Greek cities. Through laws attributed to Lycurgus the new government forged an iron straitjacket which was for centuries to contain and direct the city's energies. It follows that Spartan education during the fifth and fourth centuries is our best evidence for education of the most archaic sort – though the rigid discipline by which it had to be enforced brought about a degree of sternness in this old-fashioned system that was exaggerated to the point of caricature. Above all, it produced an unparalleled degree of interference on the State's part in purely private matters, even to the regulation of sexual congress between young married couples.

Plutarch is flying in the face of all the evidence when he tries to present Lycurgus (whom he pairs up, for purposes of comparison, with that pacific character Numa) as 'a most mild person by nature, whose prime concern was to preserve the peace'.[2] In point of fact, it is by no means certain whether Lycurgus himself ever existed as a real historical character; and if the Spartan institutions *were* the work of a single legislator, there can be no doubt that war rather than peace was uppermost in his mind. Besides, there are good grounds for supposing that Spartan education was the result of a lengthy historical process rather than the work of a single individual. An institution such as the *krypteia*, to which we shall return again presently, has parallels in other countries (comparative ethnography makes this quite clear); it was, no doubt, on account of their relatively small numbers that the Dorian conquerors of Laconia were driven to live like an occupation force, encamped in the midst of a sub-jugated but still dourly hostile population, and found themselves constrained (as the only means of establishing their rule on a permanent footing) to set about forging the future Spartan hoplite's courage and endurance from earliest childhood.

While young Athenian girls, as we have seen, lived the most secluded lives, their Spartan sisters practised numerous sports in public, on exactly the same footing as the boys. They wrestled; they learnt to throw the discus, and also the javelin, which, be it noted, was a military weapon. The purpose of this policy was, again, mainly eugenic: to train up robust and vigorous young mothers, and endow the women with elements of masculine virility. Lycurgus, so Plutarch tells us, 'would have no truck with too soft or domestic a type of training for girls (such as that given in Athens); he accustomed girls no less than boys to parading near-naked, and to dancing and singing at religious festivals in the presence of – indeed, under the immediate gaze of – young Spartan males'.[3] Such was the preparation for those well-matched unions that were to provide Sparta with such tough and daring children. It was this kind of exhibitionism which inspired Plato to arrange marriages in his Utopia – in the best general interest – 'according to the sovereign dictates of love – a very different power from that of geometry'.[4] Choirs of young Spartan girls, such as we find portrayed in Alcman's *partheneion* (maiden-song) enjoyed an unrivalled fame throughout Greece.

As for Spartan boys, they were only left with their families till the age of seven; even from infancy they appear to have been subjected to a very special training and general régime. Once again, Plutarch is our informant. 'Laconian nurses,' he says, 'were well-trained and conscientious women. Instead of tight-swaddling the babies in their care, they left their limbs and bodies entirely unimpeded. They taught them to avoid any sort of faddiness or fuss in their diet; not to be scared of the dark; not to mind being left alone; and to restrain themselves from tears, screaming fits, or any other vulgar tantrums of that sort.'[5] As a result, aristocratic families at Athens in search of a nurse for their children most often tended to look for her in Sparta.

From the age of seven the young Spartan was taken over directly by the State – to which he henceforth owed obedience till the day he died. At this point he was enrolled (rather as young Fascists or Nazis were a few years ago) in a sequence of pre-military organizations which covered his entire childhood and adolescence, and which were under the overall supervision of the *paidonomos*, a virtual 'Commissar for National Education'.[6] According to what, in my opinion, constitutes the most likely reconstruction of these successive age-groups, the boy was in turn (a) from eight to eleven, a 'youngster' or 'wolf-cub' (*rhobidas, promikkizomenos, mikkizomenos, propais*); (b) from his twelfth to fifteenth birthday a 'boy' in the full sense (*pratopampais, atropampais, meillerén*); and (c) from sixteen to twenty an *eirén*, or *ephébos* (divided into first-, second-, third-, and fourth-year grades).[7]

Children between eight and eleven were divided into 'bands' or 'troops', under the command of fully grown adolescents (the oldest grade of *eirén*), and sub-divided into patrols, each of the latter being led by its brightest member, who was known as a *bouagos*. Parallels have been noted between these 'wolf-cubs', 'scouts' and 'senior scouts' and those of the modern Boy Scout Movement: but such analogies are highly superficial, and should not be allowed to obscure one profound and fundamental difference. In Sparta these activities were no optional affair, to be pursued over weekends or during the holidays: they formed a compulsory daily routine, woven into the very fabric of a boy's life.

No doubt these children were taught to read and write, though, as Plutarch says, 'their study of letters was restricted to the bare minimum; for the rest, their education consisted exclusively in learning unquestioning obedience, superhuman endurance, and how to win at wrestling. As a result their training grew steadily tougher with the years. Their heads were close-shaved; they learnt to march barefoot and to strip off for games on most occasions.'[8]

After they were twelve they no longer wore a tunic, and were issued with one cloak only for the entire year. They slept in dormitories, on rush palliasses. They neither bathed nor applied oil to their bodies except on one or two very infrequent feast-days. For even the smallest offence they received a savage whipping. The meals they took in common were, as a matter of deliberate policy, restricted to the coarsest food, and not enough of that: the idea being to drive them into stealing extra rations, a practice which called for guile as well as audacity. We all know the tale of the Spartiate child caught with a stolen fox under his cloak: rather than admit the theft he let the beast gnaw through his belly, enduring the agony until death supervened.

'It was during the same period,' one scholar writes, 'that we first find these licensed relationships between adult men and boys – relations that were certainly erotic if not purely sensual – which seem an inevitable concomitant of any isolated community of young males. Both law and public opinion sanctioned such relationships, while imposing certain limitations on them that it is exceedingly hard for us to trace. A close bond of solidarity grew up between the lover and the boy he chose as his favourite; the lover was at one and the same time the boy's tutor and a model for him to imitate. Such close and special relationships (to be found amongst other Dorian peoples too) fostered a spirit of emulation which served to call forth even greater heights of military valour.'[9] We shall return to this topic later, when dealing with Athens, where, however, pederasty was less widespread and better concealed.

The final stage was reached at sixteen, which marked the transition from youth to adolescence. The eiréns underwent a series of initiation ceremonies which were both tests of their endurance and quasi-magical rites often accompanied by dances and masquerades. Two rival groups of *ephéboi* had to come and filch cheeses from the altar of Artemis Orthia, and this 'great game' in due course was replaced by brisk exchanges with whips – though the savage flagellation of *ephéboi* (which has become so notorious) was not practised, it now appears, till much later, in

Roman times.[10] The strangest ordeal was that of the *krypteia*, or 'period of concealment'. After a spell during which the young man lived alone, in hiding, out in the countryside, like a *lykanthropos* (werewolf), he was required to go hunting helots (ie slaves) by night, and to kill at least one of them. Such practices are attested from other periods and countries, and have origins which go back to the remote past.[11]

Apart from these tests and exercises in preparation for their military career – and to which the majority of their time was devoted – the young Spartiates received a musical training. Even this was not unconnected with warfare, since the Spartans' regular, rhythmic marching songs set a pace for the manoeuvres of their perfectly drilled troops; and we know that the Spartan army advanced to the sound of flutes (*auloi*) and lusty voices raised in some battle hymn.

If we except this musical instruction, and the elements of reading and writing which accompanied it, we can say that the whole minutely organized state system of education in Sparta was directed towards two ends only: physical training and preparation for war.

THE 'WAY OF LIFE' IN ATHENS

How does this complete subordination of Spartan education to the needs of the Spartan state compare with the situation at Athens? In the latter city we found every father allowed absolute freedom to bring his children up as he pleases – either teaching them himself or employing others to do so – till they attain the age of eighteen: at this point the adolescent becomes a citizen, and commences his civic career with a spell as a military trainee. Between the ages of seven and eighteen, then, the life of the young Spartiate and that of the young Athenian must have been radically different.

Paradoxically enough, though, during his very first months of life it was the little Athenian whose liberty of movement was most hampered. As I have already stated, Spartan nurses did not swaddle their charges. In Athens, on the other hand, the most common practice seems to have been to wrap infants up in a tightly wound spiral of cloth.[12]

To judge from the evidence of the vase-paintings, cradles most often consisted of wicker baskets or a kind of wooden trough;

but they could also, on occasion, assume very curious shapes – such as one which resembles a shoe, if this is not a piece of fantasizing to be laid at the artist's door. The practice of rocking children in their cradles was perennial, and so were the lullabies used to sing them to sleep. Plato compared these practices with the combined use of dance and music to cure the 'Corybantic disease', or, as we should say, a state of possession.[13]

Mothers more often than not nursed their children themselves – such as Euphiletus' wife who, for greater convenience, moved down to the baby's room on the ground floor, leaving her husband the upper storey normally reserved for women. This, as we have seen, enabled her to breast-feed her child during the night without any danger of tumbling down the stairs in the dark – and also, on occasion, to entertain her lover, all unbeknown to her husband, who was asleep upstairs.[14] In well-to-do families the mother was generally assisted by a nurse; this nurse would in most cases be a slave, but might also be a lower-class freeborn woman. Orestes' nurse, in Aeschylus' play *Choephoroi* (*The Libation-Bearers*), gives a highly realistic account of the cares she lavished on Agamemnon's son, and it is plain that the poet's description is adapted from contemporary Athenian practice:

Ah, my darling Orestes – how I devoted my soul to that child, right from the moment his mother gave me him to nurse as a newborn babe! Kept me up night after night he did, screaming and crying – no end of trouble, and all for nothing. Senseless things, you see, babies; you have to nurse them as though they were animals, follow their moods. A babe in swaddling-clothes can't say what ails it – whether it's hungry, or thirsty, or wants to wee-wee – though of course infants can't control their motions, it just *comes*, and that's that. You learn to guess in advance in my profession; but Lord, I was wrong often enough, and then I had to wash the child's linen – nurse and laundress in one, that's what I was.[15]

Certain painted vases show us a nurse carrying a naked (and no doubt just washed) baby to its mother, who is preparing to give it the breast. On the other hand many nurses, naturally enough, were themselves in a position to suckle the child entrusted to their care. As I have said, the strapping nurses of Laconia were particularly sought after in Athens.

The old yeoman Strepsiades, in Aristophanes' play *The Clouds*, reminds his son Pheidippides of the tender care he bestowed upon him in his infancy (as Phoenix had done for Achilles):[16] 'Damn it, you impudent devil, I brought you up – I understood all your baby talk, too, knew just what you wanted every time. *Wah-wah!* you went, and I gave you water to drink; *ma-ma* meant you were hungry, so I'd fetch you a piece of bread; and as for *caca!* – well, the minute you said *that* I had you out of the house and held at arm's length in front of me.'[17] Should we infer from these lines that an Athenian paterfamilias normally dealt with his small son's requirements in this way? Surely not: in fact, the situation must have been a most exceptional one, which Aristophanes introduced for the specific purpose of raising a laugh. Strepsiades had married a 'proper little madam', a coquette more concerned with her own toilet than her child's; perhaps Strepsiades, a stingy character, had tried to economize by dispensing with a nurse. At all events, an Athenian husband had far too many interests outside the home to take much heed of his small children. It was obviously their mother, with the assistance of her slave-women, who lavished constant care and attention on them: after all, *she* was shut up in the house with them all day long.

Later, however, when her sons began to attend school, she would be very little help to them, and indeed, would scarcely understand what they were being taught, since her own education (like that of all girls in Athens) had been sadly neglected; but so long as they were too small to attend school, they were cared for exclusively by her and the other women about the house.

Mothers and nurses did not only sing lullabies and nursery rhymes to children, but also told them, as soon as they were of an age to understand such things, all the old traditional stories: this was the first step in their education. We know very little of these songs and tales. A disobedient child, it seems, found himself threatened with all sorts of bogeys, who had names like Acco, Alphito, Gello, Gorgo, Empusa, Lamia, Mormo (or Mormolyké) and Ephialtes: a numerous and terrifying crew. The wolf also served as a bugbear, to judge from Aesop's fable 'The Wolf and the Old Woman'.[18] But good children were told amusing stories in which animals played the leading parts – those Aesopian tales which Socrates still knew by heart in his old age, and which he was busy versifying in prison shortly before he died.[19] These fables contained a moral – *docet experientia* – and therefore a lesson as well. Old Philocleon recalled one which began: 'Once upon a time there was a rat and a weasel . . .'[20] No doubt mothers and nurses alike later introduced children to their country's legends and mythology, passing on what they had learnt themselves in infancy, and had later reinforced by attendance at religious festivals and the study of works of art. This would form a grounding and preparation for the time when the children came to read Homer and Hesiod with their *grammatistés*, or primary teacher.

Plato believed that children should be allowed to play unrestricted till the age of six – though their games should be given a gentle nudge in the direction of some future trade or profession, nevertheless.[21] And Aristotle wrote, quite seriously, in the *Politics*: 'Children must be kept occupied, and the rattle (*platagé*) devised by Archytas [of Tarentum: philosopher and statesman] is rightly regarded as an admirable invention for that purpose: so long as a child is busy with it, nothing else in the house will get broken. As children are incapable of sitting still for two moments together, a rattle is a most suitable toy for them.'[22] But if the rattle made too much noise, this would not, of course, stop Mama (or Papa, if he happened to be in the house) from grumbling, regardless.

Games with balls (*sphairai*) or knucklebones (*astragaloi*) were doubtless played from early infancy onwards: they were still popular during adolescence, and we shall have more to say on this subject later. Other toys were more specifically designed for the lower age-groups – for instance, those tiny chariots, or go-carts, we see children pulling in vase-paintings. Strepsiades had bought one for his son Pheidippides: 'Obey me in this one thing,' he tells the boy, 'and then you can do as you please. Lord, I remember how *I* used to humour *you* when you were a whining infant – my very first day's jury-pay I spent on a little go-cart for you: got it at the fair during the Great Diasia [festival in honour of Zeus Meilichios], I did.'[23]

There were several religious festivals beside the Great Diasia (especially the Anthesteria, towards the end of February) that involved celebrations in which children could take part, and during which it was customary to buy them toys – either go-carts, or those miniature child-size jars, like tiny *oinochoai*, on which the artist painted pictures of little boys (nearly always naked) engaged in play, each with a string of amulets strung round his neck. These amulets (*probaskania*) were supposed to safeguard the wearer against bad luck, illness, and the evil eye. It would appear, then, that young boys were allowed to play in the *gynaikeion* near-naked, while little girls (who also appear on these vases) were ordinarily dressed in a brief tunic.

Archaeologists have dug up numerous small clay artifacts which must have been toys for young children: they include various kinds of rattle, horses on wheels, and all sorts of other animal figures such as pigs, cocks, doves, and so on. There are also a great number of girls' dolls, including some with movable limbs (*neurospasta*).[24] But perhaps the toys which children liked most were those they made for themselves. Here is Strepsiades again, telling Socrates how intelligent his son was as a child: 'Oh, he's a bright boy all right – why, when he was only so high, just a tiny nipper, he was making houses out of clay, and wooden boats, and miniature chariots from scraps of leather, and carving pomegranates into jolly little frog-figures, you've no idea how good he was . . .'[25] Similarly, the tyrant Dionysius, who had no companions in childhood because of his father's persecution mania, was reduced to 'making chariots, lamps, and wooden tables and chairs'[26] as a way of keeping himself amused.

But children were not restricted to mere make-believe animals of clay or wood (whether home-made or bought): they also had live pets – mainly dogs, as we can see from the vase-paintings, but also such birds as ducks or quails (which they tamed), mice, weasels, even grasshoppers. In such circumstances the *gynaikeion* must have tended to turn into a small menagerie.

THE EDUCATIONAL SYSTEM IN ATHENS

In Athens, as opposed to Sparta and some other Dorian cities, there was no such office as that of *paidonomos*. On the other hand, the State could hardly fail to take *some* interest in prevailing educational conditions – from the moral viewpoint if from none other. In accordance with one of Solon's laws, parents were forbidden to send their children to school before daybreak, and had to fetch them home not later than sunset, thus avoiding the dangers of a journey on foot in the dark. Similarly, young men and strangers were forbidden to set foot in the school premises when children were there; this measure was directed against pederasts.[27] But such regulations, clearly, took no note of the curriculum as such, whether in respect of classes taken by the elementary schoolmaster (*grammatistés*), the physical training instructor (*paidotribés*), or the music teacher (*kitharistés*). It is not even certain that parents in Athens were under a legal obligation to send their children to school at all; but even in the absence of a written statute, compulsory education was most certainly enforced by custom and tradition – which are just as binding an instrument.[28] Yet could the city's governing body, the *strategoi* in particular, normally disregard the education of Athenian children, which was bound to have a direct influence on the quality of Athens' future *ephéboi* – in other words, the city's prime defenders? A decree published by the deme of Eleusis, in the middle of the fourth century, pays tribute to the *stratégos* Derkylos, particularly 'for the manner in which he has watched over the education of the deme's children'. Responsibility for the engraving and setting up of the inscription is restricted to the mayor (*demarchos*) and the children's parents, who, in their gratitude, were the original instigators of this honorific measure.[29] One such document is not sufficient evidence to suggest that among the standing duties of a *stratégos* was the supervision of schools; but it does mean that he might, on occasion, turn his mind to such problems.

In any case, whether he was giving instruction in reading, music, or gymnastics – the Greek educational equivalent of the *trivium* – the master would teach his pupils in his own house, not in a public edifice constructed at the expense of the State. This is clear, at any rate, as regards the *grammatistés* and the *kitharistés*. When we are considering the *paidotribés*, we must make a distinction between the palaestras for *ephéboi* and grown men that were to be found in the various public *gymnasia*, and palaestras specially reserved for children: the latter were in all likelihood privately owned by the *paidotribai* themselves, whose names they bore, eg 'the palaestra of Taureas', or 'the palaestra of Sibyrtius'.[30]

We may assume, then, that education in Athens was virtually free from state control, and left to individual initiative. Even in the special case of 'state-supported pupils', that is, the children of citizens who had fallen for their country, whose maintenance was paid from public funds, the State did no more than farm out their education into private hands. Similarly, in 480, when the Athenians evacuated their women and children to Troezen as Xerxes was advancing on the city, 'the men of Troezen,' Plutarch tells us, 'decreed that the refugees should be fed at the expense of the State; that each of them should receive two obols; that the children should be allowed to pick fruit wherever they pleased; *and that schoolteachers' fees should be paid on their behalf.*'[31]

In ordinary circumstances, of course, parents would pay the expenses of their own children's education. One result of this must have been that the children of wealthy or comfortably-off citizens were enabled to continue their studies till the age of eighteen, when they became *ephéboi*, whereas poor children left school much earlier, often when they knew little more than the three Rs.[32] Some children, indeed, could hardly read at all. There is a pleasant anecdote, dating from 482, about one Athenian citizen who asked Aristides to write his own name in an ostracism-tablet, explaining that he himself was unable to, being illiterate.[33] But education appears to have become much more widespread in Athens during the course of the fifth century. During the last three decades – that is, throughout the Peloponnesian War – we find no analphabetics among Aristophanes' characters: even the countrified Strepsiades in *The Clouds*, and Agoracritus, the fat sausage-seller of *The Knights*, at least know (more or less) how to read and write.[34]

ELEMENTARY EDUCATION

Athens certainly had schools before the Persian Wars. In *The Clouds* Aristophanes glances back at the 'good old-fashioned education' which the men who fought at Marathon (490), the *Marathonomachoi*, received: 'First and foremost, children were seen and not heard; you could watch all the lads from one quarter marching through the streets to the *kitharistés'* house in well-drilled ranks, by the right in threes, and never a cloak between them, even if the snow was coming down in bucketfuls.'[35]

It is very likely that in some schools reading, writing, and elementary music were all taught together: at all events there is a famous cup by Douris which shows *grammatistés* and *kitharistés* in the same setting.[36] However, if we are to believe the account of education which Plato makes Protagoras give in the dialogue which bears his name, instruction from the *kitharistés* ordinarily came *after* one's primary education, and the *paidotribés* likewise took over when one's musical training was complete: 'As soon as the children have learnt to read, the master makes the whole class (all sitting on their stools) repeat aloud various verses from the classic poets, which they are then obliged to learn by heart . . . Later the *kitharistés*, as soon as his pupils can handle their instruments properly, will introduce them to other fine works of literature in the field of lyric poetry . . . At a still later stage the children are passed on to the *paidotribés*.'[37] It is very likely, in fact, that intellectual education – what the Greeks called *mousiké*, though this embraced reading and writing as well as music proper – preceded the course of gymnastic training, and that from the age of fourteen or thereabouts physical culture took precedence over intellectual, though without ousting it altogether.

As soon as a little Athenian was of an age to go to school, he passed (at least, if he came from a well-to-do family with several slaves) from the care of his nurse into that of the *paidagôgos*. This was a personal slave-attendant, whose business it was to accompany the boy wherever he went, and to teach him good manners ('honest civility of a sort befitting the young'). To this end he was permitted to employ corporal punishment as a means of enforcing obedience, particularly the birch. It was the *paidagôgos* who took the child to school each morning, and carried his satchel (containing wax writing-tablets, stylus, books, and, later, both flute and lyre).

All the time the pupil was at school the *paidagôgos* stayed there too: sometimes in a special waiting-room,[38] but more often in the classroom itself. On the Douris cup to which I refer above the cross-legged figure sitting on a stool, switch in hand, head turned towards the child reciting an epic poem, is certainly his *paidagôgos* rather than an *erastés*, or lover. Having been present during the lesson, the *paidagôgos* could later test his charge's memory at home, by 'hearing his lines'.

The masters had proper chairs, equipped with backs and short legs, throne-like seats which were the ancestors of the later *cathedra*; their pupils, together with the assistant teachers and *paidagôgoi*, were supplied with simple straight-legged backless stools (*bathra*). There were no tables or desks: with a hard-backed set of wax tablets it was easy enough to write on one's knees; they could also be used as backing for a sheet of papyrus. Demosthenes once addressed the following remarks to Aeschines, who was the son of a junior usher: 'Your childhood was spent in an atmosphere of grinding poverty. You had to help your father in his job as assistant teacher – preparing the ink [used for writing on papyrus], washing down the stools, sweeping out the classroom, and taking rank as a servant rather than as a freeborn boy.'[39]

Schoolmasters, and particularly their assistants, who had to be paid out of the fees obtained from pupils' parents, must have lived very poorly. Another vase-painting shows us a writing-master, stylus in hand, 'bending forward from his chair in a fiercely remonstrative attitude, finger raised threateningly, as though to scold the little brats entrusted to his care'.[40] We shall have to wait for the Sophists, who flourished in the second half of the fifth century, before we find really qualified teachers (at what we would call university level) whose prestige was such as to ensure an adequate recompense for their services. It would appear, too, that anyone at all could set up as a schoolmaster, provided he was capable of reading and writing himself: no kind of 'diploma' was required. If the State exercised any control over education, it was exclusively in the field of morality, and took no account of the knowledge and competence of the teachers.

The idea of a weekly holiday, Jewish in origin, was unknown amongst the Greeks. Holidays occurred at highly irregular intervals, according to the dates of each individual city's religious feasts. Certain months, however, such as that of Anthesterion (February) in Athens, contained so many holidays that they must have more or less resembled the modern schoolboy's 'long vacation'. Observe the behaviour of Theophrastus' Miser: 'When his children miss school through illness, he docks the teacher's fee proportionately; and all through Anthesterion, when holidays are so numerous, he never sends them to school at all, to avoid paying *any* fee.'[41] Moreover, every child enjoyed a number of additional holidays: family feast-days, celebrations on his own account (birthday, hair-cutting ceremony to mark the end of childhood, etc.) not to mention other important occasions such as marriages.

Obviously a child would begin by learning first to read, and then to write. He would be made to recite the letters of the alphabet — *alpha, beta, gamma, delta,* etc. – by heart, imprinting them on his mind with a series of mnemonic rhymes. These letters (*stoicheia,* the 'elements of things') were surrounded with an almost religious respect, the more so since they served to denote, not words only, but also figures, and even musical intervals. Ancient teaching methods were very rule-of-thumb, and there is no foreshadowing of modern techniques. Children progressed slowly from the easy to the more difficult, from single letters to two-letter syllables (*beta+alpha=ba*), and thence to those containing three and four letters. The pupil was trained in pronouncing especially difficult words, such as *lynx.* No effort was made to render the subject easier for him; on the contrary, the idea seemed to be that once he had conquered the most difficult bits, the rest would come without trouble. There were spelling-books in existence, with the syllables of each word divided up.

From here children moved on to reading proper: a task made all the more difficult by the fact that, in all normal texts, there was no punctuation whatsoever and the words were not even separated by spaces – as we can see, for example, in surviving inscriptions from our period.[42] The child would, of course, learn to read aloud, a practice he would subsequently keep up, since silent reading appears to have been more or less unknown: one either read aloud to oneself, or had a slave do the job for one. This is the reason why – to take a random example – Plutarch's essay discussing the way in which adolescent boys should read poetry is entitled 'How the young should *hear* [*akouein*] poems', or, in the traditional Latin: *Quomodo adolescens poetas audire debeat.*

The young scholar would now also practise writing; his wooden tablet had a layer of wax on its inner face, within a slightly raised border, and on this he would trace out letters, using a pointed instrument known as a stylus. Its other end was rounded and flattened, and could be used for erasures. These tablets – the equivalent of our modern slates – might be single-sided, double, or with several 'leaves'; in the latter case the parts were either hinged together, or bound up with loops of string inserted through holes in the frame. The master would begin by sketching the letters very faintly on the wax, and the pupil would then go over them again, applying rather more pressure. Writing could also be done in ink, on sheets of papyrus; the ink was supplied in solid form, ground up in advance, and then mixed with water by the master or one of his assistants. Pens were fashioned from split and trimmed reeds. *Ostraka*, or clay tiles, were also employed, mainly for 'rough copies'. Pupils used cross-shaped rulers (like the one that is visible on Douris' cup, hung from the wall) both to get the letters in a straight line horizontally, and also to ensure that they were directly *below* those in the line above them. This was the pattern known as *stoichedon*, to which inscriptions of the period also adhere. Perhaps there may have been handwriting competitions between schoolchildren even then, like those we know existed in Hellenistic times.[43]

With such primitive methods, learning to read and write could be a lengthy business, which took three or even four years. As soon as a child could read and write with reasonable fluency, he was set to learning poetry by heart – first single verses, then progressively longer extracts, mainly from the first of poets, Homer, the author of the *Iliad* and *Odyssey*. Indeed, what Heracleitus the rhetorician wrote in the first century AD is almost certainly valid for the Periclean Age as well: 'From his tenderest years, the child just embarking on lessons is given Homer as a nurse for his unlicked mind; and what could be better than to let our imaginations feed on the milk of his poetry when we are scarce out of our swaddling-clothes? As we grow, he always remains with us . . .'[44]

The Greeks regarded Homer as the educator *par excellence*: schoolmasters did not use him as an object-lesson in literary achievement, but drew lessons of a moral and religious nature from his text for the benefit of their pupils. These lessons might go further, might indeed take the form of general precepts for life, since in Homer was contained whatever knowledge a man worthy of the name could need: he ranged over all the various activities of war and peace, the crafts and skills, diplomacy and politics, wisdom, courtesy, courage, men's duties towards their parents and the gods. Compared with Homer, the other epic poets (those mentioned in the Epic Cycle) take a very subordinate place; but Hesiod and Solon (the latter mainly in Athens) were also studied to a considerable extent. The picture presented on the Douris cup (and on many other vase-paintings) is doubtless a typical one: the schoolmaster esconced in his classroom, un-rolling a papyrus on which are written the first lines of an epic poem, and teaching them to the boy in front of him. At this period, indeed, all books took the form of papyrus rolls.

Finally, there was arithmetic to round off this course of elementary teaching. We know that the Greeks used letters of the alphabet for figures, bringing the total up to twenty-seven by the use of three additional obsolete symbols that had dropped out of the written script: the *digamma* for 6, the *koppa* for 90, and the *sampi* for 900. This gave nine symbols for the units (*alpha* to *theta*), nine for the tens (*iota* to *koppa*), and nine again for the hundreds (*rho* to *sampi*). Above the figure 999 they either wrote out the words *chilioi* (1000) and *myrioi* (10,000), or else indicated 1000 by writing *alpha* with an *iota* to the left of it, and so on. Arithmetical calculation they found difficult: being ignorant of the 'zero-concept' they were unable to give their symbols value according to position. So for simple sums they used their fingers, following the curious rules of digital computation;[45] while for more complex problems they employed the *abacus*, a board marked out with precalculated dividing-lines to indicate the various types of numerical unit, and worked in conjunction with movable counters. This somewhat hit-or-miss method still survives in certain Eastern countries under Moslem rule. Nevertheless, children managed, somehow, to learn their multiplication tables, though they probably took a leaf from the Pythagoreans' book and used a visual aid consisting of a square of dots.

It is very doubtful whether the young fifth-century Athenian learnt even the first elements of plane geometry at school. His modest store of mathematical knowledge was almost certainly restricted to addition, subtraction, multiplication and division, together with some rudimentary ideas about simple fractions: since the drachma was worth six obols, for instance, it was important to know that a quarter-drachma was the equivalent of an obol and a half.

Such, more or less, was the sum total of Strepsiades' learning when he turned up at Socrates' 'thinkery', with the intention of 'improving himself'.

MUSICAL TRAINING

Historically, the teaching of music in Greece must predate that of reading and writing. At all periods the Greeks have been passionately attached to music and dancing,[46] and in ancient times they regarded a sound knowledge of singing and instrumental technique as the basis of any liberal education. As early as the Homeric Age the bards (*aoidoi*) who celebrated the deeds of bygone heroes were held in the highest consideration and esteem, as Odysseus reminds the Phaeacians: 'All men who dwell on earth owe a bard honour and respect: for the Muse has planted the gift of song in his heart, and cherishes all like him.'[47] The heroes themselves – even the greatest of them all, Achilles, who embodied Greece's loftiest ideals – did not look disdainfully on music: when Agamemnon's envoys reached Achilles, they found him 'playing the clear-toned lyre for his pleasure, a fine inlaid instrument with a silver cross-piece . . . His heart delighted in the music, and he sang of heroic deeds.'[48]

It is significant that the very name 'music' is derived from that of the Muses, those goddesses who preside over all man's intellectual and artistic activities: the Greeks really thought of music as the fundamental element and aptest symbol of all culture. The cultivated man was, indeed, the *mousikos anér*. Themistocles admitted that his education had been incomplete because he had never learnt to play the lyre adequately.[49] Today we admit the civilizing influence of music – *la musique adoucit les moeurs* – but for the Greeks it was the first prerequisite of civilization, and each new modification introduced to musical technique struck them as a genuine danger, something that might well upset the moral equilibrium of the entire body politic, the State as a whole.[50] We know what fundamental importance the Pythagoreans attached to music in their view of human existence, indeed of the world: a concept founded upon a universal harmony of numbers, derived from those governing musical intervals. Here Pythagoras and his disciples merely followed up, and developed scientifically, a natural inclination in the Greek psyche.[51]

The spellbound, almost hypnotized fashion in which the Greeks reacted to fine music is well caught on certain painted vases, in particular on a *crater* from the Berlin Museum which depicts Orpheus singing and playing his lyre in the presence of four visibly mesmerized Thracians. It has been suggested, with some reason, that this picture should be entitled 'The Triumph of Music'.[52] Other vase-paintings, on the white-slip funerary *lekythoi*, often portray a young man either sitting or standing in front of a tombstone, and singing to his own lyre accompaniment, while round him stand a group of people who appear to be listening in hushed and reverential awe. Such scenes, it has been suggested, are 'a musical offering made to some deceased relative or friend by those who survive him. This poor body, doomed to remain underground for all eternity, needs something more than libations: there must be solace for mind and spirit too. So even beyond the grave effort is made to give the deceased pleasure by letting him hear the sound of those melodies that delighted him when he was alive.'[53]

The *kithara*, or lyre, was a stringed instrument whose echo-chamber had originally (or so it was supposed) consisted of a tortoise-shell: the infant Hermes was said to have invented the instrument as a childish prank.[54] The hollow face of this 'box' was covered with stretched skin, and on it were fixed two upright struts, bent and secured at their upper extremity by a cross-piece (which, as we have seen, was of silver in Achilles' lyre). The strings – there were normally seven of them – ran from this cross-piece to the lower end of the instrument; there was also a bridge to lift them above the skin of the echo-chamber. Later refinements were to produce a lyre with eight and even nine strings. The instrument was played either with the fingers, *pizzicato*, or else by striking the chords with a small stick or quill called the plectrum (rather similar to the *mediator* of a mandolin) which was attached to the lyre by a length of ribbon.

As for the *aulos*, this was a wind instrument commonly described as a flute, but in fact rather more resembling an oboe – though more often than not it had two divergent pipes leading off from the mouthpiece. These stopped pipes, as well as the tongues which actually produced the vibrations, were made out of reeds. Professional players fixed the instrument to their lips by means of a leather strap-attachment (*phorbeia*) which partly covered their cheeks; but the boys depicted on the vases never have recourse to such an aid. *Auloi* and *kitharai* were manufactured in special workshops: the father of Isocrates the rhetorician made a considerable amount of money from running an *aulos*-factory.[55]

There are a considerable number of vase-paintings which show us children learning to play one or other of these instruments from their music-master.[56] The master sits on a backed chair, the pupil on a stool in front of him: either the former is playing the instrument himself, to show the child how it should be done; or making the child play, and beating time; or else they are both playing, each with a lyre across their knees. It follows that instruction was an ad hoc affair, conducted orally and without written music. This fact may strike us as somewhat surprising today, but Greek music was exclusively monodic, and therefore more easily grasped than the polyphonic variety.

The *kithara*, as opposed to the *aulos*, left the mouth free for singing; and many pictures of lyre players show them with parted lips, singing to their own accompaniment. This was what Achilles was doing, as we have seen; and the practice was so widespread that a specific word exists to denote a singer who accompanied himself on the *kithara*: a *kitharôdes*. There is a vase-painting which depicts a kind of trio, with the master singing and playing the lyre, while his pupil sits opposite and accompanies him on the *aulos* [or flute, as it is still more convenient, if not quite so musically accurate, to call it for English readers (Trs.)].

Children therefore learnt singing as well as instrumental music. The words of the songs were taken from the old lyric poets, and the lyre player had to take great care to keep the traditional rendering, free from all innovation. Aristophanes shows us young Athenians 'learning to sing some ancient ballad – in the proper posture, not with thighs glued together [an attitude considered incorrect] – like "Pallas, Terrible Stormer of Cities" or "Fierce Battle-Cry from Afar", keeping to the tune as their fathers knew it. But if anyone started fooling about and putting in trills and twiddly bits, like the tremolo stuff we get nowadays from the Phrynis School, he would get a sound drubbing for his un-Muse-icality.'[57]

The instrument that enjoyed the greatest prestige was, undoubtedly, the lyre; though the *aulos*, which was probably imported from Boeotia, had a great vogue in Athens during the fifth century. (Even in Alcibiades' day, however, we find the flute criticized: Alcibiades himself disliked an instrument which deformed one's features whilst one was puffing into it.[58]) The supremacy of the lyre was most memorably upheld by the myth in which Apollo the lyre player triumphs, in the Muses' judgment, over the flute-playing satyr Marsyas – a myth illustrated in a famous bas-relief from Mantinaea.[59] Plutarch, quoting a line of Sophocles, informs us that the *aulos* 'had originally been reserved for funeral ceremonies, at which it fulfilled a function devoid alike of prestige and brilliance'.[60] By the fourth century the *aulos* seems to have fallen out of use except amongst professional musicians and courtesans; and thus it was that the word *aulétris* (flute-girl) became synonymous with *hetaira*.[61] During this period we also find women harp players on the vase-paintings; and tambourines appear as well, especially in religious ceremonies of an orgiastic nature.

It was, too, in the fourth century that the virtuosos began to appear. Lyre playing technique grew ever more complex and diversified – so much so, indeed, that Aristotle spends some time in the *Politics* discussing the problem of whether the *kitharistés'* teaching should expand to take in the latest developments of musical art. His conclusion, a sensible one, is that such instruction should aim only to produce brilliant amateurs, not professionals.[62] Yet the 'ever-widening gulf between academic music and living art'[63] was little by little to bring about the decline of musical teaching as such.

Young Athenians occasionally utilized their musical talents to contribute to the festivity of some public occasion, in deme or tribe or city, by choral displays of singing and dancing. So it came about that in 480, after Salamis, the future poet Sophocles, then aged about fifteen, stripped, gleaming with oil, lyre in hand, led the boys' chorus that chanted the Victory Paean.[64]

In such exceptional circumstances, as well as more regularly, on the occasion of the city's great religious festivals, it was customary to appoint *chorégoi* – citizens whose election to this office depended on the fact that they were wealthy enough to defray the expenses involved – whose task it was to recruit and train (through the services of *chorodidaskaloi*, or choirmasters) groups of children for a joint performance of some lyric hymn in honour of a god. This choral offering did not require numerous rehearsals, since it was always sung in unison, or, in the case of mixed-voice choirs, in octave; the Greeks, as I have already remarked, were wholly unacquainted with polyphony. Ordinarily these performances (which combined both religious and artistic elements) took the form of competitions between several choirs drawn from each of the ten tribes. The *chorégos* of the victorious group was given a tripod as his prize; and pride (or the desire for publicity) frequently led him to commemorate the event by 'dedicating' the tripod – that is, by setting it up close to some public highway, on the top of a monument constructed at his own expense. This practice was so popular that one street in Athens, lined on either side with such offerings, became known as the Street of the Tripods [see above, p. 9]. Such is the provenance of the choregic monument of Lysicrates, which one can still admire in Athens to this day, and which bears the following inscription, datable to 335 BC: 'Lysicrates, son of Lysitheides, of the deme Kikynna being *chorégos*, the Acamantian tribe was victorious in the children's contest. The flute player was Theon; the choirmaster, Lysiades of Athens; Achon, Euainetos.'[65]

PHYSICAL TRAINING

The Greek passion for physical exercise is no less ancient (and no less strong) than their love of music: to convince onself of this one need only read the account of the funeral games celebrated by Achilles in honour of Patroclus (*Iliad*, Book XXIII), or that of the games held outside Alcinous' palace (*Odyssey*, Book VIII) or of the bow-stringing trial in Ithaca (*ibid.*, Book XXI). In any place where the Greeks founded cities, we find two buildings which between them sum up their civilization: the theatre and the stadium.

We have no firm evidence as to the age at which the young Athenian normally began to practise gymnastics under the direction of the *paidotribés*. It may have been as early as eight,[66] but was more probably about twelve, when he had already spent several years with the *grammatistés* and *kitharistés*. The physical training instructor divided his pupils into two classes: the 'little ones' (*paides*) who might be between twelve and fifteen; and the 'big boys' (*neaniskoi*), from fifteen to eighteen.[67]

Whereas reading, writing and music could be taught in more or less any reasonable-sized room, physical training required the specialized amenities of the palaestra. This was, basically, an open-air sports-ground, square in shape, with a wall running round it. On one or two sides there were covered lobbies which served as changing-rooms, rest-rooms (these were equipped with *exedrai*, or benches), baths, and shops which supplied oil and fine sand, both of which commodities, as we shall see, were essential for those physical exercises practised by the Greeks.

The palaestra was decorated with busts of Hermes, the patron deity of *gymnasia*. It could be used for the performance of all the various sports we shall discuss below, except for the foot-race, which required a far larger arena: on such occasions the *paidotribés* had to take his charges along to the stadium.

The *paidotribés* reigned supreme in the palaestra, clad in a purple cloak which he at times removed in order to demonstrate some exercise personally. He carried a long forked stick, both as a badge of office and as a means of administering sharp correctives to clumsy or insubordinate pupils: it also served to part embroiled wrestlers. He frequently was assisted by a squad of 'monitors', chosen, it would appear, from among the oldest and most talented members of the class.

Three special traits characterize Greek gymnastics: the athletes performed stark naked (our term 'gymnastics' derives from the adjective *gymnos*, meaning 'bare'); they always rubbed their bodies with oil; and their exercises were accompanied by music on the *aulos*. Thucydides attributes the first two of these practices to Spartan influence: 'The Lacedaemonians,' he observes, 'were the first to display themselves naked in public, and to rub themselves with oil for athletic contests. Previously, even at the Olympic Games, the athletes used to wear a kind of loin-cloth which concealed their private parts.'[68] The young gymnasts we see on the vase-paintings wear neither loin-cloth nor shoes, and normally go bareheaded even in the blaze of noon – though one or two are shown wearing a sort of small fur bonnet.

The essential articles which every boy had to take to the palaestra with him included a sponge for washing himself down, a small oil-flask (*alabastron*), and a bronze scraper or curry-comb (*stlengis*; *strigil* in Latin), a sort of grooved spatula with a curving end. Before his session he would wash at a fountain, or, if the palaestra was equipped with one, in a big stone tub. He would then rub oil all over his body, and finally sprinkle himself with sand, or dust, letting it run through his fingers in a fine spray. This practice was justified on the grounds that it safe-guarded health: it was supposed to protect the body against chills and sudden changes of temperature. When the period of exercise was over, the strigil was essential for scraping off the mixed coat of oil, dust, and sweat that had accumulated on the skin. After-wards, of course, the boy washed himself all over again.

It has been established that at least one flute player was permanently attached to each palaestra. His task was to set the rhythm for all athletic activities: not only those loosening-up exercises of the sort nowadays described as 'Swedish drill', but also such field sports as throwing the discus and javelin. We have vase-paintings which show these *aulétai*, their instruments fixed to their mouths by means of the *phorbeia*,[69] playing away while the boys take exercise.[70]

From the time of Peisistratus in the sixth century, the Panathenaic Festival included a competition reserved for children in the five branches of the *pentathlon*, to wit: wrestling, running, jumping, discus and javelin. Wrestling was the competitive sport *par excellence*: its Greek name (*palé*) had been responsible for the naming of the palaestra. The children began by softening up the ground with a spade, a tool frequently depicted in vase-paintings dealing with athletic subjects. Besides, digging was in itself good healthy exercise. Then the boys faced one another in pairs, heads down, arms outstretched, and tried to get a grip on each other, usually by the wrists, the neck, or the waist. The object was to tumble your adversary while remaining upright yourself. Each bout consisted of three rounds. The *paidotribés* taught his pupils all the various holds and the appropriate stance for each; and this instruction gave rise to a large technical vocabulary with which all Athenians were well acquainted. Writers adapted its terms to various metaphorical uses,[71] and Lucian, much later, was to employ it in an erotic context in the *Asinus*.[72] During competitions, whether between boys or adults, wrestlers were paired off by lot: beans were drawn, two of them marked *alpha*, two *beta*, and so on. If there was an odd number of competitors, an extra bean marked *gamma* was thrown into the urn, and the person who drew it had a bye, being held in reserve to challenge one of the first-round winners. These second-round contestants were once again paired by lot, and so till the end.[73]

There were several different types of foot-race: the sprint, the two hundred yards (the 'stade' varied from city to city, but averaged something over 180 metres), the 'double-stade' or quarter-mile (*diaulos*), the 'quadruple-stade' or half-mile (*hippios*), and the long-distance race, which might be anything up to twenty-four stades, or between two-and-a-half and three miles.

All these races, however, were run to and fro between the starting-line (marked by a row of those truncated columns known as cippi) and the further end of the stadium. When the competitor reached this latter point, he had to circle round another cippus known as the *terma*, and then run back to his point of departure, repeating the whole process if the race in question happened to be longer than the quarter-mile. These stadium cippi have been preserved (at Epidaurus, for instance) and also appear on numerous monumental reliefs.[74] Greek runners did not rest one knee on the ground at the starting-line: they awaited the signal upright, body bent slightly forward, feet close together.

As far as jumping was concerned, the only event which the Greeks appear to have gone in for with any enthusiasm was the long-jump. For this feat, as for wrestling, the boys were first made to dig over the spot where they would land after their jump. Then they attempted the jump itself, usually clutching a dumb-bell in either hand (the French word for a dumb-bell, *haltère*, is etymologically linked with the verb *hallomai*, meaning 'to jump'). These dumb-bells were made either of stone or lead, and could be of two types: a concave hemisphere, so designed that the palm of the hand could fit comfortably into the hollow, or the kind of dumb-bell we use today, in which two solid masses are linked by a bar – though the bar of the Greek dumb-bell (which served as a hand-grip) was curved. Its weight varied between two and ten pounds. Dumb-bells were also used for loosening-up exercises. During the long jump they assisted the balancing motion of the arms, and by thus employing them the athlete Phayllus of Croton was enabled to jump a distance of more than eighteen feet.

The discus was made of bronze, and weighed anything from two to eight pounds: children obviously were given much lighter ones than adults. The throwing-base was marked off at front and sides only, and the actual projection of the discus involved two successive movements: 'The discus-thrower first raised his discus in both hands. He then bent forward towards the point of release, left foot thrust forward, after which he straightened up vigorously, his torso pivoted from left to right above the hips, and his right arm described a wide circle from front to rear. In the second phase the discus descended again, the body bent forward, and the left foot (which had trailed behind during the upward movement of the discus) now moved forward again, instep turned down, toes dragging along the ground.'[75] It is this second phase which Myron's Discobolus reproduces. The discus was sanded to prevent it slipping through one's fingers. A peg was inserted at the point where it fell, so that the various contestants' throws could be measured and compared.

The javelin, a weapon employed both for hunting and in war, was also utilized for sport. The athletics javelin was about the height of a man, and as thick as a normal finger; unpointed (as a precaution against accidents) but weighted at the tip. At its centre of gravity it was fitted with a looped thong (*ankylé*), consisting of a thin leather cord between two and three feet long, which was wound round the shaft, and terminated in a ring-buckle, which the contestant slipped over the index and middle fingers of his right hand. This device, by imparting a rotary motion to the javelin, doubled or even tripled its flight. On vase-paintings we often see javelin-throwers carrying what looks like a large pair of compasses; and one picture seems to depict a trainee pacing out a prescribed distance behind his coach.[76] It therefore seems likely that the compasses were used to trace out a circle within which – at each chosen distance – the javelin had to fall. This would be a 'target-competition'; but athletes could also compete to see who achieved the longest cast.

In addition to these five classic sports, the boys might also, on occasion, go in for boxing or the *pankration*. For boxing, their hands were bound with strips of leather: there was no ring as we know it, nor any idea of rounds: the bout was unlimited as regards space, and virtually uninterrupted. The same conditions applied to the *pankration*, a still more brutal sport in which almost any kind of technique was allowed, including wrestling-holds, kicking, punching, limb-twisting, and so on; in fact, the only trick barred was thrusting your thumbs into your opponent's eyes and gouging them out. Normally the two *pankratiastai* (or all-in wrestlers) were soon rolling about in the mud (the ground was not only dug, as for wrestling or the long-jump, but watered too). The fight only ended when one of the contestants, from sheer exhaustion, raised his arm in token of surrender: and this was the alleged reason why the two sports of boxing and the *pankration* were banned at Sparta – a Spartan should never admit defeat.[77]

We see that Greek sport could be extremely rough and violent.

As H. I. Marrou wrote, 'when we try to imagine, in the words of J. M. de Hérédia, "the naked athletes under the clear Greek skies" we should do well to take the somewhat idealized renderings of the neo-classical poets with more than a grain of salt, and see them instead in the heat of the sun, and standing in a dust-raising wind, their greasy skins covered with a layer of coloured earth – not forgetting the blood-stained all-in wrestlers rolling in the mud . . .'[78]

As far as young boys were concerned, it seems likely that the *paidotribai* strove to avoid all excess, in accordance with the sensible advice given by Aristotle. Just as the philosopher warned music-masters against trying to produce virtuosi, so he also discouraged *paidotribai* from attempting to turn out athletes capable of gaining victories at the major Greek Games; counselled them to make their young charges practise every sort of sport, so that they had a well-balanced, all-round training, rather than to push them on in one particular field with a view to breaking records.[79]

Apart from the pentathlon, boxing, and the *pankration*, the boys also practised every kind of loosening-up exercise, to a flute accompaniment: arm and leg movements (*cheironomia*), games with balls or hoops,[80] even work on the punching-bag (*kôrykos*), a leather sack filled with sand and hung at chest-level, which gave good practice for boxing. Children of upper-class families also began to take riding-lessons at an early age: throughout her entire history Greece has always displayed a marked partiality for the horse. Did they also learn dancing, in the strict sense of the word? It seems very unlikely, though the exercises they performed in the palaestra would certainly prepare them to become fine dancers if they so desired. Similarly with such institutions as the *lampadédromia*, or torch-race, well-attested from several festivals: this did not, clearly, call for any special training, and any good runner could compete in it without difficulty.

One rather surprising fact is the almost total absence of any swimming contests, especially since the Greeks were a sea-faring nation, who had an idiomatic proverb defining an imbecile as one 'who could neither read nor swim'.[81] Sculling and rowing regattas are equally rare. This state of affairs may well be explained by the fact that the Greeks had originally come down from the north, from the vast Euro-Asian continent: the traditional order of contests was probably established in some remote period before they had come in close contact with the sea.[82]

PEDERASTY

We have already referred to pederasty in connection with the Spartan educational system. Distasteful though this topic may be, we cannot pass it over in silence: the love of boys played altogether too large a part in Greek education. It is to be observed, indeed, that the word for 'love' (*erôs*) is seldom employed in texts of the classical period when reference is being made to normal attraction between the sexes: it is more or less exclusively reserved for homosexual attachments. A poet such as Aeschylus, who had never taken the passionate love between a man and a woman and presented it in a play, nevertheless made his piece *The Myrmidons* hinge on the sexual love between Achilles and Patroclus (despite the fact that in the *Iliad* these two are portrayed as enjoying a warm, but quite innocent relationship). Greek tradition on this score was so strong, and so persistent, that even during the Roman period Plutarch – though himself an admirable husband and the father of a large family – felt obliged to spend several pages of his *Amatorius* proving that girls, no less than boys, are capable of inspiring passionate love.[83] It may be asserted that such a state of affairs – in Athens at any rate – was due to the fact that girls lived secluded lives, and enjoyed very little education. But at Sparta, where they pranced about half-naked in public, and where the young men were hardly likely to cultivate them for their intelligence, pederasty flourished (or was rampant) both more widely and more openly than in Athens.

On the other hand it is undeniable that the naked state of the boys during their physical training must have encouraged homosexuality. The numerous vase-paintings that portray boys and *ephéboi* taking physical exercise bear inscriptions of the *kalos* type that are little more than dedicatory tributes to *beaux garçons*. But we must go further still: I am convinced that Marrou is right in insisting on the *military* antecedents of Greek homosexuality. According to him, it began as a kind of *Kriegskameradschaft* which survived at least into the mid-Hellenic period, but was better preserved in the Dorian states, whose institutions underwent an archaizing process of ossification. The general impression one gets is that the Dorians themselves imported such customs into Greece. The Greek city-state, even at its most highly developed point (such as Athens in the Periclean Age) remains a men's club, a closed masculine society from which the opposite sex is debarred, but where a passionate attachment between an adult male (the *erastés*) and some adolescent boy of twelve to eighteen (the *erómenos*) could generate most noble sentiments of honour and bravery. The famous Sacred Band of Thebes in the fourth century is a typical instance of collective valour maintained and cemented by *amitiés particulières*. Moreover, during the sixth century in Athens the famous 'tyrannicides' seem to have acted less from love of liberty than because a son of the tyrant Pisistratus dared to cast eyes on the beautiful young Harmodius, Aristogiton's beloved. Plutarch cites several analogous instances from other cities, where the murder of a tyrant was, in reality, an act inspired by amorous jealousy or revenge:[84] a *crime passionnel*, in fact; but the 'tyrannicides' being so universally acclaimed as liberators, the honour that attached to their memory also tended to be reflected upon masculine love.[85]

From his writing-master, his music-teacher, and his physical training instructor the young Athenian learnt various concepts, techniques, and skills: but in all this there is little sign of education in the proper sense – that is, *moral* education. This side of education is, admittedly, the most difficult to achieve. Not so long ago in France the old Ministry of Public Instruction was renamed the Ministry of National Education; but it needed more than that to improve the overall training of French children overnight. Perhaps this aspect of ancient education lay in the hands of the *paidagôgos*? But the *paidagôgos* was a slave: how could he have taught his charge the virtues proper to a free man? The boy's father, who, one might think, was his natural teacher in this field, was far too busy with affairs of state. Almost the only remaining possibility, one comes to see, was the salutary influence and example of an older on a younger boy.

In Athens, it seems, Solon's laws forbade men access, not only to the school but to the palaestra as well, unless they had some specific duty to perform there. But from Plato's dialogues we see that the ban was not strictly observed: the *Lysis*, for instance, shows us Socrates, together with several of his young friends, visiting Mikkos' palaestra, for the specific purpose of admiring 'beautiful Lysis'. It was in this way that a man would first notice an adolescent, and pursue him with various attentions; if the boy responded to these advances, and an attachment grew between them, the resultant intimacy might, indeed, remain innocent, but often, doubtless, took on an altogether different character. Such a friendship was likely to prove stirring both for the older man, who would be animated by an ardent desire both to protect and to mould the character of his *erômenos*, and for the young boy, who would be full of gratitude and admiration for his *erastés*. Such, at any rate, is the ideal of 'pedagogic' pederasty as it was defined in antiquity: 'that love which settles upon some young and well-endowed youth, and by the path of friendship leads up to virtue'.[86]

Does this mean that such liaisons were actually encouraged by the State? Certainly not if any overt sexual element was involved. Even in Sparta and Crete, where pederasty flourished quite openly, any physical relationship with an *ephébos* (and, *a fortiori*, any attempt to corrupt his innocence by force) was illegal and, in theory at least, punishable by law. As far as Athens was concerned, a study of Aeschines' speech *Contra Timarchum* shows us just how strongly public opinion – quite apart from the laws on the subject – militated against the prostitution, procuring, and rape of an adolescent boy. Naturally, the partisans of pederasty used to maintain that nothing but the most innocent relationship was ever in question: it was thus that Plato could make such a relationship one condition governing the ascent of the soul towards the Good and the Beautiful, and the central principle of all truly superior knowledge.

Let us admit that Socrates' love for Alcibiades remained innocent – though not for want of trying on the younger man's part;[87] nevertheless, as Plutarch was later to remark, 'if the man who loves young boys disclaims voluptuous intentions, it is through shame and fear of punishment; since he needs an unimpeachable excuse for frequenting the company of handsome youths, he puts himself forward as a paragon of virtue and innocent friendliness. He smothers himself with dust at the *gymnasion*, takes cold baths, raises supercilious eyebrows: outwardly he gives himself the appearance of a philosopher and sage, but later, at night, when all is quiet, "sweet it is to pluck flowers in the gardener's absence".'[88] One typically Greek maxim says that physical beauty is the 'flower of virtue', as though the soul always shaped the body, and a fine body could not be sorted with anything but a fine soul.

In certain parts of the Greek world, and at certain periods of Greek history, the existence of this 'men's club' called into being, as a sort of pendant and corollary, a 'women's club', so that male homosexuality was reinforced by lesbianism. Sappho, who lived on Lesbos in the sixth century, was a teacher as well as a great poet whom ancient critics ranked almost level with Homer; she ran a kind of 'finishing school for young ladies' where mistress and pupils tended to form very close relationships.[89] But we shall find no comparable institution in Greece during the Periclean Age.

THE SOPHISTS

The instruction which the young Athenian received at school was, as we have seen, of an elementary, indeed primary nature; and it seems clear that during the first half at least of the fifth century no higher education was available in Athens. But the second half of the century saw the most radical new developments in education, thanks to the appearance of the Sophists. This word, *sophistés*, was not originally pejorative in its implications: on the contrary, it was used to describe learned, skilful men who possessed the art of passing on their knowledge and their techniques to others.

Schools of medicine had already existed for some time in various parts of Greece, on the island of Cos especially. As early as the sixth century Ionian philosophers had been speculating on the nature of the universe; and some of them (such as Xenophanes of Colophon) had had the audacity, long before Plato, to criticize the immorality of the Homeric gods. But it was the Pythagoreans, it seems, who first established a real school of higher education – the distant ancestor of our modern universities. We find such schools at two towns in Magna Graecia (Greek southern Italy): Croton and Metapontum. The subjects taught there were, primarily, philosophy and mathematics. Teachers and pupils banded themselves into a kind of religious brotherhood, placed under the patronage of the Muses and devoted to scholarship. We know that the later schools of Plato, Aristotle, and Epicurus were to adapt a more or less identical form: so true is

The Background

1 Marble head of Pericles, found near Tivoli. A Roman copy of an original Greek portrait-statue of the mid-fifth century BC

2 A restored view of the Acropolis as it was at the end of the fifth century BC

3 The Pnyx as it is today. The speaker's platform from which Pericles addressed the crowd is in the centre

4 The main underground drain, running north to south, in the Agora, Athens, as it is today

Women, Marriage and the Family

5 Preparing the bride for her wedding in the women's quarters. A scene from an Atti...

6 Hetairai depicted on an Attic vase by Smikros

ase painting

7 A wedding procession with a maid playing the flute to entertain the guests while the bride and her retinue arrive

8 A bridegroom taking his bride away by
chariot after the wedding ceremony

9 A terracotta statuette of
a woman writing

10 A terracotta statuette of two women playing knucklebones

11 (*above*) A child's toy chariot made of terracotta

12 A baby's bottle in black
glazed terracotta ware

13 A small doll
in terracotta

14 Greek girls collecting water from a fountain. Detail from an Attic vase painting

15 Grecian ladies showing the typical dress of the period. An early nineteenth century drawing

16 A Greek youth, a philosopher and a young lady wearing the *peplos*. An early nineteenth century drawing

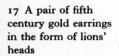

17 A pair of fifth century gold earrings in the form of lions' heads

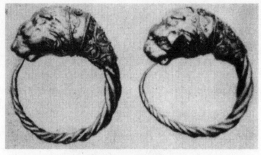

18 An incised bronze mirror cover showing Aphrodite and Pan gaming

Work and Recreation

19 (*above*) An olive harvest
with the workers beating
the trees with long sticks.
Detail from an Attic vase
painting

20 A painting thought to
represent Polynices, the son
of Oedipus, offering Eriphyle
the necklace of Harmonia.
Their dress is typical of a
pedlar and a young lady of
the period. From an Attic
vase

21 The interior of a shoe shop with an old shoemaker at work, painted on a
kylix

22 (*right*) One of the amphorai given as prizes at Greek games. The contest
for which the prize was given was illustrated on the vase

23 A potter at work fitting handles to a vase, painted on a kylix

24 A bronze figure of a Spartan girl running

25 A vase painting
of a girl tumbler

26 A wrestling
contest: bas relief

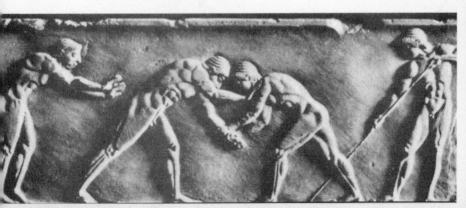

27 Boxers binding themselves with protective leather thongs before
fighting. The figure in the centre is the gymnasium master. Detail from
an Attic vase painting

28 Greek men playing a form of hockey: bas relief

29 Part of the altar at Delphi showing priestesses hanging up votive offerings

30 Part of the eastern side of the Parthenon frieze showing a religious procession. The leading figure is all that remains of a maiden carrying an incense burner followed by four girls, two carrying jugs and two carrying bowls

31 (*right*) A bas relief in the Acropolis Museum of a pensive Athena leaning on a staff

32 The altar scene at a sacrifice, a priest pours wine on the flame while another roasts the meat and a third plays the flute. Detail from an Attic vase painting

33 Part of the south frieze of the Parthenon. Heifers are being led to sacrifice

34 A rhapsode chanting an
epic poem. Detail from an
Attic vase painting

35 The Theatre of Dionysos as it stands today

36 A scene from a comedy enacted on a crude stage with a ladder leading up to it. The parody is of Blind Chiron being healed by Apollo

Warfare

37 Warriors arming before battle. Detail from an Attic vase painting

38 A warrior blowing a trumpet before battle. Detail from a kylix

39 A warrior about to leave home

it that more or less all human activities in the ancient world touched the sacred category in some respects. Theatrical performances – even when one of Aristophanes' most licentious and irreverent plays was on the stage – came under the heading of religious ceremonies; and the most freespoken philosophical discussions concerning the world and the gods took place round the altars of the Muses, who enjoyed a cult at Athens as elsewhere.[90]

But the people who were most anxious to systematize and disseminate all the new learning in the air were, undoubtedly, the Sophists. They did not teach in any particular place: these proto-professors were in fact travelling lecturers, permanently 'on circuit'. Their demonstrations of learning and verbal fluency brought them pupils who attached themselves to the *maestro* and followed him from town to town: they were, first and foremost, educators. Under the general heading of 'philosophy' they taught all the subjects then available that had not been covered by the elementary school curriculum: geometry, physics, astronomy, medicine, arts and crafts, and – above all – philosophy in the narrower sense of the word, and rhetoric.

The Sophists' claims, then, were universal, and it is here especially that they exposed themselves to a cruel flank attack (and some barbed ironies) from Socrates and Plato. Their common aim was to turn out first-class minds, men as practical as they were wise, and in particular leaders, statesmen: in short, the élite of every city-state. One of their assertions was that *areté* could be taught.[91] Now *areté* – the quality known to the Romans as *virtus* – was not primarily moral virtue, so much as that combination of qualities which make a man eminent and endow him both with practical efficiency and public fame.

Many young Athenians wanted, more than anything in the world, to acquire this knowledge, which they regarded as a necessary pre-condition of *areté*. Thus it was a great day for them when some famous Sophist arrived in their town. One of Plato's dialogues shows us the agitation and anxious impatience felt by the young Hippocrates, who has just woken Socrates up before daybreak, begging him for an introduction to Protagoras of Abdera, then passing through Athens. The two of them make their way to the house of the wealthy Callias, a patron of learning and the arts who is only too glad to offer hospitality to itinerant Sophists. There, in the lobby, Socrates and Hippocrates perceive

Protagoras strolling up and down, chatting with some extremely well-connected Athenians: Callias himself, the two sons of Pericles, Charmides:

> There was also Antimoerus of Mende, the most distinguished of Protagoras' disciples, who learnt the profession of Sophist from him and later became a Sophist himself. Others trailed along behind them, listening to their conversation: strangers for the most part, whom Protagoras had collected from all the various cities he passed through, charming them into following him by the persuasiveness of his utterance, like some new-style Orpheus. There were also some Athenians amongst them. The sight of this group [says Socrates] caused me great pleasure: I particularly appreciated the elegant patterns of movement they adopted so as never to get in front of Protagoras. They were very careful about this. Every time he made a half-turn with his front-rank companions, the audience behind him, in perfect unison, divided to left and right, wheeled about, and formed up in the rear once more. It was marvellous.

Socrates also recognizes other Sophists among those present: Hippias of Elis, omniscent and omnivorous, a forerunner of Pico della Mirandola; and Prodicus of Ceos, who was, together with Gorgias of Leontini, one of the most famous teachers of rhetoric in his day.[92]

The Sophists were not so disinterested as Socrates: they charged a stiff price for their services. On the other hand, they were the only people then capable of teaching what we would call general cultural subjects, or of giving instruction in public speaking. The common people no doubt jeered as these sumptuously clad intellectuals, with their pretentiousness and their pedantry; they certainly provided a broad target for the comic poets to snipe at. Aristophanes, in *The Clouds*, represents Socrates the Athenian as being one of them: we see him shut up in his 'thinkery' or being hauled aloft in a basket to study atmospheric and astral phenomena from close quarters. *We* know that Socrates, with his moral idealism and his fundamental insistence on truth, was in a very different category from the Sophists, who were consciously utilitarian, and far more concerned with practical efficacy than with rigorous moral or intellectual thought; but the Athenian man in the street did not draw such nice distinctions. Such mockery (the price of their success) did not prevent the Sophists from making a great deal of money, and, indeed, from launching a kind of humanist movement – which Socrates and Plato criticized and refined, it is true, but which undoubtedly contributed to the development of a Greek intellectual élite.

The most serious objection which Socrates and Plato levelled at the teaching of the Sophists was that the *areté* envisaged by them remained fundamentally indifferent to what we today call 'virtue': Callicles, in the *Gorgias*, sets his ideal of power above and beyond good or evil. The life and death of Socrates bear eloquent witness against this amoral attitude. Twelve years after he drank the hemlock, in 387, the year in which the 'King's Peace' gave the Greek city-states a certain amount of tranquillity, Plato founded his own school in the *gymnasion* of the Academy.[93] The master and his disciples spent much time pursuing truth together by means of long 'dialectical' discussions: the Platonic dialogues offer us a transposition of these into literary form. But – let us make no mistake about it – this quasi-university, the first of its kind to be opened in Greece, was not solely a centre of intellectual education: it was at the same time a kind of religious community, after the pattern of the Pythagorean School. Here philosophers and would-be philosophers, united not only in the cult of the Muses but also in their memory of that noble figure Socrates, tried to live a pure, virtuous life such as would prepare the soul – when it finally shuffled off its soiled physical envelope – for a post-mortem ascent to the contemplation of God. The 'philosophical life', in fact, was a preparation for death: it engaged one's entire being. Plato was not, it is true, altogether without interest in the idea of the Earthly City – he sketched out an ideal (and Utopian) plan for it both in the *Republic* and the *Laws* – but he was also looking above and beyond such horizons, to man's heavenly destiny.[94]

In the fourth century, the Sophistic Movement was rescued by the Athenian Isocrates, whose school of oratory was set up in rivalry to the Academy. Isocrates was a rhetorician who set himself up as a philosopher, though philosophy in the strict sense interested him only insofar as it gave the orator a good cultural background and some useful themes to expand on: he regarded it as a 'propaedeutic' to training in the art of oratory. As we know, this debate was finally decided, over the centuries, in Plato's favour: in a French *lycée*, for instance, philosophy is taught at a later stage than rhetoric, and is indeed the culminating point of a pupil's studies. What cannot be denied is that Plato is the original father of all philosophical instruction, just as Isocrates fulfils the same role for all modern classes in rhetoric.

This promotion of intellectual studies amongst a cultural élite in the various Greek city-states resulted in a certain falling-off as regards physical training. The Sophists' pupils were all too ready to criticize old-fashioned educational methods, which, they said, produced athletes with magnificent bodies but very little in their heads. We have already noted a corresponding decline in musical teaching during the fourth century.[95] On the other hand, the art of drawing enjoyed a sudden efflorescence at exactly the same time. It looks as though young would-be Athenian artists were advised to draw the human figure more than any other subject: they did so in charcoal, on panels of polished wood. Aristotle gives the drawing-master the same advice as he handed out to the music-teacher and physical training instructor: he would like to see them instruct their pupils, not with the aim of turning them into great artists, but simply so as to form their tastes and enable them to appreciate works of art.[96]

Thus, thanks to the Sophists, the intellectual side of education gradually became predominant, and broke away from the subordinate, indeed accessory role which it had played in the old-style *paideia* – though this *paideia* was preserved unchanged at Sparta.

CHAPTER FIVE

JOBS AND PROFESSIONS

The dignity of manual work – Money and usury – Agriculture – Artisans – Commercial enterprise – Medicine

---

THE DIGNITY OF MANUAL WORK

The Sophists were criticized for accepting fees; and this criticism is profoundly revealing as to the way the ancient Greeks looked upon the whole idea of professions and jobs. We say today that 'all work deserves its recompense', and payment for services rendered is a concept which strikes us as not only natural, but just. It was not so in the Periclean Age, when ideas concerning social organization still looked back to archaic times, and indeed had scarcely altered since Hesiod's day.

Now for the poet of the *Works and Days* the best sort of work – backbreaking, to be sure, but still the only kind that ensures a man full dignity – is that of the peasant smallholder, whose land provides him with the wherewithal to feed and clothe himself and his family, and to satisfy all their immediate needs. To a Greek, obsessed as he was with the idea of freedom, to be dependent on some other person for one's daily bread seemed an intolerable condition of servitude. A truly free man should be altogether his own master; and how could he be that if he was drawing a salary from someone else? Even in Homer's time the worst condition of humanity is that of the agricultural labourer, the *thés* – that is to say, the proletariat, forced by grinding poverty to hire out their services for pay.[1] The ideal, therefore, is individual (or at least family) autarky, an end not fully achievable except in the depths of the country. Hesiod makes his own plough, and all the other tools he needs. As for clothes, the women of the household first spin the wool, then weave it. The peasant of the *Works and Days* may find himself forced to dabble in trade from time to time;

but he objects to this on principle, and the whole idea of maritime commerce frightens him.[2]

Doubtless by Pericles' day economic development had brought about a whole multitude of changes. Besides, industry had been born, and the purchase of objects turned out by specialist workshops or factories became more convenient (and cheaper) than their manufacture at home. Yet the ancient distaste for paid labour persisted. In the middle of the fourth century Aristotle was still capable of writing: 'The title of citizen should be withheld from all those on whom the city depends for its livelihood . . . The perfect city will not enfranchise the mere worker (*banausos*). It is not possible to practise the civic virtues while leading the life of a worker with a pay-packet . . . There used to be a law in Thebes debarring all businessmen or traders from public office unless they had ceased their money-making activities at least ten years previously . . . By "banausic occupations" we mean all those which affect the disposition of the body, together with any performed for gain; these rob the mind of all freedom, all aspiration to higher things.'[3] Plato and Xenophon express very similar ideas.[4]

Yet it seems very probable that over this point the three writers mentioned echo the old aristocratic tradition, which had only been preserved in its pure, undiluted form at Sparta. Socrates was more realistic. Not only did he enjoy frequenting shops and craftsmen's booths (he declared there was much to be learnt in such places); we even find him, in the *Memorabilia*, attempting to persuade an Athenian to make his parents go out to work. These parents are freeborn citizens, for whom he is responsible, but whom he can no longer afford to maintain. 'Are you aware,' Socrates asks him, 'that Nausicides not only supports himself and his slaves by manufacturing flour, but also keeps large quantities of cattle and pigs? And even so his economies are such that he can often lend the State financial assistance. Take the example of Cyrebus the baker, whose trade lets him support a family and still live very comfortably; or Demeas of Collytus, who makes tunics, or Menon, whose speciality is cloaks – or, indeed, the majority of the Megarians, who derive their income from those short dresses they produce . . . Because your parents are freeborn, do you honestly believe that exempts them from all duties save eating and sleeping?'[5]

In point of fact, despite what Aristotle says, citizens with a job or profession enjoyed exactly the same rights in the Assembly (when they could get there) as anyone else. There was a law relieving a son of responsibility for supporting his father if the latter had failed to apprentice him to some trade, and another law (as we have seen) which made idleness a criminal offence. We have already quoted a passage from Plutarch which makes a very clear distinction in this respect between the ideas prevalent in Athens and Sparta.[6]

Solon himself turned merchant in order to recoup the family patrimony which his father had squandered; though Plutarch, when relating this fact, feels the need to justify it. He quotes Hesiod's aphorism to the effect that there is nothing shameful about work, and indicates that commerce, at least, was then regarded as a respectable pursuit.[7] When he writes elsewhere that no well-connected young man could possibly want to be a sculptor like Phidias or Polycletus, nor yet a poet such as Anacreon, Philemon, or Archilochus, he is simply reflecting the prejudices of aristocratic Boeotia, where he was born.[8]

In actual fact by far the larger number of Athenians took the dignity of the artist's profession for granted, and vase-painters signed their work with conscious pride. They even extended the esteem in which they held farming (when it was practised by the landowner, the *autourgos*, in person)[9] to include the banker and the high-level businessman. Demosthenes' father was an arms manufacturer, and Isocrates' father owned a flute factory – though the author of the rhetorician's *Life* is at pains to specify that the flutes were actually made by slave labour, and Isocrates' father himself merely directed their activities.[10] In Athens, as in all other Greek cities except Sparta, it was only manual labour and retail trade that were really looked down on.

Thucydides makes Pericles declare: 'Amongst us, poverty in itself is no reproach – but failure to try and improve one's position we regard as reprehensible. Here men pursue both their private interests and their public duties: we do not concern ourselves any the less with politics through having learnt a profession.'[11] A study of vocabulary is often a good and revealing guide to a people's most widespread assumptions. It is certainly true that the word *banausos*, originally used in Athens to denote furnace-workers (ie smiths and potters), and later extended to include all manual workers whatsoever, had a strongly pejorative connotation – far more so than the word *démiourgos*, which literally means 'public worker', and which we find applied not only to artisans and craftsmen, but also to those intellectual workers whom today we would include in the 'liberal professions', eg doctors. But in Ionia the worker was often called *cheirônax*, and this word – formed from *cheir* (the hand) and *anax* (leader or master), translatable perhaps as 'skilled worker' or 'master craftsman' – was never anything but an appellation of honour and respect. In many industrial and commercial cities – Corinth, for instance – workers were by no means looked down on.[12] In Athens, however, manual trades were performed mainly by slaves or metics, and freeborn citizens only undertook them in cases of dire necessity.[13]

MONEY AND USURY

In Homer's and Hesiod's times exchanges were effected by means of barter: sometimes ingots of precious metals might be employed, but not currency. The normal practice was to assess the value of an object or person in terms of cattle: a suit of armour or a woman would be worth so many head of oxen. Though money had been used in Greece as early as the seventh century, it seems to have been exceedingly cumbrous and inconvenient to begin with: it took the form of iron spits, and this is the origin of the word 'obol' (*obolos* or *obelos*='spit' or 'nail'). We know that at Sparta such currency was employed later than anywhere else; and this gave rise to the assumption, in antiquity, that Lycurgus had used the *obolos* as a device to combat luxury and corruption.[14]

Up till the time of the Persian Wars, gold and silver coins were a rarity in Greece, through lack of precious metals. The only sources of supply were the mines on the Thracian coast, and those on the islands of Thasos and Siphnos. It is true that in Attica itself, at Laurium, in the south, there were deposits of argentiferous lead – as we have seen – which the Athenians exploited; but it was not until 483 that they discovered a far richer seam, at Maronea in Thrace – 'a spring of silver, a treasure hidden beneath the earth'.[15] This discovery (which contributed substantially to the victory at Salamis, thanks to Themistocles' naval decree[16]) henceforth made it possible for Athens to have an abundant minted coinage.

The Attic drachma weighed 4.36 silver grammes, and was an excellent alloy (up to 98.3 per cent pure silver). The Athens mint (*argyrokopeion*)[17] also struck two-drachma pieces (*didrachmon*) and ten-drachma pieces (*dekadrachmon*), but above all those coins equivalent to four drachmas, commonly known today as tetradrachms. Above the *dekadrachmon* (itself fairly rare) the only larger units we know existed solely for purposes of accountancy: these were the *mina* (worth 100 drachmas) and the *talent* (worth sixty minas, or 6000 drachmas). On the other hand, the subdivisions of the drachmas had currency to represent them, and these smaller coins were also of silver. First came the obol, a sixth part of a drachma (we may note that both decimal and duodecimal systems were retained together) together with its multiplicands (pieces worth respectively three and two obols, the *triobólon* and the *dióbolon*), and its fractional parts: three-quarters (*tritémorion*), quarter (*tetartémorion*) and eighth (*hémitetartémorion*). All these coins were of the same type, with Athena's head on the obverse (helmeted, and wearing an olive-wreath), and on the reverse an owl – Athena's sacred bird – together with a crescent moon, an olive-branch, and the first three letters of the goddess' (or the city's) name. These coins were popularly known as 'Laurium owls', and there was a proverb which asserted the uselessness of 'taking owls to Athens' – or, as we would say, coals to Newcastle. The engraving of these coins for long preserved an extremely archaic format: doubtless because no one wished to alter, in any respect, a currency so hallowed by long usage, and so solidly respected on the international market.

In theory, any independent city enjoyed the right to strike its own coinage; but only one or two had succeeded in getting their currency widely accepted. Amongst the latter was Aegina (the Aeginetan stater, with its tortoise device, weighed about twelve grammes) and Cyzicus, whose staters – known as *kyzikénoi* – were stamped with the tunny and minted from electrum, an alloy of gold and silver. The difficulty was to exchange coins from these various systems one against the other. Their very multiplicity encouraged sharp practice on the part of the money-changers. The comic poet Diphilus has a scene with a stall-keeper who wants ten obols for a big fish: the customer gets out ten Attic obols, but the fishmonger says no, that won't do, what he meant was ten *Aeginetan* obols. (The Attic obol was worth only seven-tenths of the Aeginetan.)

In order to put an end to such anomalies (and, primarily, to ensure the supremacy of her own 'Attic owls') Athens, during the course of the Peloponnesian War, imposed her system of weights, measures, and coinage on every city in the League.[18] Aristophanes parodies this decision in the *Birds*, where the Statute-Seller proposes a decree according to which 'the people of Cloud-Cuckoo-Land are to use the same weights, measures and laws as the Olophyxians'[19]; similarly, in the *Peace*, he makes a joking allusion to the Athenian decree by which an allied city was fined five talents, as a result of an Athenian having died a violent death within its territory.[20]

The total amount of tribute (*phoros*) paid to Athens by the League which Aristides brought into being after Salamis was, to begin with, 460 talents per annum. During the Peloponnesian War, when the reserves which Pericles had accumulated in Athena's temple treasure had been absorbed by the cost of military operations, this tribute was raised several times, till it stood at thrice its original figure; and yet – especially after her disastrous expedition to Sicily – Athens still lacked money. The permanent occupation of Attica by Peloponnesian troops even disrupted the working of the Laurium mines, since the slaves had taken advantage of the situation to desert. At this stage solid gold statues were melted down and minted into coins, and a decree was also passed approving bronze denominations. But this currency, in the fifth century at any rate, was of short duration. In one passage of Aristophanes we find two Athenians talking: 'Do you remember the decree we passed about that bronze coinage?' says the first, to which the other replies: 'I should say so; a bad job it proved for me, I'll tell you. I sold all my grapes, and pouched away a whole stack of coppers; then off I went to the market for some barley, and just as I was holding out my sack the town crier came round bawling "Bronze coinage no longer legal tender! Only silver accepted!"' [21] (This habit the Athenians had of 'pouching' small change in their mouths has already been alluded to above.[22]) Yet bronze coinage was to re-appear at Athens in the fourth century; and this time it stayed for good.

Gold coins in circulation were mainly 'darics' (named after King Darius), minted by the Persians and bearing the device of an archer. During the final years of the Peloponnesian War, when the Great King was underwriting the Spartans financially, so many of them were circulating in Greece that the relative value of gold and silver fell from 13.33:1 to 10:1 between 450 and 336 BC.

Athenian currency, as we have seen, was not alone in being accepted by a whole group of city-states; but we only hear of one currency in the classical period that was issued, not by some individual city-state, but under the auspices of an international organization. This was the 'Amphictyonic money', struck in 338 and bearing the images of the two deities associated with the Delphic Amphictyony, Demeter and Apollo. This looks very much as though it were a remarkable attempt to achieve some sort of common currency; but it clearly enjoyed scant success.[23]

The Periclean Age also saw the emergence of usury. Hitherto loans had most often taken the form of the *eranos*, ie an interest-free loan, and otherwise people simply hoarded their capital. But the growth of economic activity came to demand investments; and to safeguard him against the risk of loss it seemed only right and fair (despite the protests of certain philosophers) that a man who loaned out capital should receive his own again with interest. From the end of the fifth century the bankers begin to appear, most of them slaves or metics; and from fourth-century court speeches dealing with disputed inheritances we learn that numbers of people lent almost their entire fortune out at interest. The most popular methods of increasing one's capital were to make high-interest loans for maritime trade, or else to buy up slaves and hire them out, either to individuals or the State.

Loans were made on a strictly short-term basis, and interest was payable at each 'new moon', ie at the close of each lunar month. Strepsiades, having run himself into debt by underwriting his son's extravagant taste for horse-racing, lies awake at night worrying about money-matters: 'I'm ruined,' he moans, 'the moon's twenty days on, the interest's mounting up . . .'[24] Normal rates of interest on a loan were one drachma per mina per month, ie 12 per cent. The five-obol rate (10 per cent) is generous; we often find nine- or even ten-obol rates, which works out at no less than 20 per cent. Usurers, indeed, went even further. The

State does not seem, in the ordinary way at least, to have bothered about limiting rates of interest. We know of one exception, however: the city of Delphi, under the archonship of Cadys, at the beginning of the fourth century, issued a decree forbidding loans to be raised at a higher interest rate than three obols per mina per month (ie 8.57 per cent) if reckoning by the Delphic mina (=70 drachmas), or at over 6 per cent if the basis for calculation was 100 drachmas to the mina, according to the most widespread usage.[25]

AGRICULTURE

The life of a peasant-farmer, working his own land, remained the Greek ideal in Xenophon's time as it had been in Hesiod's; and if the Greeks founded so many colonies all round the Mediterranean littoral, in Italy, Gaul, Spain, Africa, and even in Southern Russia, this was primarily to find land for their surplus population: the soil of Greece itself, being dry and largely barren, could not sustain them all. Xenophon's *Oeconomica* contains a hymn of praise to agriculture, which, he says, not only grows products essential for our existence, but also makes those who practise it better in body and soul alike: 'The exercise it gives to those who till the soil with their own hands induces a manly vigour in them, by compelling them to rise betimes and trudge long distances in the course of their labours . . . The earth also makes those who cultivate it eager to fight in the defence of their country, since the harvests it bears are available to all, and lie at the mercy of the strongest . . . Being a deity, the earth also imparts notions of justice . . . Agriculture further teaches us how to command others, since a good farmer must imbue his workers with the will to toil and the habit of prompt obedience . . . The man who said that agriculture was the nurse and mother of all other arts was quite right. When all is well with agriculture, everything else prospers.'[26] In other words, agriculture as an occupation produces the best citizens and the best soldiers.

The attitude to real estate varies a great deal in Greece, according to period and locality. In Lacedaemon, every full Spartiate citizen possessed a medium-sized holding (*kléros*), which was – in theory at any rate – inalienable, and which his helots cultivated for him. Naturally, since Spartans were debarred from following any profession save that of arms, other men had to till their land for them. Each Spartan received the products of his *kléros* in kind, as an annual living allowance. The official rate was seventy *medimnoi* of corn for himself, and a dozen for his wife, which makes about a hundred bushels in all, together with a proportionate quantity of fruit – olives and raisins in particular. But the *kléros* system was not enforced consistently, and it proved impossible to prevent certain families enriching themselves at the expense of the majority. The result was that in Laconia property soon became concentrated in the hands of a small number of citizens, who were continually adding to their domains.[27] In many other parts of the Greek world, such as Thessaly and Boeotia, big estates seem to have been the rule right from the beginning: smallholders such as Hesiod are rare, and frequently grumble about the big landowners whom the peasant from Ascra refers to as 'kings'.

In Attica, nearly all the great estates of the Eupatridae had been split up by the end of the sixth century, as we have seen above.[28] The great majority of Athenian citizens lived either on, or at least from, their own land. We have seen how Xenophon was careful to distinguish between the landowner who tills his soil with his own hands (*autourgos*) – aided more often than not by one or two slaves – and the man who merely supervises the work being done in his fields, such as Ischomachus, who conducts the dialogue with Socrates in the *Oeconomica*. But there was a third sort of landed proprietor: one whose entire life was spent in the city, and who entrusted his estates to a bailiff, leaving it to him to farm them, and to forward either the yield itself or its equivalent in cash. Pericles, who was kept permanently in the city by affairs of state, authorized his farm-bailiff to sell off the produce of his lands in Attica, using the money thus gained to defray the day-to-day expenses of a town house.

Before the Peloponnesian War, the position of a country landowner in Attica (even one with only a modest estate) seems to have been extremely pleasant. Such, at least, is the impression given by the nostalgic musings of that stalwart old countryman Strepsiades, when he broods over the village he was forced to leave because of the war.[29] It is true, as Glotz has pointed out, that 'the plains of the Mesogaea, Cephisus, and Eleusis all gave a good yield in corn and vegetable products; the Diacria was covered with fine vines; there were plentiful grazing-land and coppices along the lower slopes of Mount Parnes, while higher up the hives swarmed with bees; and everywhere the olive yielded an oil that was worth its weight in gold.'[30] But the 'Periclean plan' (which consisted of abandoning the countryside to the ravages of the enemy, so as to turn Athens and the Piraeus into one vast fortress, whence triremes would sally forth to raid the coast of the Peloponnese) was, in the long run, a death-blow to Attica's agriculture, especially insofar as the vine and the olive were concerned: and it was on these two commodities that the country's economy largely depended. It took time to replace those lopped vines; and the destruction of the olive-groves was a real disaster, since at least ten years must elapse before a young olive-tree begins to bear, and a good deal longer before it is at its productive peak. Other influences helped to accelerate the decline of agriculture, not only in Attica, but other areas of Greece as well, where once large estates were divided up into tiny allotments off which not even a severely reduced family could make a living any longer. On top of this, the general rise in prices tempted the smallholder to run himself into debt, and often he ended by selling his land to a speculator.

Agricultural methods remained fairly rudimentary in classical times. The only cereals cultivated to any great extent were wheat and barley, and there was not nearly enough even of these: Attica was obliged to import the larger proportion of her grain from Sicily, Egypt, Thrace, and the northern Black Sea littoral. There were normally three ploughings a year, in spring, summer and autumn. The plough, little improved since Hesiod's day, and drawn by oxen (a rarity in Attica) or mules, only permitted a very shallow furrow: the work was finished off with spade and hoe.[31]* Threshing was performed in a manner still popular in certain country districts of Greece to this day: the sheaves were laid on a paved threshing-floor, in a spot well exposed to the wind, and then trampled out by a team of horses or mules attached to a central post by a long rope, and driven round and round. The grain was then ground in a mortar (this job was normally performed by the women) with the aid of stone or wooden pestles.[32]

Translator's note: This state of affairs has not changed much with the centuries – certainly not in the Greek island where I live. Looking through my window as I type these words, I can see two oxen busy on the autumn ploughing, drawing a wooden plough at least as primitive as Hesiod's, and a great deal less complicated than Virgil's. Similarly with threshing techniques.

From the fourth century onwards, 'agricultural experts' began to study crop rotation and methods of soil improvement: they experimented a good deal with improving the yield by means of manure. But the main subject of their researches was in the field of arboriculture.

Olives were either harvested by hand, or else beaten down with long whippy reeds [again, a practice still retained in Greece (Trs.)]; they were then pressed in a kind of mortar with a spout or drainage-hole at the bottom, through which the marc (*amorgé*) was run off. This by-product was used both as a fertilizer and to render wood or leather more supple. Sometimes a real oil mill was employed, made out of two stones, one fixed, one mobile, so arranged that they fitted together, in a quern-and-mortar fashion. The resultant pulp was then fed into the olive press proper.[33]

The grape-gathering was conducted to the sound of flutes, which spurred on the harvesters just as it set the pace for exercises in the *gymnasion*. The wine press was a portable wooden vat, slightly tilted at the bottom so that the liquid drained out through a projecting pipe into the jar placed beneath it. The must was trodden underfoot – still to the skirl of the flutes – by workers who clutched a handrail running round the rim of the vat to preserve their balance.[34]

Amongst fruit-bearing trees, the most popular was, beyond doubt, the fig. Trygaeus in the *Peace* conjures up memories of fresh figs and of those cakes of preserved figs (*palasia* or *palathia*) so abundant before the war.[35] The only sugar available in antiquity was that supplied by the bees. The best-appreciated (and the dearest) honey came from the hives of Hymettus. We also find Trygaeus saying to Polemos (War), as he pours Attic honey into his mortar: 'If I were you, I'd try some other sort of honey. That stuff costs four obols. You leave Attic honey alone.'[36]

In the fifth century the vegetables most popular with Athenians (and generally regarded as a luxury) were mainly imported from the two neighbouring states of Boeotia and the Megarid. However, the farmers of Attica did manage to produce cabbages, lentils, peas, onions, and garlic; they even acclimatized the Egyptian gourd. Flowers, too, were the object of particular attention, being a *sine qua non* for the garlands and wreaths without which no festival (whether public or private) would be complete.

The breeding of cattle and horses did not flourish in Attica, since there was no lush pasturage there; but it formed one of the main economic activities on the plainlands of Thessaly and Boeotia. Donkeys and mules, on the other hand, were abundant, and used for most forms of transport.[37] Pig-breeding was widespread: Plato regarded swineherds as essential to the State,[38] and the candidates for initiation into the Eleusinian Mysteries can have had no trouble in procuring, at a cost of three drachmas, the sucking-pig that was an essential element in the ceremony performed at Phalerum Bay [see below, p. 213].[39] The mountainous frontier regions (*eschatiai*) provided pasturage for numerous flocks of sheep and goats. Strepsiades recalls how he told his baby son: 'When you're a big boy you'll bring home the goats from the fells [*phelleus*='stony district': one such region in Attica was known by name as Mount Phelleus] just like Daddy, all dressed up in a sheepskin cloak.'[40] Sheep, we should note, provided not only milk and meat, like goats, but wool too – the indispensable raw material for making clothes. On the other hand such flocks were the natural foes of all cultivation: the moment the shepherd took his eye off them they would be in amongst the crops, nibbling away, and for this reason certain cities passed laws against the breeding of goats.[41]

ARTISANS

Industry became increasingly important in Athens during the Periclean Age, and by far the larger proportion of the urban population earned their living by some sort of trade or craft. Despite this, a good number of jobs were still done at home. Yet though most Athenian women did their own spinning and weaving, and many of them baked their own bread, there were, equally, large numbers who bought loaves or cakes at the baker's – or who, having provided sufficient clothes for their own families, would then process more wool for other people to buy, and make a stock of ribbons, dresses, hats, spun thread, or ceremonial wreaths to sell in the market.[42]

The most menial tasks were primarily reserved for slaves, or, failing them, metics. The free citizen body, as has been well said, constituted a kind of 'working aristocracy',[43] and it is very seldom that we find any citizen undertaking a manual occupation, even temporarily. In any case they would frequently absent themselves from any job to attend the Assembly or the law-courts, where they were issued with tallies recording their presence.

Though there was an undeniable concentration of industry in Athens, we cannot yet speak of 'factories' in the modern sense of the word. The most important workshop known to us employed a hundred and twenty slaves: this was the armoury owned by the metic Cephalus, Lysias' father. Many businesses regarded as quite sizable had less than fifty employees. Only the mines at Laurium required a really vast slave-labour force, and the task of supplying them was shared by numerous government-licensed contractors. For all public works, eg naval and dockyard contracts, the State ordinarily supplied the raw material, and then divided the work up between a large number of small firms, none of which possessed more than the most modest facilities.

The State was in no way concerned to regulate working conditions, except insofar as it needed to do so for the preservation of order or the protection of public property. Girl musicians (both flute players and lyre players, and most of them *hetairai*) were not allowed to ask more than two drachmas a day, and in the case of several clients arguing over one woman, the *astynomoi* settled who should have her by drawing lots.[44] In the State-owned Laurium mines it was illegal to remove pit-props or cause excessive smoke in the galleries. With these few exceptions, conditions of labour do not form the subject of any legislation. The rule of supply and demand was sovereign. Unemployed persons offered themselves as casual labourers in the agora at Colonus, where they might be hired for a day or any longer period, as the employer decided. Annual contracts of employment were normally renewed on the sixteenth of the month Anthestérion, roughly corresponding with February.

The only occasional help which the State gave the proletariat consisted of reducing unemployment by means of large public works programmes. According to Plutarch, this was one of the reasons for the embellishment of the Acropolis under Pericles' administration; and the well-known passage (from his *Life* of Pericles) also gives us an impressive list of the various trades which benefited from such a windfall:

As for the working population, Pericles did not want such people to go unpaid; but he was equally anxious that they should not get money for doing nothing. Consequently he put a series of firm proposals before the Assembly involving large-scale construction projects and plans for various buildings, which would keep numerous trades fully employed for some while to come . . . The basic raw materials – stone, bronze, ivory, ebony, cypress-wood – were to be worked and assembled by a whole range of craftsmen: carpenters, pattern-makers, smiths, stonemasons, dyers, gold-smelters, ivory-workers, painters, enamellers, engravers, drivers and waggoners, merchants, sailors and harbour-pilots, wheelwrights, wainwrights, coachmen, rope-makers, weavers, curriers, and navvies . . . Thus the requirements of the scheme would bring prosperity, as it were, to people of every age and aptitude . . .[45]

Very often, in the skilled trades, a father would train his son up to succeed him, passing on all the techniques and secrets of his craft. Often, too, children were apprenticed to some local master craftsman, an arrangement sealed by a contract; and in order to promote a spirit of healthy rivalry among the apprentices, competitions were sometimes organized for their benefit, eg in the potters' workshops.[46]

In Athens there were about sixty public holidays per annum, though these were distributed very unevenly over the various months. Work began early in the morning, and did not end till sunset. It was not only that obsessional juror Philocleon who got up at cockcrow:[47] 'When [the cock] sings his dawn song, up they all spring and hurry off to work – coppersmiths, potters, shoemakers, tanners, bathmen, millers, lyre-makers-cum-shield-turners; why, some of them are shod and abroad when it's still quite dark.'[48]

By the end of the fifth century the normal daily wage of an unskilled labourer was one drachma, but this rose during the fourth century along with the cost of living. Some craftsmen were paid piece-work rates, as we can see from certain surviving inscriptions which record building accounts. Such a wage would just about support an unmarried worker, but was hardly adequate for a family man, even bearing in mind the exceptionally plain diet of the average Greek, who would often make do for a day on a hunk of bread, two onions, and a small handful of olives.

Apart from unskilled labouring jobs, most occupations called for intelligence and skill, and were much more than a mere repetition – as monotonous as it was mechanical – of certain routine actions. The dividing-line between artist and artisan was often a very fine one; many crafts demanded good taste and a degree of aesthetic perception. Many workers had a habit of singing as they went about their tasks, and in some workshops the rhythm of production was controlled by a flute player. But negligent or idle slave-workers were liable to brutal floggings, and great care was taken to see that they did not pocket the fruits of their labour themselves. The opening scene of Aristophanes' *Peace* shows us Trygaeus' two slaves collecting and kneading a repulsive array of turd-cakes for their master's giant dung-beetle: one of them exclaims: 'There's one thing I don't run any risk of in this game, mates: no one's going to accuse me of scoffing the pastry I make.'[49] We know that in order to stop slave pastry-cooks eating the cakes and pastries they baked, their masters sometimes fitted a wide circular disc round their necks, the diameter of which was more than their arm's length, and which acted in the same manner as a muzzle.

Tools and equipment were simple, indeed primitive; and their efficiency in output was correspondingly low. Miners were issued with an oil-lamp (made of lead or baked clay) which they stood in a niche in the rock-face beside them, and which would burn for about twelve hours. A round-the-clock shift system was worked. The galleries were seldom more than a yard high, and often less, which meant working on one's knees, or even lying down. In order to avoid the risk of the roof caving in, the miners would leave standing pillars of ore at irregular intervals, which fulfilled the same function as the modern pit-prop; but greedy contractors would have these pillars removed, thus seriously endangering the men working the gallery. The State was obliged to threaten extremely severe sanctions against such behaviour. Air-vents were infrequent, and it must have been very difficult to breathe. Behind the miner himself, who worked with pick, hammer, and chisel, were other workers (some of them possibly women) who gathered the ore into baskets and carried it, bent double, to the main shaft, round which there ran a wooden staircase by which they could regain the surface. There the ore was pounded up in mortars, milled, washed, and finally smelted down in the furnace. The lead thus obtained was sold commercially in pigs of about thirty pounds' weight, each stamped with the trademark of the smith who had cast it. The silver was refined and dispatched to the public mint (*argyrokopeion*), where it was used for striking off fresh currency.[50]

Ceramic workers were very numerous, and mainly centred, in Athens, on the appropriately named Ceramicus quarter. Clay was the raw material in antiquity not only for those utensils which we still produce as pottery or china today, but also for many others now made with some quite different material, such as wood, glass, or metal. Instead of barrels the Greeks had large clay jars known as *pithoi*; clay drinking-cups (*kylikes*) filled the place of our modern glasses; and clay cooking-pots (*chytrai*) were employed where we would use saucepans. An immense variety of different jars and vases was turned out, adapted for every conceivable purpose, lamps included.[51] There is a votive stele from Corinth[52] which illustrates the process of clay extraction. There were several clay pits in Attica, notably at Cape Colias, seven miles south of Athens. To make the clay redder and less porous, it was treated with ochre (*miltos*) or vermilion; we know from an inscription that in the fourth century Athens enjoyed a monopoly of the vermilion from the island of Ceos.[53]

The potter's wheel was in use as early as the Homeric Age, but it had remained a very rudimentary affair – just a flat wheel revolving on a vertical spindle, which the potter either turned by hand himself or employed an assistant to operate for him. When a pot had been modelled it was set in the sun to dry, after which it was polished and, finally, decorated. At an early period the decorators painted black figures on the red ground of the pot; in the fifth and fourth centuries they left their figures the natural colour of the clay, sketching the outline in black and finally black-glazing the entire background. These were the red-figure vases, which succeeded the black-figure technique. As well as black and red, the artists had several other colours available: white, which sometimes served as a ground, eg in numerous funerary *lekythoi;* purplish red, and, more rarely, blue, pink, gold and brown. The black glaze, with iron oxide as its main ingredient, had a fine metallic sheen and was extremely lasting: it was applied with a coarse brush. Afterwards the pot was oven-baked – an extremely delicate operation. When the piece was an artistic creation (many of the vases we admire in museums never served any practical purpose, but were made simply to be looked at and enjoyed) the potter would sign his name on it: *made by so-and-so*, we find, and the same with the decorations: *painted by* ——. Thus we know the names of many such craftsmen, several of whom at least were great artists in their own right. All the paintings proper of the classical period have perished, but these vases enable us to form some sort of notion of them.

Blacksmiths' forges are occasionally depicted on vases. The furnace is always shown as being higher than a man, ie at least six feet from ground to summit, the fire in which is worked up with a bag-like bellows made from goatskin. One worker holds a piece of metal down on the anvil with a long pair of pincers' while another hammers it out. In almost all the forges thus depicted we see one or two jars hanging from the wall: these doubtless contained water to refresh the thirsty smiths, who most often appear stark naked, or at the most very lightly clad. We also see a group of craftsmen casting the separate pieces of a bronze statue prior to its assembly (the latter being effected by a system of lug-joints). There is another scene which shows us a colossal statue receiving a final polish.[54]

Greece originally possessed some fine forests, but by the classical period these had already been sadly depleted, and timber had to be imported, from Macedonia, Thrace, Asia Minor, and Magna Graecia (Southern Italy). The bulk of Athens' navy was built with Thracian timber. The tools employed by joiners are depicted on one bed-maker's funeral stele: they included set-square, compasses, and curved moulding-guides. Various vase-paintings show us such scenes as a carpenter squaring off a beam with a long-handled, hammer-like instrument, or an ivory-worker piercing a hole in a casket with a bow-operated auger, or a sculptor chiselling out a wooden Herm.[55]

The dressing and polishing of cut stones had been brought to a fine art. Greece, as we know, possessed some magnificent marble quarries, notably on the island of Paros and, in Attica itself, on the flanks of Mount Pentelicus. There was also an attractive bluish limestone, such as we find in great quantities at Delphi. The quarrymen left projecting 'haulage lugs' on two sides of each rectangular block (or in the case of column drums, on the flat periphery) so as to allow for hoisting. This operation was carried out with rudimentary equipment consisting of several long beams, a cable, and a block and tackle; the lugs, of course, were removed at the end of the journey. Stones were close-jointed with one another by means of lead clamps; the shape of these clamps varied from age to age (some are dovetailed, some in the form of a T) and provide archaeologists with useful evidence for dating a site. We know, too, that the Greeks were very fond of painting on stone: most of their marble statues and bas-reliefs were picked out in vivid colours, blues and reds especially. Stelae, both the incised and sculptured types, were also painted, and the letters of an inscription were not only engraved, but also painted, normally in red.

Leather was prepared by the tanner or currier (*skytodepsés, byrsodepsés*) before passing into the cobbler's hands to be fashioned into shoes. Some tanners were important figures of industry, and went in for politics: one thinks of Cleon and Anytus. In one vase-painting we see a cobbler setting about a 'made to measure' job by simple, not to say primitive methods: the customer has placed his foot on a sort of plinth (whether of stone or wood is uncertain) on the workshop bench; one of his hands rests on the cobbler's head. The cobbler himself is cutting the leather round the customer's foot with a paring-knife. On another vase we see a shoemaker working up a piece of leather, cutting it to shape: hanging from the wall are a paring-knife, some scraps of leather, and several shoe-patterns.[56] Men's and women's shoes were made in different workshops.[57]

Spinning and weaving were mainly done by women in their own homes; but there were also workshops which specialized in 'treating' baled wool. First it was washed in warm water; then the tufts were 'carded', by teasing them out and rubbing them close against one's outstretched leg. For this operation a gadget known as an *onos* or an *epinétron* was also sometimes employed: its purpose was revealed by the picture on one particular specimen. This semi-cylindrical object, of baked clay, was designed to fit over the knee and the lower part of the thigh. The woman using it would rub the tufts of wool over its slightly rough outer surface. Next, the wool was put on the spindle. Spinners did not always work sitting: there is a vase-painting of one who appears to be managing both spindle and distaff with great adroitness while on her feet. Last of all, the wool was woven on a primitive loom, of the upright or vertical type. Once the warp had been set up, the weft was threaded through by means of the shuttle (*kerkis*).[58]

The dyer (*bapheus*) subjected his material, whether wool or linen, to a long and meticulous preparation before actually dipping it in the dye-bath: this was to ensure that the colour should be wash-resistant and non-fading.[59] Lastly there was the fuller, or *knapheus*, who gave a special finish to new cloth, and also – like modern dyers – cleaned up used garments. He placed them in large vats filled with water and potash, or else in receptacles containing 'fullers' earth', otherwise known as smectite, and then subjected them to heavy pressure. When Theophrastus' Mean Man 'takes his coat to the fuller's, he tells him to use plenty of earth, so as to make the coat stay clean longer'.[60]

COMMERCIAL ENTERPRISE

Farmers and craftsmen very often sold their products directly, without any need for a middleman. The Acharnian brought his own sacks of charcoal to market, and the peasant did the same with his fruit, vegetables, cheese, oil and wine. The lamp-maker, the cobbler, armourer or the potter had examples of the work turned out by his slaves on sale in the front of the workshop. Thus Kerdon, the shoemaker in one of Herodas' mimes, is both craftsman and retail trader. Various vase-paintings show us a passer-by examining a potter's wares, fishermen bringing their catch to market, and oil-sellers hailing potential customers, telling them – as they top up a jar – what first-class stuff they've got for sale.[61]

But there also existed large numbers of professional retailers, who bought from the producer and resold to the general public. All those persons in retail trade were known as *kapéloi*, a word which carried a decidedly pejorative connotation, and did not include the *emporoi* – these being merchants dealing in wholesale business, which meant, nine times out of ten, maritime trade.

All shopkeepers were *kapéloi* – not least those who dispensed food and drink. Tavern-keepers were followed by the sellers of 'grain, vegetables, and mash' and of 'garlic and bread, with all who keep hostelries'.[62] The main area where such people congregated was the Agora itself, and the nearby streets. As Glotz put it, 'all those with any produce to sell – slaves bearing their hand-woven fabrics, craftsmen from the Ceramicus or Melité or Scambonidae, peasants who had left their country village before dawn, Megarians with their pigs, the fishermen of Lake Copais – from every side they came crowding in. Down the tree-lined avenues they streamed, to the various quarters reserved for each particular commodity, and separated one from another by a movable barrier. In quick succession, at their officially appointed times, the various markets opened: vegetable-market, fruit-market, markets for cheese and fish and meat and *charcuterie*, for game of every sort, flesh and fowl, for wine, timber, pottery, old clothes, and hardware. There was even a corner set aside for books. Each stallkeeper had his own pitch, reserved for him on payment of a special fee, where, under the shade of awning or large umbrella, he would lay out his wares on a trestle-table, close to his cart and his resting beasts. Shoppers wandered round, much solicited by the various stallkeepers, with porters and errand-boys eagerly offering to assist them. The air was always loud with shouts and oaths, and arguments in which the *agoranomoi* could never be sure whose side they ought to hear first. When the open-air markets closed, customers moved across to the covered arcade, a sort of Oriental-style bazaar with the money-changers at the lower end of it.'[63]

Small traders had a bad reputation for honesty: they were regularly accused of giving short change and short measure, despite the watch kept on them by the *metronomoi*, and the quality of their goods came in for sharp comment as well. Even though they might, individually, be as honest as the day, the occupation they pursued was the object of general obloquy. Aristophanes never missed an opportunity of reminding his audience, maliciously, that Euripides' mother had sold vegetables in the market; and it was true that women who made a living this way, whether in the Agora or down one of the market streets, were even less well thought of than their male colleagues, and very often suspected of personal misconduct. Aristophanes' sausage-seller, in *The Knights*, is told by one of the servants of Demos (ie 'The People'): 'You've got all the qualities needed to be a demagogue – coarse, brutal voice, low birth, and guttersnipe manners.'[64]

Despite the appalling roads, which were often no more than mere tracks, with fords instead of bridges at each river-crossing, there were plenty of itinerant pedlars who made long trips with their bales and pack-animals, normally either donkeys or mules. These sometimes carried the whole load themselves, and sometimes were harnessed to a light cart or a four-wheeled waggon. They might, for instance, be bringing the products of lush Boeotia to Athens: Aristophanes shows us an Athenian haggling with a Theban, who had brought a whole load of game and fish in, including some of the famous eels from Lake Copais, so prized by Athenian gourmets.[65] But since overland communications were so difficult and costly, the bulk of international commerce was handled by sea, through the agency of the *emporoi*.

During the fifth century the Mediterranean had been cleared of pirates, mainly as a result of the Athenian thalassocracy, which had remained unshaken even since the victory of Salamis and the birth of the maritime league at Delos. Her warships – the famous triremes with their triple banks of oars – simultaneously upheld Athenian naval supremacy and acted as a police force on the high seas. This meant that merchantmen could enjoy undisturbed sailings from port to port, faced with no dangers apart from those of wind and weather. These vessels were known as 'round' or 'hollow' ships (*ploia strongyla*) to distinguish them from the long, narrow-beamed, shallow-draft triremes. Another difference between the two was that whereas the triremes owed their speed primarily to their oars, the merchantmen (which moved much more slowly) were, for the most part, dependent on sail, and only used oars as an auxiliary form of power. The Greeks understood the use of anchors, but had failed to discover the principle of the capstan winch; and it has been argued that this ignorance was a contributory factor in limiting the tonnage of their ships: even their largest merchantmen had a displacement of under four hundred tons, ie about three times that of a trireme. But there were other reasons for this top limit on tonnage: for instance, with the rudimentary haulage devices then available, how could a large vessel be hauled up on the slips for the winter, or even beached at night when there was a high sea running? The absence of any reliable charts, compasses, or reasonably powerful lighthouses made navigation by night a decidedly hazardous business; as a result all sailing tended to be done in the hours of daylight, and then only during the summer. No captain ever got out of sight of land if he could possibly help it: the favourite technique was to hug the coast as long as possible, and then take a 'stepping-stone' route from island to island, so as to always find some shelter by nightfall. The trip from the Piraeus to Sicily was normally made by way of Corcyra and Tarentum: ships were hauled overland by means of a 'false keel'. In order to avoid the long haul round the Peloponnese, it was customary to cross the Isthmus from the Saronic Gulf to the Gulf of Corinth by means of a 'roller-slipway' known as the *diolkos* (hauling across). The rollers were made of wood: the course of the *diolkos* ran very close to that of the present Corinth Canal, actually crossing it here and there.[66]

The Piraeus, with its vast roadstead and well-protected inner basins, had already eclipsed both ports of Corinth, its old and long-standing rival Aegina, and indeed every other maritime city of Greece. It was the centre of activities even more vital than those carried on in the Agora: Athens' maritime trade far outstripped her shore-based commerce, and the fortunes of her *emporoi*, whether citizens or metics, were immeasurably greater than the modest gains with which the *kapéloi* contented themselves. Since these merchants had to make enormous capital outlays and ran very considerable risks, they were on occasion aided by the bankers, who lent them money at high rates of interest. Though the State allowed free enterprise its head in all these activities (except, as we shall see, for the marketing of grain) it nevertheless derived a steady benefit from them: through the agency of a tax-farming syndicate it levied customs duty, first at one, later at two per cent, on the total value of all merchandise passing through the Piraeus.

Athens' political hegemony enabled her at the same time to maintain supremacy in the field of commerce. To begin with, so that the dockyards of the Piraeus should be able to keep up a non-stop ship-building programme, it was essential to import timber from Thrace, and several other sorts of raw material from various places abroad; and Athens' preponderance in Greek affairs guaranteed her a monopoly of supply – either *de iure*, as in the case of vermilion from Ceos, or *de facto*. The author of *The Constitution of Athens*, a most instructive little monograph which has come down to us amongst the works attributed to Xenophon, has some apposite remarks to make on the subject [this is the acidulous diehard often referred to as the 'Old

Oligarch' (Trs.)]: 'In the whole of Greece, and indeed amongst the barbarian nations too, is there any people with such a talent for self-enrichment as the Athenians? Consider the facts. If such-and-such a city has good timber, if this one is noted for its iron-ore, or that one for its copper or its flax, how are such commodities to circulate freely if the mistress of the seas is not given first pick of them? That is the way we get our navy: one city supplies us with timber, another with iron, this one sends us copper, that one flax, yet another provides our tallow . . . I have no need to till my land; I can get all I want by sea.'

Another passage in the same work gives us some idea of the abundance and variety of goods that poured in from every quarter to the Piraeus: 'The disasters which Zeus inflicts on crops and harvests have serious consequences for inland cities, but are easily borne by a maritime people, since not all regions suffer simultaneously. The result is that goods flow in from fertile countries to whatever power dominates the high seas. Furthermore – if I may mention so minor a point – the opportunity which this maritime supremacy, and the trade it fosters, offer for enlarging the richness and variety of our dinner-tables is quite incalculable. Every choice local delicacy from Sicily and Italy, the varied products of Cyprus, Egypt, Libya, the Black Sea, the Peloponnese and many other regions, all converge on one point, thanks to this thalassocracy of ours.'[67]

But what was more vital to Athens than all these luxury goods was her grain supply, since Attica produced far too little wheat and barley to feed her population. The Cornmarket of the Piraeus (*alphitopôlis*) always had to have sufficient reserves available to meet the needs of the city and the armed forces. At the first session of each *prytaneia*, ie ten times a year, the Assembly was presented with a report on the state of public provisioning. Extremely stringent laws defined the obligations of corn-merchants and small wholesalers (*sitopôlai*), not to mention those of all millers and bakers; they were particularly stern on any kind of hoarding or stock-piling that would produce a bread shortage, and thus engineer a rise in prices. The enforcement of these laws was entrusted to the 'college' of *sitophylakes*, or grain comptrollers, who supervised not only all trade in cereals, but also the sale of flour and bread.

The chief grain-exporting countries, Egypt, Sicily, the Black

Sea littoral – were all at a considerable distance from Athens. It is safe to say that the question of the corn supply always dominated Athens' policies, since the military expeditions to Egypt and Sicily during the fifth century (both of which ended disastrously) were undertaken at least partially for economic reasons and it was her desire to safeguard the cargoes of wheat from the Black Sea which compelled Athens to regard the Thracian Chersonese, and her other possessions on the Hellespont and the Bosphorus, as vital outposts, to be held at all costs. Certain fourth-century inscriptions concerning the doings of petty princelings on the Cimmerian Bosphorus are most revealing: we find both Satyrus, and his son Leucon, and his grandsons Spartocus and Paerisades, either granting or ratifying extremely generous privileges and concessions to Athenian importers.[68] In 354, at the outset of his oratorical career, Demosthenes declared before an Athenian court:

There is, I imagine, little need to remind you that we import more wheat than any other country in the known world. Now the quantity of grain that reaches us from the Black Sea littoral is at least equal to that which we obtain from all other sources combined. The reason is easily understood. Apart from the fact that the region [the present Crimea] is exceedingly rich in wheat, its ruler, Leucon, has granted special tax-exemptions to the merchants who import that wheat to Athens; indeed, an official is on hand at the docks to ensure that merchantmen destined for this country are given loading priority . . . Now this monarch normally levies a three-and-one-third per cent duty on all grain exported from his country. The total amount of wheat reaching Athens from the Black Sea has been calculated at some 400,000 *medimnoi* [roughly half a million bushels], a figure which can be checked against the books of the *sitophylakes*. What this means is that on the first 300,000 *medimnoi* he is giving us 10,000 for nothing, and on the remaining 100,000 something like 3000 more. And so far is he from withdrawing this concession that, having established a new trading-post at Theodosia (which, if we are to believe our merchant-seamen, is just as good as the one on the Bosphorus [ie Panticapeum, the modern Kertsch]) he has proceeded to grant us similar duty-free privileges there too . . . Moreover, two years ago, at a time of universal dearth, he sent us such quantities of corn that when all your needs had been met there was still fifteen talents' worth over, a sum of which Callisthenes had the administration.[69]

We can see that even after the loss of her political empire in 404, Athens still retained a great deal of her commercial ascendency. In this sphere she was not to be eclipsed by Alexandria and Rhodes till long after the end of the period with which we are here concerned.

MEDICINE

The professions (if such we may call them) of schoolmaster and public lecturer have been discussed in the previous chapter. When we come to law and justice we shall have occasion to consider those quasi-advocates the *logographoi*; and mention will also be made, apropos the religious and the creative life, of such persons as priests, seers, and artists. Apart from these, there is only one example of what we today call the 'liberal professions' which it seems apposite to introduce at this point: and that is medicine.

Plato, indeed, does not appear to regard medicine as a liberal art,[70] a fact which may be due to the prevalence of charlatans in his day who were all too ready to pass themselves off as doctors. Since there were no such things as degrees or diplomas, anyone who so cared could set up in practice. Many would-be healers operated by means of magical spells or dream-interpretation: this latter method was extensively practised in the great sanctuary of Aslepius at Epidaurus, which I shall discuss in more detail presently. But there were also genuine doctors, for the most part freeborn citizens, though it might happen that some rich man had one of his slaves given instruction in medicine so that he could subsequently look after his master's health. On the other hand, doctors themselves possessed slaves, who acted as their assistants and thus acquired practical experience in the healing art.

Medicine had flourished in Egypt for many centuries before Pericles' day, and even in Greece itself boasted a tradition going back at least as far as the Homeric epoch.[71] The Ionian philosophers were much concerned with medical theories, and we saw in the previous chapter that a number of fifth-century sophists claimed to teach, amongst other things, mecidine. There was a medical school at Cnidus, and perhaps also in Croton, the city of the celebrated Democedes, who served as public medical officer on Aegina and in Athens before entering the service of Polycrates of Samos – from whom he moved on to the court of King Darius.[72] But it seems fairly certain that scientific, as opposed to merely empirical medicine had its first beginnings on the island of Cos, where the Asclepiad family handed down their acquired knowledge from father to son – though they were also willing to communicate them to other medical students outside the family circle.

The famous medical writer Hippocrates of Cos was born about 460 BC: he was, if not the father of medicine, at least the originator of a method based wholly on observation and reason, and also of an attitude which we can fairly label 'medical humanism'. This creed finds remarkable expression in the 'Hippocratic Oath', the treatise 'On Ancient Medicine', and the *Aphorisms* of the Hippocratic Corpus. Here are some of the provisions of the Oath: 'I shall administer no poison to any person, even at their request; I shall never administer abortifacients to a woman. Whatsoever house I enter, I shall go there for the healing of the sick, and abstain from all wilful wrong-doings or misdemeanours, and in particular from any seduction of women or boys, slave no less than free.'

It was now that medical deontology reached its apogee; Louis Bourgey observes, with some justice, that 'a general respect for one's fellow-man, without distinction of class or origin, was not a habitual attitude in Graeco-Roman antiquity, even on the level of moral didactics; and in this respect we cannot but recognize the Hippocratic medicine, both as regards its practice and its ethics, was well in advance of the times'.[73]

The *paidotribai*, already discussed in the preceding chapter, were led by their occupation to develop a species of *gymnasion*-centred physical therapy. They had to be health experts and dieticians in order to advise an athlete as to the best general régime he should follow; they also had to possess some skill in massage and manipulation if they were to deal with, and reduce, the various fractures, sprains and dislocations incidental to violent physical exercise. Thus Herodicus of Selymbria, after a long career as a *paidotribés*, quite naturally turned to the profession of medicine.[74] There were 'athletic medical advisers'[75] and also military doctors, who, as we see from the *Iliad*, accompanied an army in the field to succour the wounded: the same was true in Xenophon's time, and can be confirmed from the *Anabasis*.[76]

Medical students attached themselves to some well-known doctor for training in diagnosis and prognosis; they also learnt from him all practical procedures such as bleeding, cupping, or the application of purges ('cupping-glasses' in horn and bronze have been turned up by the archaeologists). They were taught, in addition, to perform certain minor surgical operations; but anatomical knowledge remained very defective, largely because contemporary *mores* and religious susceptibilities were opposed to the dissection of human cadavers, and surgeons could, therefore, only practise on animals.

Medical treatises were available to the general public,[77] who could also (whatever may have been said on this topic) obtain drugs directly from the pharmacist (*pharmakopôlos*).[78] He in his turn had recourse to the *rhizotomos* ('root-cutter') for his supplies, since the cutting of medicinal plants had been regarded, for countless centuries, as an essential element in the art of healing. Most often, however, doctors themselves dispensed the drugs which they prescribed for their patients. They had surgeries, and some were even able to provide accommodation for patients they wished to keep under observation during treatment. There were also itinerant doctors, who went from town to town like the Sophists, offering consultations to those who might need them.

One well-attested and characteristic institution is that of the public medical officer (*démosios iatros*). We have already mentioned the example of Democedes of Croton. There is also a bronze plaque from Idalion in Cyprus, datable to the middle part of the fifth century, which tells us of a contract signed between this village and one Onasilus, a doctor, and his brothers, who agree, in return for an overall fee, to treat local war casualties.[79] In Athens, the public medical officers were selected by the Assembly, before which they declared their qualifications.[80] The city paid them a fee, and put premises at their disposal which served as surgery, operating theatre and nursing home in one. Medical supplies were paid for by the State. The cost of this social service was defrayed by means of a special tax known as the *iatrikon*.

So patients who lacked the means to consult a private doctor were still given every care and attention, just as in a modern hospital [and in Britain, naturally, by the National Health Service (Trs.)].

In Greece medical specialists were a rarity, whereas in Egypt, if we are to believe Herodotus, there were large numbers of them. The best attested branch of specialized medicine is the oculist's: his main stand-by was the salve or the eye-bath. We hear of dentists whose technique ran to lead or gold fillings; and one Aristophanic joke suggests that there may possibly have been specialists in diseases of the rectum.[81]

Women might have a medical career, but for the most part they confined themselves to such jobs as nursing or (their main function in this field) midwifery. Socrates was the son of a midwife, and Plato makes him discuss this profession at some length, apropos his own sort of maieutics, which consisted of delivering *minds* in labour.[82] For the more intimate sort of complaint, too, women might hesitate to call in a male doctor, and would find it easier to turn to someone of their own sex. Phaedra's nurse, who talks as though she were a contemporary of Euripides, says to her mistress: 'If you are suffering from some unmentionable complaint, here are women who can help you to ease it; but if it is the kind of thing that may be properly revealed to a man, tell us what it is, so that your case may be referred to the doctors.'[83] But qualified midwives apart, self-styled 'healers' of the female sex were even more liable to employ magical cantrips and old wives' remedies than their male counterparts.

CHAPTER SIX

DRESS AND TOILET

Hygiene and care of the body – Male dress – Feminine dress –
Jewelry and toilet accessories – Footwear – Headgear

HYGIENE AND CARE OF THE BODY

Greek doctors attached considerable importance to personal hygiene, care of the body, and physical exercise. Men (and in Sparta, at any rate, women too) regarded the practice of gymnastics as indispensable to one's general health and well-being (*euexia*). Socrates himself, at a comparatively advanced age, took a course of physical training 'so as to reduce his belly, which was more than its proper size'.[1] Children learnt at a very early age to bathe and swim in the sea or the nearest river (though the latter were rare in Greece, and dry as often as not). Spartan children took a daily dip in the Eurotas, winter and summer. Grown men did the same, though Nausica and her serving-girls, who bathed in the river after doing their household washing, were to have few imitators in the classical epoch, when women never bathed in public except on the occasion of certain religious festivals. It must have been during the Posidonia or the Eleusinian Mysteries – in the latter case, no doubt, down at Phalerum Bay, on the occasion of that odd ritual known as *haladé mystai* ('To the sea, Mystae!') – that the painter Apelles saw Phryne in the water, and conceived the notion of his Aphrodite Anadyomene.[2]

Pisistratus and his sons, in the sixth century, had furnished Athens with a series of monumental fountains where the women came to fill their water-jars; but when the spout was set high enough, it was also possible to take a shower at one of these fountains by standing directly under the jet. Several black-figure vases show scenes of this nature, though it is to be remarked that they become exceedingly rare during the red-figure period. If the fountain was constructed with a lower basin, it would obviously be forbidden to bathe in it, so as to avoid pollution. The reason why fountain-bathing was a rarity in fifth-century Athens must be ascribed to other facilities having by then appeared on the scene.

This was the period when palaestras and *gymnasia* were springing up everywhere; and these establishments were equipped with fountains, washing-basins, and even swimming-pools (*loutra*). The circular bath attached to the *gymnasion* at Delphi is nearly ten yards in diameter and little short of six feet deep, which would be perfectly adequate for swimming. The athletes doubtless first washed themselves down in the basins beneath the fountains, and then plunged into the bath for a communal swim.[3] Whenever it was humanly possible *gymnasia* tended to be built within easy distance of the sea, a river, or a spring (that at Delphi is quite close to the Castalian Fountain), so as to make the job of fixing bath installations that much easier. Towards the close of the fifth century open-air baths were generally abandoned in favour of the more comfortable indoor variety, with running water, lead pipes, and efficient waste disposal; they even had something very like slipper-baths for washing one's feet. At the time when Aristophanes' play *The Clouds* was first performed, in 423, it seems there were not, as yet, any hot baths in the *gymnasia*, only in those public bath-houses about which I will have more to say in a moment;[4] but later *gymnasia* came to be fitted up with sweating-rooms, in which the heat provoked violent perspiration. The *gymnasion* certainly made a large contribution to the spread of clean personal habits in Greece.

Greeks of the classical era were also acquainted with the other, more individual, sort of bath, used for purposes of washing and relaxation, as the Homeric heroes had employed it before them. This bath (*pyelos*) was generally made of moulded baked clay, and hence very fragile, though it could also be carved from a single block of stone or built with small bricks, the latter being mortared together and then given a coating of pitch. The baths found in Olynthus are very nearly square, and have the rear portion of their bottom raised like a seat, a practice which recalls the modern hip-bath; they are not fitted with any sort of waste-plug. In such a bath the body cannot be totally immersed: the occupant must either wash himself down, or get some minion to perform the task for him, with a jug of water or a sponge.

The more roomy, deeper sort of bath, in which one could stretch out and be completely covered by water, were said to have been invented by the Sybarites.[5]

There were also various tanks or basins, some round, some oval, made of either metal, baked clay, or wood, which could be used either for standing wash-downs or as children's baths. The usual type of foot-bath consisted of a shallow metal pan, standing on three feet fashioned to resemble lion's paws. But the most popular type of washing vessel during the classical period appears to have been the large, deep, circular basin, supported on a single pedestal which raised it a fair way off the ground, hollowed out below so that it resembled a gigantic wine-glass, and crowned with a capital (usually Ionic). In red-figure vase-paintings this is the most common feature both of private and of palaestra-owned baths. Such basins were frequently carved out of solid stone, but sometimes modelled in clay. They had to be filled by hand (except for those in the *gymnasia* that were placed directly beneath a fountain) and emptied in the same way. The water poured into them during the winter months was first heated in a bowl. However there were certain people – especially those who avidly admired the Spartan régime – by whom hot baths were regarded as a decadent, enervating institution. Aristophanes hints that many Athenians took this 'laconizing' fad so far as to despise, not luxuries merely, but common cleanliness and self-respect.[6]

Public baths existed in Athens as early as the fifth century, and became considerably more numerous during the fourth. Customers used either low hip-baths of the type described above, or the swimming-pool, or both. Individual baths were generally arranged round the periphery of a circular chamber, and some of these rotunda-style bath-houses were also equipped with sweating-stoves. Even in the absence of such stoves, public bath-houses certainly had some form of general heating, not to mention warm water for clients to wash in. They were run for their proprietors by a bath attendant (*balneus*) who collected the small entrance fee – two 'coppers': the *chalkous* was worth one eighth of an obol – kept the place in order, and supervised the activities of his 'bath-slaves', who kept the furnaces going, scrubbed down the customers, and afterwards rubbed them with oil. The *balneus* was very often a picturesque, loud-mouthed character with a decidedly dubious reputation.

Most people – at least those who enjoyed plentiful leisure – did not merely go to the baths to wash, but also to meet their friends and exchange gossip. Those of a thrifty or puritanical disposition, such as Phocion, never appeared there at all;[7] but the common people thoroughly enjoyed the relaxation and sense of comfort a bath gave them, and would linger there for hours, especially during the winter, when they had no fire at home and wanted to get warm.[8] In several of these establishments there seem to have been special rooms set aside for women; but these were doubtless patronized only by courtesans, slaves, and free-born women of the lowest classes. Athenian ladies took their baths at home, either in a tub or, more often, gathered round a pedestal basin which stood in one part of the *gynaikeion* – a scene frequently represented in vase-paintings.

The Greeks were not acquainted with soap. As we saw in Chapter Four, athletes in the *gymnasion* rubbed themselves over with oil and fine sand, and then scraped this mixture off with a strigil before washing. Bathers either used a coarse carbonate of soda, extracted from certain types of earth, or else a potassium lye obtained from wood-ash (no doubt the same as the *konia* or *litron* employed to clean fabrics); there was also a special clay known variously as *smegma*, *chalestraion*, or *kimôlia gé*. Aristophanes makes Dicaeopolis say: 'Never since I first washed my face have my eyes smarted as they do today – what a lye!' Elsewhere he speaks of 'that little monkey Cleigenes, the wickedest bath attendant who ever served out a mixture of old ashes and bad nitre, swearing it was real lye and first-class Cimolian chalk'.[9] Cimolus is one of the Cyclades, and still produces a type of chalky stone known as *kimôlia*, very rich in nitrous content. Theocritus' Syracusan Women, in the third century, seem to have used a kind of soft cream for their hands in lieu of soap.[10]

Most people took a bath before the evening meal: the practice was so widespread and regular that the words 'to take a bath' became more or less synonymous with 'to have dinner'. Socrates, as we know, was more concerned with the care of his soul than of his person; but when he was invited out to dine, he too had a bath before presenting himself at his host's house: 'I met Socrates all freshly washed, and with sandals on his feet – two most unusual things for him. I asked him where he was off to, that he looked so spruce. "To supper at Agathon's," he replied . . . "I agreed to be his guest this evening, and that explains these embellishments in my toilet; when you are asked out by such a nice boy you must look nice yourself." '[11]

On such occasions a visit to the barber was also customary. Athenians much enjoyed passing the time in barbers' shops, gossiping and passing on the latest news (as Lysias' Cripple observes[12]); but they also attached considerable importance – as did Homer's 'long-haired Achaeans' – to the nice ordering of their beards, hair, and moustaches. Beards were worn full or clipped according to the social class of their owner, or the particular age in which he happened to live. The barber also acted as a manicurist and pedicurist.

It was only after Alexander's day that the Greeks began to shave beard and moustache off completely. When we read about razors during the classical period, it is always as a toilet-accessory for women rather than men. In order to get rid of superfluous hairs, women would depilate themselves by means of singes or special face-packs, but also on occasion with a razor. In Aristophanes[13] it is a woman who, anxious to pass herself off as a man, remarks: 'I've started by throwing away my razor, so that I'll get all hairy, and quite unlike a woman'; and when, in another comedy, Euripides remarks to Agathon: 'You must always have a razor about you: just lend it me for a moment', this is a pointed allusion to the poet's effeminate habits. When Praxagora tells her companions to disguise themselves before going to the Assembly and taking over power, she makes them show her the false beards they were instructed to bring along with them.[14]

'It was not all that long ago,' Thucydides says, 'that older persons of the upper classes in Athens, out of affectation and elegance, were still wearing long linen robes and pinning up their hair in a bun with golden "grasshopper" brooches.'[15] It is still not certain whether these were brooches, or pins, *shaped* like grasshoppers (none such have been found) or golden spirals which produced a sound vaguely like that of the grasshopper as one walked along. If one examines that famous early equestrian statue in the Louvre, it is impossible not to admire the rider's elaborately curled locks, one tress arranged in careful symmetry behind each ear. Men in those days took as much trouble over their coiffure as did the *korai* whose statues have been unearthed on the Acropolis.

But after the Persian Wars, hardly anyone in Athens continued to wear their hair long apart from the children; when they reached their majority they cut off these youthful tresses and dedicated them to the gods. The situation at Sparta was exactly the opposite: there the children had close-cropped heads, and it was the grown men who wore those long and elegant locks which only upper-class dandies affected amongst the Athenians. Theophrastus' Mean Man gets himself a crew-cut on economic grounds, so as to avoid too many visits to the barber.[16] Slaves invariably had shaven polls, and most free Athenian citizens of the classical era wore their hair fairly short, as we can see from the public officials depicted on the Panathenaic Frieze.[17] As for the beard, this had quite often been cut, during the archaic period, in what the Victorians referred to as a 'Newgate frill'; but in the Periclean era it was allowed to grow full on the cheeks, and merely trimmed to a point or spade-shaped.

In earlier centuries there had been very little difference between men's and women's hair-styles; but during the classical period Athenian women preserved, and even added extra refinements to, those complicated coiffures which their husbands had thankfully abandoned. They only let their hair down and wore it loose over their shoulders at certain special festivals. Slave-women, as a rule, were supposed to wear their hair short, but it would seem that *hetairai* and flute-girls were exempt from this regulation: the flute-girl on the Ludovisi Throne wears her hair in a chignon, all done up with the *kekryphalos*, a sort of hairnet or bandeau which gathered up one's hair from the forehead to the nape of the neck, and kept it well back out of one's eyes. Freeborn women only cut their hair on some special occasion, especially as a token of mourning. Young girls often wore a simple hair ribbon to hold their tresses up on the top of the head, or off the forehead. Whereas the hair of the Acropolis *korai* was often plaited onto long tresses which hung down low over back or breast, that of Athenian women in Pericles' day was normally frizzed and curled into a stable mass, and piled up, by various methods, on the back or top of the head. Archaeologists have found various combs from this period, eg the double comb made of olive-wood that turned up in the Athenian Agora, with thirty-one fine teeth on one side and twenty rather coarser ones on the other, the centre being decorated with an intaglio motif of the familiar egg-and-dart pattern.[18] Other combs have survived made of bone, ivory, bronze, or tortoise-shell. Some are so exquisitely decorated as to be genuine works of art in their own right.

The main object in dyeing one's hair was to make it blonde, the eternally favourite colour: wigs and false switches were also employed for this purpose. Reference has already been made to the use of razors and depilatories to remove superfluous hair; in addition women also employed beauty creams, make-up, and a great variety of scents, which could be bought at the *myropólion*. Ischomachus observes of his young wife: 'One day I saw her all plastered with ceruse, to make her complexion look even paler than usual; farded with alkanet, to improve the natural rosiness of her cheeks; and wearing high-heeled shoes, to exaggerate her natural height.' These efforts earned the poor girl a long sermon from her husband; and yet, being a thoroughly nice and respectable creature, she had only done such things in an attempt to give him extra pleasure.[19] Courtesans not only employed white-lead ceruse and alkanet rouge, but also emphasized their eyes and eyebrows with black or brown liners, and were well acquainted with the use of the *strophion*, or brassière. A coquette of the Periclean Age, we see, was not entirely without resources; and so far we have not made any reference to the subject of jewellery, which will be discussed later.

MALE DRESS

In the field of textiles, the Greeks had some vague acquaintance with the existence of exotic products such as silk,[20] and cotton, which Herodotus refers to as 'vegetable wool',[21] or, more literally, 'wool obtained from a tree'; but ordinarily their only available raw materials were flax, wool, and the fleece of various other animals, especially the goat, whose hair was woven into a coarse material known as *sakkos*.

The spinning and weaving of wool – one of a Greek woman's immemorial tasks – has been discussed in a previous chapter. Flax was cultivated in the East and in Asia Minor, from where the European Greeks first imported it, either raw or processed. Later the plant was acclimatized in several parts of mainland Greece such as Thrace, Macedonia and Achaea, and on some of the islands, including Crete, Cyprus, and Amorgos. The stems of flax were dried out in the sun, and then 'retted', or steeped in warm water; after a second drying process the flax was beaten out on a stone surface with a mallet to separate the husk from the inner fibres, which were finally spun and woven.

Ancient dress, both Greek and Roman, was not cut and tailored, as modern garments are, to fit the individual body: it was, essentially, a draped costume, based on a plain rectangle of fabric, just as it left the hands of the weaver, after treatment by the dyer and fuller. It covered the body very loosely, in some cases only being held together by a belt, some pins, or one or two sewn corners. 'The mere fact of such loose drapery,' one scholar writes, 'produced a kind of accidental, intermittent semi-nakedness that was evident in every sphere of outdoor life, such as we see it depicted on ancient vase-painting and sculptures, and which was taken completely for granted.' Slaves, workers, peasants and sailors must have provided a constant spectacle of bare shoulders and torsos, with arms and legs burnt brown by sun or wind, and taking on a kind of patina from their continual exposure to the air around them.[22] This semi-nakedness, which climate and custom had rendered perfectly comfortable, would hardly cause any raised eyebrows in a country where athletes habitually paraded themselves without a stitch on. Quintilian was to say of the toga: *nec strangulet nec fluat* (let it be neither too tight not too loose), and it was true that ancient dress should neither be so close-enveloping as to hinder free movement, nor so free-floating as to cause embarrassment.

Men wore no kind of underwear; instead of a shirt they had the tunic, which they wore directly over their bare skin. The most simple and primitive type of tunic (which also very often did duty as a coat too) was the *exômis*, a garment which left one shoulder exposed (*ex-ômos*). The *exômis* was, primarily, a working-costume for slaves, all citizen-labourers, and most sorts of soldier. It was short, caught in at the waist by a girdle, and fastened on the shoulder with a fibula or a simple knot: it might be either open or sewn together down the right thigh. In any case it left the whole right side of the torso largely exposed. Megara was particularly famous for the quality of the *exômides* it produced.

The tunic proper, or *chitôn*, when worn short, only differed from the *exômis* in being normally fastened at both shoulders with hooks or loops. At the outset of a particularly fierce engagement – in fact, just as he was storming into Alexandria, sword in hand – King Cleomenes 'burst the stitches which held his tunic together on the right shoulder',[23] thus more or less transforming his *chitôn* into an *exômis*. When the tunic was worn with a girdle it fell into a series of heavy folds round the waist, known collectively as the *kolpos*; this was sometimes accompanied by a second, wider girdle called the *zôstér*, worn rather higher up the body, a military-type belt made of leather which formed yet another *kolpos*. We can see an example of this in a horseman on the Panathenaic Frieze, who is standing beside his mount.[24]

At night the tunic was kept on – it also performed the function of a nightshirt – and only the girdle was removed. 'If some accident befalls you in the village,' Hesiod remarks, 'your neighbours come hurrying out ungirt, while your kinsmen stop to put on their belts.'[25] Children wore short tunics with no girdle, like that of the young Theseus depicted on the celebrated cup by Euphronius, in the Louvre.[26] Nevertheless, the long tunic-robe of the ancient Ionians (which, as the old epithet *helkesipeplos* indicates, fell right to their feet) was not completely abandoned during the classical period, though it seems to have become a formal, ceremonial garment worn by priests, minstrels, and certain competitors in the public games. The Delphic Charioteer is clad 'in the long charioteer's tunic, the traditional white *xystis* worn for races. It falls to the ankles in long parallel folds from a high waist, well above the stomach . . . The upper part of the tunic is loose and comfortable, like a blouse, especially at either side. It forms a V-neck both in front and behind, and is gathered together in a series of small pleats on the shoulders and arms. The combination of these gathered pleats and the braid that was threaded beneath the armpits formed "sleeves" coming practically down to the elbow.'[27] Even the shorter type of tunic sometimes had these long sleeves, which must have been sewn up, doubtless a fashion copied from the Persians.[28]

The common Greek outer garment, the *himation*, was a single piece of woollen cloth, rectangular in shape, and without loops or attachments of any sort. A plain *himation*, of coarse material and without a coloured pattern, such as the philosophers wore, was known as a *tribôn* ('coat for everyday use'), while the *himation* made from fine wool, often with coloured stripes in it, such as was affected by dandies, was called a *chlanis*. Those who wore this garment often also carried a long crutch-headed stick, and when they stood still they would lean on it, so that it held the fold of the *himation* in place under the armpit – a posture familiar to us from frequent representation on bas-reliefs and painted vases.[29]

Spartan children, as Plutarch says, 'wore no tunic after the age of twelve, and only had one coat to last them the whole year through'.[30] Many Athenians, too, whether in imitation of the Laconian fashion,[31] or because they simply could not afford more, similarly wore a *himation* next the skin, and nothing more. Socrates did so, and many other philosophers followed his example: 'You go about barefoot and tunicless,' Antiphon told him.[32] However, the *himation* was voluminous enough to envelop the entire body; it was only if a violent gust of wind blew it up that the absence of a tunic became noticeable. However, it seems clear that to wear a *himation* next the skin was, generally speaking, regarded as an oddity.

The *himation* was put on as follows. First, the wearer spread it over his shoulders and back, letting the two lower corners hang down in front of him. Then, with his outstretched right arm, he grasped the free folds and passed them either over his left arm (which was bent to accommodate them) or else over his left shoulder, whence they hung down behind *en pointe*. This was the process which the Greeks described as 'dressing to the right' (*epi dexia*); the fold of the *himation* was grasped in the right hand, brought across to the right, and finally passed back over the left shoulder. In Aristophanes' *Birds*, Poseidon says to the god Triballus, who, being a barbarian deity, is presumed ignorant of Greek customs: 'My dear fellow, what *are* you playing at? Dressing yourself to the left, that'll never do. You want to redrape your *himation* so, to the right. Oh, you poor chap, what's *this*? You're a regular Laespodias!'[33] [There is a play upon words here which suggests that Poseidon has the *membrum virile* rather than a leg in view – a regular Aristophanic joke. (Trs.)]. The Athenian *stratégos* Laespodias had ulcers or varicose veins on his left shin, and therefore let the fold of his *himation* hang down on the right to conceal them: if he had draped himself in the normal manner, his left leg would have been visible as he walked (provided he wore nothing but a short tunic underneath). In Plato's *Theaetaetus*, Socrates sneers at country bumpkins 'who do not know how to fold their *himation* over the left shoulder like freeborn citizens'.[34]

Ancient orators, such as Solon, Pericles, Themistocles or Aristeides, were wrapped up in their *himation* when they spoke from the public rostrum: since both arms were enveloped, and only the right arm peeped out from the folds, they were effectively prevented from employing all the more expansive varieties of gesticulation or oratorical 'business'. Such, according to Aeschines, was the attitude of Solon's statue at Salamis: he is citing this instance of reserve in public speakers of a bygone age the better to attack those vehement and agitated gestures employed by Demosthenes – the 'wild beast' (*thérion*), as he terms him.[35] An identical attitude may be remarked in the replica of a supposed statue of Sophocles.[36] The fold of the *himation* could, alternatively, be tucked under the chin or even taken over one's head like a cowl. But in Aeschines' and Demosthenes' day, speakers in the Assembly held forth from the rostrum with the fold of their *himation* tucked under their right armpit and carried across their chest diagonally, like a sash, to their left shoulder, which left the right arm completely free, 'outside the *himation*'. In the *Women in Parliament*, Praxagora says to her companions: 'We must vote by raising our hands – that means uncovering one arm right to the shoulder.'[37] It was quite true that this method of voting (*cheirotonia*) meant freeing one's right arm and shoulder from the draped *himation*: otherwise it could not be managed at all.

Sometimes, in order to hamper one's physical movements less when violent activity was contemplated, the *himation* would be folded in two lengthwise; but this doubling meant that one had to pin it at the left shoulder to make it stay put, like an *exômis* or a *chlamys*. After the defeat at Chaeronea (338 BC), when even old men had been mobilized to defend Athens against Philip's threatening advance, 'the whole city,' the orator Lycurgus tells us, 'was swarming with elderly, enfeebled dug-outs, bent double, tottering on the very brink of the grave, *their cloaks folded double and pinned at the shoulder*'.[38] In this way they had, by improvisation, adapted their civilian *himatia* to the requirements of a military existence.

The *chlamys*, a cloak specially associated with soldiers, *ephéboi*, and horsemen, and probably Thessalian in origin, was made of thicker and stiffer material even than the *tribôn*, and was always pinned up at the shoulder. It was a comparatively short garment, liable to balloon out in the wind behind runner or rider – a phenomenon which artists turned to good effect, as we may see from the exquisite free-flowing folds on the Panathenaic Frieze.[39] Being so open and loose, the *chlamys* could not be wrapped round the body like the *himation*, nor did it make the tunic an optional garment. By shifting the position of the fibula to the other side of one's neck and shoulders, it was very easy, if one so desired, to free the left arm instead of the right. The *chlamys* could also be wound round one's left arm as a kind of rudimentary shield: this is what Alcibiades[40] did, just before he was killed, as he charged out of his burning house. The *chlamys* (which was normally dyed purple) remained the most common type of military cloak throughout antiquity: Pontius Pilate's soldiers, before crowning Jesus with thorns, wrapped him in one of their own cloaks, 'a scarlet *chlamys*' [St Matthew, 27.28-9].

Slaves in Athens wore no distinctive costume: they must have dressed very much as metics or poorer-class Athenian citizens did.

FEMININE DRESS

Women's dress did not differ very much in basic principle from men's. Special techniques of drapery and the accumulated experience of feminine coquettishness might transform its appearance; but the staple garment was still, fundamentally, a rectangular piece of woollen or linen fabric, just as it came from the loom, and loosely fitted to the body by means of fibulas or sewn-up corners. Phocion and his wife, we are told, were so poor that they possessed one outdoor cloak between them, which they took turns to wear when they went out. However, the arrangement, colour, and method of wearing this basic wardrobe varied considerably between the sexes: in the *Women in Parliament* Praxagora and her companions do not only borrow their husbands' sticks and big walking-shoes (*embades*), but their cloaks too; and Blepyrus, being thus reduced to donning his wife's small saffron-coloured cloak (*krokoté*), cuts a ridiculous figure.[41]

The most rudimentary feminine garment was that worn by young girls at Sparta, about which the Athenian poets had so many rude jokes to make.[42] This was the short open *peplos*, which performed a double role as tunic and cloak combined. It consisted of a fairly narrow length of woollen fabric, rather like a shawl, which was pinned up on each shoulder by means of a fibula; it had no girdle and was unsewn. Only one side of the body was really covered by this vestigial garment; the other was revealed by the slightest movement. Young Lacedaemonian girls, Plutarch tells us, wore 'these quasi-tunics, the skirt of which, not being sewn from the hem, fell open as the wearer walked, revealing her thighs; whence the nickname they were given, *phainomerides*, or "thigh-displayers" '.[43]

If it was long enough, this open *peplos* might have a fold in it: 'When a woman had woven a larger piece of material than that employed by a Spartan girl for her skimpy *peplos*, she was naturally forced to bunch all the extra material – all, that is, which taken vertically exceeded her own height – under the clasps of the fibulas. So while the woollen "shawl" remained open at one side, it now had to be folded double at the top: the result was an upper garment of variable length coupled to a single, unsewn skirt. Similarly, if the width of the draped *peplos* exceeded that of its wearer's chest measurement, the extra material hung down the line of the lateral opening in cascade-like folds which made the costume appear extraordinarily full and ample.'[44] A woman dressed in such a *peplos* could easily pass one hand under the double fold – a characteristic gesture found in a number of statuettes, especially those that form the pedestal of a looking-glass.

If the fold was big enough, the rear portion of it could be draped over the head as a kind of veil or hood. Women portrayed on funeral *stelai* are draped in this manner. When the fold hung in its normal position, it might be divided in two by the use of a girdle at the waist: to judge from the replicas that have survived, this was the costume worn by Pheidias' Athena Parthenos.[45] The girdle not only kept the pleating well-arranged (thus preventing the wearer's right leg from being exposed when she walked) but also defined the outline of the torso more clearly – a factor which contributed not a little to the added nobility and austereness of her general appearance. It could, in addition, (if the material was not pulled straight down over her bosom) help to preserve the arrangement of full, hanging folds which the Greeks termed a *kolpos*.

The *peplos* could, lastly, be half sewn up, from hip to ankle, or, indeed, all the way, from the shoulder down, so that only a pair of arm-holes were left free. The arrangement of the open *peplos* was necessarily asymmetrical, whereas that of the closed *peplos*, which more or less resembled a cylinder, achieved, *per contra*, a quite remarkable symmetry. The closed *peplos* could also be designed with fold and girdle, just like the open type. This is the splendidly impressive garment worn by the 'garment-workers' (*ergastinai*) in the Panathenaic Frieze from the Parthenon.[46]

During a war between Athens and Aegina (we do not know its precise date, but it must have been some time before 485 BC), Herodotus tells us, the Aeginetans won so crushing a victory that all the Athenians perished save one: 'In due course this man made his way back to Athens with the news of the disaster. When the women whose husbands had sailed for Aegina learnt what had happened they crowded round the wretched survivor, furious at the fact that, of them all, it was *he* who had come back, and stabbed at him with their shoulder-pins, each one asking as she did so what had become of her husband. In this manner he was done to death, and the Athenians considered the revenge taken by their womenfolk a more terrible thing than the disaster itself. Not knowing what punishment to inflict upon them, they eventually changed the dress they wore for that common amongst the women of Ionia: previously, Athenian women had dressed in the Dorian manner, and very similarly to the women of Corinth. Now they were forced to adopt the linen tunic, for which no pins were necessary. In actual fact, however, this costume is not Ionian in origin, but Carian: the dress originally worn by Greek women was the same everywhere, that is, what we call the "Dorian style".'[47] This final assertion is highly arguable; indeed, we are not obliged to take any of this Herodotean anecdote *au pied de la lettre*. The change of fashion in women's dress at Athens was, almost certainly, the result of a long evolutionary process rather than directly attributable to some dramatic incident such as that recounted by the historian. But we should, equally, accept the distinction he draws between the *peplos* (ordinarily made of a woollen fabric, and held together by pins) and the sewn linen tunic, and concede that the latter was a more recent innovation.

The Greeks of every period had used the wool of their sheep to clothe themselves with, whereas flax (as I have pointed out above) was at first imported, notably from Ionia, before being

acclimatized in various parts of Greece. For a long while, therefore, linen must have been regarded as a 'luxury textile', and its
use only spread gradually, beginning with the more elegant
members of the leisured class. But there is also good reason to
suppose that the ancient woollen *peplos*, even after it was abandoned
by women of fashion, remained the characteristic garb of peasants
and most women of the people – not to mention slaves. Just as
Athenian architects united the Dorian and the Ionian frieze in
the Parthenon, so Athenian women sometimes wore the so-called
Dorian *peplos*, and sometimes the fine close-pleated linen tunic
known as 'Ionian'. There is a bas-relief from Eleusis, datable to
the middle of the fifth century, which portrays Demeter as
severely clad in the *peplos*, while her daughter Koré wears the
elegant linen tunic.[48]

This linen tunic, like the *peplos*, was made from a rectangular
piece of fabric, just as it left the loom; but the two long hems
of the rectangle were sewn together, and the two upper borders
were stitched on either side, over the shoulders and down the
arms, in a double seam (sometimes augmented by fibulas) so as
to form loose and roomy sleeves. The girdle was adjusted to form
a *kolpos*, which varied in depth according to the length of the
material. The linen tunic was pleated by the primitive method
known nowadays as *plissage à l'ongle*, or thumb-pleating, since
the use of the goffering-iron appears not to have been known in
antiquity. This long tunic-robe could – again like the *peplos* –
embody a double fold at front and back.

The tunic was not so warm a garment as the *peplos*, and in
winter women wore various sorts of additional coverings over it.
These might take the form of a plain shawl, pinned sashwise
across one shoulder, or a circular cape (*enkyklon*), or else a *peplos*
used as an outer coat, or even a long draped *himation*, like a
man's, but with its folds arranged, rather more elegantly, so as to
fall in front rather than behind (*chlanis*). Sometimes this mantle
was folded in several thicknesses lengthwise, and draped back
over both arms, thus taking on the appearance (as we can see
from the vase-paintings) of an elongated scarf or stole.[49]

During the fourth century, elegant young women (as portrayed
in a group of terracotta figurines from Tanagra) wrapped
themselves up in vast and artfully draped mantles which
covered almost the whole of their tunics; and they would

sometimes draw a fold of this mantle over their heads to form a hood.[50]

Though Athenian women of the poorer classes continued to weave and make their own clothes, it was only natural that the craftsmen of certain cities should make a considerable name for themselves in some specialized type of garment. The island of Amorgos exported richly worked linen tunics, which sold at very high prices; while it was possible to make one's own, a good deal cheaper, using Sicilian flax.[51] The long linen robes turned out in Corinth, and known as *calasireis*, were also much valued. Chios, Miletus and Cyprus exported their embroidered garments over a wide area. Pellene in Achaea produced very popular mantles, and the extra-fine linen known as *byssos*, which was processed at Corinth, enjoyed a great vogue amongst fashion-conscious women.

Euripides shows us a woman of his day trying on a new dress in the *Medea*: a messenger arrives with the story of how Glaucé, the King of Corinth's daughter who has just married Jason, received the poisoned crown and tunic, those lethal gifts brought her by the children of the jealous sorceress whom she had supplanted:

> At the sight of the fine apparel, she could restrain herself no longer, but yielded wholly to her husband's solicitations. Almost before your children and their father were out of the house, she had seized the embroidered robes and put them on; then she set the golden crown upon her tresses, and tidied her coiffure in a bright-gleaming mirror, smiling at her own insubstantial reflection. This done, she rose from the throne and tripped across the hall, white feet twinkling daintily, overjoyed with your gifts; again and again she would rise on tiptoe and glance down at herself . . .[52]

This last and most picturesque touch is easy enough to understand: Glaucé turns and glances down at her heels as she rises on tiptoe to see how her robe hangs – and what it looks like from behind.

JEWELLERY AND TOILET ACCESSORIES

Princess Glaucé's golden crown was just the sort of rich trinket which Greek women liked to adorn their hair with when they were 'dressing up' for a festival or some private entertainment. As we have seen, male Athenians of the Persian War period, with their *krobyloi* and their golden grasshopper-brooches, were just as dandified as their wives; but subsequently – except for certain special occasions such as religious ceremonies or formal banquets – masculine fashion tended, very quickly, to become much more austere. Young fops from the wealthier classes, or Aristophanes' long-haired 'Knights' – such folk, indeed, might still not disdain such ornaments, and there were some who even wore metal anklets. A homosexual dandy like the poet Agathon, who, we are told, enjoyed dressing up as a woman, no doubt wore jewellery; but he was noticed precisely because he was something out of the ordinary. During the classical period, under normal conditions, jewellery was more or less exclusively the prerogative of women, except for signet-rings, which men wore in order to place their seal (*sphragis*), in clay or wax, on any document the contents of which they wished to remain a secret.

Women, on the other hand, commonly wore necklaces, bracelets, earrings and anklets. Those heavy pendant necklaces characteristic of the Mycenaean and the Greek archaic periods (such as the necklace of Harmonia for which Eriphyle betrayed her natural duty) had become rare by Pericles' day, and were replaced by much lighter types, sometimes with amulets suspended from them. Bracelets were normally worn round the wrist, but also appear on the upper arm, between elbow and shoulder, when the arm and shoulder are disengaged from the *peplos*. They may either be helical in pattern, or else plain rings of gold or silver, sometimes with a clasp in the form of a figurine. Very often, too, this type of ornament is shaped like a serpent coiled round on itself.

The practice of piercing the ear-lobe and hanging jewelry from it dates back to time immemorial. The Greeks of the Periclean era did not weight their ears down with the heavy, intricate gold ornaments popular amongst the Mycenaeans; they preferred, for the most part, small circular studs of precious metal wrought in various patterns, such as the rosette. Sometimes they hung tiny animal figurines from them as amulets. The fashion of wearing a ring round the ankle or calf was very widespread and seems to have possessed a religious, or rather a magical significance, in the apotropaic sense. Women, as we might expect, kept their jewellery locked up in a casket, and sent a slave-girl for it when they wanted to dress up: this is a motif which turns up frequently in vase-paintings, and also on funerary *stelai*, eg the remarkable *stele* of Hegeso.[53]

When discussing the various articles essential to feminine well-being we should not forget the fan and the parasol – both of them extremely useful in so hot and sunny a country as Greece. The Greek fan (*rhipis*) had nothing in common with our modern fan, the pleated type which folds in on itself and can be extended to form a half-circle. It was a simple, flat instrument with a handle, ordinarily either heart-shaped, or else fashioned to resemble some sort of leaf – arum lily or palm – with the stalk serving as a hand-grip. Such, it would appear, are those non-folding fans (probably made from thin sheets of wood) with which the elegant young ladies portrayed in the Tanagra figurines are cooling themselves.[54] Sometimes we find circular fans, too, or palmetto-shaped ones; and they all display a remarkable range of colours – green, blue, white, and occasionally gilded.

On the other hand, to judge from the evidence of several fifth-century bas-reliefs and painted vases, the parasol (*skiadion*) had a structure almost identical with that of a modern umbrella, being constructed from a circular piece of material stretched over a number of radiating ribs, which converged on a sliding ring free to move up and down the stick that served as the handle. In especially elegant specimens the ribs sometimes ended in little spikes, which protruded beyond the rim of the opened parasol: we may note that it is seldom depicted in the shut position. Parasols could also be used as umbrellas. They were nearly always carried by a slave, who walked behind the lady to be shaded. Such parasols seem to have had a religious significance analogous to that of the dais in certain processions, eg those of the Panathenaic Festival and the Skirophoria, during which a white parasol was borne before the priest of Poseidon and the priestess of Athena; but they were also put to a completely secular use – enabling elegant young ladies to preserve their delicate white complexion.

FOOTWEAR

Socrates, together, doubtless, with a whole host of slaves and poorer people, walked barefoot about the Athens streets and the roads in the immediate vicinity of the city. Characters depicted in vase-paintings are very seldom shod, and there can be no doubt that Athenians – both men and women – habitually went barefoot indoors. But for outdoor use, sandals and shoes were customary. Theophrastus' Mean Man, we may note, only put his shoes on for the afternoon, as an economy measure.

Our main difficulty with Greek footwear (as indeed with Greek hats, which will be discussed shortly) is to make some correlation between the various names preserved in our literary texts and the visual illustrations to be found on vase or stele: many proposed identifications must remain a matter of conjecture. Shoes were often made to measure, and in such a case the cobbler would cut the sole directly round his customer's foot.[55] Sandals consisted of a plain sole (which might be made of cork, wood, or leather) held on by thongs that were wound round ankle and big toe, leaving the upper part of the foot exposed. The *embas*, a modern-looking boot worn by men on journeys of any length, was ankle-high, laced up in front, and fitted at the top with a kind of turnover, so that it much resembled a cut-down thigh-boot. The *endromis* was very similar, but without the turnover. The *kothurnos*, which Aeschylus (or so we are told) adapted for theatrical use, originated in Lydia: it was a high-soled buskin, less fitted to the wearer than those types already mentioned, since it could be worn equally well on either foot. Hence the nickname of 'Cothurnus' given to the statesman Theramenes by his enemies, who accused him of changing parties with undue facility.[56]

Women's shoes were far more varied and elegant in design. The names of some types, such as *persiká* or *lakonikai*, offer a clear indication of their origin: but to describe them is a far harder matter. We know that women who wanted to increase their height employed a kind of 'elevator' which they placed between their foot and the inner sole of the shoe, since Greek cobblers seem not to have been acquainted with the use of high heels in the strict sense, ie attached externally to the shoe. One comic poet remarks that if a woman is too short, she puts cork inside her boots. The leather used for women's shoes was dyed various colours, black, red, white or yellow. Just as different localities specialized in different garments, so several towns boasted superlative shoemakers, whose fame went far and wide – those of Argos, Sicyon and Rhodes were among the best-known.

One mime by Herodas takes us into the premises of a cobbler, who, like so many of his ilk, also sells shoes over the counter. It is true that this mime only dates from the third century; but it seems very probable that fashionable ladies in Athens were able to choose among a wide range at their retailer's at least a hundred years earlier, and that the scene Herodas draws for us could have taken place, virtually unchanged, during this earlier epoch. Two customers enter the shop, and the cobbler, Kerdon, instantly bustles forward to serve them. He makes them sit down, sends his assistants scurrying in all directions, and displays the various models in his collection, to the accompaniment of much high-pressure sales-talk. He informs us, *en passant*, that he has thirteen slaves working for him. Then he goes on:

KERDON: A wide range here, ladies, just you look at them all – Sicyonian, Ambracian, Nossian canary-yellow, Chian, 'parokeets', espadrilles, mules, slippers, Ionian bootees, party overshoes, high button-boots, 'crab-tops', Argos sandals, scarlet pumps, walking-shoes, sneakers: something for each of you, just say what you'd like, now . . .

CUSTOMER: That pair you picked up just now – how much are you asking for them? Don't pitch it too high, now, or we'll be straight out through that door again.

KERDON: You name the price, lady, *you* tell *me* what they're worth. But make it fair – I got a living to earn, remember . . .

CUSTOMER: Why the hell can't you stop drivelling and tell me the price, straight out?

KERDON: Lady, this pair is worth a mina [100 drachmas: a considerable sum] – give them a good looking-over, that's right, I tell you I couldn't knock a clipped farthing off the price, no, not if Athena herself was wanting them.

CUSTOMER: I can see why this sweat-shop of yours is so stacked with good stuff, Kerdon – and as far as I'm concerned, you can keep it . . .

The bargaining continues, on the same bantering note.[57]

HEADGEAR
Lastly, we come to hats. Men normally went about the streets bareheaded, and only wore a hat out in the country: the only people who were liable to carry any sort of headgear in the city

were visiting strangers. On the battlefield, a metal helmet was worn, while pugilists – boxers, as we would say – had leather headguards.

The *pilos* was an attractive hat, tall and roughly conical in shape; sometimes it had a peak to keep off the sun, and also, on occasion, various ornamental devices. It was normally made of felt, but high-quality, semi-stiff felt, to prevent its being too easily flattened. It might also be made of leather, and even of metal. Herodotus describes the lofty Persian tiara as a *pilos*.[58] This headgear might also be used as a kind of military helmet.[59]

The word *pilidion*, a diminutive of *pilos*, in fact was applied to quite a different type of hat (just as in French a *casquette* is not the same thing as a *petit casque*). This plain felt or woollen bonnet was, in the first instance, used as a kind of night-cap, which doctors sometimes prescribed for their patients to ensure that they kept their head warm.[60] This same bonnet, without any peak or other decorative additions, was also worn in the countryside by slaves and working-class people – peasants, shepherds, craftsmen, sailors, boatmen. It is the headgear adopted by Hephaestus, as patron deity of all workers. An Athenian of any social standing would have been ashamed to show himself on the streets of Athens wearing so vulgar and common a headgear: Solon once did so, but in very special circumstances – he wanted to convince people he had gone off his head.[61] The *kyné* was a leather (literally, a 'dogskin') bonnet very similar in shape and purpose to the *pilidion*.

The *pilos*, even when equipped with a peak, offered little protection against the scorching rays of the sun. The favourite headgear worn by travellers – it was also that of Hermes, the Heavenly Messenger – was the *petasos*, a low-crowned, broad-brimmed affair of felt or straw, fitted with a chin-strap that enabled the wearer to push it to the back of his head or carry it slung between his shoulders. Such a hat had to be fastened to one's head in some way, since it could so easily be blown off by the wind; but it was a very effective protection against both wind and rain.

Women, as we have seen, covered their heads with a fold of their tunic or overmantle, which they arranged like a hood. The *kekryphalos*, which has also been mentioned earlier, was a kind of sash or headscarf knotted over the hair, not a hat in the true sense. But women also wore a circular, broad-brimmed hat with a pointed crown, the *tholia*, which was really a variant form of the *petasos*. The statuettes from Tanagra show us just how elegantly a woman of fashion could wear the *tholia*.

CHAPTER SEVEN

FOOD, GAMES AND RECREATION

*The sub-divisions of the day – Food and drink – Banquets –
Plato's* Symposium *– Xenophon's* Symposium *– Adult amusements – Big-game hunting – Fishing – Expressive mime*

THE SUB-DIVISIONS OF THE DAY

The working day, and also every kind of public meeting, such as
those of the Assembly, the law-courts, and the various religious
festivals, began, in the normal way, at daybreak. Before the
Athenian went out into the early dawn he would have a small
breakfast (*akratismos*), which normally consisted of some bread –
either barley or wheat – soaked in a little undiluted wine (*akratos*).
He might also supplement this sparse fare with a few olives
or figs.

The sub-divisions of the day – the hours as we know them –
could not be reckoned with any accuracy in ancient Greece.
Originally the various moments of the day were designated in a
very vague way: people spoke of 'dawn', of 'the market rush-
hour' (about mid-morning), or noon, afternoon, and evening.
From the middle of the fifth century, however, the Greeks had
two devices available for telling the time: the sun-dial, or *gnômôn*,
an import from the East, and the *klepsydra*, or hour-glass water-
clock, which indicated the passage of time by a drip-level. The
hydraulic clock, which was based on the same principle as the
klepsydra, had not yet appeared during the classical period. For
all practical purposes in Athens it was the obelisk-type *gnômôn*
erected on the Pnyx by the astronomer Meton, or various other
sun-dials (some of which were portable) that people consulted –
calculating the time from the variable length of the shadow they
cast – in order to be on time for an appointment or invitation.
In the *Women in Parliament* Praxagora tells her husband: 'All
you'll have to do when the shadow's ten feet long is primp

yourself up and go out to dinner.'¹* In a fragment by the comic poet Eubulus we read of a glutton who, 'having been invited to dinner by a friend for the hour when the shadow was twenty feet long, took the measurement as the morning sun was coming up, and appeared when the shadow was actually two feet longer than had been prescribed in the invitation: he turned up soon after daybreak, apologizing for being late, and saying he had been held up by business.'² Since all dinner-parties were held in the evening, this is rather as though he had been invited for eight, and turned up at eight am. Even when the *gnômôn* had become a commonplace, the Greeks still do not appear to have made a habit, as the Romans did, of numbering the hours from sunrise. Their time-keeping therefore remained very vague and approximate, a fact which surely influenced the basic rhythm of their existence.

Towards mid-day, or soon afterwards, the Greeks had a quick, perfunctory meal which they called *ariston*. Some of them also took a snack early in the evening (*hesperisma*); but the most substantial meal of the day normally occurred at sunset, or even later, when it was quite dark. This was dinner, or *deipnon*.

FOOD AND DRINK

What did the Greeks eat in the ordinary way, at home? Most of them, and notably the Athenians, were well-known for their moderate appetites – a phenomenon for which the climate and the thin, semi-barren soil were, between them, largely responsible. Yet the inhabitants of lush Boeotia were traditionally reckoned great gluttons, and their gourmandizing no less than their thick-witted oafishness provided a constant target for malicious jokes. This supposed predilection of theirs for good food and rivers of drink may, however, have been mainly due to jealousy and prejudice on the part of their neighbours.³ The Spartan régime, on the other hand, was considered even more frugal than that of the Athenians; but perhaps this verdict was produced by a similar sort of self-deception, only in reverse.

Translator's note: This primitive type of dial indicated time by the length rather than the angle of the shadow. As Benjamin Bickley Rogers, that most amiable of Aristophanic editor-translators, found by personal experiment, 'an object casts a shadow of "over twenty-two" times its own height at sunset, and a shadow of ten times its own height about thirty-one minutes earlier. It is plain therefore that the gnomon . . . of an Athenian dial was one foot in height, rising vertically from the ground.'

As early as Homer's day men could be described as 'grain-eaters'. Cereals – essentially wheat and barley, which, as we know, the Athenians were obliged to import in large quantities – formed the basis of their diet. When Plato, in the *Republic*, wishes to draw a picture of the good, healthy, primitive life, he writes: 'As for nourishment, men will, no doubt, make themselves flour, either from barley or wheat, which they will knead or cook on a griddle, thus producing fine loaves and scones. These they will serve either on straw or nice clean leaves.'[4] Barley-flour made into flat griddle-cakes was called *maza*, and was a staple element in people's daily diet. According to one of Solon's ordinances, wheaten bread proper (*artos*), which was baked in round loaves, should only be consumed on feast-days. But in Periclean Athens both *maza* and *artos* were, it seems certain, obtainable from the baker daily (in the old days every family had baked their own bread), though *maza* was cheaper, and poor folk had to content themselves with it for the greater part of the time.

All solid food that accompanied bread at a meal went by the generic name of *opson*: green vegetables, onions, olives, meat, fish, fruit or sweetmeats. Vegetables were scarce, and (in the city at least) relatively expensive, except for beans and lentils, which were most often mashed up into a sort of purée (*etnos*) or soup: this was the coarse but filling dish to which, as Aristophanes tells us, the gargantuan Heracles was especially addicted.[5] Garlic, cheese and onions were also eaten in large quantities, especially in the army, where those more delicately nurtured found such a diet both coarse and monotonous.[6] Olives – at least before the Peloponnesian War – were plentifully abundant in Attica; and though they mainly went to the production of oil, quite a large proportion of them were eaten in their natural state.

Meat was expensive, except for pork (a sucking-pig cost three drachmas[7]) and the urban proletariat only ate it occasionally, after some great religious sacrifice: almost every feast-day involved a climactic scene of slaughter-house butchery, sacrifice followed by general feasting and revelry. Out in the country, on the other hand, well-to-do landowners could enjoy a regular varied diet of pork, mutton, goat's meat, and table-fowl – not to mention the game they picked up out hunting.

Most Athenians in the city were obliged to rely on fish more often than meat. It is significant that the word *opson*, which, as I have said, covered anything one ate with bread, should gradually have come to mean fish in particular – indeed, the word for 'fish' in modern Greek derives from it [or rather, from its diminutive, *opsarion*, which, by a regular process of abbreviation, was shortened to *opsari*, then to *psari*, its present form. (Trs.)]. Bread and fish between them were probably the staple diet of the urban populace. Any rise in the price of sardines or anchovies at Phalerum alarmed the man in the street, who was scared of losing one of his regular favourite dishes. The fish-market was one of the most crowded and picturesque in the whole of the Agora. Some particularly tasty and sought-after species were too expensive to appear on a poor man's table – for instance, the famous eels from Lake Copais, since Athenians appreciated freshwater fish no less than those, such as the tunny, that were caught out at sea. They were also very fond of shellfish and molluscs of every sort, not to mention squid and octopus, which were abundant off the shores of Euboea, and provided the fishermen of Eretria with so valuable a livelihood that the town took a squid as its numismatic device.[8] Salt-provision dealers (*tarichai*) sold both fish and meat either smoked or pickled in brine. The meal would be rounded off by a dessert (*tragèma*): fresh or dried fruit, most often figs, nuts, and raisins, or honey-cakes.

It was the women of the house, especially the slaves, who ordinarily did the cooking. From the fourth century on, however, professional chefs and pastrycooks begin to appear on the scene: some of them even produced tracts on the 'culinary arts'. Plato mentions 'Thearion the pastrycook, Mithaecus, the author of a treatise on Sicilian cuisine, and Sarambus the wine merchant – three eminent connoisseurs in their several fields'.[9]

Most food was eaten in one's fingers, since the use of forks was still unknown. The flat 'scones' of *maza* or wheat bread could very well do duty as plates, but bowls and platters in wood, terracotta or metal were also used, and for purées or soups the Greeks had soup-spoons very like ours, sometimes with richly chased handles. For meat, a knife was essential.

The most popular Spartan dish, which they took in their communal 'messes' (*syssitia*), was the famous black broth, a sort of thin stew the ingredients of which included pork, blood, salt and vinegar. Plutarch relates how, in order to sample this cele-brated dish, 'a certain King of Pontus bought a Laconian cook, and had him serve up black broth: he found it not at all to his liking, which elicited the following remark from the cook: "King," said he, "this soup should only be taken after a dip in the Eurotas." '[10] This anecdote, incidentally, confirms the practice of taking a bath before dinner – even in Sparta, where, as we have seen, hydrotherapy was not thought much of.

A form of nourishment somewhere between solid food and true liquid was the *kykeôn*, which, besides being the ritual beverage at the Eleusinian Mysteries, was very popular with Greek peasants. This was a porridge-like substance made from barley meal and water, which could be given an aromatic flavour by the admixture of various herbs such as pennyroyal, mint, or thyme: a frugal dish, but one supposed to possess certain medicinal properties. Delatte, who has made a special study of the *kykeôn*, writes: 'In Aristophanes' *Peace* Trygaeus, who is scared that over-indulgence in fruit will give him indigestion, is advised by Hermes to drink a *kykeôn* flavoured with pennyroyal.' This appears to have been a traditional country recipe. Elsewhere in the same play the *kykeôn* is extolled by the Chorus as a rural speciality. Among the benefits of peace which the peasant finds on returning home, again, is the *kykeôn* (with thyme), which he regales himself on during the summer. A passage in Theophrastus' *Characters* shows very clearly that the *kykeôn* was a 'popular' beverage, a rustic tipple from which the upper classes abstained. His Rustic has drunk a *kykeôn* before going to the Assembly, and when those on either side of him find his breath disagreeable, he stoutly maintains that no flower, no perfume is so pleasant as thyme.[11]

The place of drinking-glasses was taken by goblets such as the Laconian *kôthôn* (presumably made of wood or metal) which, Plutarch informs us, was highly suitable for military use: 'Its glaze disguised the filthiness of the water which soldiers found themselves obliged to drink, and the sight of which would have filled them with disgust: besides, the mud that fouled the liquid was caught and held by the inner rim of the goblet, and the water thus actually reached one's mouth in a slightly purer state.'[12] But for general domestic use in Athens terracotta cups were the normal thing.

The most common drink was certainly water, and connoisseurs learnt to relish its flavour and freshness. Milk was also drunk, especially goat's milk, besides a species of hydromel, water and honey mixed. But it was the vine that provided the drink of kings, the 'gift of Dionysus'. In the countryside, after the vintaging, the must was duly sampled. The method of making wine differed a great deal from our modern procedure: there was, for instance, no prolonged or systematic fermentation in vats, so that to preserve the precious liquid for any length of time was extremely hazardous. In order to solve this problem, the wine was adulterated with salt water or various other ingredients, which calls to mind the modern Greek processing of resinated wine, or *retsina* – though as far as is known resin was never used as a preservative in antiquity. Aromatic herbs such as thyme, mint, or cinnamon were also added, and sometimes honey. The Greeks were acquainted with the production of *vin cuit* (ie by heating the must), and each region known for the superlative quality of its local *cru* had a different way of maturing it.

Wine destined for on-the-spot consumption was stored in leather 'bottles' sewn together from the skins of pigs or goats, while that scheduled for export was decanted into large baked clay jars (*pithoi*), which served the same purpose as modern casks, and subsequently into amphoras (also of baked clay) the inner walls of which had been coated with pitch. The amphora-handles were stamped with the wine merchant's name, together with those of certain local officials, whose seal was some guarantee of quality, like a modern *appellation contrôlée*. The wines of Thasos, Chios, Lesbos, Rhodes, and certain other localities were held in particularly high esteem. The export and import of wines were regulated (notably on Thasos) by various laws which imposed heavy penalties on fraud, and seem to have underwritten some sort of protectionist system.[13]

Wine was very seldom drunk undiluted (*akratos*). Before every meal a mixture of wine and water, in varying proportions, was made in a large bowl called a *kratér*. In the *Iliad*, when Achilles receives Agamemnon's envoys he says to Patroclus: 'Take the largest *kratér*, son of Menoetius, mix the wine strongly, and give drinking-cups to all.'[14] During the classical period the wine was similarly diluted with more or less water according to the occasion. Attendants would dip into the *kratér* either with long curved ladles of metal or clay, or else with *oinochoai*, and go round filling the guests' cups. Wine was also employed during religious ceremonies for libations in honour of the gods; but in the cult of certain deities wine was proscribed, and these were offered libations of milk instead.

BANQUETS

The Spartans might make a regular practice of their communal meals (*syssitia*), but all Greeks thoroughly enjoyed a banquet, especially one designed to celebrate some special family or civic occasion, or indeed any notable event: various successes, most often in the field of athletics or that of poetical contests; the arrival or departure of a friend. Such banquets (*symposia*) even gave birth to a new literary *genre*, as can be seen, *inter alia*, from such writers as Plato and Xenophon, both of whom wrote a *Symposium*, and, much later, from the *Symposiaca* of Plutarch or Athenaeus' *Deipnosophistai*.

The word *symposion*, which we translate 'banquet', more literally means 'drinking-party'. In order to understand this we must bear in mind that every formal dinner, and all banquets given by a religious brotherhood or any other association (*thiasos*) consisted of two successive stages: first came the satisfaction of one's hunger by the banquet proper, and secondly – though this part of the proceedings, despite coming second in time, was far from being regarded as secondary: it lasted far longer, and the *symposion* derived its name from it – secondly, there was the business of drinking (drinking wine, that is, for the most part), a process accompanied by all sorts of incidental entertainment, which was enjoyed by all but naturally varied a good deal from one place and period to another. It might consist of anything from good talk and intellectual puzzle-games to music, dancing-girls, and similar titillations. But it should not be supposed that the first half of the proceedings excluded drink, while the second half, *per contra*, excluded solid food: far from it. We know that guests could have wine during their meal if they so desired, and that afterwards, during the *symposion* proper, they often continued to nibble at titbits (*tragémata*) to stimulate their thirst: fresh or dried fruit cakes, grilled beans or chick-peas, and so on.[15]

In Athens, as in the Spartan *syssitia*, these banquets were strictly all-male affairs. Here we get a clear glimpse of that aspect of Greek society already alluded to above, in Chapter Four, apropos education and pederasty: freeborn women were rigorously debarred from these social occasions, just as they were from any participation in political affairs. It is true that, as a sort of compensation, they had feasts of their own, in connection with certain religious festivals, which were equally strictly reserved for women: for instance, the Thesmophoria in Athens. In Plato's *Symposium* Diotima, the 'wise woman' from Mantinea, does not join the feast as a guest: Socrates merely reports what he claims to have heard from her lips – words which, despite this palpable literary fiction, are obviously an expression of his own thoughts, or, more likely still, those of Plato himself *qua* author.[16] During the Periclean Age, in fact, women were only present at banquets, as a rule, to wait on the male guests, and in particular to amuse them, during the latter half of the evening, with music, dancing, and seductive charm.

Various friends, or the members of an association (*hetairia*), sometimes arranged to meet at their several houses in turn, each providing his share of the feast, victuals and drink alike: this was known as an *eranos*. But more often than not, banquets were given to a group of invited guests by some host rich enough to defray all the expenses of the occasion himself. These invitations seem to have been, for the most part, quite casually issued: the host met his friends on the street, or in the Agora, and asked them home to dinner, on the spot. It sometimes happened, too, that a guest would, on his own initiative, bring a friend along, without any prior notification to the master of the house. Parasites – those perennial butts of the comic poets – were always waiting for the chance to free-load at a good square meal with drink laid on.

When a guest reached his host's house, he would remove his shoes, and slaves would wash his feet before he proceeded into the banqueting-chamber. The guests were often crowned with garlands of flowers or leaves, and might also wear certain similar decorations, known as *hypothymides*,[17] hung round their necks. Generally they ate in the lying position, or, to be more exact, with their legs stretched out on a couch and their body either upright, or propped at an angle on cushions and bolsters, as one can see from the numerous vase-paintings and bas-reliefs which portray *symposia*. The number and arrangement of the couches seems, clearly, to have been variable: it was common practice for two, and sometimes three, guests to occupy the same couch. There were the same delicate questions of etiquette and precedence as bedevil dinner-parties today. The most honourable place was on either side of the host, who could (but did not invariably) decide where each guest was to sit. The tables were small, portable affairs: there might be one per guest or merely one for each couch. Some were square or oblong, others round, with three legs. Slaves set out the food on them, ready to eat, on platters or in bowls.

As soon as the guests had seated themselves, attendants brought round ewers and basins for them to wash their hands (*chernips*), a very useful custom when one recalls that the bulk of the meal would be eaten with one's fingers. Dinner often began with a *propôma*, which it is tempting to translate as 'apéritif': this was a cup of herbally infused wine that the guests passed round before they started on the food.[18] Table-napkins as we know them did not yet exist: one wiped one's fingers on pieces of bread, which were afterwards thrown on the floor (along with meat-bones and other such scraps) for the dogs of the house. These used to prowl expectantly round the tables and couches – a common motif in the figurative art of the period.

Some guests might only have been invited for the *symposion* proper, and these would arrive when dinner was over. Drinking would begin with the usual libations to the gods, especially to Dionysus, the 'good divinity' (*agathos daimôn*) who bestowed the gift of wine on men. A libation meant drinking a little undiluted wine and sprinkling a few drops of it on the ground, invoking the god's name as one did so. Then a hymn to Dionysus was sung. Finally a 'Lord of the Feast' (*symposiarchos*) was chosen, often by throwing dice. His main function was to determine the proportion of wine to water in the *kratér*, and to decide how many cups each guest should be required to drain. The common practice was to toast each person present in turn. Anyone who disobeyed the Lord of the Feast was required to pay some sort of forfeit, eg to dance stark naked, or go three times round the room carrying the flute-girl in his arms. (There always had to be at least one flute-girl.) Often the party would end in general drunkenness; and certain vase-paintings show us these revellers, in a very sorry state indeed, being laboriously helped home (half-led, half-carried) by the long-suffering women.

PLATO'S *SYMPOSIUM*

In Plato's *Symposium,* we get our first glimpse of Socrates going off – washed and brushed and wearing sandals, *not* a usual thing with him, as we may recall – to the house of the poet Agathon, who had invited him, and several other friends, to come and celebrate his having won a prize in the tragedy competition. On the way there Socrates takes it upon himself to invite a friend of his own, Aristodemus, who has not been asked by Agathon; and as Socrates suddenly drops behind to think about a problem that has just occurred to him, Aristodemus gets there first. Agathon makes him welcome, however, and sends a slave to look for Socrates. He then shows Aristodemus to his place on a couch already occupied by a doctor named Eryximachus, and a slave washes the new arrival's hands. Agathon orders dinner to be brought in without waiting any longer for Socrates, who finally turns up half-way through the meal. 'After which, when Socrates had taken his place on the couch [next to Agathon, and so in the place of honour], and dined, and everyone had finished, they all made libations, sang the hymn to the god [Dionysus], and performed the other usual rites. Then they began to drink.'[19]

We then hear, in turn, the views of Phaedrus, Pausanias, Eryximachus (the poet Aristophanes stands down in his favour because of a persistent hiccup – which earns him a 'prescription' from the doctor himself on various ways to cure this affliction), Aristophanes (his hiccup now cured), Agathon (after a short interlude), and, finally, Socrates himself, who first conducts a 'dialectical' discussion with Agathon, in his usual manner, and subsequently expresses his ideas on the subject – or rather, Plato's[20] – by putting them into the mouth of the priestess Diotima.

Socrates had scarcely finished speaking when suddenly 'there came a loud banging at the street door, and from beyond it what sounded like a crowd of uproarious revellers, amongst whom the voice of a flute-girl could be distinguished'. Agathon tells his slaves to see what the trouble is:

A moment later the voice of Alcibiades could be heard in the outer court; he was completely drunk, and shouting at the top of his voice 'Where's Agathon? Someone take me to Agathon!' So they brought him into the guests, with the flute-girl and some of his other companions supporting him. He stood there in the doorway, wearing a thick-plaited wreath of ivy and violets, all hung about with ribands. 'Good evening, gentlemen,' he said. 'Drunk. Very. Will you let an in-inebriated p-person join you? Or must we be on our way again after we've put this wreath and stuff on Agathon? That's what we came round for, really.'[21]

Alcibiades is invited in, and plumps himself down on the host's couch, between Agathon himself and Socrates, whom at first he fails to recognize. Agathon tells the slave to remove his shoes.

Then Alcibiades announces that he must have some more to drink, and proclaims himself, with the proper authority of the inebriated, Lord of the Feast. He demands a large cup of wine – no, he says, that *psyktér* will do better. (The *psyktér* was a wine-cooler, which, as the narrator tells us, held eight *kotylai*, or nearly two quarts.[22]) It is filled up, and he drains it completely, after which he forces Socrates to follow his example. Then, being invited to speak, he pronounces his famous encomium on Socrates: *in vino veritas*.[23] Then Socrates asks to be allowed to speak in praise of Agathon, and demands a reshuffle on the couch, so that he and Agathon are beside each other again. 'But suddenly a new and numerous band of revellers appeared at the street-door, and finding it open – someone was just going out – they marched straight in and sat down on the couches beside us. A general uproar now unsued, and all semblance of order vanished: we just had to drink enormous quantities of wine.'[24]

Some guests now take their departure, while others fall asleep: only Agathon, Aristophanes and Socrates are left still drinking and arguing. Finally first Aristophanes and then Agathon succumb to sleep. At this point Socrates, who could absorb a remarkable amount of liquor without being any the worse for it, 'got up and departed; he took the road to the Lyceum, and when he had bathed, he spent the rest of the day in his normal fashion, as though nothing out of the ordinary had happened. Having done so, he went home in the evening, and retired to sleep.' Thus ends Plato's *Symposium*.

XENOPHON'S *SYMPOSIUM*
Xenophon's work of the same name begins (after a short preamble) as follows: 'During the great Panathenaea, there were

various horse-races. Callias, the son of Hipponicus, went along with young Autolycus, to whom he was very attached, and who had just won the prize in the *pankration*. After the races were over, Callias went home to his house in the Piraeus, together with Autolycus, his father, and Niceratus. He met a group which included Socrates, Critobulus, Hermogenes, Antisthenes and Charmides,' and proceeds to invite them all to dine with him that evening, along with Autolycus and his father, doubtless to celebrate his young *erômenos'* victory in the *pankration*.

In the banqueting-chamber Autolycus (whose beauty makes him the cynosure of all eyes) is seated next to his father. The guests are eating in silence when, suddenly, there comes a knock at the door. This is a clownish parasite called Philippus, accompanied by a slave, who demands a free dinner for himself and his servant. Callias invites him to join them: 'Look at these long-faced guests of mine,' he observes. 'You've come just in time to cheer them up.' But to begin with Philippus' wisecracks completely fail to get a laugh out of the diners. So he stops eating, muffles up his head, lies out flat on his couch and pretends to cry, which makes those present feel sorry for him. They beg him to go on with his dinner, and even promise to laugh at his jokes.[25]

'When the tables had been cleared away, and the libations were made and the paean chanted' – that is, when the *symposion* proper began – a Syracusan mountebank appears, to offer the company an entertainment (*kômos*), bringing with him a troupe of three young artistes: a first-class flute-girl, another girl, a dancer-cum-acrobat, and a very good-looking boy who both dances and plays the lyre. (It is more than probable that the wealthy Callias had in fact engaged the Syracusan and his troupe in advance, to amuse his guests: Xenophon hints as much by merely remarking that this impresario hired out dancers and musicians as a money-making concern.)

First the guests hear a performance on flute and lyre. Callias suggests having perfumes brought in, but Socrates opposes this, saying that the use of perfume is only suitable for women. (In banqueting-chambers, as in every *gynaikeion*, there were tall *thymiatéria*, or incense-burners, which also served a purpose during religious ceremonies. The Greeks made lavish use of perfume, or incense, on every possible occasion.[26]) After this the acrobat takes over. First she juggles a dozen rings in time to the flute; then she does a dangerous turn, somersaulting through a hoop bristling with swords, and each of her numbers elicits astonished comments from the guests. Finally it is the dancing-boy's turn, and his performance leads Socrates to pay a droll tribute to dancing as such, or rather, to eurhythmics – which, he says, he would like to take up in order to reduce his somewhat over-protruding belly to more reasonable proportions. The clown, Philippus, then proceeds to parody the two dancers in a most grotesque manner. Socrates decides that the drinking shall be moderate, not such as will produce general intoxication; and after the boy has sung a piece, accompanying himself on the lyre, the old philosopher initiates a discussion. Each of the guests must name that virtue or art to which he attaches most value, and then attempt to justify his choice. This gives rise to a series of frivolous and disjointed speeches, rounded off by an amusing 'beauty contest' between Socrates and Critobulus.

A little later some of the company propose that they shall play the 'portrait game', but others are against this, and Socrates reconciles the factions by bursting into song himself. The girl acrobat is about to launch into a new number, this time on a potter's wheel, but Socrates asks the Syracusan to put on a less risky and nerve-racking spectacle. While the impresario and his troupe are outside making the necessary preparations, the guests launch into a discussion on the subject of love. This, fundamentally is the central theme of Xenophon's *Symposium*, just as it is of Plato's. Afterwards young Autolycus retires, together with his father; and the Syracusan now presents a kind of mime, in which the two dancers, boy and girl, play out the roles of Ariadne and Dionysus, to a flute accompaniment. This elegant spectacle very soon takes on a lascivious turn: 'The two performers resembled a pair of lovers, impatient to satisfy their urgent and long-standing desire. At the spectacle of them clasped in so close an embrace, as though they were on the point of going to bed together, the unmarried guests swore they would wed without delay, while the married ones saddled up their horses and galloped straight home to enjoy their own wives. Socrates, and a few more who had stayed on with him, went off for a stroll with Callias, to rejoin Autolycus and his father. On this note the banquet ended.'[27]

Xenophon's *Symposium*, for all its transposition of reality into literary terms, would seem to have caught the characteristic atmosphere of these cheerful and convivial occasions rather more accurately than Plato's essay in the same genre. We even see Socrates giving the company a song; it was, primarily, at such banquets, and at religious ceremonies, both public and private, that Greek men made some use of the musical education they had acquired as children. 'At feasts in particular, songs formed a natural expression of happiness. The lyre was handed round among the guests, and sometimes each of them in turn – holding a branch of laurel or myrtle in his hand – would sing a stave while his neighbour accompanied him on lyre or flute. All those present made some personal contribution to the fun; and it is pleasant to see, on various case-paintings, the spectacle of portly, balding, respectable citizens (whose increasing girth cannot rob them of a curious robust elegance) refreshing themselves between a couple of drinking-songs. The kind of thing these educated topers would quote was Simonides' poem in honour of Crios, the Aeginetan athlete, or "Drink, now is the time to drink", or verses of a more elevated nature, such as "Dear Harmodius, death cannot destroy you". There were the songs of Cratinus – "Fig-sandaled tell-tale Doro", "Makers of wise ditties"; there were snatches from Aeschylus or Euripides, a stanza or two of Sappho or Alcaeus. Others whose work contributed to these improvised concerts (which often went on long into the night) were popular poets such as Theognis, Anacreon, or Cydias of Hermione.'[28]

These parties might, as we have seen, be supplemented with what amounted to a cabaret show, such as that put on by the Syracusan impresario; but the host had to be wealthy enough to afford to hire a troupe of artistes. More often the guests entertained themselves, which was much less expensive. Apart from music and songs, they would either have free-ranging discussions and debates (which, no doubt, in the ordinary way bore a much closer resemblance to the disjointed, daggers-drawn arguments of Xenophon's *Symposium* than to the carefully worked out speeches on similar themes in Plato's), or intellectual parlour-games, riddles, charades, portraits and the like – these three are mentioned by Xenophon – a pastime to which the quick, subtle Athenian mind was naturally drawn; or, lastly, games of skill, the most popular, as far as we can judge, being that known as the *kottabos*.

Every *symposion*, as we have seen, began with libations to the gods, Dionysus in particular: one drank a little unmixed wine, and spilt the dregs on the floor, invoking the deity as one did so. During the course of the party the drinkers, instead of merely pouring their libation on the ground, amused themselves by aiming the dregs at an agreed target. During this novel type of libation one did not invoke the name of a god, but that of one's beloved: if the drops fell in the dish or bowl one was aiming at, it was regarded as a favourable omen, announcing that one's amorous hopes would be crowned with success. Women, too, played this 'erotic' *kottabos*-game at their own all-female banquets, and so did the courtesans invited to male reunions: on a certain vase by Euphronius there is a picture of a naked woman, sprawled on a banqueting-couch, holding a cup in her right hand by one handle and saying: 'This throw is for you, Leagros.' Theramenes' gesture as he died was a parody of this sport: being condemned to death by order of Critias, one of the Thirty Tyrants, he is said, when the time came for him to drink the hemlock, to have thrown the last drops on the ground as in the *kottabos*-game, with the words: 'Good health to noble Critias!'[29]

The *kottabos* enjoyed such a vogue that several variants on the elementary form described above passed into currency. The bowl which formed the target might be filled with water, and a number of tiny clay saucers set afloat in it: the game then consisted in aiming at these minuscule 'boats' and throwing the wine so skilfully that it made them overset and sink. The *kottabos* prize went to whoever caused the largest number of 'shipwrecks'. Eventually someone had the idea of setting up a tall vertical rod of metal, with a pointed tip, on which a tiny disc was balanced: the player now had to knock the disc off with the dregs from his cup, and it appears that a throw was regarded as particularly successful if the disc, when it fell, struck a kind of sconce or upturned cup fixed on the rod about two thirds of the way from the bottom.

This Dionysiac amusement (it was, naturally, accompanied by copious draughts of wine) was practised above all at banquets, but also in those public places where the idle tended to gather, such as the public baths. The prize for the winner might take the shape of eggs, apples, cakes, a pair of sandals, a necklace, ribbons, a cup, a ball, or simply a kiss from his beloved. It seems that the player was judged, not solely by his accuracy in hitting the target, but also by the elegance with which he handled his cup while throwing.

ADULT AMUSEMENTS

In Chapter Four we were exclusively concerned with the toys and games appropriate to early childhood; so far we have scarcely touched on the amusements of older children, adolescents, and grown-ups – who were by no means less addicted to games than their juniors. The basic games of childhood and youth vary little from nation to nation, or from one age to the next; most of those in use today were already known to the ancient Greeks, in an identical or near-identical form. Athenian children – and indeed Greek children generally – played with balls and bladders, hoops, tops, and knuckle-bones; they even knew about hopscotch. They had see-saws and swings; they played leap-frog and *ephedrismos*, the ancient equivalent of piggy-back riding, besides marbles (or rather, in their case, nuts) for which they had various rules and variations: 'One version consisted of throwing your nut at three others, which were probably set up – this must have taken some skill – in the form of a pyramid . . .; the winner took all four nuts. In the game known as *homilla* or *delta*, a circle or triangle was traced on the ground, and the nut had to be pitched inside it. It seems a fair assumption that the player who scored a "bull" won all the nuts that had previously fallen outside the target area. There was yet another version, which substituted a bowl or chuck-hole for the outline in the dust . . .; the method of play would remain as before.'[30] Children also played with pebbles or pot-sherds, seeing who could get them closest to a line drawn on the ground.[31]

The device known to us as a yo-yo was also in use among the ancient Greeks: they had the same double disc joined by a short cylindrical bar, round which a string was wound, its other end being looped over the user's finger. Perhaps the Anticythera *ephébos* was practising this game.[32] The yo-yo could be made either of wood or metal, and our museums also contain 'votive yo-yos' in terracotta: as we know, when young Greeks of either sex attained their still-adolescent majority, it was customary for them to offer up to certain deities either their real childhood toys or else votive substitutes which exactly reproduced their shape.

Both children and *ephéboi* went in for balancing exercises: there is a cup in the Louvre which depicts a young man juggling a sharp-bottomed jar on his raised left foot.[33] *Askoliasmos* was a contest between young people to see which of them could keep their balance longest on a full, greased wine-skin: the skin – and its contents – went to the victor. This event was particularly associated with certain rural festivals in honour of Dionysus.[34] The use of stilts was also known.

Ball games were not by any means restricted to children: as early as the *Odyssey* we find Nausicaa and her girl companions playing one sort, and, just as today, there were numerous varieties. A bas-relief from the Cerameicus shows us a group of completely naked adolescents playing ball with curved sticks, a scene which cannot but suggest the modern sport of hockey.[35] Adults, too, played ball in the *gymnasia*, where a special area was reserved for this pastime. It is difficult to draw a hard and fast distinction between these 'games' and various exercises prescribed by the *paidotribés*, in the sense that the games, too, were played in the open air, and helped to make the body strong and supple.

Everyone in antiquity, young and old alike, derived a great deal of pleasure from domestic animals – often in a decidedly cruel manner. One archaic bas-relief shows us two *ephéboi* sitting face to face, each with an animal on a lead: one has a dog and the other a cat, and the two animals are clearly squaring up to fight. Behind each of the youths there stands a man, leaning on his stick, and taking a passionate interest in the battle: these, no doubt, are the 'fans' – or the punters.[36] Yet true cats (as opposed to dogs) were rare in ancient Greece. What the Greeks generally had in their houses were domesticated weasels, which hunted mice for them. The most common type of staged fight between animals involved a pair of cocks, each primed with garlic and onions to put it in fighting fettle. Their spurs were tipped with bronze barbs to make the blows they delivered draw more blood. Such cock-fights, of which we have several representations on vases, gave rise to much betting, and people would pay high prices for a first-class pedigree fighting-cock. In Athens, indeed, an official cock-fighting jamboree was organized annually by the civic authorities.

As for games of chance, these were legion, ranging from 'odd or even' played with small bronze coins (*chalkinda*), knuckle-bones, or beans, to all the various games involving dice (*kyboi*). Plato's *Lysis* gives us a glimpse of children in a palaestra on the feast-day of Hermes, patron god of *gymnasia*: 'Having offered up sacrifice, they were playing odd-or-even with large quantities of knuckle-bones, which they took from baskets, while others stood round in a ring and watched them.'[37]

Dice games were normally played with three terracotta dice, the six faces of which were marked either with letters bearing numerical values (A=1; B=2, etc.), or else with the names, in a more or less abbreviated form, of the numbers one to six. The one, or 'ace', was called *kybos*.[38] The best throw, known as 'Aphrodite's throw',[39] was a treble six; the worst, a treble *kybos*, or three ones, known as 'the Dog'.

The so-called 'five-line game' was a contest between two players, who moved their pebbles, like pawns, from line to line in accordance with the scores they threw at dice.[40] The Greeks also knew a game similar to the French *jeu de l'oie*, or 'goose game' [played with two dice on a squared board marked with a goose at every ninth square: landing on the goose gives one the right to a double throw (Trs.)]. As for the Greek *petteia*, or *pesseia*, this much resembled backgammon or draughts, and went back to a period of remote antiquity: we find Homeric heroes – and Penelope's suitors – 'delighting their hearts with draughts'.[41]

Athenians who daily frequented the Agora and other public meeting-places never lacked for entertainment: this was especially true of the *gymnasia*, where many citizens continued to take exercise throughout their adult years. The most common, but by no means the least popular amusement was to idle one's time away strolling about the streets and the Agora, gossiping in the barber's shop, or indeed any sort of shop or work-room: this was the proper setting for exchanges of news or a good long discussion, and Socrates regularly came here in the hope of meeting people. The Agora was also a 'pitch' for tumblers, jugglers, mimes, conjurors, dancers, and clowns of every description. Athens certainly had its puppeteers, and a 'shadow-theatre' that was a forerunner of the Oriental Karageuz; Plato may well have had this in mind when he excogitated his famous myth of the Cave, and the shadows that flitted across the rock-face. Concerts were regularly held in the Odeon, mainly on feast-days.

In his tribute to the men who died on the field of honour (which is also a tribute to the whole city, its laws and its customs) Pericles – as reported by Thucydides in his own words – had this to say: 'As a respite from our labours, we have many kinds of recreation available: we can restore our spirits with the numerous

contests and religious festivals that succeed one another throughout the year, and in our domestic lives there is a seemliness which
daily turns our depression to joy.'[42] We shall have more to say
about these civic festivals later, in the chapter devoted to religion.

BIG-GAME HUNTING

Hunting and fishing were then, as they still are today, a full-time
occupation for one section of the community, but for others
merely a pastime. Xenophon, in his *Cynegetica*, regards hunting
as a necessary and important part of a boy's education, since it
exercises the body, inures one to danger, and thus acts as a
preparation for military combat; but such notions were more
popular in Laconia than in Attica, and were inspired, in Xenophon's case, by his admiration for Spartan *mores* – though these
included the hunting of helots, regular manhunts, in fact.[43] However, many well-to-do Athenians certainly went in for hunting as
a sport, though Attica was one of the poorest game areas in Greece.

During the Mycenaean and archaic periods, there had still been
large numbers of wild beasts roaming the mountains and forests
of Greece, lions in particular. Big-game hunting left a considerable mark upon Greek mythology, which contains a very large
number of gods, goddesses and heroes specifically associated with
this pursuit – all of whom are piously enumerated by Xenophon
at the beginning of his *Cynegetica*. In the classical period there
may have been one or two wild beasts still surviving (there were
certainly wolves, which have not entirely disappeared even to this
day), but the main game hunted consisted of boars, stags, hares –
which were particularly plentiful – and birds such as partridges,
quails, larks, thrushes, and so on. Aristophanes' comedy *The Birds*
lists numerous species, but it is not always easy to identify them.

Among the various methods of catching game in use during
the Periclean Age, trapping was probably the most ancient. For
birds and small animals snares, springes, and spring-traps were
employed.[44] To these must be added – especially as regards the
larger game that one hoped to capture alive – the pit-trap described
by Xenophon. A deep pit was dug, with sheer sides, and then
branches and leaves were laid across it by way of camouflage. In
the middle an upright stake was rigged up, with a lamb tethered
to it: the lamb's bleatings attracted the carnivore, the branches
gave way under its weight, and it crashed through to the bottom

of the pit. In order to get it up, an open cage was lowered into the bottom of the pit, with a hunk of meat inside it: the moment the animal entered the cage, the door was dropped shut and the cage hauled up again.

Birds could be shot either with bow and arrow or sling-stones: the hunter's other weapons included javelin, hatchet, bludgeon, dagger and stick – the latter being commonly used for hunting hares. As Chantraine rightly observes, 'the ancient world had no powerful or accurate shooting weapons, and riding was the exception rather than the rule. In consequence the game had to be caught in snares or nets and only then finished off by the hunters. In this respect Xenophon's *Cynegetica* is most instructive. When hunting hare, the hunter (assisted by a hound from his pack) himself flushed the quarry from cover and did his best to drive it, like a beater, towards the nets. These nets were watched by a keeper (*arkyôros*), and either he or the hunter might finish off the netted hare, unless it was pulled out alive. There were three distinct types of net: the *arkys*, a small, fine-meshed type, made from three-ply cord, about four feet long and just over a yard high; those known as *enodia* (so called because they were stretched across roads and set at the junctions of paths), which were tougher – twelve-ply cord – and also much longer: anything from four to nine yards, in fact; and, lastly, the *dictya*, made from sixteen-ply cord and used for the capture of all types of game. These measured not less than twenty yards in length, and might be anything up to fifty. They were also used for forming temporary stockades, and the posts on which they were rigged stood more than a yard high.[45]

The use of hunting dogs was pointless when snares or traps were in question; but for the netting method they proved indispensable, and indeed, they were so widely employed that the Greek word for 'hunter', *kynégos*, means, literally, 'leader of dogs'.[46] In Xenophon's *Cynegetica* much emphasis is laid upon the breeding and training of hounds and retrievers. Certain breeds of dog from Laconia had a particularly high reputation for speed and sureness. Hunting dogs with thin pricked ears and sharp muzzles are depicted on various vase-paintings and *stelai* from the classical period. 'One black-figure vase shows us a hunter, head crowned with a fur bonnet (*pilidion*), wearing a high, girt-up tunic (*euzônos*) to leave him free for immediate action, and carrying a hunting-stick (*lagobolon*) over his shoulder, with a hare and a fox slung from it. The dog crouching beside him appears to be one of those Laconian hounds which Aristotle describes as a mixture of dog and fox.'[47]

FISHING

Fishing, rather more than hunting, was a full-time occupation; we have already noted the preponderance of fish in the average Athenian's diet. It would not, in all likelihood, have occurred to Xenophon to write a treatise on fishing to complement his *Cynegetica*, since the Greeks regarded fishing as a far less noble pursuit than hunting. Plato, when making a comparison of their educative value in the *Laws*, addresses the following exhortation to young people: 'My friends, may you never acquire a taste, much less a passion, for sea-fishing or angling; or indeed for the pursuit of aquatic creatures in any way whatsoever; or, lastly, for that most idle form of fishing in which the pots do the work for you, whether you are awake or asleep.'[48] Plutarch was merely reiterating and emphasising an opinion already widely held in the classical era when he wrote that fishing was an inglorious pursuit, unworthy of a free man, because it required more cunning than strength, and did not, like hunting, provide one with healthy exercise.[49] We have to wait for Oppian's *Halieutica*, which did not appear till the second century AD, before we find a Greek treatise devoted to the art of fishing. However, from literary allusions and figurative art we can get a pretty clear notion of ancient fishing techniques, which much resemble those still current today, and have undergone considerably less development than those of *la chasse*.

Angling with hook and line, mentioned by Plato, was very much like its modern counterpart, involving a rod (generally some sort of reed or cane) and a line woven from flax or horsehair to which was attached a cork float, a lead sinker, and, finally, the hook. Small fish were baited with worms or insects, and the larger sort with small fry. The Greeks also anticipated current practice by employing artificial baits, such as 'flies' made from scraps of red wool. They sometimes dispensed with the rod and used a ground-line instead. One fifth-century cup shows us a boy squatting on a rock that overhangs the sea: he has a fishing-line in his right hand and a creel in his left. In the transparent water the painter has sketched in some fish, an octopus, and a lobster-pot.[50] These pots were a kind of wicker basket, sometimes large and round, sometimes elongated, with pointed ends. The principle was the same as today: once the fish was inside, a series of sharpened sticks prevented it from getting out again.

Fishing-nets, like those used for hunting, were of many different sorts. The main distinction was the same then as now, between the *épervier*, or cast-net, a funnel-shaped affair fitted with lead weights, which was flung into the sea spread flat, and closed immediately, and the *senne*, or tow-net, a long rectangle which the fishermen made fast at either end and pulled along, thus driving the shoal towards a predetermined spot. Several boats might take part in the one operation.

One method which combines the principles of net and pot is that known by the French as *à la madrague*; it consists of a permanent installation, a kind of labyrinth constructed with nets and sunken posts, through which the fish are lured to a central enclosure, a 'death-chamber' lined with netting, which is hauled up when full. The Greeks also used the harpoon or trident, not only against cetaceans, but also to hunt medium-sized fish, especially tunny. Tunny-fishing required a more complex organization than most, and numerous willing hands to help. Watchers were posted in certain look-out stations to let the fishermen know when a shoal of tunny was sighted. Some of the latter would then act as 'beaters', and drive the fish towards the nets – no doubt in the manner adopted by modern Greek fishermen today, who 'accompany this part of the business with a tremendous hullabaloo, beating small drums, banging the surface of the water with stones on the end of strings, splashing and churning the sea with their feet, or thwacking pieces of wood with sticks.'[51] Finally the boats drew in close to each other; and the netted tunny were hauled up to the surface and dispatched, either with harpoons or gaffs.

When sword-fish were sighted a net was cast into the sea and then brought back shorewards by the fishermen in such a manner that it formed a vast semi-circle; when the neck was near enough shut, men plunged into the water and harpooned the sword-fish. The Greeks also went in for torch-fishing or lantern-fishing, which Oppian describes as follows: 'If certain types of fish are best captured at daybreak, others yield more readily in the evening:

as the first shades of night fall, the fishermen light a torch, and, with skilful manoeuvring of their trim craft, bring grim death to the unsuspecting fish: these, delighted by the resin-fed flame of the pine-torch, leap up around the boat to see this deadly evening light, and expose themselves to the strokes of the pitiless trident.'[52] This method is still in use today, most notably round the coast of Lesbos.[53]

EXPRESSIVE MIME

Several of the games described above involved some expressive sort of mime, and we have seen how sensitive the Greeks were to elegance in any gesture, from the draping of a robe to the way one threw the contents of one's cup at *kottabos*.[54] Today Mediterranean peoples as a whole, and the Greeks in particular, accompany – even, on occasion, replace – their words with a whole host of lively and expressive gestures. They are said to 'talk with their hands', and also with the movements and positioning of their heads, indeed of their bodies as a whole. Was this so in antiquity?

The Greeks of Pericles' day, like their modern counterparts, said 'no' by raising the chin and tossing the head back (*ananeuô*)' not by turning the head alternatively to right and left. When they met one another, they raised the right hand in greeting, but did not exchange the 'salutatory kiss' which was to become customary among the Romans. As for the handshake, this was reserved for certain acts of a specifically religious nature, and considered as symbolizing a solemn obligation.[55] On the funerary *stelai* we often see some surviving relative clasping the dead man's hand.

In the theatre of the Assembly, applause was expressed by clapping (*krotos*) or cheers, and disapproval by whistles and cat-calls.[56] It appears, however, that these noisy demonstrations (*thorybos*) were rare during Pericles' administration, and did not become at all frequent till after his death. We know, in any case, that public speakers of Solon's day delivered their speeches without any rhetorical gestures, hands hidden under their *himation*, while in Demosthenes' and Aeschines' day they gesticulated as freely as they pleased, and constantly emphasized the vehemence of their remarks with vigorous oratorical tub-thumping.[57] It may be inferred that this change in public speaking was matched by a different attitude in the public who listened to it; that audiences grew progressively noisier and more violent. Aristophanes, who admired the dignified reserve of Athenians in the good old days, was shocked by the vulgarity of his contemporaries.

Certain gestures in common daily use had a symbolic significance. People snapped their fingers, hand held aloft, as an expression of joy: perhaps this is what the Marathon *ephébos* is doing. In order to express contempt or derision for someone, it was not customary to thumb your nose at him, but to fold in all your fingers except the middle one, and point that in his direction, an action for which the Greek verb is *skimalizô*. Now as we know, 'the middle finger was regarded, by the Greeks no less than the Romans, as the *infamis digitus*, and this gesture was, therefore, a piece of guttersnipe obscenity, analogous to what is known in France as *faire la figue*' [or, in Britain, to the reversed V-sign (Trs.)].[58]

Many gestures were dictated by religious or superstitious motivations. People turned their eyes away from any sight which they believed could bring defilement on them, and spat to avert evil omens, or the consequence of any word or encounter regarded as unlucky. The Superstitious Man in Theophrastus 'always takes fright on meeting a lunatic or an epileptic, and spits in the fold of his robe'.[59] When a Greek was weeping or in pain or – *a fortiori* – knew himself on the point of death, he would muffle up his face in a fold of his cloak, partly out of decency and self-restraint, partly to prevent anyone else being forced to witness so ill-omened a sight.[60]

Lastly, there was the matter of mourning; and this gave rise to demonstrations which today would seem decidedly excessive: 'The women wail and lament,' Lucian wrote. 'Everyone is in tears. Breasts are beaten, hair is torn out by the handful, cheeks are nail-raked till they bleed. Sometimes a mourner will even rend his garments and spread dust on his head; and indeed, the living deserve more commiseration than the dead, for very often they roll about and beat their heads on the ground, whereas the corpse is togged up in all his finery, with wreaths galore, and laid out on an elevated bier, as though about to take part in some solemn procession.'[61] This sketch of Lucian's is several centuries later than the classical epoch; but from numerous textual allusions and artistic representations it seems clear that mourning practices in Pericles' day were scarcely less violent.[62]

CHAPTER EIGHT

RELIGIOUS LIFE AND THE THEATRE

Religious traditions and rites – The religious calendar – The theatre – 'Benefactors of the people' – Mystery religions – Divination – Superstition – Magical practices

---

RELIGIOUS TRADITIONS AND RITES

The Greeks are often regarded as rationalists, and this is true enough in the sense that they created philosophy and science as we know them; true, too, inasmuch as several Greek philosophers submitted the religious traditions of their nation to sharp and corrosive criticism.[1] But the Greek people as a whole, like all people in antiquity, were imbued with a sense of the sacred[2] which the word *thambos*, pre-Hellenic in origin, expresses extremely well. *Thambos* is that reverential terror and awe aroused by the proximity of any supernatural force or being which one discerns, or thinks one can discern, in nature or the world of men.[3] The whole universe, for the men of antiquity, was peopled by a host of divinities, large and small, benevolent and fearful: this was the source of the polytheism which (after an early animistic phase) soon took on so markedly anthropomorphic an appearance in Greece. In those days,

> when the sky above the earth
> Did move and breathe with a race of deities,[4]

men believed firmly in the existence of countless immanent, almost tangible divinities, on whose pleasure depended not only men's happiness or misery on this earth, but also their fate after death, in the realms of Hades. Their whole life was adjusted to the rhythm of countless religious festivals – some domestic, others associated with deme, tribe, or city – and punctuated by the meticulous performance of rites inherited from their ancestors (*ta patria*).

It is true that in Greece, from the sixth century onwards, there appeared one or two bold spirits amongst the philosophers who embraced atheism; and though these were at first isolated, their numbers increased during the second half of the fifth century, the age of the Sophists, which in a sense foreshadows the eighteenth-century *Aufklärung*, with its *illuminati* and anti-clericalism.[5] Such men as Pericles and Thucydides, though they conformed outwardly to all prescribed civic and family ritual, seem to have had a very qualified faith in the efficacy of religious ceremonial, and, *a fortiori*, in that of superstitious observances or the veracity of oracles. When Pericles was confined to bed and sick of the plague that was soon to carry him off, in 429, 'he showed a friend, who had come to visit him, an amulet which the women had hung round his neck; and remarked that he must be in a bad way to stand for *that* kind of nonsense'.[6] But men far more nearly like 'the average Athenian', even a *stratégos* like Nicias or a writer such as Xenophon, were imbued with a piety that bordered on the superstitious. Even philosophers like Socrates and his disciple Plato, who made such sharp criticisms of Homeric mythology, certainly believed in the existence of the supernatural[7] – yet it was for 'impiety' that Socrates was made to drink the hemlock!

Many philosophers, like the neo-Platonist Plutarch some centuries later, steered a course mid-way between unquestioning simple faith and scepticism, following a *via media* that tried to avoid superstition and atheism alike, both of which they regarded as equally culpable errors. It was only from the third century BC onwards that the Epicurean school attracted large numbers of unbelievers: even so, the philosophers of the Garden were not atheists, though the gods they recognized were relegated to a position far from the world of men, and took not the slightest interest in human affairs. This led Epicureans to a practical disregard for religion, and often to open expressions of hostility where traditional observances were concerned.[8]

The city-state of antiquity was, as we would say nowadays, a totalitarian régime. Any attempt to drive a wedge between temporal and spiritual functions was unthinkable: the priests did not need a 'vocation' when they were civic officials. It was logical, therefore, that those philosophers who made an open profession of atheism, or whose beliefs were in any way suspect, should be regarded as violating the laws of the city and its 'social covenant'. No man could be a good Athenian without believing in the puissance of Athena, the city's patron deity, and that of her father, Zeus. This is why during the fifth and fourth centuries several philosophers were put on trial charged with impiety. The trial of Socrates is the best known amongst these: in 399 he was accused 'of not believing in the gods recognized by the city, of attempting to introduce new divinities, and, by so doing, of corrupting the young', and in due course condemned to death. Before him three other men – all non-Athenians, but with considerable influence in Athens – had been similarly brought to trial for impiety: Anaxagoras of Clazomenae, who was Pericles' old tutor; Protagoras of Abdera; and Diagoras of Melos.[9] Tragic poets such as Aeschylus and Euripides were by no means immune from persecution of this sort, though – with a somewhat surprising inconsistency – comedy enjoyed far greater licence. Aristophanes could, with impunity, challenge Demeter to make a single grain grow when the birds had eaten all the seed (*The Birds*), and, in *The Frogs*, present Dionysus – the very god, be it noted, in whose honour any play, whether tragedy or comedy, was performed, the theatre's patron deity – as an arrant cad, braggart, and buffoon. But in these burlesque extravaganzas nothing was taken seriously.

The most ancient ceremonial known to Greek religion – a religion that lacked both dogma and scriptures – was, beyond any doubt, those pastoral and agrarian rites designed to guarantee fecund flocks and fertile fields. 'Let us picture a Greek peasant,' says Professor Nilsson. 'Like humble folk in all ages, he rose early, before the dawn. In the still half-dark sky he would look up and seek the stars . . . He would kiss his hand in greeting to the rising sun, just as he would similarly welcome the first swallow or the first kite . . . But he longed for rain more often than sunlight, and sometimes he yearned for coolness, too. He would raise his eyes to the highest peak in sight – it might be cloud-capped on occasion – since there, on the very summit of the mountain, sat Zeus, the cloud-gatherer, the thunderer, the rain-giver. He was a mighty deity . . . The growl of the thunder was the sign of his power and his presence; sometimes of his wrath.'[10] Even linguistic usage testifies to the force of these beliefs: the Greeks never said 'it rains' or 'it thunders', but 'Zeus rains' and 'Zeus thunders'.

Water is rare in Greece, and therefore doubly precious. This is why springs and streams were regarded as sacred. An army never crossed a river without offering sacrifice to it, for the river itself was a god. Hesiod says that one should never cross a river without saying a prayer and washing one's hands in its waters. The 'nymphs' (a word which merely means 'maidens') haunted mountains, cool grottoes, thickets, meadows, and springs; sea-nymphs were known as Nereids, and we know that Achilles' mother, Thetis, was one of them. They were beneficent deities, but might turn very nasty if one offended or even neglected them; when a man went mad he was said to have been 'taken by the nymphs' (*nympholeptos*). Similarly, the deaths of men and women alike were attributed to the invisible arrows of the divine archers, Apollo and Artemis.

The cult of the gods consisted, fundamentally, of prayer, sacrifice, and purification. One generally prayed standing, with arms upraised to the sky, when addressing Zeus or the other celestial deities, and prostrate on the ground if one's appeal was to Hades or the other gods of the underworld. First came the invocation of the god or goddess concerned; then followed a 'reminder' of the pious acts the appellant had performed in the past; last of all the request was formulated. This is the formula observed in Book I of the *Iliad* by the priest, Chryses, when he addresses his god Apollo: 'Hear my words, O thou of the silver bow, protector of Chryse and divine Cilla, mighty lord of Tenedos, O Smintheus, hearken! If ever for thee I have built a shrine to thy pleasing, if ever I have burnt fat thighs of bulls and goats on thy altars, then grant my prayer: let the Danaans suffer thy arrows for these my tears.'[11]

When one approaches the gods, it was nearly always on a *quid pro quo* basis, one's offering being made in order to obtain some personal favour, or assistance against one's enemies. In the official prayers of the city, Athens asked the gods, and above all Zeus and Athena, to ensure 'the well-being and safety of the citizens of Athens, and of their wives and children, and of the whole country together with her allies'. The offerings which normally accompanied one's prayer might be either a libation of wine or

milk, or some cake or pastry (*pelanos*) laid on the altar, or vegetables and other harvest-time first-fruits. But the most important
sacrifices were blood-offerings. In the most archaic period it was
believed that the gods demanded human victims; the sacrifice of
Iphigeneia, for instance, is a legendary memory of such human
sacrifices, which were replaced – well before the classical epoch –
by the immolation of animals. Rams, ewes, cows, oxen, pigs, goats
and deer were all slaughtered for this purpose. Each deity had
his or her special preference: Poseidon was mainly honoured with
bulls, Athena with cows, Artemis and Aphrodite with goats, while
Asclepius required cocks or hens, and other gods would accept
doves, dogs, and even horses. The 'hecatomb' – that is, literally,
'the sacrifice of a hundred oxen' – and the triple sacrifice to
Poseidon of a bull, a ram, and a boar (known in Rome as the
suovetaurilia), were both attested as early as Homer's day.[12] The
victims had always to be *teleioi*, that is, healthy and without
blemish. Their sex and colour were also matters of importance:
goddesses normally had female animals sacrificed to them, the
celestial deities were honoured with white or near-white beasts,
while the chthonian gods of the underworld preferred (appropriately enough) black or dark-fleeced offerings.

The ceremony was most often performed in the morning, at
dawn. The altar was decorated with flowers and garlands of
leaves: the white-clad priests, together with their acolytes, all
wore wreaths. The victim itself was wreathed too, and adorned
with bunches of woollen ribbons: sometimes its horns were gilded.
Both victim and sacrificers were sprinkled with lustral water from
a vessel known as a *chernips*. A fire would then be lit on the altar,
into which was thrown a few grains of barley and some hair
clipped from the victim's head. After the prayer, the sacrificing
priest pulled back the victim's head and slit its throat with one
stroke of his knife. The blood which spurted out had to spatter
the altar. Only a small portion of the animal thus slaughtered was
normally burnt in honour of the god: a slice from the thighs, and
a little fat, the smoke (*knisa*) of which, according to Homer, the
Olympians loved to savour.[13] The meat from the quartered beast
was shared out amongst the priests and the faithful, who might
either consume it on the spot or take it away with them. However,
in certain special sacrifices made to the dead, or to the gods of
the underworld, the victim was completely consumed by fire: this

was the 'holocaust'. Often a soothsayer took part in the ceremony: he would examine the still-warm entrails of the beast, the liver in particular, and from various marks on them deduce the will of the gods. A sacrifice might be summed up as a slaughter-house spectacle with a meal as its usual climax.

The holocaust was also employed as an individual or collective purificatory sacrifice. Like all peoples in antiquity, the Greeks made a formidable bugbear of ritual defilement – defilement of the whole being, body and soul alike – though without introducing the comparatively recent notion of moral error or 'sin'. Unclean, in particular, was anything connected with birth or death; and all murderers, even if they had killed in justifiable self-defence. One could only approach the images of the gods, or take part in their ceremonial cults, if one was in a state of ritual purity; otherwise, by virtue of that sense of *thambos* described above, one might inevitably expect to be overtaken by divine wrath and divine vengeance. Not only every sacrifice, but also, as we have seen, every session of Athens' political Assembly began with rites of purification and lustration. Every house in which a death had occurred must be purified, and all its inhabitants with it, as happened to Odysseus' palace after the slaying of the wooers. For these purificatory ceremonies sea-water was often employed, and if a sacrifice was involved, the victim was generally a pig, the blood of which was used for the lustration. The god of Delphi, Pythian Apollo, who, according to legend, purified Orestes after the murder of his mother, was regarded as the 'purificatory god' *par excellence*: he himself had been obliged to undergo ritual purification after slaying Python. Every impious word had to be expiated on the spot, if only by spitting, an act which possessed purificatory powers.[14]

The cult of the dead, as Fustel de Coulanges has demonstrated in his *Cité antique*, played a great part in the lives of those who survived them. It began on the third day after the funeral.[15] On every anniversary a procession was made to the graveside, where libations and sacrifices were offered to the deceased, and followed by a funeral meal. The libations, both of wine and milk, the various other offerings – salt, cakes, fruit – were placed in special bowls with pierced bottoms, so that food and drink could drain through to the dead person. The dead were supposed to live on in the underworld, and to enjoy the offerings made them by those on

earth – witness the shades called up by Odysseus in the 'Nekyia'
(*Odyssey*, Book XI), who pounce so eagerly upon the black blood
of the slaughtered victims, to drink and regain a little strength.
A statuette or picture of the dead man was kept in the house,
beside the domestic altar: from a second-century BC inscription
we learn that this representation had to be crowned with laurel
twice monthly, on the seventh day and at the time of the new
moon;[16] it is more than probable that this rite, or something very
like it, had been observed during the classical period.

THE RELIGIOUS CALENDAR

Festivals (at once religious and civic, the two elements being
indissolubly bound up together) were especially numerous and
brilliant in Athens – a point emphasized by Pericles, as we have
seen, during the Thucydidean Funeral Oration.[17] All of them
helped, simultaneously, to boost religious feelings and patriotism,
belief in the gods and national pride. Only war could temporarily
suspend the cycle of these great periodical festivals, or at least
diminish their splendour: that is why Aristophanes, in the comedy
which bears her name, shows us a personified Peace, escorted –
when the efforts of Attica's labourers have at last released her
from imprisonment under piles of stones in a cave – by two
'maids of honour' who are Opôra, the harvest-goddess, and
Theôria, goddess of shows and festivals. The pleasures of peace,
to an Athenian of the Periclean Age, meant, above all else,
material plenty and the excitement of the great festivals, or
panégyreis. One thinks ahead to the watch-cry of the Roman plebs,
panem et circenses – though Theôria conjures up pleasures of a
somewhat more elevated order than the Games in the Circus.

Most, if not all, of these festivals included competitive contests
(*agônes*) of some sort, most often in the field of gymnastics or
athletics. These we have already mentioned apropos of education.[18]
But there were also contests in music or lyric poetry, in tragedy
and comedy, and even, on occasion, 'beauty-contests' – judged on
figure and bearing, and held between men as well as women.

Let us now go through the main dates in Athens' religious
calendar, and briefly describe the most important festivals.[19]
During the Peloponnesian War a reform of the calendar, introduced in order to abolish the discrepancy between lunar months
and a solar year, caused a certain amount of trouble in the

celebration of festivals. This gave Aristophanes the opportunity to make his Chorus of Clouds, on the Moon's behalf, address the following light-hearted complaints to the Athenian people: 'You do not arrange your days properly, but turn them all upside down, any old how: and the result (she says) is that the gods are always taking it out on *her* when they're cheated of their dinner and have to trudge home on a festival-day without getting what they're entitled to, while you lot are still arguing and bickering in the courts as to when sacrifice should be made. Often when *we're* observing fast-days, say in memory of Memnon's death, or Sarpedon's, *you're* cheerfully pouring libations.'[20]

The official year, both civil and religious, began in July, during the month of Hecatombaiôn; this month was originally known as Kronion, since on its twelfth day, in thanksgiving for the harvest now safely gathered in, a feast was held in honour of Kronos, Zeus' father, and his wife Rhea, the Mother of the Gods. The Kronia, like the Saturnalia at Rome, brought masters and slaves of every family together in a gay and uproarious domestic banquet; but the festival also had its public, national side. On the 16th of the same month was celebrated the sacrifice of the *Synoikia*, which recalled the *synoikismos* accomplished by Theseus – that far-off inauguration of Attica's unity and Athenian power. Right at the end of Hekatombaiôn there came the great national festival of Athena, the city's patron goddess: this was the Panathenaea.

The Panathenaea was celebrated annually, and lasted for two days; but once every four years it was celebrated with particular solemnity, and then lasted at least four days. The victors in the athletic contests (which included the famous torch-races, or *lampadedromia*[21]) received as their prizes oil from Athena's sacred olive-trees, in special amphoras known as '*panathenaika*'. These were decorated on one side with a representation of Athena Promachos (ie 'who fights in the front rank') standing between two pillars, and on the other with a picture of the particular contest (eg the foot-race) for which the prize had been won. Afterwards there took place the great Panathenaic Procession (represented in marble on the frieze of the Parthenon) which set out from the Ceramicus, made its way through the centre of Athens, and finally reached the Acropolis, solemnly bearing the embroidered robe destined for Athena's cult-statue – a robe made annually by certain specially chosen young girls. The procession, which included priests and representatives of every civic body, metics included, was most carefully marshalled into position, and escorted on its way by mounted *ephéboi*. When they reached the Acropolis, they first sacrificed four oxen and four sheep before the old temple of Athena Polias (ie 'Protector of the City'), and then, moving across to the great altar which stood before the Parthenon, they slaughtered enough cows to feed the entire city. It was no doubt this mass-sacrifice which gave the month its new name of *Hekatombaiôn*.

In Boedromion (September) there were celebrated the Eleusinian Mysteries, about which we shall have more to say presently, and the Boedromia, the feast of Apollo Boedromios, ie 'helper in battle'. This feast included a sacrifice and a procession. But the month with the greatest number of festivals in it was Pyanopsion (October). On the 7th took place the Pyanopsia, a feast in honour of Apollo. This was connected with the sowing, and accompanied by some odd and immemorially ancient ritual. The god was offered a dish of beans (*pyanoi*) and several other vegetables, all mingled with wheaten flour; a special branch of olive, the *eiresioné*, was afterwards borne in procession, wrapped about with wool and loaded with first-fruits – clearly a fertility talisman – while a cheerful boys' choir sang:

> 'The *eiresioné* bears figs and fat loaves,
> A small pot of honey, and oil to anoint it,
> A cup of neat wine to befuddle and lull it.'[22]

Another somewhat similar procession took place during the Oschophoria in honour of Dionysus: a group of adolescents, led by two boys who were *amphithaleis* (ie who had both parents living),[23] marched along bearing vine-branches with the grape-clusters still hanging from them. Sacrifice and libation were accompanied by the ritual cry of '*Eléleu iou iou!*' Afterwards there was dancing, and races between the *ephéboi*.[24]

On the 11th, 12th and 13th of the same month there took place the Thesmophoria, or feast of Demeter Thesmophoros. In this capacity the goddess watched over the fertility of crops and the fecundity of women. Only married Athenian women might take part in this festival, and men were rigorously debarred from it.[25] Women prepared themselves beforehand by abstaining, for several days, from any sexual contact.[26] On the first day, called Anodos ('the Going Up'), there were brought out to the light of day the remains of certain sacred objects (sucking-pigs, pastry shaped to resemble serpents, or the sexual organs) which had been buried some four months previously. This piece of agrarian magic is analogous to the ritual performed in Athena's honour by two small girls called *arréphoroi*. During the second day, Nesteia ('the Fast'), the women abstained from all food. On the third, which was called Kalligeneia ('Fair Fertility'), they offered up to Demeter all kinds of fruits of the earth, together with bowls of broth and cheese. Then they uttered various obscene gibes at one another, manipulated small figurines which portrayed the female sexual organs, ate pomegranate-seeds, and flagellated themselves with green branches – all of these being rites deemed favourable to conception.

The Apaturia, or civic festival of the phratries, also lasted three days. The first two were taken up with sacrifices and banquets. On the third, called Koureôtis, fathers presented the legitimate children, born to them during the past year, before the members of their phratry, for official enrolment. On this occasion each paterfamilias would sacrifice a sheep or a goat on the altar of Zeus Phratrios and Athena Phratria.

Finally, on the thirtieth day of Pyanopsion, Athena Ergané ('the Worker'), patron goddess of artisans, and Hephaestus, patron god of smiths, were honoured by bronze-workers (*chalkeis*) and other craft-guilds in a festival called the Chalkeia.[27] The workers freely offered to Athena (just as peasants dedicated the first-fruits of their crops) some product of their particular industry, some masterpiece specially executed for the goddess. Such votive offerings to Athena Ergané have been unearthed by the archaeologists: for instance, that of a certain Bacchius, from whose epitaph (likewise preserved) we learn that he was a potter, and that he had won first prize in a craftsmen's competition: 'Bacchius offered this [ex-voto offering] as a tithe to Athena Ergané after having received the victor's crown from the fellow-members of his *thiasos*.'[28]

In the month Poseidaion (December) there was held the feast of the Haloa (derived from *halos*, the threshing-floor or ploughed field). The purpose of this was to safeguard the grain germinating beneath the soil, just as the aim of the Thesmophoria had been to prosper the sowing. On this occasion sacrifice was made to Demeter, to her daughter Koré, and also to Poseidon, who gave his name to this month, and who had been a chthonian deity (*Gaiéochos*) before becoming Lord of the Sea. Men played no part in the Haloa, except for certain officials whose task it was to supervise the ceremonies; on the other hand courtesans were admitted, though they, like the men, were barred from the Thesmophoria. The male generative organ, the *phallos*, seems to have played a central part in this rite: a certain vase (*péliké*) now preserved in London shows us a woman scooping up powder from a box and scattering it over a row of terracotta phalluses, planted in the ground like corn-stalks.[29]

The phallus also played an important role in the festivals of Dionysus, which took place (the most ancient of them, at any rate) during the winter months. In Poseidaion there was celebrated the agrarian or rural Dionysia, during which the *phallos* was borne in solemn procession through the fields behind a girl basket-bearer (*kanéphoros*).[30] An Athenian decree concerning the colony of Brea, in Thrace, datable to about 445 BC, stipulates that the inhabitants of this city shall send to Athens 'for the Great Panathenaea, a cow and a *panoplia* [suit of armour]; and for the Dionysia, a *phallos*'.[31] This feast gave rise to such popular junketings as can still be seen at a modern village *kermesse* in France. Young peasants would try to balance on greasy inflated wineskins, a sport known as *askoliasmos*,[32] while cheerful, noisy bands of revellers (*kômoi* – the origin of the 'comic' Chorus) would traverse the streets and alleyways of the town, dancing, singing, and flinging cheerful or obscene ribaldries at everyone, whether men or women, they encountered en route. From the fifth century onwards, the more wealthy demes reinforced these celebrations with dramatic performances.

In Gamélion (January), the marriage month (*gamos*), was held the festival of the Gamélia or Theogamia, which recalled the divine union of Zeus and Hera; and also another festival of Dionysus, the Lenaea. This last was not, as has sometimes been supposed, a feast to do with the wine press (*lénos*): the vintage season was several months past. It was, rather, an orgiastic feast in honour of the Lenai, another name for the Maenads or Bacchants, women possessed by Dionysiac frenzy. In the sacred precinct of the *Lenaion* they performed their ecstatic and

dishevelled dances.[33] Since Dionysus was the god both of the
dithyramb and the theatre, this festival also included recitals of
lyric poetry and dramatic productions: several plays by Aristophanes, among them the *Acharnians*, the *Knights*, and *The Wasps*,
were played during the Lenaea, to an exclusive audience of
Athenians and metics, whereas during the Greater Dionysia, in
March, the audience would include large numbers of delegates
from the allied cities, who had come to Athens with their tribute
quota. It was this absence of allied delegates which allowed
Aristophanes to attack his *bête noire*, Cleon, so much more freely
in the *Acharnians*: 'We are on our own; this is the Lenaea, and no
strangers are yet amongst us: no tribute or allies have reached us
from the cities. We here are clean-winnowed flour, and our
resident aliens the civic bran, if I may so put it.'[34]

Another great festival of Dionysus, as God of Wine, took place
during Anthestérion (February). This was the Anthestéria, which
(like Demeter's Thesmophoria in Pyanopsion) stretched over the
11th, 12th and 13th days of the month. On the first day in this
triduum, called Pithoigia ('the Opening of Jars'), the terracotta
pithoi in which the wine had been stored since the autumn
vintaging were opened. On that day or the next, known as Choés
(the Feast of Wine-pitchers: cf. *Choéphoroi*) there was a drinking
competition, at which, when the trumpet sounded, one had to
down a potful of wine as fast as possible. The victor received a
crown of leaves and a full wineskin. Many of these pots, or
pitchers, have survived: they are often decorated with scenes of
small children playing with toys and garlands, since the Anthestéria also incorporated a children's festival.[35] On the second day
a procession took place, in which Dionysus, mounted upon a
boat-shaped float, was escorted through the town. Those taking
part in the procession appear to have worn masks, and comparisons
have been drawn between this cheerful ceremony and the modern
carnival. The role of the god had to be taken by the King Archon,
since the Basilinna, or queen (ie the King Archon's wife) had to
be united with him in a *hieros gamos* (sacred ritual marriage).
But the third day of the festival, known as Chytroi ('the Feast
of Cooking-Pots'), had a quite different character: this was
devoted to the dead and the dying. A stew of vegetables and
various kinds of grain (*panspermia*) was prepared in terracotta
cooking-pots: this had to be consumed before nightfall. The

principal sacrifice was offered up to Hermes Psychopompus, the 'conductor of souls' on their way to Hades. In order to avert bad luck, people uttered the following phrase at the end of the third day: 'Outside, Kéres (goddesses of death): the Anthestéria is over!'[36] Anthestérion was also the month of the Chloia, the festival of Demeter Chloé; and of the Diasia, the major Athenian festival in honour of Zeus.

During the month Elaphébolion (March) which marked the end of winter and the coming of spring, thanksgiving sacrifices were offered up to Athena (*Procharistéria*), and – most important event of all – the Greater Dionysia took place. This formed a second theatrical 'season' after the Lenaea, and attracted large numbers of foreign visitors, since by then the winter storms were over, and ships once more sailing the Aegean. The festival, which for sheer magnificence came second only to the Great Panathenaea, lasted for five days. On the 9th, the dithyrambic contest was held; on the 10th it was the turn of the comedies; and from the 11th to the 13th came the tragic trilogies, each followed by a satyr-drama. We shall return to these presently when discussing the theatre.

In Munychion (April), on the sixteenth day of the month, there was celebrated the festival of the Munychia, which included a procession in honour of Artemis. Cake-offerings were borne to the goddess's shrine, surrounded by flaring torches. Thargelion (May) saw the celebration of the Thargelia, in honour of Artemis' brother Apollo, the supreme 'purificatory' god. On the first day, the 6th, the town was purified by the ritual of the *pharmakoi*, which has certain parallels with the Jewish practice of finding a 'scapegoat'. Two men ran through the streets, with everyone whipping them as they went, using fig-branches and bunches of sea-onions, or squills, for the purpose. This was done so as to drive out of the city, along with the men, all the defilement, the *miasmata*, with which they were supposed to be laden. On the 7th Apollo received an offering known as the *thargelos* – that is, a cake or a mash of various cereals, a first-fruit dedication from the coming harvest. On the 25th was held the Plyntéria, or the feast of 'Athena's bath'. The ancient wooden image (*xoanon*) of Athena Polias was carried in procession to Phalerum, and plunged into the sea, peplos and all; after this immersion the goddess was offered cakes of dried figs. Naturally, because of the cult attaching to images, the statue was regarded as embodying the goddess herself, and its 'bath' guaranteed the purification of the entire city under her tutelary protection. The main festivals held during Thargelion, then, saw to the corporate lustration of Athens, a process that would make her worthy of the divine benefits of harvest-time.

The last month in the Athenian year was called Skirophorion (June), and in it were held the Skirophoria, a festival the ritual of which is more or less unknown, but which appears to have involved a common sacrifice to Demeter, her daughter Koré, Athena, and Poseidon; the Dipolia or Bouphonia, during which a plough-ox was sacrificed to Zeus; and the Arrétophoria, a feast in honour of Athena, which contained certain rites, performed by two small girls known as *arréphoroi*, similar to those of the Anodos, during the Thesmophoria.

It will be noted that we have mentioned ten months only of the Athenian year. The two remaining months, Metageitnion (August) and Maimaktérion (November) were certainly not altogether devoid of religious ceremonial; but the eponymous feasts of the Metageitnia and Maimaktéria are scarcely referred to in the evidence available to us. However, enough has been said to prove that Thucydides was in no way exaggerating when he made Pericles declare that Athens celebrated religious festivals from one end of the year to the other. Even so, we have omitted the feasts of certain minor deities such as Asclepius, and those of the heroes (eg the Theseia), not to mention those foreign cults imported by the metics, such as the Bendidaia, celebrated during the fifth century, in the Piraeus, in honour of the Thracian goddess Bendis.

THE THEATRE

When discussing the agrarian Dionysia, and the two urban festivals of the Lenaea and the Greater Dionysia, we have had occasion to mention dramatic representations. The theatre, together with the stadium, forms the most characteristic monument in every Greek city of any importance. In Attica, we know that besides the theatre on the southern flank of the Acropolis, in the sanctuary of Dionysus Eleuthereus, there were others, scattered through a number of demes – most notably the Piraeus, Collytus, Salamis, Eleusis, Thoricus, and Rhamnous. Such theatres were used to put on plays during the agrarian, or rural, Dionysia.

It is both logical and convenient to discuss the theatre in a chapter devoted to religious life, since every dramatic perform-ance took place in a sanctuary of Dionysus, during a festival devoted to the god; Dionysus' priest presided over it, and – like those athletic events which accompanied other festivals – the occasion was organized by the civic authorities in the form of a play-contest.

As is well known, Greek plays were put on in the open air, normally on the slope of a hillside, which could support the curving tiers of seats (*theatron*) surrounding the circular *orchestra*, where the Chorus danced round Dionysus' altar, in front of the *proskénion*, a stage, with porch, standing out from the *skéné* (the latter having originally been a simple tent where actors and *choreutai* dressed). The Theatre of Dionysus in Athens dates, in its present shape, only from the Roman period: the magnificent theatre attached to the sanctuary at Epidaurus, in the Argolid, has better preserved the appearance it wore in classical times.[37] In all these theatres the acoustics were excellent.[38]

In Athens, before the Lenaea and the Greater Dionysia, the city's highest officials – the Eponymous Archon and the King Archon – began preparations for the dramatic festival long in advance. The first step was to appoint *chorégoi*, rich citizens whom the State required to recruit, support, and equip, at their own expense, the various Choruses, both tragic and comic. (The former consisted of fifteen *choreutai*, the latter of twenty-four.) Poets desirous of taking part in the contest – foreigners, ie non-Athenian Greeks, were also eligible – 'asked for a Chorus' from the Archon, who was allowed to accept or reject their application as he pleased, but subsequently had to justify his decision to the people. The poet was his own producer, and it was he who trained the Chorus; however, he could, if he wished, be assisted (or even replaced) by a chorus-master (*chorodidaskalos*), since this task was a heavy one, and demanded a considerable variety of talents. The Chorus both sang and danced, to a flute accom-paniment, so that an ancient tragedy or comedy was an all-round spectacle, which – at least from this external viewpoint – some-what resembled the modern opera or comic-opera. The Archon, moreover, was responsible for selecting the leading actor, the *protagonistés*, who himself had charge of the second and third supporting players, the *deuteragonistés* and *tritagonistés*. There were no actresses, either in tragedy or comedy: all feminine roles were taken by men, which makes the use of the mask a little less odd.

Once the three important lists – of *chorégoi*, poets, and *protagonistai* – had been established, they next had to be sorted out in groups, ie every poet must be provided with a *chorégos* and a *protagonistés*. During one session of the Assembly, the names of the *chorégoi*-designate were placed in an urn, and the lot determined the order in which each of them should be called upon to select their poet. Thus in 472 the young Pericles was appointed *chorégos*, and chose Aeschylus, who that year presented the trilogy of which *The Persians* formed one part. The *protagonistai* were appointed to the various poets by lot; later, each *protagonistés* was required to interpret a tragedy for every poet in turn, a system which put the competing authors on a more equal footing.

All these preliminaries concluded with the *proagôn*, a general 'presentation' of the poets and their companies, which took place in the Odeon, a covered building near the theatre, mainly employed for putting on musical concerts. Each poet in turn went up on a dais and proclaimed in turn his own name, the titles and subjects of his plays, and the names of his various performers. This ceremony, then, formed a sort of substitute for bill-posting.

The actual performances, like any other official meeting, began in the morning, shortly after daybreak. This was indeed essential if some four or five plays were to be crammed in before sundown (each including dances and choral lyrics), and a brief breathing space left between each: the play itself, whether tragedy or comedy, was performed without any breaks or intermissions. The following was the daily 'theatrical ration' of the spectators, for four days on end, during the Greater Dionysia: after one preliminary day devoted to the Dionysiac Procession, and another to the purely poetical dithyrambic contest, the third day was allotted to the performance of comedies, three poets – later five – presenting one each. The three days after that were set aside for tragedy, each in turn being devoted entirely to the work of one of the three poets selected by the Archon. This would mean a tetralogy, to wit, a trilogy of three tragedies, followed by a satyr-drama.

The Athenians who stuck through the Greater Dionysia to the end, then, in four days saw fifteen, perhaps seventeen plays (not to mention listening to dithyrambs), or in other words, were subjected to something like twenty thousand lines of verse, either spoken or sung. Such powers of endurance may astonish us, but lengthy recitations of the Homeric poems (eg during the Panathenaea) had trained the audiences to a point where their concentration was more or less inexhaustible.

Women, even though they could not be actresses, were certainly admitted to the theatre as spectators.[39] The price of a seat was two obols (one third of a drachma); but the State itself paid the admission fees of indigent citizens, setting aside a special 'entertainment fund' (*theôrikon*) for the purpose. Seats in the front row were reserved for priests and civic officials, as well as for those (whether Athenian or non-Athenian) who had been granted the privilege of *proedria*, that is, of privileged seating accommodation. *Bouleutai*, *ephéboi* and metics had seats reserved for them in the wings of the *theatron*, while the women, it seems, were restricted to the very topmost tiers. Each of the ten tribes had its own block. But despite these precautions, the audience did not always settle down peaceably; sometimes there would be confusion and brawling, and then the *rhabdouchoi* (staff-bearers or beadles) responsible for keeping order in the theatre were obliged to intervene. It seems quite certain that for such lengthy sessions the Athenian audience (despite that well-known Athenian moderation in such matters) would bring along something to eat and drink *in situ*. Sometimes particularly generous *chorégoi* would make distributions of cakes and wine to the crowd, and it looks as though the plays must have been received in a fairly festive mood.

Yet these performances had a definitely religious character: they began with a purificatory ceremony, performed with the blood of a sucking-pig, and the priest of Dionysus sat in the centre of the front row, facing the altar of his god that stood, similarly, in the middle of the *orchestra*. When the lustration was over, the order in which the competitors' plays were to be performed was decided by lot. At the beginning of each performance a herald blew a trumpet. Despite the religious nature of the occasion, the audience made their reactions known with noisy abandon, clapping or whistling or stamping their feet.[40] Certain poets, we are told, hired a claque to applaud their efforts. We may also find the extreme licence of ancient comedy somewhat surprising, but we should not forget the special character of the Dionysiac cult. The Dionysia opened with a procession in which the *phallos* was carried like a national flag; as for the *kômos* (whence our word 'comedy' derives), it had always been characterized by an overplus of unbridled and decidedly broad gaiety.

At the end of the contest came the judges' verdict and the distribution of prizes. Before the festival a list of eligible judges was drawn up, and this was reduced by lot, when the proceedings opened, to a panel of ten. These ten judges had special reserved seats in the theatre. At the close of the presentations they voted; but yet another selection by lot was employed to reduce these ten personal votes to the final, decisive five. The procedure was as follows. In one urn were placed the ten tablets on which the judges had recorded their votes, and in another, five little black cubes and five white. A voting-tablet and a cube were drawn out simultaneously, and only the vote which matched with a white cube was valid. These precautions were, clearly, taken to prevent the possibility of dishonest pressurizing on the part of the poets and the *chorégoi*: when we come to discuss the machinery of justice, in the next chapter, we shall find an even more remarkable array of such devices. Even so, the crowd did sometimes attempt to put pressure on the jury, and this was liable, once again, to produce uproarious scenes which the beadles had some difficulty in controlling. Plato, with aristocratic disdain, labelled the public audience at dramatic festivals a 'theatocracy'.[41]

Three prizes were presented in each category, ie tragedy and comedy: to the poet, the *chorégos*, and the leading actor. These prizes consisted of a plain ivy wreath. Only the victors in the dithyrambic contest, it appears, received a tripod. We must not confuse with these prizes the fees – no doubt proportionate to the success of the play – which author and leading actor received. Victorious *chorégoi* sometimes commissioned a monument commemorating their victory (and a perennial reminder of the fame it brought them) which they then dedicated to Dionysus: that of Lysicrates has been preserved.[42]

Two days after the end of the festival, there was a public meeting in the theatre to scrutinize the conduct of the Archon who had organized that year's contest, and he was either given a vote of thanks, or a vote of censure.

'BENEFACTORS OF THE PEOPLE'

The *chorégia* we have had occasion to discuss in connection with the theatre was a *leitourgia*, that is to say, a public service, and – at the same time – a kind of supertax aimed at the wealthiest citizens. But there was a certain amount of honour and prestige attaching to it, since a victorious *chorégos* did not hesitate, on occasion, to spend yet further money in erecting a permanent reminder to his fellow-citizens of the occasion on which 'his' poet had, partly thanks to him, borne off the prize.

Other rich citizens would be selected for the remaining *leitourgiai*: the *trierarchia* (upkeep and command of a warship, ie a trireme); the *gymnasiarchia* (organization of athletic games, and provision of the oil necessary for the competitors); or the *hestiasis* (defrayal of the expenses for a public banquet given to the members of a tribe). During the performance of their appointed duties these citizens were regarded as sacrosanct officials, and anyone who insulted or struck them – for example one Meidias, who hit Demosthenes actually in the theatre, in full sight of the audience, when Demosthenes was *chorégos* – exposed himself to the severest penalties. If they showed themselves generous in their functions, and devoted to the public good, they were regarded as *euergetai*, ie 'benefactors of the people'; and though some Athenians must have been highly involuntary benefactors, who found such expense went very much against the grain, others recognized the *leitourgiai* as a means of acquiring real popularity for themselves and their families, and pounced on them eagerly. We should not forget that *philotimia*, the desire for honours and renown, was a deep and widespread emotion in Periclean Athens; and it is easy to cite instances of wholly voluntary and spontaneous 'euergetism'.

Cimon, Miltiades' son, employed his own wealth and the plunder acquired during his military campaigns for the benefit of his fellow-citizens: he removed the boundary-fences on his estates so that metics and indigent Athenian citizens could come in and pick the fruit, and every day he provided a plain but sufficient meal for large numbers of poor people. He ran, in fact, what we today would call a soup-kitchen. In this way, Plutarch remarks, thinking of the custom of providing free meals at the City Hall (*Prytaneion*) for particularly distinguished citizens, Cimon turned his house into a 'common or free-for-all *prytaneion*'.

Cimon even ordered the rich young sprigs who served in his personal bodyguard to exchange clothes with the aged and ill-clad citizens he encountered, and made them distribute largesse, in the Agora, to those who were ashamed to beg.[43]

But it was, above all, the festivals and public competitions which provided the occasion for really spectacular generosity. Nicias had got himself very much in the public eye by his lavish spending when he led the Athenian 'embassy' (*theôria*) to Delos; he was even said to have prefabricated a bridge in Athens, complete with splendid decorations in the way of gilding, pictures, crowns and tapestries, and shipped it across to link up the islands of Delos and Rhenea during the festival.[44]

Similarly, at the four great Panhellenic festivals of the Olympian, Pythian (Delphic), Isthmian and Nemean Games (the victors in these Games are the ones celebrated by Pindar in his *Triumphal Odes*), rich and ambitious Greeks strove to see who could best glorify himself and his country by quite lunatic prodigality, which sometimes ruined the donor. Alcibiades' conduct at the Olympic Games in 416 excited the admiration of all Greece. Not only, thanks to his large and magnificent racing-stables, was he able to enter no less than nine chariots in his own name, and thus carry off the first, second, and fourth prizes – an unheard-of feat – but he also erected a vast marquee in which, after sacrificial thanksgivings, he offered a sumptuous banquet to a vast crowd of pilgrims.[45] It was true that those who envied this munificence did their best to minimize it: it was said that the city-states of Ephesus, Chios and Lesbos, Athens' technical 'allies', had been obliged to furnish Alcibiades, gratis, with sacrificial victims, wine, and marquee, and even that one of the chariots he entered did not, in fact, belong to him.[46]

The sanctuary of Zeus at Olympus, near the banks of the Alpheus, was the scene, every four years, of a ceremonial gathering (*panégyris*) attended by Greeks from all parts of the country. The importance of this 'penteteric' festival ('penteteric' means 'recurring every fifth year', or, as we would say, 'every four years' – like the Great Panathenaea) was such that the only chronological system valid throughout Greece was based on the period covered by the 'Olympiads', beginning in 776 BC. Thus the battle of Salamis (480 BC) was dated to the first year of the 75th Olympiad ($74 \times 4 = 296$, and $776 - 296 = 480$). Even slaves or barbarians were admitted to the Olympic festival – though married women were not. It was at Olympia, above all, that the Greeks became most aware of their profound unity, despite all the political divisions which kept them apart. A regular fair seems to have been held around the sacred precinct of Zeus; there were amusements – by no means all of them athletic or sporting – to suit every taste. Many Sophists and writers used this occasion to give public readings of their latest works: notably Herodotus, Gorgias, Lysias, and Isocrates. The last-named, however, did not read his own piece – which he called *Panegyricus* because he had specially composed it with an eye to the *panégyris* at Olympia.

The festival lasted for seven days. On the first, sacrifices were offered up on the altar of Zeus and the six double altars, popularly supposed to have been set up by Heracles. Libations were poured over the tomb of the hero Pelops, eponymous founder of the Peloponnese; and then the preliminary formalities for the Games themselves were dealt with. The next five days were mainly devoted to sporting events: ten for grown men, three for under-age boys. The former competed in four foot-races: the *stadion* (about 200 yards); the *diaulos*, or quarter-mile; the *dolichos*, or 'long haul', about two miles; and the race in armour. There were also wrestling, boxing, the *pankration*, and the *pentathlon*, or 'five-item contest'.[47] Lastly, there was the four-horse chariot-race, held in the Hippodrome (the event in which Alcibiades triumphed in 416) and the mounted horse-race. For the boys there were the *stadion*, wrestling, and boxing only. All these events were competed for under the supervision of the *Hellanodikai*, or 'judges of Greece'. The seventh and last day was marked by a solemn procession and a banquet. The names of the victors – the *Olympionikoi* – were proclaimed by the herald, together with their father's name and that of their country. The prize they received was a simple crown of wild olive, but their prestige was enormous, and their family and city both basked in the glow of it. Athens rewarded those of her citizens who triumphed at the Olympic Games with 'free meals at the *Prytaneion*';[48] and the story is told of how one town, determined to welcome home their *Olympionikos* in a really unprecedented way, actually tore down a section of the ramparts, so that he might enter through a gate where no person had set foot before him.

MYSTERY RELIGIONS

But were the city-cults and those centred on the Panhellenic sanctuaries sufficient to meet the religious needs of the Greek people? It is true that an Athenian might show a really fervent devotion to his goddess Athena, just as Hippolytus – in the play by Euripides which bears his name – nurses a quasi-mystical pious adoration for Artemis: but this Hippolytus is also an Orphic. These public cults, often with grandiose ceremony attaching to them, were always a little cold, a little impersonal: the prayers they addressed to the gods were for the collective well-being of a city, even for that of Greece as a whole, and they concerned themselves very little with the happiness of individual persons in this life or the next. Even the cult of the dead was mainly concerned to supply the 'shades' with nourishment; it gave no assurance concerning their well-being – or otherwise – in the underworld.

Contrastingly, the 'mystery religions' promised their adherents immortal bliss, provided they underwent initiation and observed the prescribed ritual requirements: there was no question of meritorious or sinful conduct involved. These cults, then, were concerned with the salvation of the individual. The Greek word *mystérion*, like the French or English words deriving from it, contains the idea of a secret restricted to a privileged minority; and the connected notions of 'mystic' and 'mysticism' were to be found in several of these sects, advanced well beyond the merely germinal state. Some were regarded as suspect by the State; others, such as the Eleusinian Mysteries (which Athens not only recognized but actively supported) enjoyed specially favourable conditions, and thus became of exceptional importance throughout the course of antiquity.

I said earlier that the Great Mysteries of Eleusis were celebrated in Boédromion (September) in honour of Demeter and her daughter Koré.[49] These goddesses watched over cereal crops; they were also responsible for the dead, who – like the grain – were buried underground. The Mysteries seem also to have undergone a certain amount of Orphic and Dionysiac influence. The Homeric Hymn to Demeter, which has been preserved, tells the myth of Koré's rape by Hades and the 'quest' of her grieving mother, who was welcomed at Eleusis, agreed to confer immortality on young Demophon, and then founded her Mystery

Cult. These lines, near the end of the Hymn, constitute a kind of 'Beatitude': 'Happy is he among mortal men who has beheld these Mysteries; but the non-initiate who has no part in them gets no share of such blessings when he is dead and dwells below, amid murky darkness.'

Eleusis, a deme of Attica, lies some fourteen miles from Athens. On the fourteenth day of Boédromion, the 'sacred objects' (*hiera*), contained in a basket, were borne in procession, with great pomp and ceremony, from Eleusis to Athens, where they were deposited in the Eleusinium. On the 15th, candidates for initiation were assembled in the Painted Portico (*Stoa poikilé*): all, even slaves or barbarians, were eligible, the only exceptions being unpurified murderers and those whose speech was not 'intelligible', that is to say, in all likelihood, those who could not speak Greek and therefore were unable to pronounce the ritual formulae correctly. On the 16th the *mystai* went down to the harbour at Phalerum for a curious ceremony of purification. At the signal given by the priests, crying 'To the sea, Mystae!' each had to run down and dip himself in the water, trailing a sucking-pig behind him: the pig was subsequently sacrificed.[50] Then, on the 19th, a great and solemn procession conveyed the Basket of the Mysteries back from Athens to Eleusis, along the Sacred Way, to the sound of hymns and cries of 'Iacchos! Iacchos!' Finally, after a day of fasting, the two nights of initiation proper took place at Eleusis, between the 21st and the 23rd.

But what transpired on those two nights had to remain a secret, and whoever revealed what he had seen or heard was liable to the death penalty. The secret was so well guarded that only a few late texts, mostly of the Early Church Fathers, enable us to get some idea of what the initiation comprised. The great hall where the secret rites took place, the *telestérion*, has been uncovered by excavation: it is a vast square chamber, with sides fifty yards long, containing six rows of seven columns, their bases still visible: the tiers of seats, some of them carved in the rock, provided accommodation for about three thousand people.

On the first night the lower degree of initiation was conferred. The fast of the *mystai*, like that of Demeter in the Homeric Hymn, was broken by the consumption of the *kykeón*, that ritual beverage compounded of pulse, water, and pennyroyal.[51] Then the sacred objects hidden in the basket were revealed to the *mystai*, and

handled by them. It is presumed that these were mainly representations of the sexual organs, both male and female. The *mystés*
was required to pronounce this ritual formula: 'I have fasted; I
have drunk the *kykeón*; I have taken the sacred object from the
basket; the act accomplished, I have placed it in the casket; then
transferred it again from the casket to the basket.' Sacred hymns
were also chanted, led by priests of the Eumolpidae ('good
singers') family.

The second night was that on which the previous year's *mystai*
became *epoptai*, or 'seeing' *mystai*, and thus attained the highest
degree of initiation. The great hall of the Telestérion was plunged
into absolute darkness, and the *mystai* were obliged to move about
in an atmosphere of terror and alarm, fostered by eerie chanting.
Then, suddenly, torches – the characteristic attributes of Demeter
and Koré, and symbols of revelation – blazed out with brilliant
light, illuminating the centre of the hall. Then there was shown
to the initiates 'that most great and wonderful mystery: a
reaped corn-ear', together, in all probability, with a genuine
'liturgical drama', a *hieros gamos*. A precious fragment by the
rhetorician Themistius (wrongly attributed to Plutarch[52]) has this
to say:

> The soul, at the moment of death, experiences the same im-
> pressions as those who are initiated into the Great Mysteries ...
> First comes a grim and interminable struggle through darkness,
> with random sallies and laborious detours. Before the end a
> peak of terror and alarm is reached, with trembling and cold
> sweats; but then a marvellous light suddenly dazzles the eyes,
> and one is transported to pure and holy places, meadows where
> the air is full of song and there are dances in progress, with
> sacred utterances and divine epiphanies to inspire religious awe.
> Then, at last, initiated and made perfect, free, and walking
> unrestrained, a man can celebrate the Mysteries, a crown on
> his head; he lives amongst pure and holy men; he sees the
> crowd of non-initiates on earth, wilfully plunging into filth and
> darkness, and dallying with evil through their very fear of death,
> instead of believing in the bliss of the life to come.

The mysteries of Dionysus, like those of Demeter, doubtless held
out a promise of happiness beyond the grave; their adherents,
who were grouped in *thiasoi* to which entrance was by initiation,

practised the rite known as *ômophagia* – that is, eating the raw flesh of a slaughtered animal.

It is more difficult to determine just what Orphism consisted of during the classical period. By 'Orphism' I mean the congeries of religious ideas that attached themselves to the Thracian singer Orpheus, prophet of Dionysus, who had swayed men with the magic powers of his music, and had descended into Hades before being finally torn to pieces and devoured by the Maenads. Orphism had its charlatans, who got short shrift from Plato,[53] and who (according to him) promised the wealthy, in return for a considerable fee, personal protection from all ills through certain magical sacrifices and incantations, besides various unpleasantnesses to their enemies. Yet Plato himself elsewhere drew inspiration from Orphic notions, which proves that he at least had some respect for the beliefs themselves, if not for their practitioners. It has been maintained, however,[54] that 'Orphism, during the classical period, was not a doctrine, and indeed scarcely a cult . . . About the Orphic books we know next to nothing.' Despite this, it remains probable that during the fifth century there existed, if not an 'Orphic religion', at least various small groups who practised the 'Orphic way of life'; and that it was they who provided the theologians and moralists for the great mystical movement connected with Dionysus in his 'orgiastic' aspect.

The whole Orphic theology, especially the myth of Dionysus-Zagreus and the Titans, is odd, to say the least of it. According to the Orphics, because of an ancient crime (the murder of the young Zagreus by mankind's ancestors, the Titans) which suggests the concept of original sin, the human soul is locked in the body as though in a prison or tomb (*sôma* (body)=*séma* (tomb)), and has to go through a whole cycle of successive existences and reincarnations. But to those acquainted with the revelations of Orpheus a way of salvation lies open. The Orphic must lead a life of abstinence, renunciation, and asceticism. He is a vegetarian, for belief in the transmigration of souls implies a respect for every kind of living creature. The soul must rid itself of all that is material and carnal in order to break free from earth and aspire towards the Divine Abode (which, we may note, exactly parallels the conclusion of the *Phaedo*). Certain gold-leaf amulets found in tombs on Crete and in Magna Graecia have preserved for us the words which the initiate must address to the gods of the underworld (though their Orphic character has not been irrefutably established):

> I come from a communion of pure initiates, O most pure and sovereign Lady of the Underworld . . . I esteem myself a member of your blessed fellowship, but destiny has struck me down . . . I have fled the cycle of heavy pains and sorrows, and have sped with eager feet towards the long-desired crown; I have sought refuge in the bosom of the Lady, Queen of the Underworld . . .

And the goddess replies:

> O fortunate and blessed one, you who were man have become god.

The initiate finally utters the mysterious formula:

> A kid, I have fallen into milk.[55]

DIVINATION

In the official state religion, prayers and sacrifice were offered the gods for the prosperity of the city; whereas in the mystery cults, the individual attempted to obtain, by way of initiation, some guarantee of happiness in the life after death. But in Greece as elsewhere in antiquity, men wanted still more than this: they desired to know the will of the gods, both for the present and the future, to get advance information on approaching events. This is where divination comes in. The Latin word *divinatio* itself indicates how central a role divination played in ancient religion, since it embraces, etymologically speaking, all the *divina* – that is, anything to do with the gods; and it is a fact that divination was, perhaps, the most *alive* element in Greek and Roman religion. In Greece, a diviner was called *mantis* and his art *mantiké*: this term was particularly applicable to intuitive or 'inspired' divination, and appears to derive from the same root as *mania* (madness or ecstasy) and *Mainas*, a Maenad. But the Greeks were also familiar with inductive or rational divination (*entechnos*, *techniké*), which depended on the seer's observation of certain phenomena regarded as sure signs (*sémeia*) of the divine will.

Omens were of various sorts. They might be prodigies or portents: any abnormal or extraordinary sight, such as a monstrous birth, whether human or animal,[56] was a formidable 'sign'. They might be atmospheric: rain and thunder were both 'signs from Zeus' (diosémeiai). They might be visual – any unexpected encounter, especially when you went out in the morning, was either a good or an unlucky omen; or aural, in the sense that any sudden, unexpected word, noise, shout or sound of whatever sort was a klédôn (aural omen) capable of interpretation. They might even be physiological: any involuntary movement brought about by epilepsy (the 'sacred disease'), or such simple phenomena as a buzzing in one's ears, or a sneeze, had some significance, since the individual will did not produce or control them. When Telemachus sneezes, his mother Penelope regards it as a good omen,[57] and similarly in the Anabasis, when a soldier sneezes after one of Xenophon's speeches, 'at this sound, with unanimous alacrity, the whole army made obeisance to the god'.[58]

At Dodona, Zeus' sanctuary in Epirus, which was probably the most ancient of all the oracular shrines in Greece, the Selloi (priest-diviners) predicted the future from the way the wind rustled the leaves of the oak-trees (which were sacred to Zeus), or set various bronze basins clashing, which they hung close together in the branches for that purpose. But the bulk of omens were drawn from animals, whether living or dead. The flight of birds, and their cries, were particularly informative concerning the divine will, for reasons explained by Plutarch: 'In the science of divination, what we call ornithomancy, or augury by birds, is . . . one of the greatest and most ancient branches; since a bird's quickness of apprehension, its ready response to any phenomenon, makes it a natural instrument for the divine purpose, which controls its movements, its various calls or cries, and indeed its flight in formation. Now the god will hold it suspended in midair, now he will send it skimming down-wind, according as he wishes to speed some human undertaking to its allotted end, or to cut it short. This is why Euripides commonly calls birds "the heralds of the gods".'[59] The eagle, Zeus' sacred bird, gave a sinister or favourable omen according to whether it appeared on the left or the right. Ornithomancy enjoyed such a vogue, from the Homeric epoch onwards, that the Greek words signifying 'bird' (ornis, oiónos) carry the alternative meaning of 'omen'.

When discussing sacrifices we have already had occasion to mention *hieroskopia*, a method of divination probably imported from Etruria, which consisted of examining the entrails of a freshly slaughtered animal and deducing the divine will from the signs so revealed. There were three things to be observed in particular when examining the liver: the state of the lobes, the gall-bladder, and the portal vein. In Euripides' *Electra*, Orestes, before killing Aegisthus, assists him perform a sacrifice, where deadly omens presage the imminent act of murder: 'Aegisthus took the sacred entrails from his hands, and examined them. The liver was lacking a lobe; the portal vein and the vessels round the gall-bladder revealed ill omens to his scrutiny . . . "Why this downcast air?" Orestes asked. "Stranger," Aegisthus replied, "I fear some treachery at my gates; for I have a mortal enemy, Agamemnon's son, the sworn foe of me and mine." '⁶⁰ A missing lobe in the liver was the most unequivocal sign that this entrail-examination could reveal: so Cimon, Agesilaus, and Alexander the Great were all warned of their impending doom.⁶¹

But the very title of *mantiké*, under which the Greeks subsumed every branch of divination, suggests that for them the most valued method was that of inspired or ecstatic prophecy, in which a man – or a woman – received a direct 'message' from the gods. An intermediate technique between inductive and intuitive divination was that known as oneiromancy, or divination by dreams. The belief which regards certain dreams as divine revelations is an exceedingly ancient one, and not yet altogether obsolete: the sale of pamphlets with titles like *A Key to Your Dreams* remains steady. In Homer we find the gods sending men a variety of dreams, and the same is true of ancient tragedy (whence it passed into eighteenth-century French drama). But *oneirokrisia*, the interpretation of dreams, was a complex art, since many dreams were deceptive.

One great sanctuary in the Argolid, that of Epidaurus, which flourished especially during the fourth century, was famous for the miraculous cures that took place there. When evening came, the pilgrims would retire for the night under the 'incubation portico' (*abaton, koimétérion*) and fall asleep there. During their sleep they were cured, most often after a dream in which they saw Asclepius, Apollo's son, the God of Healing, come to them: he would either touch and manipulate the affected part of their body, or else prescribe them some specific cure which they would lose no time in applying when they woke up. The *stelai* at Epidaurus – a most curious collection – have recorded for us numerous detailed instances of such 'miracles'. We read of a one-eyed woman who recovered her full sight, a dumb child who suddenly began to speak, a man who was cured of an ulcer, and so on.[62]

During sleep a person attained a state of unconsciousness propitious (it was thought) for divine intervention. Approaching death also developed those divinatory powers which existed, in latent form at least, in every individual. Both Patroclus and Hector, in the *Iliad*, when at their last gasp, prophesy the circumstances of their killer's own, not too far distant death: yet neither of them is a professional seer, like Calchas or Helenus.[63]

Fully qualified prophets, or prophetesses, could also pass into a state of ecstasy (*ekstasis*) or 'enthusiasm' (*enthousiasmos*) – that is, what the Greeks would regard as divine possession – during which they were able to reveal the will of Zeus, transmitted most often via his son Apollo, the god of divination *par excellence* – just as he was also the supreme 'purificatory' god (see above).

In the second century AD that sceptical writer Lucian, in a passage as ironical as it is amusing, set down the following list of the main oracular shrines of Apollo (the speaker is Zeus himself): 'Having chosen so all-engrossing a profession, Apollo now finds himself practically deafened by importunate bores who come and clamour for oracles everywhere. At one moment he has to be in Delphi; the next he is hurrying off to Colophon; from there he moves on to Xanthus, and then – always at the double – to Claros, after which it's Delos or Branchidae: in short, whenever a prophetess (having swigged her sacred water, chewed up some laurel-leaves, and wriggled about on the tripod for a bit) invokes his presence, he must rush straight off there and mug up the right oracles, or else ruin all his carefully built-up professional prestige.'[64] We find a case of prophecy directly inspired by Apollo in the Trojan Cassandra, whose divinatory trance state Agamemnon portrays on-stage during the *Agamemnon*. The same is true of the various Sibyls, and also, very probably, of the prophets known as 'Bakis'. It is certainly the case with the Pythia at Delphi.

The Panhellenic sanctuary of Pythian Apollo at Delphi in Phocis – the site lies at the very heart of central Greece – had several claims to fame. It was the scene of the Pythian Games, celebrated, like those of Olympia, every four years. There was its 'Amphictyony', or League, of the cities and tribes close to the sanctuary, which played a large and sometimes ill-fated part in the history of the Greek states as a whole. But its main attraction was, undoubtedly, its oracle, the most famous and widely consulted oracle of all the many in operation during the classical period. It has been asserted that the Pythia – a simple peasant-woman of Delphi, impeccable in her life and conduct, who was required to maintain complete chastity during the exercise of her office – did no more than draw lots, with beans, to provide answers to questions (which must, then, have always been posed in a form that could be answered Yes or No). It is true that the system of drawing lots was one often employed in ancient Greece when people wished to ascertain the divine will; it is also known that such 'cleromancy' was practised at Delphi during the classical era. But what cities and individuals alike sought at Apollo's sanctuary was an inspired response from the lips of the Pythia, who – seated on the prophetic tripod, in an ecstatic state, down in the underground *adyton* (taboo place) of the temple, proclaimed the will of Zeus as revealed through his son Apollo. How was this state of *enthousiasmos* produced? Here we have no precise information. The most popular current theory is that we have to do with a species of auto-suggestion or self-hypnotism, a religious phenomenon quite distinct from hysteria, and of which numerous instances can be adduced.[65]

Anyone wishing to question the oracle first paid a fee called the *pelanos* (cake), and then made a preliminary sacrifice of a she-goat. Before the goat was slaughtered it was sprinkled with water, and if it shivered and trembled when this cold douche struck it, Apollo was presumed to be willing to prophesy.[66] Then the Pythia, after purifying herself at the Castalian Spring, went into the temple, where she first burnt laurel-leaves and barley-flour on an inner altar, and then descended to the underground part of the temple reserved for divination, and known as the *manteion*. Those consulting the oracle followed her, their order of precedence being determined partly by lot, and partly by the right of *promanteia* (privileged consultation) which some of them had been granted. However they, together with the priests and the seers, halted in a special anteroom reserved for this purpose, while the Pythia proceeded alone into the nearby *adyton*. Priests and visitors could hear her when she prophesied, but they could not see her. She then pronounced the 'truth-telling' and 'infallible' oracular utterances of Apollo Loxias – the epithet, meaning 'ambiguous' was apt enough, since the responses were often decidedly equivocal. In the *adyton* there stood the golden statue of Apollo, the tomb of Dionysus (whose cult was taken very seriously at Delphi, a fact which may partly explain the Pythia's trance state, Dionysus being so closely associated with the ecstatic and the orgiastic), and, finally, the *omphalos* or 'navel of the earth', an archaic betyl (sacred stone) roughly conical in shape, together with the tripod, on the top of which the Pythia seated herself.

This is not the place in which to discuss the immense influence, religious, moral and political, which the Pythian oracles exercised – especially during the period (ie the sixth and fifth centuries) when religious faith was strong and unquestioning. The rise of the Sophistic movement coincided with a certain diminution of religious ardour, and, in consequence, of faith in the oracles. Yet it was well on in the fourth century that the philosopher Plato, when planning his Ideal City, decided that all questions of faith and morals should be referred to the Delphic Oracle. There can be no doubt that this great thinker regarded the Oracle as exercising a beneficial influence on the development of Greek civilization.[67]

SUPERSTITION

Divination, then, was not – as it is today, at least in all civilized countries – a clandestine business conducted by clairvoyants, mediums, and other such people; it was an official institution, recognized by the Greek city-states, which themselves consulted the Pythia and numbered seers among their civil and military officials. Lampon, the friend of Pericles (who appointed him a sort of Minister for Culture) was a diviner, for instance.

The border-line between religion and superstition is often very uncertain: that is why Theophrastus' portrait, in his *Characters*, of the Superstitious Man contains many allusions to ritual we have already met when discussing religion, though here some of them are carried to absurd lengths. Here it is:

On the day of the Feast of Pots, the Superstitious Man washes his hands and asperges himself with lustral water in the temple; he puts a bit of bay-leaf in his mouth before coming out, and keeps it there all day, wherever he goes.[68] If a weasel crosses his path,[69] he will not proceed till some other person has gone by, or else till he has thrown three pebbles across the road. Suppose he sees a snake in his house: if it is of the reddish-brown sort he will invoke Sabazius,[70] but if it is a sacred serpent, then he will build a shrine on the spot, without delay. When he passes one of those smooth stones set up at cross-roads, he will not go on his way till he has poured oil on it from his flask (lékythos)[71] and knelt down and prostrated himself before it [the act of proskynésis]. If a mouse gnaws into one of his flour-sacks, he will hurry off to the official diviner (exégétés)[72] to find out what he should do. If he is simply told to get a fresh patch put in it, he neglects this advice and performs apotropaic rites instead.[73] He is for ever purifying his house on the grounds that it has been haunted by Hecate.[74] If he hears an owl hoot when he is out, he is much perturbed, and will not go a step further till he has cried 'Athena forfend!' He is very careful not to tread on a grave, or go anywhere near a corpse or a woman in labour, saying how important it is for him to avoid pollution. On the fourth and twenty-fourth days of every month,[75] he has mulled wine served up for his household, and hurries off to buy myrtle-branches, incense, and a sacred picture [or 'cake': the text is dubious]; when he gets back he spends all day sacrificing to the images of Herma-phroditus and putting garlands on them.[76] Whenever he has a dream he is straight off to some dream-interpreter or seer or augur, asking what god or goddess he should propitiate. When he is under instruction for admission to the Mysteries, he goes to see the Orphic priests (Orpheotelestai) once a month, taking his wife with him – or if she has not the time to spare, his children and their nursemaid. He is one of those people always down at the sea purifying themselves. If he sees one of those garlic-wreathed fellows[77] [or, garlic-wreathed images of Hecate: text uncertain] that are to be found at cross-roads, he hurries home, summons the priestesses, and makes them go round him with sea-squills or a puppy-dog to take off the defilement. At the sight of a lunatic or an epileptic, he shudders, and spits in the fold of his robe.[78]

If one broke a shoe-lace when putting on a shoe, this too was an omen: right foot lucky, left foot unlucky.[79]

It would be quite wrong to suppose that all superstitious people were uneducated or of the lower classes. A wealthy statesman such as Nicias, or a writer and disciple of Socrates like Xenophon, surrounded themselves with diviners and *chrésmologoi* (oracle-mongers), and went in for ritual scarcely less niggling than that practised by Theophrastus' Superstitious Man. We know that because of an eclipse of the moon – a major portent – Nicias lost his army and himself perished miserably in Sicily: 'What would Athenian reaction be to the news of the disaster?' Fustel de Coulanges asked.[80] 'They knew Nicias was a solid, reliable man, whose personal courage was not in doubt. Nor did it occur to them to criticize him for his inactivity, since this had been dictated by a religious taboo. The only thing they blamed him for was employing a seer who did not know his business. For the seer interpreted the eclipse wrongly; he should have known that when an army wished to retreat, an eclipse of the moon was a *favourable* portent.'

MAGICAL PRACTICES

Magic, which claimed to provide effective ways of controlling both the inanimate world and living persons – even, indeed, of compelling the gods to put their divine power at man's disposal – was by no means unknown in classical Greece; but it was yet, if I may put it that way, in its infancy, by comparison with the vast development it was to undergo in the Hellenistic and Roman periods. The Greeks themselves regarded it as being foreign in origin, an import from the East: the greatest sorceress in Greek mythology, Medea, was a barbarian, born in Colchis, and it is noteworthy that when Aeschylus stages an act of necromancy, the evocation of a dead man from his tomb, it is in the *Persians*, and the ghost thus called up by the Chorus of Elders, in a truly spellbinding scene, is the old King, Darius. Despite this, there are numerous traces of magical practices in the *Iliad*, and even more in the *Odyssey*; and the witches of Thessaly were famous from the classical period onwards. They were credited with the power of 'calling down the moon', a belief which provided some sort of explanation for the satellite's eclipses.[81] It is true that Medea was said to have settled in Thessaly with Jason, and may supposedly have passed on her secret knowledge to others there.

The *orpheotelestai* mentioned by Theophrastus were the same low-level Orphics whom Plato criticized for exploiting the rich, claiming they could guarantee them a happy life (with confusion to their enemies) by special incantations. Their rites properly belong to the sphere of magic, as does the 'circle of purification' which priestesses traced with the body of a dead dog. This latter ceremony must be connected with the cult-ritual of Hecate, a goddess mentioned elsewhere by Theophrastus in his portrait of the Superstitious Man. Hecate is a vaguely disturbing deity: she was the patron goddess of magicians and Orphics, and seems – like Bendis and Sabazius – to have originally come from Thrace. Her nature was both lunar and chthonian. Popular superstition created a very formidable version of her – infernal in the worst sense, the sender of ghosts and nocturnal terrors. An unrivalled sorceress, she was well acquainted with love-spells of every sort, and her cult was primarily practised by women.

One kind of magical device to compel love was certainly current during the fifth century, since it is indirectly attested by Pindar (who attributes its invention to Aphrodite rather than Hecate). He mentions it apropos the love Jason must needs inspire in Medea, the princess of Colchis, if he is to win the Golden Fleece: 'Then first did the Cyprus-born goddess, whose darts strike keenest home, bind fast to the four spokes of a wheel the dappled wryneck (*iynx*), and bring down that maddening bird from Olympus to mankind . . .'[82] The wryneck owes its name to the mobility of its head and neck, which it can turn about in any direction. We note that it is here associated with a wheel, and the *iynx* can mean either the bird alone, or bird and wheel in conjunction. The wheel has the power of a 'magic circle': one vase-painting, from the third quarter of the fifth century, shows us the mother of a young Athenian girl, on her daughter's wedding-morning, busily spinning the magic wheel round on a stick in order to endow the newly-married couple with Aphrodite's gifts.[83] Such 'bird-wheels', mostly fashioned in terracotta, have been identified in modern museum collections, and must have been employed for magical rites of this sort.[84] Theocritus, writing in the third century, shows us (the poem is called *Pharmakeutriai*, 'The Sorceresses') a young woman, abandoned by her lover, and determined to 'bind' him to her by strong magic. She asks her maid for the laurel-branches and potions; then she invokes, amongst other divinities, the Moon, Hecate, and Medea. Finally she chants the incantatory refrain which must accompany each turn of the *iynx*: 'Wryneck, wryneck, draw that man to my threshold.'

From the first half of the fourth century the use of curse-tablets – *defixionum tabellae*, as the Romans called them – became widespread in Attica. This was a magical device for working harm on one's enemies, especially opponents in a court case, by 'devoting' them to the infernal deities, Hermes, Hecate or Persephone. Literally, it meant 'binding' them, 'nailing' them down in the realm of the dead by the process of *katadesis*. We find frequent enumerations of the various parts of the enemy's body, together with his intellectual faculties and his occupation, the object being to attack him in every aspect of his personality. The name of the person thus 'devoted' to death was enclosed in a lined square; then the lead tablet on which the curse had been scratched was rolled round an iron nail and buried in the ground.[85]*

*Translator's note: There is no comprehensive – or even remotely adequate – history of Greek and Roman magic in existence. The Greco-Egyptian magical papyri have been edited by Karl Preisendanz (Leipzig, 2 vols: 1928–32): this otherwise excellent work remains incomplete, and now badly needs bringing up to date. Otherwise the most useful survey for the general reader is still that by K. F. Smith in Hastings' *Encyclopedia of Religion and Ethics*, Vol. VIII, s.v. 'Magic (Greek and Roman)'.

CHAPTER NINE

LAW AND JUSTICE

Justice and ostracism – Court procedure – 'Blood-tribunal' – The Heliaia – Punishments – The worth of Athenian justice

---

JUSTICE AND OSTRACISM

It is only in Athens that we have any detailed knowledge of the machinery of justice. For the other Greek city-states our evidence is scrappy and inadequate. At Sparta, an aristocratic society must have ensured that justice was a good deal more rough and ready in its application than at Athens: for instance, in his detailed account of how Pausanias was accused of treason, Thucydides mentions his confrontation by the ephors, and the way he was walled up alive in the temple of Athena Chalkioikos, where he had sought sanctuary, but says nothing about his having been brought before any sort of tribunal.[1]

The right to dispense justice was originally a royal prerogative; in Homer and Hesiod it is the kings, the sceptre-bearers, who pronounce judgments (*themistes*). In the democratic Athens of Pericles' day, this royal power was exercised by the people, who stripped the ancient Court of the Areopagus of all its authority except that of trying certain murder cases. As Philocleon proudly proclaims in Aristophanes' play *The Wasps*: 'This authority of ours is as great as any king's: can any happiness or good fortune match that of an Athenian juryman? . . . Do I not rule a fine kingdom, no whit worse than that of Zeus himself?'[2] However, before describing the workings of the courts, I think this an appropriate place to make brief mention of one quintessentially Athenian institution, that belongs, perhaps, to the political rather than the judicial sphere. This was a device by which the people were enabled to send one of their number into temporary banishment, without bringing him to trial or even formulating any specific charge against him: it was known as ostracism.

'Ostracism,' it has been said,[3] 'was a penalty peculiar to Athenian law, a form of exile which Athens imposed, in a purely arbitrary manner, by taking a general vote on potsherds (*ostraka:* hence the name given to the proceedings).' It was Cleisthenes, after Solon the chief architect of Athenian democracy at the end of the sixth century, who instituted ostracism as a safeguard against any attempts to establish a tyranny: it was essential that those who might wish to emulate Peisistratus should be prevented from seizing power. It is both ironic and amusing to note that amongst the first victims of ostracism were the elder Alcibiades and Megacles – the first a close colleague of its inventor, the second his nephew. Ostracism was a preventive measure: it did not seek to punish a crime but to make the commission of that crime impossible. It was directed against any real or supposed attempts to establish a tyranny, and any display of overweening ambition, or what appeared as such: it thus rested wholly on the principle of 'trial by presumption'.

Not more than one ostracism-vote could be held per annum, then only if a preliminary committee of the Ecclésia had decided that a prima facie case lay for proceeding to the *ostrakophoria* in that particular year. Both the preliminary hearing and (if deemed admissible) the actual vote, several weeks later, took place during the course of the sixth and seventh *prytaneia* – that is, in winter, in the months of Poseidaion and Anthestérion, both with a fair crop of festivals,[4] so that the peasants of Attica, freed from their heavier labours, would be glad enough to come to town.

The *ostrakophoria* was considered an extraordinary session of the Assembly; but it was presided over by the nine Archons and the Council of Five Hundred, the Boulé, instead of the usual officials. Moreover it was not, like a normal session, held on the Pnyx or in the theatre, but in the Agora, the original ancient place of assembly. That day 'the Agora was boarded up with a wooden barrier, in which ten entry-gates had been left; the citizens filed through these by tribes, and so registered their votes.'[5] Large numbers of these inscribed potsherds have been found, especially since the Americans began excavating the Agora.[6] The vote was secret, but illiterate citizens had to get some friend or neighbour to write the name of the man they wished ostracized.[7]

The sorting and counting of this great heap of sherds must have been a long, irksome business. According to Plutarch, 'the Archons began by counting the total number of *ostraka*. If less than six thousand votes had been recorded, the ostracism was declared null and void. If the figure was higher, the *ostraka* were then sorted according to name, and the man whose name appeared most often was, by proclamation, sentenced to ten years' exile.'[8]

The person thus ostracized had a ten-day stay of sentence in which to take leave of his friends and make arrangements for accommodation beyond the frontiers of Attica. He was allowed to retain control over the disposition of his financial assets – the factor which distinguished ostracism, as a penalty, from ordinary exile (*phygé*), the latter involving the confiscation of one's goods as well. The ostracized person might come no nearer Athens than Euboea or the Argolid; but this proviso apart, he was free to reside where he pleased, and to change his address at will. Sometimes an ostracized person might be recalled, by special popular decree, before his ten years of exile had elapsed. Thus, when the Athenians felt that Xerxes' invasion plans constituted a terrible threat to them, shortly before Salamis, they proclaimed a general amnesty in order to establish a 'sacred unity', a common front against this imminent peril. Under the amnesty, all those in exile as a result of ostracism returned to Athens: they included Megacles, who was Pericles' great-uncle; his father, Xanthippus; the Elder Alcibiades; and Aristides, known as The Just. Later victims of the *ostrakophoria* included Themistocles, the victor of Salamis; Cimon, the son of Miltiades; Thucydides, son of Melesias, Pericles' adversary (not to be confused with the historian of the same name); and, towards the close of the Peloponnesian War, the demagogue Hyperbolus. After this ostracism fell into disuse.

COURT PROCEDURE

One fundamental difference between the administration of justice in antiquity and in any civilized country today is that Athens, at least, had nothing resembling a Public Prosecutor's department. Justice did not take direct cognizance of an offence, and magistrates seldom initiated prosecutions themselves: there was no equivalent of a Grand Jury or the French *chambre de mise en accusation* to 'find a true bill'. In all private lawsuits (*dikai*) only the plaintiff or his legal representative (in the case of minors, women, metics and slaves) could enter an action, cite witnesses, or plead in open court – sometimes with the assistance of a quasi-advocate known as a *synégoros*. In the case of a public indictment (*graphé*) – that is, when some act presumed contrary to the general interest was involved – any member of the community who so chose (*ho boulomenos*) could regard himself as an injured party *qua* citizen, and as such had the right, indeed, the duty, to 'come to the aid' of the law by laying a charge with a magistrate. One consequence of such a state of affairs was that the State found itself virtually obliged to encourage denunciation, which favoured the rise of numerous *sykophantai*, or common informers [the origin of this term, which literally means 'fig-revealers', is obscure, and all attempts to explain it mere guesses (Trs.)].

In a case where material loss was occasioned to the city by some infraction of the laws concerning commerce, customs and excise, or the mines, the individuals who brought the prosecution were 'interested parties' in the trial they initiated. If the accused was found guilty, they received a proportion of the fine imposed by way of recompense: three quarters during the fifth century, and half in the fourth. But to prevent the frivolous (or merely malicious) multiplication of charges, in all private suits both parties were required to deposit a certain sum towards the defrayment of legal costs (*prytaneia*); in public hearings only the accuser had to make such a deposit (*parastasis*). If he withdrew charges, or did not obtain at least one fifth of the votes when it came to a verdict, he was liable to a fine of 1000 drachmas. In both cases the actual trial (*agôn*) was exclusively fought out between the interested parties: the presiding magistrate's duties were restricted to collecting sworn statements, recording the testimony and evidence assembled by either side, and then, as a rule, acting as combined judge and jury foreman. The jury (whatever its constitution) took no vocal part in the proceedings; they simply listened to the two sides of a case and then decided between them. However, with so many jurymen involved, it was not unknown for them to demonstrate their sympathies, on occasion, by 'murmuring' (*thorybos*).

These presiding magistrates were, as a general rule, one or other of the Archons: the King Archon for cases involving homicide or questions of religion, the Eponymous Archon for civil suits brought by private citizens; the Polemarchos, for cases involving metics or foreigners; and the *thesmothetai*, when the city's material interests were at stake. Such is the background of Plato's *Euthyphro*, with Euthyphro himself (a diviner) and Socrates meeting outside the Royal Portico, where the King Archon's court was convened. Euthyphro has just laid a charge against his own father, whom he regards as guilty of murder by neglect, in that he left a slave of his (himself a murderer) to die in his bonds of cold and hunger. Socrates, on the other hand, has been summoned to appear before the King Archon as a result of a charge brought by one Meletus, accusing him of impiety and corrupting the young – an indictment which subsequently led to his death.

Yet Athens did maintain a police force. It was controlled by those magistrates known as 'the Eleven', or the 'Criminal Commissioners', whose task it was to apprehend any thief or other malefactor caught *in flagrante delicto*. A murderer who confessed his guilt was executed on the spot; other cases had to be brought to court. The Eleven were also responsible for the state prisons, and brought all summary charges which carried a penalty of preventive detention. They intervened in certain other cases, notably when a citizen personally laid hands on a criminal and arrested him (*apagôgé*), or when a magistrate was requested to come and effect such an arrest himself (*aphégésis*), or, lastly, in cases of denunciation. They were also in charge of executions: it was a servant of the Eleven who brought Socrates the hemlock in prison.

'BLOOD-TRIBUNAL'

There were a large number of courts in Athens. The most ancient and venerable, beyond any doubt, was that of the Areopagus, which had lost all its political power by Pericles' day, but which continued to judge cases of premeditated murder, wounding with intent to kill, arson (if the house was inhabited at the time), and poisoning. In the case of murder it was entitled to impose the death penalty; physical violence was punishable by exile and confiscation of property.

The fifty-one *ephetai*, or criminal court judges, were divided amongst three separate tribunals. At the Palladium cases of manslaughter and incitement to murder were heard, and the maximum penalty that could be imposed was limited exile without confiscation of property. The Delphinium heard such cases of homicide as the King Archon (who acted as examining magistrate) decided were justifiable, or contained mitigating circumstances. A third tribunal, held at Phreattys by the sea, dealt with those in temporary banishment for manslaughter who had subsequently committed murder with intent. Since the accused was still ritually defiled as well as under decree of banishment, he presented his defence from a boat, while his judges sat on the shore.

Finally, there was a fifth 'blood-tribunal', consisting of the King Archon and the ten tribal 'kings', which sat outside the Prytaneion. The type of case heard by this court suggests that its origins go back to remote antiquity. As Glotz says, 'it condemned unidentified murderers *in absentia*, and pronounced a solemn judgment upon the animal or object, be it of wood, metal, or stone, which had occasioned the death in question. This agent was then transported or cast beyond the boundaries, and the land freed from defilement as a result.'[9]

But it was not the homicide courts which gave Athens her special position in the field of justice, or distinguished her from the rest of the Greek city-states; this role was reserved for the popular jurisdiction of the Heliaia, the Supreme Court, which – murder apart – was entitled to deal with almost every conceivable sort of case. However, various offences touching men in public life came before the Boulé; and really serious crimes against the security of the State were judged by the Assembly itself, convoked in plenary session. This is how, in 406 BC, the victorious generals who fought the sea-battle off the Arginusae Islands, but were afterwards accused of neglecting to rescue troops lost overboard during a storm, came to be tried – and convicted – in two dramatic sessions of the Assembly.[10]

THE HELIAIA

Though the Assembly of the People possessed plenary powers, in the sphere of justice no less than elsewhere, they could hardly deal with all court business; and it was a sub-committee of the Assembly, the Heliaia (itself a fairly large body) which was responsible for most cases, allotting them between various specialized 'benches'. Any citizen above thirty years of age, who had not been deprived of his civil rights by *atimia*, was eligible to serve in the Heliaia. The number of *heliastai* and *dikastai* was fixed at six thousand – the same figure as a quorum for plenary sessions of the

Assembly, and that which was regarded, for all practical purposes, as fairly representative of the whole peoples' will. (We have already seen that six thousand, again, was the minimum number of votes required to validate an *ostrakophoria*.) If every Athenian who so desired stood a fair chance of becoming a *bouleutés* or *prytanis* at least once in his life,[11] he had an even better chance of becoming a judge, since the Boulé consisted of five hundred members only, and the Heliaia contained over ten times that number.

Every year the nine Archons assisted by their secretary, would select by lot six hundred names from each of the ten tribes. These names were taken from lists of candidates submitted by the demes, each in proportion to the size of its population. The procedure of drawing lots was analogous to that in use for the designation of *bouleutai*.[12]

The various courts of the Heliaia (several could be in session at the same time) had juries of 501 (the most usual figure) which might rise on occasion to 1001, 1501, or even 2001 members. The distribution of the *heliastai* between the various tribunals was hedged about with an infinite wealth of precautions, the prime object being to prevent any defendant knowing beforehand who any of his judges were to be. Today it has become possible to describe these complex operations in detail (as they were practised during Aristotle's lifetime, at any rate), thanks to the discovery and identification of fragments of the *klérôtéria* (lot-drawing machines) in the newly excavated Agora. This archaeological evidence has enabled us to make perfect sense of three chapters of Aristotles' *Constitution of Athens*, which we possess in somewhat mutilated form, and which, until this discovery, had not been fully elucidated. The *Constitution of Athens* was first published in 1891, from a papyrus which provided the sole available text. Here, then, we have one of those numerous instances in which two disciplines (here papyrology and archaeology) combine and complement one another.[13]

On the day when the courts were sitting, the 'heliasts' would rise while it was still dark, and make their way to the court-house by the light of lanterns carried for them by their slave-boys.[14] When they got there they would present themselves at the entry reserved for their own particular tribe, each bearing his heliast's 'identity card' – that is, a tablet of bronze or box-wood (according to the period) on which was engraved his name, together with his patronym and his deme, and also one of the first ten letters of the Greek alphabet, from A to K, showing to what section of his tribe the heliast belonged, the six hundred heliasts of each tribe being divided into ten sections of sixty apiece. Naturally, through illness and various other causes, the number of heliasts in one section who actually showed up must often have been a good deal less than sixty. Philocleon, for instance, in *The Wasps*, was shut in his house by his own son, and can hardly have been present! Such 'heliasts' tablets' have been rediscovered during excavations, for instance that of 'Dionysius son of Dionysius, of the deme Coelé', which bears in one upper corner the letter A: it follows that Dionysius belonged to the first section of his tribe. Everyone would know that the deme of Coelé was included in the Hippothöon tribe.

At the entry allotted to each tribe stood one of the nine Archons, the tenth being watched over by the secretary of the *thesmothetai*; they were assisted by doorkeepers, the latter being public slaves. On either side of the door at each of these entries there was a *klérôtérion* – two of a tribe, or twenty in all. The *klérôtérion* was a high marble pillar, the front face of which was pierced with a series of small horizontal slots designed to accommodate the heliast's tallies. These slots were arranged one above the other in five vertical columns. Above each of these columns, on the left-hand *klérôtérion*, was engraved one of the first five letters in the alphabet, A–K; and the next five, Z–K, similarly appeared on the right-hand pillar allotted to each tribe. Down one corner of all these pillars ran a vertical conduit, hollowed out like a funnel at its upper end; the voting tallies dropped into this funnel, and passed out at the bottom, but only one at a time, their progress being controlled by a stopper or some other mechanical device rather like a tap, set at the lower end of the conduit. We might have assumed that spherical tallies like marbles would be more convenient for this purpose, but Aristotle is quite specific: what they used were *cubes*, similar to those employed as dice. They were made of bronze, and were finished in either black or white.

At each entrance-gate there were, in addition to the two *klérôtéria*, ten special boxes, each being marked with one of the first ten letters of the alphabet. Each juryman deposited his tally in the box which bore the same letter as was marked on the tally itself. Then the beadle shook up the boxes, and the Archon drew a tally at random from each of them. The first heliast whose name was drawn from each box was known as the 'tally-man', since it was his duty to insert the various tallies, his own and those of his colleagues as the Archon drew them, into the slots of the *klérô-térion*. Each of the 'tally-men' from the ten tribes thus proceeded, starting from the top, to fill the slots in the vertical column (*kanonis*) which bore the letter corresponding to his particular section. In this way it was not long before the names of all jurymen present were slotted into the *klérôtérion*.

The Archon then proceeded to count up the number of names on the column with most gaps in it (ie where the absentees were most numerous); he already knew the number of jurymen required for the day's various hearings, and from this could determine the number of white and black cubes that must be dropped into the funnel of each *klérôtérion*. The heliasts whose names were included on the shortest list then knew that they had been eliminated by the luck of the draw, and could soon return home. Let us assume, for purposes of demonstration, that on this particular day it was necessary to make up four juries of five hundred members each, ie that two thousand heliasts had to be selected, making two hundred per tribe, or one hundred from each *klérôtérion*: the Archon would then drop into the funnel $100 \div 5 = 20$ white cubes. Let us also assume that the shortest column of names had forty-five tallies in it: he would then put in $45 - 20 = 25$ black cubes. Naturally the white and black cubes were all dropped into the funnel together, in such a way that they would be fed into the conduit at random.

Each white cube that emerged from the machine was valid for a horizontal cross-row of five tallies, and the same for each black cube: so that if the first cube to emerge was white, the top person in each column (ie the 'tally-men' of each section) was on that day's jury-roster, and his name at once proclaimed by the herald. If the next cube was black, the five heliasts whose tallies were slotted in second place on each column were dismissed for the day; and so on.

Besides the *klérôtéria* and the ten boxes which contained the tallies of each tribe's heliasts, the Archon also disposed of two urns, and a number of other boxes proportionate to the number of courts that happened to be sitting. The two urns, set one beside each *klérôtérion*, contained a quantity of acorns corresponding to the number of jurymen required from the five sections of each tribe: these acorns were marked with letters of the alphabet, beginning with the eleventh, lamda, which indicated the various courts to be provided with juries. (These letters, too, had previously been distributed by lot.) Let us return to our previous example, four juries of five hundred members each: it follows that each urn allotted to a *klérôtérion* would have to contain a hundred acorns, twenty-five marked Λ, twenty-five M, and similarly with N and O. The juryman held up the acorn he picked out, so that the presiding Archon could see the letter it bore. The latter, having scrutinized it, put the juryman's tally into the box marked with the same letter as was on the acorn. Then the heliast showed his acorn to the beadle, who issued him with a baton – token of jury membership – which not only bore the 'colour of the day' allotted to the court in question, but was also marked with the letter on the heliast's acorn. This meant that he was compelled to attend the court allotted him, and not wander off into some other one. If he did this, the colour of his baton would at once give the game away, since each courtroom had its door-lintel painted a different colour, and the juryman had to present himself at the one which matched the colour on his baton and had a letter corresponding to that he had drawn.

The 'tally-men' now added their own tallies to those drawn by lot, and the beadles carried off to each courtroom the boxes containing the names of those citizens from each tribe who were allotted for jury-service there. These tallies were handed over to certain heliasts (themselves appointed by lot) so that after the session they could be returned to their colleagues in the jury. Only by presenting them could jurymen claim their jury-fee (*misthos dikastikos*); this fee varied between one and three obols *per diem* according to the period.

In Chapter LXVI of *The Constitution of Athens*, Aristotle proceeds to give an equally detailed account of how the name of the magistrate presiding over each court was selected. It will have been observed that although the number of jurymen serving was always an odd one (usually 501), so as to avoid the possibility of a split vote, nevertheless the number elected by means of the *klérôtéria* came out at an even figure (eg 500): how the last heliast was appointed we do not know. Did the presiding magistrate perhaps hold a casting vote? This is a possibility, but it cannot be regarded as certain. Aristotle goes on, in an equally detailed manner, to explain how various special duties were allotted amongst the jurymen. There was one who had charge of the water-clock (*klepsydra*), which measured the time allotted for speeches by litigants and their advocates, and was rather like an hour-glass. Others supervised the distribution of voting-tablets, while others again, as we have seen, returned each juryman his tally so that he could claim a day's attendance fee. But we will not pursue Aristotle's analysis any further. I thought it worth while to scrutinize the selection of heliasts in some detail, however, to show what meticulous attention the Athenian democracy bestowed upon the machinery of justice, with the evident object of avoiding any possible fraud and, above all, any collusion between the interested parties and members of the jury sitting in judgment on their case. With such a system no plaintiff could possibly have prior knowledge of the composition of the jury before which he would have to appear.

The courts of the Heliaia could not, of course, sit on a day when the Assembly was in session, since all the heliasts were citizens and members of the Ecclésia. Nor did they sit (for religious reasons) on feast-days, or days that for any reason were regarded as unlucky. The administration of justice was thus often held up.

At last, however, the heliasts did actually reach the court assigned to them. They were issued with one token (*symbolon*) which was exchanged for another when the voting took place, and it was this second tally that entitled them to collect their pay when the court rose. They sat on rush-covered wooden benches. The presiding magistrate sat on a raised dais (*béma*) at the far end of the courtroom, flanked by his secretary (the Clerk to the Court), a public usher, and a posse of those Scythian archers who kept order both in the courts and the Assembly. Before him was the bar of the court, with benches for the litigant parties on either side of it. There was also a table on which the votes were counted. The public were admitted to all cases except those specifically held *in camera*, and crowded into the space by the entrance, which was railed off from the jury-box. As soon as the court was in session, the presiding magistrate had the doors closed.

A case was opened by the Clerk to the Court reading out the

charge and a written statement by the defence, both of these being in the dossier. Then the presiding magistrate allowed plaintiff and defendant to present their case in turn. Any citizen involved in legal proceedings was obliged to speak in person. If he felt unable to compose his own speech, he would call in a professional brief-writer (*logographos*) to do the job for him, and learn the result by heart. Many such briefs that have survived to this day, by authors like Lysias or Demosthenes, were written at the request of a client, in just such circumstances as I have described. A litigant could also ask the court's permission (which was generally forth-coming) for some more eloquent friend (*synégoros*) to help, or even deputize for him: such a person would not be a professional lawyer, nor would he expect a fee. Athenian minors, women, metics, slaves and freedmen were represented in law by father, husband, legal guardian, master or patron (*prostatés*) respectively.

Except when cases of bad weather-omens, as in the Assembly, caused the session to be suspended, the hearings went on without interruption and were supposed to be got through in a single day. Accordingly the time allowed each party for speaking was limited, though they also had the right to reply. Here was where the water-clock or *klepsydra* came in.

Throughout the entire session the heliasts merely sat and listened. Immediately afterwards the herald summoned them to vote. Each of them had to do so as his conscience dictated, in accordance with the terms of the oath he swore, without consultation or deliberation. In the fifth century, each juryman deposited a pebble (*pséphos*) or shell in one of the two urns before which he passed, the first being for an acquittal, the second for a conviction. During the fourth century, to make the voting still more secret, another system was devised. Each juryman was issued with two bronze discs, which had a metal rod running through them. One of these rods was grooved, and the other plain. Some of these discs have been discovered, with the phrase *pséphos démosia* ('public vote') engraved on them. The heliasts, as before, would file past the two urns, but now only the first urn had any significance. They would hold their discs by the rod, between thumb and forefinger, thus concealing their intentions, and deposit one or other in the first urn (grooved rod for a conviction, smooth for an acquittal): the remaining disc went in the second urn.

When the accused was found guilty by a majority of the votes, either he was sentenced accordingly to a fixed penalty, or else there now took place an 'assessment of punishment' which called for yet another vote. One famous instance of the latter procedure was that of Socrates' trial in 399 BC. The accused was himself allowed the chance to state what he considered a fair sentence. Socrates declared that, far from feeling he merited punishment, he rather was of the opinion that he deserved some recompense for the services he had rendered his fellow Athenians, and he proposed that he should be given free dining-rights in the city-hall, like Olympic victors and other notable benefactors of the State. Such a statement on the part of a defendant who had already been found guilty was perilously near contempt of court, and Socrates was accordingly condemned to death. Heliasts did not care to be made a mock of in this way.

When the accused was acquitted, and his accuser did not obtain one fifth of the votes cast, the latter had to pay a fine, or might even suffer *atimia*, ie loss of civic rights. This is what befell Aeschines in 330, when he lost his case against Ctesiphon (which meant, really, against Demosthenes) in the affair of the Crown: he was condemned to pay the very heavy fine of a thousand drachmas. This provision, it is clear, was regarded as necessary in order to limit the activities of professional informers, who were always ready to accuse a fellow-citizen. Nevertheless, as we have seen, in the absence of a Public Prosecutor's department, the law encouraged informers by guaranteeing them a part of the accused person's confiscated property, in the event of his being found guilty. The corresponding risk they ran themselves, if they failed to make their charges stick, formed a logical counterweight to this advantage, and must have made them weigh up their chances very carefully before going to law.

It is obvious that so idiosyncratic a system of justice, which required the co-operation of whole shoals of jurymen, was peculiarly calculated to develop a taste for litigation and pettifogging chicanery in many Athenians – so much so that Athens could be represented as a 'Dicaeopolis', or 'City of Legal Wrangling' [its secondary meaning, 'City of Just Men', can be ironically implied (Trs.)]. Aristophanes' play *The Wasps* – which Racine had in mind so often when composing his *Plaideurs* – launches a comic attack in this dangerous tendency. What Aristophanes hits at hardest are the consequences of the jury-free system, instituted as compensation for the time lost by assiduous attendance in court: every bonehead and layabout in town goes rushing off to sit on a case and collect his attendance-tally. It seems clear enough that justice could have been just as well administered with a less cumbersome apparatus and a smaller number of jurymen. But in Athens' judiciary as elsewhere, we have to recognize that same democratic instinct which sought to involve all citizens in the business of the government. The Assembly, as we have remarked, possessed judicial authority in addition to its other powers, and there were numerous political cases which it tried itself – particularly if the accused happened to be *stratégoi*. But it could not possibly deal with them all. The Heliaia, being a delegation of the assembly composed, like the Council, of citizens drawn from every tribe (and therefore truly representative of the Athenian people) had to contain sufficient members to preserve its irrefutably 'popular' character. It was this – since no appeal lay against its verdicts – which alone justified its sovereign authority.

During the hearing no evidence from slaves was admissible unless it had been obtained under torture (by whip, rack, thumbscrew or wheel); but the employment of this method was always preceeded by some sort of official notice. One side would offer to put its own slaves to the torture, or request that its opponents did so. It may be that this kind of 'judicial torture' a comparatively mild affair, consisting in the first instance of 'a formal procedure demanded by the position of the slave himself, who might well have feared his master's wrath had he spoken otherwise than under duress'.[15] But what we can be quite sure of is that, be this as it may, no free man, whether Athenian, metic or foreigner, was ever 'put to the question'.

PUNISHMENTS

Just as court procedure differed according to the status of the litigants – freeborn parties were not treated in the same way as cases in which one, or both, contestants were metics or slaves – so too did the nature of the sentence. Financial penalties included fines, damages, and partial or total confiscation of property. Personal punishments ranged from banishments (either temporary (*phygé*) or permanent (*aeiphygia*)) to loss of civic rights (*atimia*); imprisonment – a penalty reserved, in the ordinary way, for non-citizens, except when a person had been condemned to death and was awaiting execution, like Socrates; whipping on the wheel,[16] branding with red-hot irons, or confinement in the pillory (*xyla*), these last being reserved for slaves; and, finally, the death penalty, which will be discussed presently. There also existed various ignominious penalties of an archaic and religious nature, such as the ban on adulterous women wearing jewellery or entering a temple, the solemn curse pronounced upon sacrilegious persons *in absentia*, the shaming and permanent inscription set up on a stele, and, finally, deprivation of burial rights.

The presiding magistrate would have verdict and sentence recorded by the Clerk to the Court, and dispatched to the officials responsible for its enforcement: that is, either to the Eleven, who had charge of the prisons and carried out executions, or else to the *praktores*, who collected fines, or, lastly, to the *pôlétai*, whose business it was to sell confiscated goods at public auction, and then in due course remit part of the proceeds to the prosecutor, setting aside the proper judicial tithe for the Treasurers of Athena.

Many citizens and foreigners, when sentenced to fines that were beyond their means to pay, were able to avoid the prescribed penalty by going into voluntary exile: this is what Aeschines did after the Crown case, and Demosthenes himself after the Harpalus affair [in which he was accused, and convicted, of accepting bribes from Alexander's rebel general Harpalus, then in Athens; but his guilt seems uncertain, to say the least – Pausanias for one expressly denies it – and he may well have been made a scapegoat for the Macedonian party (Trs.)]. We know that Socrates, even after being condemned to death, could have got out of prison with his friends' help and gone into exile. [Demosthenes, too, appears to have escaped from prison with the magistrates' connivance. (Trs.)] He drank the hemlock, which was not the cruellest form of execution, but a kind of privileged suicide. It may be as well to enquire here how those condemned to death in Athens were normally treated.

In Aeschylus' *Eumenides* Apollo, when driving out of his temple at Delphi the hideous Chorus of Erinyes who are pursuing Orestes, has this to say to them: 'It is not fitting for you to set foot in this abode. Your place is where justice is executed with beheadings and eye-gougings and slit throats, where the fullness of youth is cut away with their seed, where there are mutilations

and stonings, and men moan in the long agony of impalement.'[17]
We can hardly suppose that Aeschylus is alluding here to current
Athenian practice, as so often is the case with the tragedians: the
castration of young boys, in particular, was an Oriental custom
unknown amongst the Greeks.

This being so, what was the most common form of capital
punishment in Athens? In 1915 a common grave was discovered
at Phalerum, dating from before the classical period; and in it
were seventeen skeletons, each with an iron collar round the neck
and fetters on wrists and ankles. These were, beyond any doubt,
men who had been pegged out on a high palisade by means of
the collars and gyves (remains of wood were found still adhering
to the latter) and left to die: they may well have been pirates
who were executed after being captured.[18] Now Herodotus tells
us that in 479 the Athenians, 'having captured the Persian
Artayctes, governor of Sestos, pegged him out alive on a board'.[19]
Plutarch relates how Pericles, after crushing the revolt on Samos
in 439, had a number of Samians fastened to stakes in the market-
place of Miletus, and left there for ten days on end, after which
he had them dispatched with clubs.[20] Aristophanes shows us
Mnesilochus 'pegged to the plank' by a Scythian archer and left
there, like Andromeda on her rock.[21] Elsewhere he refers to the
'five-holed wooden instrument' on which Cleon would be
stretched:[22] these five holes obviously correspond with the iron
clamps in which neck, arms, and legs were confined.

As Gernet says: 'From the combined archaeological and literary
evidence a very clear picture of this . . . appalling torture can be
formed. The condemned person was stripped naked and fastened
by five clamps to an upright post. It was forbidden to help or
relieve him in any way whatsoever; he was simply left there till
death supervened. This treatment has something in common with
crucifixion, the only difference being that in the latter case feet
and hands were nailed, and the resultant loss of blood must have
considerably shortened the victim's agony. Moreover, one
essential part [of this torture] was the iron collar, which sat close
under the lower jaw and, by the sheer weight of the victim's
body, added appreciably to his sufferings. One may well imagine
what agony he must have suffered – agony that might well be
dragged out for several days. The fact that such a mode of
execution was practised among the Athenians cannot but modify,

to some extent, our notions concerning their penal code. More-over, it was in use throughout the classical period . . . and can be traced as late as the end of the fourth century.'[23] Are we then to identify this torture with the *apotympanismos*, the word most often used in Athens to denote capital punishment? Some are inclined to think so, but it is far from certain. If not, what was the *apotympanismos*? Flogging to death? Or perhaps decapitation? In the present state of our knowledge it is impossible to tell.[24] [The references given in Liddell-Scott-Jones all suggest some variant on crucifixion. (Trs.)]

At all events, the scene of such punishments was outside the actual city, beside the northern Long Wall between Athens and the Piraeus. One day, Plato tells us, 'Leontius, returning from the Piraeus by the road outside the northern wall, perceived some corpses in the place of torture.'[25] This place is not to be confused with the pit known as the *barathron*, a former quarry situated to the west of the Acropolis, down which, from remote times, it had been the custom to cast certain types of malefactor whose crime carried the death sentence.

The *barathron* would appear to have been employed only in cases of sacrilege or treason; and death by stoning – a rarely attested penalty – was reserved for the same purpose, though it could also be used as a rough-and-ready method of summary execution, carried out by the people as a whole, in an upsurge of mass anger. Thus in 479 we find the *bouleutés* Lycidas being stoned to death on the spot by his colleagues and any other citizens present for proposing that the terms of the Persian general Mardonius should be accepted.[26] Exposure in chains, tied to an upright plank or post, was a punishment mainly applied to pirates, and to offenders caught *in flagrante delicto* while stealing or engaged in some act of gross indecency. Other criminals who were condemned to death either drank the hemlock or underwent the mysterious punishment known as *apotympanismos*.

THE WORTH OF ATHENIAN JUSTICE
There can be no doubt that the machinery of justice in Athens was far from perfect, and that many of the criticisms levelled against it by Aristophanes in *The Wasps* were well-founded. Indeed, one must go further than this, and recognize the fact that the principles of Athenian law were neither as clear nor as

consistent as could be desired. The absence of any penal code gave far too wide a scope to 'popular juries', which, being so large, lacked any training in jurisprudence, and, like all crowds, were far too easily swayed by their passions and prejudices, either for or against the defendant. One needs only to read a few ancient court speeches to realize that their *captatio benevolentiae* normally worked through flattery of popular self-esteem and by representing the plaintiff, as far as possible, as a modest fellow, a man of the people, the natural enemy of wealth and power. The 'Apology' of Socrates, if Plato has preserved its main outline for us with any degree of fidelity, must have been a well-nigh unique exception to this rule, when one considers the tone of aristocratic hauteur with which it is permeated. The Athenian judicial system likewise encouraged the growth of informers.

But we must also bear in mind that the legal system was constantly developing: from the seventh-century reforms of Draco onwards – these in themselves marked a considerable advance on what they had replaced – law and justice had made great progress in Athens. The most important reform was the abolition of collective punishment and the recognition of personal responsibility: in former times not only the guilty party, the murderer himself, had been liable, but his entire family with him.[27] The old principle of the law of retaliation – 'an eye for an eye and a tooth for a tooth' – was very rarely applied in Periclean Athens, where personal punishment was now more and more tending to be replaced by financial penalties, at least as far as the citizen body was concerned.

What may be most justly criticized is not so much the aims as the practical efficacy of this judicial system. In fact the Athenians were at very great pains to render justice with equity, by providing endless guarantees of impartial treatment and conforming, insofar as they could, to the moral principles of their times. Every heliast took an oath before serving on a jury, and the words of this oath can be roughly reconstructed from evidence supplied by several ancient authors: 'I shall cast my vote in accordance with all laws and decrees promulgated by Assembly and Council alike. In a case unprovided for by existing legislation I shall adopt the most just solution, not allowing myself to be swayed by favour or enmity. I shall vote solely and exclusively on the basis of the evidence put before the court. I shall hear both parties with equal attention. All this I swear, by Zeus, by Apollo, and by Demeter. If I am faithful to my oath, may my life be happy; if I am foresworn, a curse on me and all my family!'

Why, in the last resort, should there be this modern tendency (discernible in the work of Glotz and many other scholars) to idealize not only Athenian justice, but also every other democratic institution of the Periclean era? A judicial system which could bring about the condemnation of Socrates – 'a man who, we may safely assert, was the best and wisest and most upright in his generation'[28] – was hardly perfect, even if viewed exclusively against the context of its own period. We would do much better to admit, frankly, that in the sphere of justice, despite meritorious effort, Athens did not attain that *acmé*, that pitch of perfection which she reached in her arts, her literature, and her philosophy. Doubtless she lacked that special flair for law which the Romans possessed: it is only right that we should acknowledge Rome's share in the making of that general civilization from which our own derives.

CHAPTER TEN

WARFARE

Athenian imperialism – The Spartan army – Military organization in Athens – The infantryman – The religious significance of war – Strategy and tactics – The maritime power of Athens – The trierarchia *and naval tactics – War dead and wounded – Civil war: the scourge of Hellas*

ATHENIAN IMPERIALISM

It is generally assumed today that the democratic régimes are more pacific by nature than those under a dictatorship. This was not so in antiquity, when Athenian democracy – during the Periclean Age at any rate – showed itself bellicose, expansionist, and imperialistic.[1] Athens' policy after the Persian Wars – during which she had contributed more than any other city to the defeat of the invaders – was to acquire an overall hegemony in Greece, and then to keep it, despite any aspirations to independence on the part of her so-called 'allies' (who were in fact her subjects), and despite the hostility of Sparta and her Peloponnesian allies, who refused to acknowledge Athenian supremacy.

In order to acquire and maintain her domination over the islands of the Aegean and many maritime cities on the coast of Asia Minor – besides guaranteeing free passage for her grain-supplies, most of which came from the Black Sea and had to be transported through the narrows of the Hellespont[2] – Athens needed both a powerful fleet and a large merchant marine. As we know, thanks to the decisive action of Themistocles in the years before Salamis (480),[3] the Athenian thalassocracy controlled the whole eastern end of the Mediterranean till Athens' collapse in 404 BC. During the fourth century, Athens was to attempt to regain her lost maritime empire, especially in the period after 377, when she formed her second maritime league.

Over and above this, throughout the entire classical period Athens also needed a land army to defend her against attacks by neighbouring cities, in Boeotia or the Peloponnese, and, on occasion, to initiate such attacks herself. Yet on land Athens was more often than not forced into a defensive position when faced by the Spartan or Theban hoplites. When Isocrates, in an attempt to stop this suicidal internecine feuding between Greek states, proposed a joint hegemony by Athens and Sparta, he naturally associated the naval power with Athens, and the military with Sparta.

THE SPARTAN ARMY

This military supremacy of Sparta's depended, in the first instance, on a system of education, from childhood on, geared exclusively to preparation for war, as we have already observed.[4] From his sixteenth to his twentieth year, the Spartan youth was an *eirén* of the first, second, third or fourth grades. This category was the equivalent of the Athenian *ephébia*, except that the latter was only half as long, lasting for a mere two years.

At twenty, every Spartan citizen was enrolled in the regular army, but his military training was not yet regarded as complete: 'the education of Spartans continued well into their maturity', we are told.[5] From twenty till thirty these young warriors, even if they were married, continued to lead a communal existence with their 'tent-companions', and to mess together for meals (*syssitia*). They were still forbidden access to the Agora, and did not exercise any political rights. It was only after the age of thirty that they began to lead any sort of family life, and even so it was still broken up by the practice of communal messing. At sixty the Spartan was finally released from military service and could become a member of the senate (*Gerousia*); but he still spent much of his time in the *gymnasia*, supervising children's exercises or the wrestling-bouts between eiréns. It is, therefore, no exaggeration to say that his whole life was devoted to war.

The Spartan army, under the command of one of the two kings (often with an ephor to keep an eye on him), consisted basically of 'hoplites', citizens with full rights, and *perioikoi* ('the dwellers round about'), whose arms and equipment (*panoplia*) will be described presently. This heavy infantry was divided into five regiments (*morai*) commanded by *polemarchoi*, under whose orders came lesser officers such as *lochagoi*, roughly equivalent to staff-majors, *pentekontarchoi*, or company commanders, and *énomotarchoi*, junior subalterns. The various units carried out their manoeuvres with great flexibility and adroitness (Xenophon the Athenian much admired them for this) – in particular when they deployed from column of march to battle formation. The leading section halted, and a quick series of orders brought all those behind up into line with it. If an enemy detachment then appeared in the rear, each file would execute a dexterous countermarch so that the crack troops were still left in the front rank, facing the enemy.[6]

Spartan hoplites could be distinguished at a glance from those of any other city by two things: the colour of their tunics, and the way they wore their hair. Their tunics were red, or rather purple, throughout, the object being, it was said, 'to prevent bloodstains from showing'. In the Athenian army, for instance, only an officer's dress had purple bands or stripes on it. The Spartans also wore long hair, which in Periclean Greece was regarded as a remarkable, indeed a notorious anachronism. Before a battle they would dress and comb these locks with great care (in the normal way of things they cannot have paid much attention to them): before the battle of Thermopylae, a Persian horseman sent by Xerxes to see what was going on in Leonidas' camp managed to get a glimpse of the Spartan troops, of whom (in Herodotus' words) 'some were exercising themselves, while others were combing their hair'.[7]

Sparta relied entirely on her hoplites, who would if need be die where they stood rather than retreat. She had very little in the way of cavalry. Camp discipline was tough, and the slightest offence punished by a flogging: serious misdemeanours might carry the death penalty, or military degradation and loss of civic rights. Sparta's one weakness from the military viewpoint (but this weakness in the end proved her undoing) was lack of manpower, *oliganthrôpia*. Her hoplites remained first-class, but their numbers dwindled. The caste of the *Homoioi* ('Equals'), whose material survival was bound up with the country estates (*kléroi*) worked for their benefit by the lower classes, remained a narrowly exclusive group, which furthermore, for selfish reasons, tended to limit the numbers of its children – so much so, in fact, that it progressively failed to make good its losses in battle, and in the end, quite literally, foundered. At Plataea, in 479, there were five thousand full Spartan hoplites in the field (together with another five thousand hoplite *perioikoi* and a host of light-armed helots numbering some 35,000);[8] but a century later, at Leuctra, in 371, there were no more than seven hundred Spartiates available.[9] Yet despite the smallness of their numbers, the Spartan hoplites, through their perfect training, and their ingrained sense of honour and discipline, nearly always were left undisputed masters of the field of battle – till the battle of Leuctra, where they were defeated by the Theban army under Epaminondas.

Boeotia had always possessed one of the finest cavalry arms in Greece. Her hoplites did not carry the usual round buckler, but one that was slightly indented on either side.[10] During the fourth century Gorgidas created the famous Sacred Band of Thebes, a crack body containing only three hundred men, but planned to operate like modern 'shock troops'. The hoplites in this battalion, like those of Sparta, were often bound to one another by *amitiés particulières* which, we are told, did much to augment the unit's courage and homogeneity. When a young Theban came of military age, it was his *erastés* who provided him with his *panoplion*, or complete military equipment.[11] Finally, Epaminondas managed to supersede the old unchanged Spartan tactics by a new method of combat, the oblique-order attack, and it was thus that he managed to defeat the Spartan warriors – though indeed, there were few enough of them.

MILITARY ORGANIZATION IN ATHENS

At Athens, as we have seen, the young were allowed to develop more freely during childhood and early adolescence, in conditions altogether different from those prevailing at Sparta,[12] without the same exclusive and driving obsession to produce nothing but crack warriors. Nevertheless, the young Athenian took constant exercise in the palaestra under the direction of his *paidotribés*, and gymnastic training was a normal preparation for military service. Wrestling, running, jumping and discus-throwing all developed his strength and suppleness, and as for the fifth element in the *pentathlon*, throwing the javelin, that was a purely military skill. For grown men who had passed the age of *ephébia* gymnastics represented the best possible way of 'keeping fit' and training themselves between one campaign and the next. In the fifth century it seems fairly clear that most Athenians, whatever their age, spent a good deal of time over such 'fitness exercises', which kept them constantly ready for the rigours of active service; but from the fourth century on, we may observe a lessening of enthusiasm for athletics. Xenophon remarked that 'those who go in for physical culture in the cities are now comparatively rare',[13] and it was precisely at this period that the Greek city-states began more and more to rely upon professional soldiers, often foreign mercenaries, to protect them for pay, whereas before the Peloponnesian War Greek armies consisted almost wholly of citizens.

Every Athenian was liable for military service between the ages of eighteen and sixty. From eighteen to twenty he was an *ephébos*, and underwent recruit training. From twenty to fifty he remained a member of the regular forces, on the reserve either as hoplite or cavalryman. At the outset of every military campaign abroad (*exodos*, ie beyond the frontiers of Attica) some classes, and occasionally all, were mobilized. Between fifty and sixty a citizen was numbered amongst the veterans (*presbytatoi*) who (together with *ephéboi*, and metics of all age-groups) formed a kind of territorial army, or Home Guard, responsible for manning the frontiers and fortresses of Attica. In peace-time, the bulk of the army remained on the reserve, with the exception of the *ephéboi*, who for two years did full-time training, and were therefore exempt from all political duties – and even from legal prosecution – during this period: they were citizens, technically, as soon as they joined the *ephéboi*, but did not exercise citizens' rights for a further two years.

An Athenian, therefore, was liable in all to forty-two years' military service, and each one of these forty-two 'classes' was named after some eponymous hero. Citizens who attained their sixtieth year were discharged from all military obligations and became instead *diaitétai*, or public arbiters, something rather like a Justice of the Peace.[14]

At the time of her entry into the Peloponnesian War, in 431 BC, Athens possessed a regular army of 13,000 hoplites and 1000 cavalry, together with a 'territorial army' including 1400 *ephéboi* (the annual intake was roughly 700), 2500 veterans, and 9500 metics: in all, some 27,400 men.[15]

Despite a long-standing German theory to the contrary, there can be no doubt that the *ephéboi* did in fact exist during the fifth century. The hoplites who fought at Marathon had certainly received a military training. We may, however, ask whether at this period *all* Athenians were liable for two years' military service, ie whether those of the poorest class, the *thetes*, who mainly served as rowers in the fleet, were not exempt from it. Aristotle gives us a detailed account of the *ephébia* as it was in the fourth century, though by then it may have undergone certain modifications which did not apply during the Periclean Age.

At the beginning of the Attic year, in the month Hecatombaiôn, these young eighteen-year-old Athenians were enrolled among their fellow-*démotai*, that is, the members of their fathers' demes. The deme-assembly checked their ages and decided, by a show of hands, whether they were regarded as legitimate and freeborn. Any contested case was referred to a special court of the Heliaia, and a youth found guilty of imposture was promptly sold into slavery by the State. The Council then subjected the *ephéboi* to a fresh scrutiny. Their physical aptitudes were certainly taken into account by these various 'recruiting boards' – first by the deme-assembly, latterly by the Council, and again in court if a case of contested status came up.[16]

Then the *ephéboi* proceeded to the temple of the goddess Aglauros (the Bright One) on the north side of the Acropolis, and took the following oath, hand outstretched upon the altar: 'I shall not dishonour the sacred arms I bear; I shall never desert my fellow-soldiers; I shall fight in the defence of my country and her sanctuaries; and I shall hand on to posterity, to the best of my strength and with all my comrades' help, a city in no way diminished but rather made greater and more powerful. I shall obey the magistrates, the laws now in force, and those that may duly be enacted henceforward; if any person attempt to subvert them, I shall use all my strength, and the assistance of all men, to prevent this. I shall honour the cult of my ancestors. To this oath I ask the following divinities to bear witness: Aglauros, Hestia, Enyo, Enyalios, Ares and Athena Areia, Zeus, Thallo, Auxo, Hegemone, Heracles, the Boundaries of my country, the spirits of Corn, Barley, Vines, Olives and Figs.'[17] This catalogue of deities, especially Aglauros, Thallo, Auxo (all eponymous goddesses of increase), together with the inclusion of Attica's boundaries and staple crops, betrays markedly archaic elements: such a form of oath must certainly go back well before the fifth century.

As officers in charge of *ephéboi* the people chose a *sophronistés*, or general superintendent, from each of the ten tribes, a short list of three names being chosen and put up by the fathers of the *ephéboi* themselves. They also elected a *kosmétés*, or director, who had final authority over the whole body of *ephéboi*; they likewise nominated their gymnastic trainers (*paidotribai*) and various special instructors who taught them heavy-armed combat techniques (*hoplomachia*), as well as archery and javelin-throwing: in Aristotle's day a further instructor had been added to teach them how to handle that new-fangled weapon the catapult.[18] The *ephébos'* distinctive dress was the *chlamys*, which in his case appears to have been a regulation black.[19]

The year of military service began some two months after the civil year, in Boédromion. Director and superintendents 'began by taking their *ephéboi* on a conducted tour of the various sanctuaries in Attica [which they would be called upon to defend at need], and then marched them down for garrison duty in the Piraeus, some being stationed at Munychia, the rest at Acté . . . The *sophronistés* received an allowance for the *ephéboi* in his tribe [four obols per head per day] and bought what was needed for their common sustenance, since they messed by tribes.'[20] Perhaps the *ephéboi*, as a body, were already divided into cavalry and infantry, though this is not certain; what we do know is that the *kosmétés* was responsible for making the *ephéboi* competent horsemen, and teaching them to shoot while mounted.[21]

This accounted for the first year's training, at the close of which 'a meeting of the Assembly was held in the public theatre, where the *ephéboi* were paraded and drilled in close formation; they then received from the State a spear and a round buckler, were sent on route-marches through Attica, and posted for garrison duty to the various fortresses'.[22] For the rest of this second year the *ephéboi* acted as *peripoloi*, or 'patrolling troops', at the fortresses of Eleutherae, Phylé, and Rhamnous.[23]

At Rhamnous especially, various fourth-century inscriptions enable us to evoke the life led by the *ephéboi* in picturesque detail, even down to their relations with the local population: 'For the peasants and fisherfolk of Rhamnous, the presence of a sizable contingent of young men must have supplied a very useful market for the sale of their farm-produce and fish. Deme and garrison worked together in close co-operation . . . The *ephéboi*, despite their military duties, often must have been a rowdy and ill-disciplined body of troops . . . These young men were more enthusiastic over their athletic training (a necessary complement to their more specifically military occupations) than they were over field-days and drill; and such gymnastic exercises called for a high consumption of oil . . .' To this end citizens of Rhamnous made generous financial contributions – which earned them official thanks and honours (in the form of crowns) from the *ephéboi* and their leaders. The little theatre of Rhamnous must also have enjoyed especially lively audiences, thanks to the presence of the *ephéboi*. 'Esconced in the seats of honour [*proedria*], local officials and garrison officers alike watched the performances put on there', mainly it seems, festivals of comedy: 'The god of the Lenaea brought a breath of gaiety to townsfolk and troops alike: this was a somewhat coarse and countrified audience, better suited to appreciate the slapstick caricature of ancient comedy than the sophisticated subtleties of a tragedy by Euripides . . . The life of these peasants took an upward turn through contact with the *ephéboi*: more civilized urban fashions were introduced, and these in turn created fresh needs, to which the archaeological remains testify.'[24]

THE INFANTRYMAN

The hoplite, the heavy-armed infantryman of Athens and Sparta, who preserved his supremacy on the battlefield throughout the fifth century and a decade or two longer, was equipped with a *panoplion*, which consisted both of weapons and defensive armour.[25]

The Athenian helmet of the fifth century (*kranos*) was lighter than those worn in earlier periods, and adorned with a less cumbersome crest. It consisted of a roughly hemispheric metal headpiece, lined with felt and topped by a crest that reproduced the line of its curve, plus jointed cheek-plates and, though not invariably, a nasal visor and a neck-guard. The cuirass, or *thôrax*, generally made of bronze, was in two parts – breastplate and backplate – joined by hooks or buckles; it stopped short just below the waist, leaving the thighs more or less completely exposed. It was often decorated with line-engravings or intaglio-work which emphasized the thoracic muscles. Instead of this metal cuirass a kind of jerkin was sometimes worn, made from leather or linen, and reinforced with metal strips. Finally the legs were covered from knee to ankle by brazen greaves (*knémides*), the use of which was gradually abandoned during the fifth century. As for the Athenian shield (*aspis*), this, in contradiction to the laterally intended Boeotian buckler, was ordinarily a circular bronze affair, somewhat less than three feet in diameter. It could also be made of several layers of ox-hide, stitched together on a wood or metal base and fronted with metal plates. The outer surface was always convex, and had a central boss (*omphalos*), this being carved on occasion into the likeness of a Gorgon's head (which possessed religious or magical significance as an apotropaic, a protection against bad luck) or other such emblems (*episéma*). Such devices could be richly wrought, though they could hardly vie with that on the shield of Achilles, which was the work of Hephaestus himself. The inner face was furnished with one, and later with two handles or loops, through which the hoplite passed his left hand and arm. When he was not actually fighting, the shield was slung across his shoulders by means of a baldric, a thong being passed through the arm-loops to facilitate this. Sometimes the shield was fitted with an extension, a sort of fringed apron (doubtless made from leather), designed to protect the combatant's lower limbs. The hoplite of the classical period normally went barefoot, as opposed to the archaic 'man of bronze', who was shod in metal.

Offensive weapons had undergone fewer changes since Homer's day than protective armour. The spear and the sword were still unrivalled. The spear (*dóry*), a weapon designed for shock-encounters, consisted of a wooden shaft some six feet in length, fitted at one end with a metal point, which was sometimes flat and leaf-shaped, and sometimes a massive affair like a thin, elongated pyramid. The shaft was normally made of ash, and bound with leather at the grip: beyond this it contained a metal heel designed to counterbalance the point. The heel was sometimes pointed itself, so that the spear could, at a pinch, be used by either end. The sword (*xiphos*) was not merely a dirk, but a weapon designed to supplement the spear in close combat. The hoplite's sword had a straight, double-edged blade, and its length, hilt included, might be anything up to two feet. It was worn slung from the left shoulder in a baldric. After the Persian Wars the hoplite was also equipped with a short stabbing-sword, little larger than a dagger.

The supreme command of all Athenian troops was vested in the War Archon (*polemarchos*) and the *stratégoi*. Below this level the Athenian hoplites were divided into ten units (embodying the foot-soldiers of each of the ten tribes) commanded by ten *taxiarchoi*, officers elected by the people, whose cloaks were trimmed with a wide purple stripe;[26] each *taxiarchos* appointed his own company commanders (*lochagoi*).

The fourth-century Athenian *stratégos* Iphicrates created a body of light-armed troops known as *peltastai*: apart from the fact that their equipment was less weighty than that of the hoplite, we know very little about them. It appears that their buckler (*pelta*) was an indented wickerwork structure, shaped rather like the crescent moon, while the metal cuirass was replaced by some sort of linen tunic. These 'peltasts', being so much more mobile than the hoplites, acquitted themselves with great distinction in battle.

The peltast, however, was really no more than a lightened hoplite: his offensive weapons were still the spear and sword. Greek armies also had other light-armed troops, who possessed no defensive armour at all, save possibly a flimsy buckler. These included slingers, javelin-throwers (*akontistai*), and archers – not to mention the crews of a new invention called the catapult, who made their first appearance in the second half of the fourth century, and constituted a sort of artillery arm. The catapult worked on the torsion principle, obtaining its propulsive force from twisted ropes of hemp or horsehair which naturally tended to straighten out when released: in this way it was able to project missiles on an almost flat trajectory.

The ancient sling (*sphendoné*) consisted of two long cords made from wool or horsehair, with a leather pouch between them. In this pouch was placed either a stone, or else a cylindrical sling-shot made from clay, lead, or bronze. The slinger swung this device rapidly round his head, and then abruptly let go of one end: the stone or sling-shot was projected for anything up to two hundred yards by the centrifugal force thus generated. The javelin as used in battle (*akontion*), a sort of miniature spear, was fitted with a propulsive thong, much resembling that described earlier apropos the practice javelins used by young men in the palaestra.[27]

Before the Persian Wars there were certain archers (*toxotai*) in Athens who wore Scythian costume; though those, in all likelihood, were not barbarians but Athenians, who attired themselves thus by way of amusement. They acted as squires to the hoplites and cavalry, and also served as light-armed troops. Yet at Marathon, in 490, the Athenian army contained neither archers nor cavalry;[28] it was the strong contingents of both in Xerxes' army which forced Athens to raise similar bodies herself. Athenian archers fought at Salamis and Plataea (480–479); and during the Peloponnesian War they reached an effective strength of 1600 men. These archers were recruited from the poorest citizen class, the *thetes* or proletarians, and used the traditional double-curved bow: 'They were bare-armed and bare-legged, their bodies and the upper parts of their thighs being protected by a jerkin or short tunic. They occasionally wore boots, their heads were covered with a light helmet or a sort of bonnet like that worn in Thrace. As a normal rule archers carried no defensive weapons; they wore their quiver slung across their back.'[29]

A careful distinction must be made between this corps of foot-archers, together with the mounted archers, or *hippotoxotai*, and the Scythian archers whom Athens first began to purchase when she formed her maritime league in 477. These slaves, of barbarian origins, were Athens' police force, with a special duty to guard the courts, the Assembly, and every other official meeting-place: their function was civil, not military. They wore trousers (*anaxyrides*), which came down to their ankles and were regarded by Athenians as the distinctive characteristic of barbarian costume, together with a tall and generally pointed bonnet, which covered the back of the head and had a flap protecting the neck; they were armed with a bow, *górytos* (not the normal type of quiver, but a case with a loose leather flap-top, hung from the left side of their belt), a short scimitar, and, on occasion, a hatchet. There were about a thousand of them: originally they camped in the Agora, but finally they occupied a permanent barracks on the Areopagus. From here they had a commanding view of the lower city, their most important beat.[30]

After Marathon a cavalry arm was also raised, which numbered three hundred horses: this total was subsequently raised to six hundred, and in the end reached a thousand. This corps was recruited in a special way, from the two most wealthy census-classes – of which the second was, in fact, known as the 'Cavaliers' or 'Knights' (*hippeis*). Horses were not provided by the State, and horse-breeding was a luxury which only a rich Athenian could afford. Boys of good family 'very early learnt to gallop through the fields round Colonus, or ride in processions, and when they reached military age they were already experienced horsemen; it naturally came about that after their two years' training they were drafted into the cavalry.'[31] The commander-in-chief of the Athenian cavalry division (*hipparchos*), elected by the Assembly for a year, was responsible for recruiting new troopers (apparently from those whose *ephébia* was just over); but his choice had to be ratified by the council, before whom the cavalry annually paraded for inspection (*dokimasia*). The *hipparchus* had ten squadron commanders (*phylarchoi*) under him, each squadron being recruited from one particular tribe, and having a nominal strength of one hundred men.

The Athenian cavalryman was armed with two spears and a sword, the latter a curved, sabre-like weapon (*kopis*). He only wore a hoplite's cuirass and shield on parade, and the brazen greaves that would have galled his horse's flanks were replaced by a pair of high leather thigh-boots. (At one period Athens adopted Thracian cavalry equipment: thick woollen cloak, tops and bonnet of fox-fur.) He rode bareback, without saddle or stirrups, and his horse wore the minimum of harness, with no protective caparisoning. By the fourth century, however, cavalry equipment was tending to grow heavier, and we find Xenophon advising troopers to wear a made-to-measure breastplate and gauntlets, besides protecting their horse – mainly under the belly – with padded quilting.[32]

The cavalry, by the very nature of their recruitment, were regarded as the aristocratic cream of the services, in contrast with the 'rabble' of hoplites and light infantry. They had all the *hauteur* that horsemen naturally acquire by sitting astride their noble beast and looking down on other men from a great height. Xenophon, writing in the fourth century, shared this attitude. They were enthusiastic 'laconizers' (ie admirers of Spartan customs and discipline) and let their hair grow long in the Spartan manner. (They cut a fine figure on the Panathenaic Frieze from the Parthenon.) In his comedy *The Knights*, Aristophanes represents them with a certain sympathy, though this is tinged with ironical undertones: his 'Knights' are sterling fellows, firmly attached to the old ways and a somewhat outdated kind of patriotism, the natural enemies of a demogogue like Cleon.

The Athenian army contained all sorts of auxiliary bodies, such as the 'Courier Corps', whose members were known as *hémero-dromoi*, because, in order to perform their liaison missions or carry news to Athens, they had to be capable of running for an entire day (*hémera*) before passing on their message to another courier.[33] There were also medical officers to care for the wounded, as we see in Agamemnon's army before Troy; and military diviners who, as we shall see, had an important role to play. In order to transmit important news fast, the Greeks did not rely exclusively on couriers, but also on signal-fires, which, thanks to a good relay-system, formed a sort of 'visual telegraph network'.[34]

THE RELIGIOUS SIGNIFICANCE OF WAR

At Athens in particular the oath taken by the *ephéboi*, and their tour of the sanctuaries, made embarking on military service an act of religious significance. There were numerous other rituals performed by the armies of every Greek city, both at the beginning of each military campaign and at various stages of a war. Before committing oneself to hostilities, it was customary to consult the gods, perhaps by consulting the oracle of Pythian Apollo, or some local shrine or seer. When war had been decided upon, hostilities still did not commence till the herald – whose person was sacrosanct – had announced the severing of relationships in a solemn and formal declaration. It was this same herald who, if things went badly, would bear proposals of truce or armistice to the enemy. A state of war between two states was defined as existing, legally, only after all relationships between them had been broken off by means of heralds (*akéryktoi*).

Before actually embarking on a campaign, it was vital to consult the gods yet again, and sometimes to debate their ambiguous or contradictory responses. Thucydides, who had little time for oracles himself, was nevertheless obliged to make some reference to the *chrésmoi* current in Athens during the Peloponnesian War, because of the very considerable influence they exercised upon the opinions and sentiments of the man in the street.

Even when the army was ready to march, it could not set out on any day, regardless. The reason why the Spartans only reached Marathon after the battle was over was because they had a religious taboo upon starting a campaign before the full moon. The Sicilian expedition set forth on an ill-omened day, and we know how catastrophic a conclusion it had: the gods visited any negligence of this sort with the direst retribution.

On the eve of the army's departure its leader offered sacrifice and made the prescribed prayers. If, like Nicias, he was a devout person, he would take care to bring images of the Athenian gods with him, and a portable altar on which burnt a perpetual flame lit at the city's altar-hearth. He also had several diviners on his staff, since throughout the campaign no important decision would be taken without first sounding the will of the gods.

Finally the two armies would manage to get themselves drawn up in battle order, and confronting one another. On either side the commander-in-chief, assisted by his diviners, would offer up prayers to the gods and 'devote' the persons and property of the enemy to them. He would also make sacrifice, and the diviners would attempt to presage the outcome of the battle by examining the still smoking entrails. It might happen that when one side had already engaged for action the other dared not defend itself because the gods had not yet made their purpose clear: at Plataea, the Spartan army stood motionless, arms grounded, shields lying at their feet, exposed to a hail of arrows as they waited for the gods to give utterance.[35]

During the actual struggle the gods and heroes did not abandon their faithful suppliants, but fought at their side. 'At the battle of Marathon, against the Persians, many Athenian soldiers believed they saw the armed ghost of Theseus, charging at their head against the barbarians.'[36]

In the archaic period, as we see from the *Iliad*, the only reason for taking prisoners was to immolate them afterwards; the gods had been promised a human sacrifice, and were entitled to it. This rule was only broken if there seemed a chance of extracting a ransom which made it worth the risk. Even during the classical period, a defeated enemy was very often slaughtered without mercy on the field of battle, or even – which seems even more cruel to us – when the fighting was over, and they had actually surrendered. The wounded were finished off where they lay. After the city was sacked, its inhabitants – old men, women and children included – were put to the sword. Any persons spared were sold into slavery. Such was the ancient rule of war, sanctioned – indeed, enjoyed – by religious authority. Only the dead received any sort of consideration, if one can call it that. The victor was responsible for burying his own fallen, and had to grant his opponents – if any survived – a truce for the like purpose.

The defeated enemy, whether dead or captured, was relieved of his arms, a practice we find as early as the *Iliad*. These weapons and armour, either piled up on the battlefield or hung from the branches of trees, formed the 'trophy' (*tropaion*) that was dedicated to the gods and became thereafter a sacred cult-object. The scarecrow-like figure hung about with battle-spoils was regarded as a divine image.[37] To erect a trophy was to proclaim one's victory for all to see, since one could not do it unless one had been left undisputed master of the field. It sometimes happened that after an indecisive conflict *both* sides erected a trophy.

By the classical era it was no longer the sum total of booty captured from the enemy that one dedicated to the gods, but merely a tithe, the tenth part (*dekatê*). This is the origin of those often grandiose monuments, statue-groups or 'Treasuries' which line the Sacred Way leading to various Panhellenic sanctuaries, such as that of Delphi, and which, centuries later, shocked the patriotic susceptibilities of Plutarch, himself a priest of Pythian Apollo: 'When you see the god surrounded on all sides with tithes and spoils got by murder and war and rapine, and his temple chock-a-block with Greek arms and Greek booty, does it not strike you as intolerable? Do you not feel pity for the Greeks when on these fine offerings you read such disgraceful inscriptions as "Brasidas and the Acanthians: won from the Athenians", or "The Athenians: from the Corinthians", or "The men of Phocis: from the Thessalians"?'[38] [The reader should, perhaps, bear in mind that the speaker here is not Plutarch himself, but a character in one of Plutarch's dialogues. (Trs.)]

Just as the enemy's territories were ravaged during a campaign (armies lived off the land), so that it was common practice to destroy crops and trees, even olive-trees, which took so long to reach maturity after re-planting; so, similarly, after the victory the defeated side's lands belonged to their conqueror, who dealt with them as he pleased, and might, if he so wished, raze every house to the ground and destroy every living thing within their boundaries. When a peace-treaty was concluded, it was natural that the gods should preside over this solemn act, just as they had over the declaration of war which preceded it. They were invoked as witnesses in the formulaic oath, an oath sealed by a special sacrifice.

STRATEGY AND TACTICS

The army lived off the land; but it was advisable, nevertheless, to take some initial provisions with one, if only to have some means of subsistence before the enemy's frontiers were crossed. Therefore every Athenian citizen, on mobilization, was required to bring in his knapsack (or, more literally, his basket – *plekos*) enough to live on for three days: this meant staple items such as bread, cheese, olives, onions and garlic. Hence the frequent appearance, in Aristophanes, of the 'haversack which stinks of stale onion', and which symbolizes all the nasty discomfort of active service.[39]

Most set battles during the classical period were brutal head-on clashes between armed ranks who charged one another at the double, chanting the *paean*, as soon as the trumpet sounded the 'Attack': such were the tactics of the Athenian hoplites at Marathon. This brisk advance was designed to reduce the time in which the enemy's light-armed skirmishers could cause casualties with their missiles, and also to make the initial impact as violent and irresistible as possible. Even the Lacedaemonians, renowned throughout Greece for their rigorous training and skill at manoeuvres, formed up before facing the enemy and kept the same formation throughout the engagement unless it was absolutely vital to change it, since any alteration in tactics while actually engaging the enemy was regarded as most dangerous. The battle latterly resolved itself into a series of individual actions, or cheek-by-jowl duels known as *monomachiai*. Strategy remained primitive at least till the time of Epaminondas and Iphicrates. The normal depth of a Spartan battle-line was eight ranks, with each man occupying about a square yard of ground – unless the commander gave the order to close ranks and fight shoulder to shoulder, with overlapping shields. Fundamentally, if we disregard the use of chariots (which even in Homer serve little purpose except to get the leaders to the battlefield promptly, and enable them to leave it with equal speed) an infantry battle in the Periclean Age differed very little from those described throughout the *Iliad;* and one sees how Homer could be regarded as a still up-to-date master of military science.

Nevertheless, the appearance of the cavalry arm after Marathon did change the structure of an engagement in some respects. The original task of the cavalry was to go on scouring and reconnaissance expeditions, and to make contact with the enemy. In the year 394, before Corinth, a young Athenian named Dexileus, together with four other troopers, died while on a particularly hazardous mission that had been entrusted to them. His funeral stele in the Ceramicus cemetery shows him running his spear through a foeman who has fallen beneath his horse's hooves.[40]

The cavalry was also employed to pursue and slaughter an enemy army on the run. On such occasions, only a man with the bravery and self-control of a Socrates had any chance of surviving amid those fleeing infantrymen – especially the hoplites, who were weighed down by their heavy armour. Here is Alcibiades, in Plato's *Symposium*, describing the philosopher's conduct after the disastrous battle of Delium in 424 (Socrates was forty-six at the time):

> I happened to run into him during the retreat. I was in the cavalry, and he was serving as a hoplite. Our troops were in headlong flight; and there was Socrates, stumping along with Laches. At this point I rode over, the moment I spotted him, shouting 'Don't lose heart, I'll see you through all right,' or some such encouragement. I had a better opportunity to observe Socrates' conduct here than I did at Potidaea – for one thing, being mounted, I was in less of a fright – and the first thing that struck me was how much more composed and sensible he was than Laches. Furthermore – this is to your account, Aristophanes – he was stalking along just the way you wrote, 'proud as a flatfoot pelican, pop-eyes rolling', with the same calm stare for friend and foe alike, but making it very clear, even to someone a mile off, that he would give a good account of himself if molested. It was this that enabled both him and Laches to get clear away: no one cares to tangle with his sort of character in a battle when there are frantic fugitives to be chased.[41]

After Athens' capture and sack by Xerxes' troops in 480, the city's walls had been rebuilt and strengthened, primarily through Themistocles' insistence. Military architecture was to make enormous progress during the fourth century, as the ruins of Messene testify. The various fortresses in Attica were of no more than secondary importance; that of Rhamnous, for instance, which had originated as a mere watchpost, did not really merit the title of stronghold till after the fortification-work begun on it in 412, during the Decelean War. (Its towers and ramparts were subsequently reconstructed several times.[42])

Since fifth-century armies had very little effective siege-artillery, a well placed citadel with strong fortifications and garrison was extremely difficult to take by direct assault. During the whole of the Peloponnesian War – and it lasted very nearly thirty years – though the Lacedaemonians and their allies ravaged Attica time and again, they never once tried to storm the powerfully defended central fortress of Athens and the Piraeus, linked by the Long Walls. If a city was determined to defend itself, nothing could break its resistance save a surprise attack, or a siege maintained so closely that the garrison was starved into surrender: occasionally, too, treachery might open the gates from within. In order to shorten the long agony of a siege, the assailants had no compunction in cutting off the fresh water supply to those within the walls, so that they were forced to surrender through thirst; however, this trick was regarded as unfair, and banned by the Amphictyonic League of Delphi.[43]

In the fourth century one Aeneas Tacticus ('The Tactician') wrote a work, which has survived, on the art of defending a stronghold under siege. It contains all sorts of detailed and astute advice on the securing and patrolling of posterns, on passwords and signals, on what sort of look-out posts should be established and when best to effect a sortie (at night); it deals with sentries' rounds, and siege-engines (which were beginning to be used at the time) and other machines with which the besieged garrison could counter them; it tells one how to set fire to the assailants' towers or artillery (which were, therefore, mainly made of wood), how to prevent a surprise assault, and, in short, every possible stratagem with which to frustrate the wiles of the enemy. Aeneas also advises tethering dogs outside the walls, especially on dark or stormy nights: they will not only spot spies or traitors from a considerable distance, but may well wake a drowsy sentry with their barking when they do so. We know that in fact dogs played a not inconsiderable part in the defence of such fortresses.[44]

During the period under discussion we are not yet concerned with the Macedonian phalanx or the development of siegecraft (*poliorkétiké*), which between them were to give the warfare of the Hellenistic Age a very different character, far removed from the battles of the *Iliad*. In this respect the fourth century is a period of transition, during which rapid advances were made in the art of war.

THE MARITIME POWER OF ATHENS

But it was as a maritime power that Athens dominated the Aegean, especially during the fifth century, when, as we have seen, she established a veritable thalassocracy. Yet as late as 490, the year of Marathon, she had no fleet worthy of the name, just as she had no cavalry. Behind the rise of Athens' naval strength stands one man – Themistocles. He knew very well (long before the Pythian Oracle pronounced that 'only wooden walls would be unassailable') that if Athens was to defend herself against the fleet of Aegina, and, above all, against a threatened invasion by Xerxes, she must possess large numbers of warships. It was he, too, who presently drafted a good many Athenians from the heavy infantry to the navy or the marines – so much so, indeed, that he was later accused of having turned noble warriors into 'vile galley-slaves'.[45] Taking advantage of the discovery of a new and richer seam in the Laurium mines – 'that silver spring hidden underground'[46] – he persuaded his fellow citizens not to share out the resultant profits, as they had intended – the gross sum capitalized was a hundred, or perhaps even two hundred talents[47] – but instead to lend this amount to the hundred richest Athenians for the purpose of building triremes. Furthermore, he planned and carried out extensive harbour works at the Piraeus, which now replaced the unsatisfactory roadstead of Phalerum as Athens' main port; the basins of Zea and Munychia, which later served as arsenals, were equipped and fortified. This construction-programme was pushed through so fast that in 480, at Salamis, Athens had no less than 147 triremes on active commission, with a further 53 probably held in reserve: a total fleet, that is, of some two hundred vessels. During the course of the fifth century, thanks to the funds made available by tribute from the subject-cities of the Athenian empire, this fleet was increased still further. From the fifth to the fourth centuries its average strength was between three and four hundred triremes – a sufficiently large number to guarantee Athens control both of the Aegean and the Narrows.

Originally Greek warships had been for the most part *pente-konteroi*, that is, ships of fifty oars with the rowers seated on one long bench, one man to each oar (*monérés*). In the fifth century, and indeed down to the Roman period, the regular type of warship was the trireme, a craft with three banks of oars. Its hull dimensions can be estimated from the size of the Zea docks: it was some 150 feet long, and about 20 feet in the beam. The proportion of length to beam was, therefore, a little over 7:1, while in merchantmen (known as 'round ships') it might be less than 4:1:[48] the triremes were, appropriately, referred to as 'long ships'.

The hull was built on a keel-and-rib skeleton: the keel curved up astern to deck level, while under the bows it was constructed in such a way that a ram or 'beak' could be fitted to it. The timber employed was generally pine, except for the keel, which was of oak: this was to enable the trireme to be hauled up in the slips, a common naval practice in antiquity. The seams were caulked with tow and wax. Finally the hull was given a coat of pitch (or more wax) and then had various emblems painted on it: two great eyes, for instance, on either side of the bows, which had a similar apotropaic to the *episéma* on the hoplite's shield. The poop was finished off with a volute or swan's-neck device, known as the *aphlaston*: this, together with the beak, constituted a naval 'trophy' in the event of the ship being captured. The beak was occasionally combined with the painted eyes on the hull to represent some animal's head – that of a boar, for instance.[49] The trireme normally had only the one mast, with a yard and a square-rigged sail: when the mast was not in use it could be unstepped and laid out towards the stern, on a crutch. The trireme only travelled under sail when well out of range of the enemy, and in such circumstances might use both sail and oars if speed was called for; but during an engagement manoeuvres were carried out by the rowers alone. Steering was by means of two large oars fixed on either side of the poop.

The most puzzling thing about the trireme is just how the three banks of rowers were organized. Couissin's account gives the following explanation: 'Above the thwarts or cross-beams which joined the upper part of the hull were set benches (*thranoi*) . . . A second bank could be accommodated by seating the rowers on the thwarts themselves (*zygoi*) and piercing thole-ports for the oars . . . Lastly, down under the thwarts, in the bilge (*thalamos*), there was room for a third bank of oars, again with matching thole-ports. The Athenian trireme carried 170 rowers: of these 62 were *thranitai*

(31 on either side), 54 *zygitai*, and 54 *thalamitai*. The thole-ports were probably staggered, in which case the rowing-benches would be too.'[50] The oars, naturally, varied in length, according to the height of each bank above the sea: those of the *thranitai*, whose thrust required most effort, were about ten feet long, while those of the *thalamitai* were less than five. Every rower had to bring with him his oar, the leather loop with which it was held in the thole-port, and, finally, the cushion – again of leather – which he put on his wooden bench.[51]

Besides the 170 rowers, a trireme carried some 30 more men to bring the total complement up to two hundred. There were a dozen or so topmen (*perineô*) whose task it was to handle the stays and sail, and also to bail out the bilge; a dozen marines (*epibatai*), armed like hoplites, who were stationed at prow and stern during a close engagement to fight off boarders or lead the attack on to the enemy's own decks; the commanding officer (*trierarchos*) and his 'First Lieutenant'; the helmsman; the quartermaster (*keleustés*), who passed on orders to the crew and set a striking-rate for the rowers with the assistance of a piping bosun (*trieraulés*); the forward look-out (*prôreus*) stationed on the foredeck; a steward's mate in charge of the commissariat; and one or two petty officers to keep discipline among the rowers.

THE *TRIERARCHIA* AND NAVAL TACTICS

The institution of the *trierarchia* (literally, 'command of a trireme') also appears to date from the time of Themistocles. It was a *leitourgia*, or public service, in the same category as the *chorégia*.[52] The *trierarchoi* were nominated annually by the Board of Generals (*stratégoi*) from a list of such citizens as could afford this extremely expensive responsibility: wealth, rather than naval skill or experience, was the prime criterion. Though the State provided the hull and, in all likelihood, the rigging of a trireme, together with the crew, the *trierarchos* still had heavy expenses to meet. He was required to fit the boat out, if necessary making good any deficiencies in her gear; he also had to pay for maintenance and repair-work during the course of a campaign. Though he was in titular command of the vessel, he always had an experienced sailor as his helmsman: the helmsman was the senior member of the crew, and acted as the captain's technical adviser.

Towards the end of the Peloponnesian War, citizens found

themselves too impoverished to bear the added burden of the *trierarchia*. At this point it was declared that two men (*syntrierarchoi*) might club together and split the expenses of fitting out one trireme. Each of them spent six months as its commander. In the fourth century the financial situation grew steadily worse, and a system of *symmoriai* (syndicates or companies) was devised to spread the burden of this onerous public service more evenly.

The rowers were, for the most part, Athenian citizens drawn from the lowest census-class, the *thetes*; sometimes metics served at the oars, and when the shortage of manpower became really acute, the authorities employed slaves, promising them their freedom if they distinguished themselves in action. We should not forget that to put a mere two hundred triremes into commission required no less than 40,000 men. The daily rate of pay varied between three obols and a drachma.

The departure of an Athenian fleet from the Piraeus was a great occasion, especially when it was bound on so crucial a venture as the armada which, in Hecatombaiôn (July) 415, set sail for Sicily:

The Athenians, together with such of their allies as were in the city at that time, marched down to the Piraeus at dawn on the appointed day, and embarked ready for departure. With them there came almost the entire remaining population of Athens, citizens and foreigners alike: there was no Athenian but had some loved one to see off, some kinsman, son, or comrade. High hopes and lamentation were mingled in their hearts: confidence in victory with agonized doubt as to whether they would ever see their relatives again. But the sight of that vast navy made them more optimistic . . .

. . . No expense had been spared either by the *trierarchoi* or the State in fitting out the fleet. Each sailor was being paid at the rate of a drachma a day out of public funds. The city had further provided sixty fast warships (minus crew and equipment), and forty more complete with picked crews and a full complement of marines. The *trierarchoi* were supplementing the official rate of pay with a special allowance to top-bank oarsmen and officers; they had also been at pains to fit their vessels out with first-class gear and spare no expense in decorating them. Each had striven to the utmost to make his own ship the best-equipped and fastest in the fleet . . .

When the embarkation was complete, and all supplies stowed aboard ready for departure, a trumpet sounded, and the crowd fell silent, this being the signal for the usual prayers before sailing. For once, however, instead of each individual ship offering up these prayers separately, the whole fleet prayed in unison, with a herald leading them. Wine had been mixed in bowls throughout the host, and the troops and their officers made libations with gold and silver cups. The whole crowd watching from the shore, citizens and other well-wishers alike, joined in these prayers. When the paean had been sung and the libations performed, the fleet left harbour; to begin with they sailed in line astern, and then fanned out, racing one another to be the first past Aegina . . .[53]

But alas, all too soon the trireme *Salaminia* (which, like its sister-ship the *Paralia*,[54] was specially employed to carry official State communications) set forth bearing orders to Alcibiades, one of the three supreme commanders, to return to Athens and stand trial for sacrilege; and this proud armada suffered, ultimately, total and absolute defeat. Book VII of Thucydides' history, which describes the naval battles before Syracuse that brought about the destruction of so vast and magnificent a fleet, is also extremely instructive for the study of ancient naval tactics and strategy.

Naval strategy was a difficult art. The Athenians excelled at it, just as the Spartans had no rivals when it came to the deployment of infantry. The main object was to ram the enemy amidships: to achieve this end it was advisable, first, to break up and outflank the opposing squadron, and profit by the resultant confusion. One hazardous manoeuvre was to close-haul an enemy vessel at full speed, shipping one's own oars as one overtook it, and shearing off the enemy's oars with one's prow, thus crippling the vessel and making it an easy prey.

In order to carry out such precise manoeuvres at sea, the crews, it is plain, must have undergone a lengthy training. Xenophon relates how the fourth-century commander Iphicrates (who not only invented the peltast, but was also a great admiral, or *nauarchos*) taught his squadron to manoeuvre fast and efficiently: 'To start with, he left his large sails behind, since he expected to fight . . . Often, when the squadron was about to make shore for lunch or dinner, he would lead them out to sea again just as they reached their landfall. Then he would bring the triremes about so their prows were facing landwards once more, and, at a given signal, send them all racing for the shore. The prize was well worth while: those who landed soonest were the first to get water and anything else they needed, and the first, consequently, to have their meal . . . He divised various signals for use at sea during the hours of daylight, by which he could deploy his squadron in line ahead or battle formation . . .'⁵⁵

From this passage we can see how closely a Greek fleet tended to hug the coast, since the crews as a rule took their meals ashore.

WAR DEAD AND WOUNDED

Spartan warriors who fell in action were buried in their scarlet cloak, which also served as their shroud, and covered with branches of olive. Their graves were inscribed with their names, whereas the tombs of all other Lacedaemonians remained anonymous.⁵⁶ At Athens, after every campaign, the bones of her dead soldiers were piously brought back to the city, and honoured with a civic funeral: 'Three days before the ceremony a tent was erected and the bones deposited inside it, so that the bereaved could bring some offering for their own dead [most often these took the form of woollen ribbons, wreaths and garlands of flowers or leaves, fresh branches and funeral urns]. For the actual funeral procession hearses were provided, with cypress-wood coffins, one to each tribe. One empty bier was borne in the cortege, decked out in memory of those who were missing, and whose bodies had not been recovered. All who wished could walk in this procession, whether citizen or alien; and the women would crowd round the graveside, wailing bitterly. The coffins were laid to rest in the public cemetery, which lies in the most beautiful of the city's suburbs [the Ceramicus], where all war-casualties are buried, save those who fell at Marathon . . . When they were committed to the earth, some orator chosen by the State . . . pronounced a fitting tribute to them . . .'⁵⁷ In 431 it was Pericles himself who delivered this *epitaphios logos*, the gist of which has been preserved for us by Thucydides.

On the funeral stele the names of the dead were engraved under their several tribes, with a very simple inscription above them: 'List of Athenian dead from such-and-such campaign: tribe of . . . [eg Erechtheus]'; but often there would also be a brief quatrain attached, a funerary epigram extolling their heroism and the magnificent example they set for posterity.[58] War-orphans were cared for by the State, which undertook to support them till they came of age. Then there took place the solemn ceremony of presenting each orphan with a full set of weapons and armour (*panoplion*) – a gift they were offered by the State, the occasion being the Greater Dionysia, and the place of presentation the theatre: '... When the tragedies were about to begin ... the herald came forward and presented a group of young men accoutred in armour, orphans whose fathers had died on the battlefield; then he would deliver that splendid proclamation which has so often fired others to like valour: "These young men, whose fathers died fighting like the brave warriors they were, have been supported by the State until now, when they come of age: so today the State puts this armour upon them, and sends them forth into life, wishing them all good fortune, and invites them to seats of honour in the theatre (*proedria*)." '[59]

As for those citizens who recovered from their wounds, but remained crippled or otherwise handicapped, they too received assistance from the State: there was a law, attributed to Peisistratus, which decreed that disabled ex-soldiers should be supported at the public expense.[60] This law should not be confused with another, which guaranteed a daily pension of two obols to all civilians fallen into indigence as a result of ill-health:[61] the 'cripple' for whom Lysias wrote so delightful a plea was certainly no war-casualty. If he had been, we can imagine the way he would have blown his military trumpet the moment there was talk of stopping his pension!

CIVIL WAR: THE SCOURGE OF HELLAS

The Athenian hoplites of Marathon, those of Sparta at Thermopylae and Plataea, together with Athens' sailors and marines at Salamis, between them saved Greece. If it had not been for their efforts, the civilization described in these pages would have perished before it was full-grown, and Hellas have become a Persian satrapy. But after the Persian Wars, Greece turned all her energy and hard-won military experience against herself. One of the most atrocious – and most significant – episodes in the Peloponnesian War was the affair of Melos, in 416. This small Dorian island in the Aegean (where, in 1820, the Venus di Milo was to be unearthed) had what Athens regarded as a wholly unjustifiable desire to remain neutral when the two 'Great Powers' were at war with one another. We must turn to Thucydides for the tragic 'dialogue' between Athenian envoys and Melian government, a discussion the moral of which much resembles that in an Aesop fable, and can be summed up in three words – 'Might is Right'. When the Melians refused to yield, an Athenian expeditionary force laid siege to the city. The siege lasted over a year, for this tiny garrison, so jealous of their independance, resisted heroically, and in the course of one sortie wrought great slaughter amongst the besieging forces. The Athenians actually had to send home for reinforcements; and that, as Thucydides tells us in his tersely laconic account, was the end of it: 'The citadel was more closely beleaguered; treachery intervened, and the inhabitants surrendered at discretion to the Athenians, who proceeded to kill all males of an age to bear arms, and sold the women and children into slavery.'[62] These Melians were not barbarians, but Greeks.

Massacres of this sort, coupled with battle-losses by sea and land, weakened Greece to such an extent, and produced so chronic a shortage of manpower, that in the century that followed the city-states were obliged to hire, for their own protection, an ever-increasing number of mercenaries – that is to say, foreign soldiers who did not fight out of patriotism, as a citizen-militia would, but simply for pay, as a means of earning their living. As early as 399 we find a striking instance of this: the 'Ten Thousand' Greeks of the *Anabasis*, (amongst whom was the Athenian, Xenophon, who afterwards chronicled their exploits) were professional soldiers, ready to put their swords at the service of those who paid them best. Their story 'clearly illuminates the fatal consequences of a long war, which left the former combatants so weakened that they were forced to hire any mercenary aid they could get; it marks the advent of a "brute licentious soldiery" '.[63] But all too soon these adventurers no longer needed to go abroad in search of a livelihood, taking service under some Persian prince: the city-states of Greece herself, their old quarrels flaring up once more, were soon competing for them at cut-throat prices. It was in vain that Demosthenes kept exhorting his fellow-citizens to serve aboard the triremes themselves, or don a hoplite's armour: they preferred, more often than not, to send mercenaries against Philip, and when they at last changed their minds it was already too late. Chaeronea

(338) saw the best troops of Athens and Thebes go down before the Macedonian phalanx.

War had preserved this civilization; and now war was to weaken and imperil it. The fratricidal struggles between Greek and Greek had slowly destroyed the cream of the nation's manhood, leaving Hellas a defenceless victim for Macedonian and Roman conquerors to despoil.

A SUMMING UP

The Periclean Age, as arbitrarily defined at the beginning of this book, ie the classical period of the fifth and fourth centuries, constituted one stage only in the historical development of ancient Greece, which took, from first to last, more than a thousand years. In many respects it was a specially privileged and brilliant period. But no account of it – certainly not mine – can afford to ignore altogether what went on before and after it: neither the archaic and Homeric epochs, nor yet that 'Hellenistic' civilization which, from Alexander's time onwards, began to spread beyond its narrow national frontiers till it embraced the larger part of the known world, and can be regarded as the final flowering of the Greek spirit. The fact is that Greek civilization displays certain constant factors, which first appear in Homer's day, and never completely vanish, even under the Roman Empire.

But *was* the Periclean Age quite so brilliant, quite so specially privileged? I am by no means sure that the foregoing chapters give all that flattering a picture of it. When one undertakes to reconstitute the daily life of any given country, at some particular moment in time, one is obliged to concentrate above all on the outer appearances of things – and in their most commonplace form, too, which is the condition most nearly approximating to 'daily life'. We have made a close study of the lower city in Athens, with its stinking, crooked, ill-lit alley-ways, and its third-rate, architecturally graceless private houses; but there is very little in this book about the Acropolis, or the peerless monuments that crown it: the Propylaea, the temple of Wingless Victory (*Niké Apteros*), the Erechtheum, and the Parthenon, the ruins of which are still Athens' greatest glory today. We have gone through the humblest trades pursued by the lowest artisans of the community – a community endowed by nature with unswerving good taste and industrious perseverance; yet there have been few allusions to the masterpieces of Greek painting and sculpture. We have seen, in great detail, just how heliasts were allotted to the various courts, but have heard nothing of the eloquence which a Lysias or a Demosthenes could achieve. We have had quotations from various ancient authors – Aristophanes in particular – which struck me as illustrative of some aspect of daily life; but not a word about Pindar's poetry, or Plato's philosophy, or the historical achievement of Thucydides. We have had a description of the theatrical performances staged during religious festivals – but how much have we learnt about the finest tragedies of Aeschylus, Sophocles, or Euripides? When examining the topic of education and schooling, we have touched on methods of calculation, but almost wholly ignored the development of geometry and pure mathematics in Plato's day – a development which contained the seeds of that magnificent late-flowering phenomenon, Hellenistic science.

It is true that this book, such as it is, may provide some sort of corrective to that literary tradition (current in France and elsewhere) which, ever since the Renaissance, has presented readers with a picture of Greece that is idealized, imaginative, dream-like – and quite unreal. Are we *really* to 'believe in all sincerity', as has been suggested, that 'each person's daily life had the rhythm and serenity of a fine Sophoclean drama'?[1] Can we *really* 'approve, in a general sense, the admirable hygiene and healthy vigour' of a people who, when we get down to facts, never cleaned their teeth, never used handkerchiefs, wiped their fingers on their hair, spat everywhere regardless, and died in swarms of malaria or tuberculosis, even supposing they survived those terrible years that brought famine or plague? It is in sheer stupefaction that one finds so level-headed a critic as Taine conjuring up a Greece of religious festivals and country pastimes, with beauty contests where every competitor 'was another Venus di Milo'.[2]

Indeed, the first thing that strikes any historian who makes a study of ancient civilizations is the similarity, direct influence, or even virtual identity which he finds when examining the customs and *mores* of quite different peoples, who knew very little about each other, but who enjoyed much the same conditions as a result of roughly parallel development in technical knowledge, social conventions, and even, up to a point, intellectual thought. Many facets of daily life described in this book (not to mention a whole host of religious ceremonies and beliefs) can be paralleled from other ancient peoples such as the Persians, the Mesopotamians, the Egyptians and the Hebrews – though, of course, they go hand in hand with equally well-marked differences. But the special mystery of Greece – the 'Greek miracle', as people like to call it – lies in the fact that a country which, by and large, enjoyed material conditions very little different from those of its neighbours could, nevertheless, develop a culture both intellectually and artistically far superior to theirs, and indeed far more enduring.

The inevitable gaps in the present work on such topics as Greek literature, philosophy, science and art are easily filled, since excellent studies exist in all these fields. But I would, in the matter of art at least, like to cite a passage by that great modern Greek writer Nikos Kazantzakis, since it both completes and extends my remarks concerning craftsmen (see Chapter Five, pp. 130 ff.): in ancient Greece there was no absolute division between artisan and artist:

When you take a really good look at a piece of sculpture from the high classical period you see that it is not a static object: an imperceptible frisson of life runs through it, it quivers minutely, like the wing of a gliding falcon. A practised eye can discern the fact that this sculpture gave perfect expression to a sense of movement which had dominated the work of the preceding generation, and simultaneously pointed the way to future developments. The statue lived and moved: with a kind of well-disciplined audacity it both preserved tradition and hinted at new ideas. The ancient world did not take kindly to brusque innovation. Men accepted traditional patterns with respect, and if they went beyond them it was in a spirit of conformity. When a creative artist happened on a new technique or approach, a new smile perhaps, everyone welcomed and absorbed his discovery as though it were a common benefit . . . Art was not an individual, personal affair; the artist represented his city and his race, and had no other aim than to immortalize some supreme moment experienced by those entities as a whole. His links with the people were close.[3]

How, then, must we view the Greeks? A sober, hard-working people, of immense bravery on the battlefield – and this quality they have not lost over the centuries: witness their national struggle for independence in 1821, and their superb record during the last war – who also, through the intermediacy of Rome, passed on an imperishable heritage of wisdom to our own civilization: a *ktéma es aei*, as Thucydides called it, a possession for ever. Yet the glorious light of Hellas has not only dazzled latter-day writers into giving a falsified ideal picture of it, as we have just observed; it has also blinded quite a few serious historians. In our day there is not merely (as there was in antiquity) a 'Spartan mirage',[4] but also – and pre-eminently – an 'Athenian mirage', coupled to a generalized 'Greek mirage'.

One often reads enthusiastic tributes to Greece which, in their crude lack of subtlety, come perilously near platitude. Periclean Athens, we are told, presented a matchless example of perfect democracy. The moral virtues of the ancient Greeks, as represented by Plutarch's 'heroes' and the Stoic sages, are unsurpassable. The Greeks are supposed to have been both rationalists and meliorists, trusting in the unaided strength of human reason, and convinced that this earth was anything but a 'vale of tears' as far as man was concerned. Let us see how much truth there is in these assessments of Greek politics, Greek morality, and the Greek way of life as a whole.

The Athenians did invent the notions of civil liberty and democracy, and that is vastly to their credit; and (under Pericles' régime at least) they were prepared to accept wise authority, Pericles being a most distinguished leader who knew how to win their support – in itself a remarkable achievement. But can we forget those countless slaves, or Pericles' aggressive, expansionist imperialism, or the savage cruelty with which he put down any rebellion? Even in Pericles' day the Athenian régime was already suffering from a number of serious faults; and to off-load all responsibility for these on to the great man's successors, such as Cleon, is a dangerous over-simplification. We may grant that Athens was the most liberal of the Greek city-states; yet does she not, even so, very often appear in a self-centred, cruel, intolerant guise barely distinguishable from totalitarianism? And how grudgingly she bestowed the much-coveted title of Athenian citizenship!

Greek morality as most generally practised during the classical period was very far from that of 'Plutarch's heroes'. It is true that the 'fine and noble' (*kalos kagathos*) Athenian, that well-bred gentleman of antiquity, identified beauty and virtue while bracketing evil with ugliness, and naturally abstained from falsehood or vile conduct of any sort: he was too careful of his reputation (*doxa*) and too eager for esteem and honour (*philotimia*). But it seems clear that this morality rested, ultimately, on public opinion, on what people might *say* about one; and this, surely, is a very flimsy sort of foundation – as Plato for one demonstrated. The young men who appear in his dialogues are decent, likeable, indeed charming people; but nothing (save the teachings of Socrates – and how seldom they were applied!) could stop them, in later years, from taking the path of an Alcibiades or a Callicles. With them the desire for fame, the ambition to achieve power and renown outweighed all other considerations.

The sanctuary of Pythian Apollo at Delphi did, certainly, exercise a vast moral and religious influence. Yet the wise aphorisms engraved in the entry to the temple do not in any sense embody a dynamic morality: there is no committal here, no *dépassement*. 'Know yourself', the maxim which Socrates adopted and to which he gave a new twist, implies no more than: 'Understand your human condition and its limits: do not, by excess, expose yourself to the vengeance of divine Nemesis.' The other two precepts, 'Nothing too Much' and 'Go Bail and Ruin is near', meant that one was to observe measure in all things, and to avoid, above all else, the stirrings of intemperate zeal on behalf of others – what we, in fact, would describe as 'charity'. Lessons of wisdom, perhaps: but a very cautious, middle-class sort of wisdom.[5]

The only kind of morality which seems to me at all elevated is that of certain philosophers, disciples of Socrates, who also had precursors among the Orphics and Pythagoreans: the morality of a Plato, for instance, who aspired to make man one with the Absolute Good (ie with God) by a process of self-denial and contemplation,[6] or that of an Aristotle, founded on the key virtue of magnanimity.[7] But how many true disciples did these great philosopher-sages produce? In a general way of speaking, we may say that polytheism was far more prone to degenerate into mere superstition than to raise the moral tone of the man in the street.[8] Even the mystery-cults, such as that associated with Eleusis, did not require their adherents to live a virtuous life in order to attain blissful immortality: this was guaranteed them, whatever their vices, by the magical rite of initiation. Diogenes had great fun at the expense of eternal beatitude which was granted to a common brigand (if he had been initiated) but refused to an upright man such as Epaminondas, who, if he omitted to undergo initiation, would wallow for all eternity in the mire of the underworld.

Finally, this 'love of life' which so many writers go on about when discussing ancient Greece did, indeed, exist: the Greeks – like countless people in other countries throughout history – had a zest for life, above all for the sunlight and brilliant clarity of their seldom-clouded skies, which it was so hard a thing to abandon for the gloomy underworld of Hades. But if they relished the pleasures of existence, it was without illusions or foolish optimism; they kept their eyes wide open to the true condition of mankind, which by and large tends to contain at least as much ill as good. As Festugière rightly remarks, 'we do the ancient Greeks a great injustice when we represent them as cheerful and carefree in their attitude to life. The truth is quite the reverse. Their most commonly held belief was that life is hard, that the gods are jealous and pitiless, sending men more misery than happiness, and that man's one inalienable possession, which remains when all else is lost, is that magnanimity or greatheartedness with which he masters the contrariness of fate. Perhaps the final notion of Greek wisdom is embodied in the man who rises above his destiny.'[9]

In this respect the Greeks seem not to have changed since the *Iliad*: in the allegory of the two jars, Achilles, when addressing the mourning Priam, does not even consider the possibility – which would have struck him as so unlikely as to be quite unreal – that Zeus would ever bestow unmixed blessings on a man. It was a great deal, indeed, to have been granted even a few years' happiness by this supreme deity – as Peleus and Priam himself had been – since many men knew nothing but misery throughout their entire life.[10] 'Of all the good things on earth,' Theognis proclaims, 'never to have been born is best, never to have seen the bright rays of the sun; or else, being born, to pass as soon as may be through the gates of Hades, and lie beneath a thick earthen shroud.'[11] Herodotus, too, is of the opinion that 'those whom the gods love die young'.[12] In tragedy, the Chorus frequently advises against calling any man happy till he is dead – for who knows what the gods may have in store for him? And Euripides, echoing Theognis, declares that we should weep for those entering the world, since such misfortunes await them, but raise joyful songs over the dead, whose sufferings are now ended.[13]

It has been my aim to show the ancient Greeks, above all the

Athenians, as they really were, minimizing neither their squalor nor their greatness. The greatness, indeed, so far outshines their failings that there seems no possible point in whitewashing such a people with bogus idealism. It is true that the Athenians put Socrates to death unjustly. But Socrates was himself an Athenian – and what man, taken simply as a human being, was ever greater than Socrates?

NOTES

CHAPTER ONE, THE BACKGROUND: TOWN AND COUNTRY

1. See Plutarch, *Life of Theseus* 6. 3–7. According to legend, various savage brigands did haunt the overland route, eg Periphetes, Sinis, Sciron and Procrustes. But in any case it was a shorter and quicker trip across the Saronic Gulf than making a detour through the Megarid

2. Thucydides, 2. 15

3. G. Fougères, *Athènes* (1912) p. 125

4. Plutarch, *Life of Cimon* 13

5. Lysias, *On the Refusal of a Pension to the Invalid* 19–20

6. Demosthenes, *On the Crown* 169 [284]

7. Pseudo-Dicaearchus, *On the Cities of Greece* [Fr. Hist. Gr. Vol. 2 p. 254]

8. Demosthenes, Olynthiac 3. 26 and 29

9. Aristotle, *Constitution of Athens* 50. 2

10. Xenophon, *Symposium* 2

11. *Sylloge Inscr. Graec.* 281

12. Plutarch, *Life of Pericles* 5. 2

13. Aristophanes, *Wasps* 219 248–57

14. See above, p. 9

15. Antiphon, 1. 14

16. Plutarch, *Life of Demosthenes* 11

17. Thucydides, 2. 3

18. Teles, ed. O. Hense, pp. 15, 41

19. Aristophanes, *Plutus* 535

20. See V. Svoronos-Hadjimichalis, *Bull. Corr. Hell.* Vol. 80 (1956) pp. 483–506

21. Herodotus, 4. 103

22. Xenophon, *Memorabilia* 3. 6. 14

23. See R. Martin, *L'Urbanisme dans la Grèce antique* (1956) p. 223

24. Aeschines, *Against Timarchus* 124

25. See David M. Robinson, *Excavations at Olynthus* Fasc. VIII (1938) and XII (1946); also J. Chamonard, *Exploration archéologique de Délos*, Fasc. VIII

26. Xenophon, *Memorabilia* 3. 8. 9

27. See Demosthenes, *Against Euergus and Mnesibulus* 57: 'When they heard the shouting, the other servant-girls (who were on the upper floor, where their quarters are) locked themselves in'

28. Aristophanes, *Wasps* 139–141

29. R. Ginouvès in *Bull. Corr. Hell.* Vol. 76 (1952) pp. 560–1

30. Demosthenes, *Against Androtion* 53

31. Lysias, *On the Murder of Eratosthenes* 9–10

32. Ps-Aristotle, *Oeconomica* 2. 2. 4

33. Polyaenus, *Strategemata* 3. 9. 30

34. Plutarch, *Life of Phocion* 18

35. Athenaeus, *Doctors at Dinner* 2. 39 f.

36. Andocides 4. 17; Plutarch, *Life of Alcibiades* 16

37. Jean Hatzfeld, *Alcibiade* pp. 128–9, citing Inscr. Gr.² Vol. 1 p. 330; cf. Tod, *A Selection of Greek Historical Inscriptions*, Vol. 1 p. 80. On the meaning of the word *anaclisis* see L. Robert, *Hellenica* Vol. IX p. 46

38. Plato, *Protagoras* 314c–316a

39. See Aristophanes, *Wasps* 935; *Thesmophoriazusae* 633; Eupolis, quoted by Athenaeus, *op. cit.* 1. 17 e

40. Demosthenes, *Against Conon* 4

41. Aristophanes, *Lysistrata* 915–36; *Clouds* 12–14

42. Plutarch, *Life of Cimon* 13

43. Aristophanes, *Clouds* 1002–1008

44. R. Martin, *op. cit.* p. 276. Cf. Hans Herter, *Platons Akademie* (Bonn, 1952)

45. Plato, *Phaedrus* 230 b–e. This passage was frequently imitated, as we can see from the opening of Plutarch's *Amatorius* (*Erōtikos*), *Moralia* 749 A: 'Just for once try and keep your discourse free of meadows and shady trees and other such poetic stuff – all that twining ivy and bindweed, I mean, and indeed anything resembling those descriptions of landscape which lead certain authors – with rather more zeal than felicity – to borrow Plato's stage-properties: his Ilissus, his famous *agnus castus*, and that gently sloping bank of turf . . .'

46. Aristophanes, *Birds* 493–8

47. Aristophanes, *Frogs* 108–15

48. Plutarch, *Life of Cimon* 10

49. Plutarch, *Life of Pericles* 33

50. Xenophon, *Anabasis* 5. 3. 7–12; cf. E. Delebecque, 'Le site de Scillonte', in *Annales de la Faculté des Lettres d'Aix*, Vol. 29 pp. 5–18

51. Aristophanes, *Clouds* 43–52

52. Aristophanes, *Acharnians* 32–6

53. Aristophanes, *Peace* 569–79

CHAPTER TWO, POPULATION: CITIZENS, RESIDENT ALIENS, SLAVES

1. A. Aymard, *Recueils de la Société Jean Bodin* 6. 1 (Brussels 1954) pp. 52–3

2. On these trials for impiety see below, Chapter VIII, pp. 192–3

3. Herodotus, 7. 104

4. Plato, *Crito* 50 a–b

5. See J. A. O. Larsen, *Representative Government in Greek and Roman History* (University of California, 1955)

6. Plutarch, *Life of Aristides* 7. 6. It would seem that the figure 6000 indicated the necessary quorum of voters rather than the minimum vote needed to secure the ostracism of any individual; but the question is still debated

7. See above, pp. 27–32

8. See Aristophanes, *Thesmophoriazusae* 277–8

9. Demosthenes, *First Philippic* 10

10. *Acts of the Apostles* 17. 21

11. Cf. Aristophanes, *Women in Parliament* [*Ecclesiazusae*] 131, 148, and 163

12. On these Scythian archers

see further below, pp. 50, 230, and 255

13. Aristophanes, *Clouds* 577–586

14. Xenophon, *Hellenica* 1. 7. 7

15. See G. Glotz, *La Cité grecque* (1928) p. 221

16. See above, p. 11

17. Aristophanes, *Constitution of Athens* 63. 1; see below, Chapter IX, pp. 232–50

18. Thucydides, 2. 39

19. See R. Flacelière in *Fouilles de Delphes*, Fasc. III. 4, no. 204

20. Homer, *Iliad* 18. 373–7, 417–21, 469–73

21. Thucydides, 5. 116

22. Athenaeus, *op. cit.* 8. 289 d

23. Xenophon, *Oeconomica* 9. 5

24. A. Aymard, *L'Orient et la Grèce antique* (1953) p. 329

25. See Demosthenes, *For Phormio* 45; cf. his speech *Against Stephanus*

26. Lysias, *On the Refusal of a Pension to the Invalid* 6

27. See A. Plassart, in *Rev. Et. Gr.* Vol. 26 (1913) pp. 151–213,

a study entitled *Les archers d'Athénes*

28. For this rite of *katachysma*, see Aristophanes, *Plutus* 768, 795–799

29. Fustel de Coulanges, *La Cité Antique*, pp. 127–8

30. See above, p. 14

31. See A. Aymard in *Rev. d'Hist. de la Phil. et d'Hist. Gén. de la Civil.* (1943) pp. 124–46: 'Hiérarchie du travail et autarcie individuelle dans la Grèce archaïque'

32. Plutarch, *Life of Lycurgus* 24. 3

33. See R. Joly, *La Thème Philosophique des Genres de Vie dans L'Antiquité Classique* (Mémoires de l'Académie royale de Belgique, 1956)

34. Plato, *Phaedrus* 248 e. The list of categories is as follows:– (1) Philosophers (2) Virtuous monarchs (3) Statesmen (4) Athletes (5) Seers (6) Poets (7) Agricultural workers and craftsmen (8) Demagogues (9) Tyrants

CHAPTER THREE, WOMEN, MARRIAGE AND THE FAMILY

1. See G. Glotz, *La Civilisation égéenne*, pp. 166–70

2. See E. Mireaux, *La Vie Quotidienne au temps d'Homère*, pp. 204–27

3. Cf. Plutarch, *Comparison of Lycurgus and Numa* 3. 5–9

4. Euripides, *Andromache* 597–598

5. Xenophon, *Oeconomica* 7. 5

6. Herodotus, 6. 122

7. Naumachius *ap.* Stobaeus Vol. 3 pp. 22, 68, 234 [ed. Gais-

ford]: his poem *Advice to the Married* 12

8. Menander, *The Arbitration* 490 ff., and fr. 651

9. Xenophon, *Symposium* 8. 3

10. Plato, *Symposium* 179 b–c

11. Cf. Plutarch, *Amatorius, passim*, and R. Flacelière, *Les Epicuriens et l'amour*, in *Rev. Et. Gr.* Vol. 67 (1954) pp. 69–81

12. Plutarch, *Life of Themistocles* 32

13. Demosthenes, *Against Eubulides* 20–1

14. Hesiod, *Works and Days* 696–8

15. See above, p. 56

16. See M. Durry, *Le mariage des filles impubères à Rome*, in *Comptes rendus de l'Académie des Inscriptions* (1955) pp. 84–91

17. Aristotle, *Politics* 7. 14. 5–6, sets the optimum marriage age for girls at eighteen and for men at thirty-seven

18. Menander, *The Rape of the Lock* [*Perikeiromené*] 435–7 (ed. A. Koerte)

19. Demosthenes, *Against Boeotus II* 12–13

20. Demosthenes, *Against Aphobus* 3. 43

21. Cf. Dio Chrysostom 7. 70 [p. 113]

22. Cf. Aristotle, *Politics* 7. 16 [p. 1335 a 36]

23. Cf. the Greek Anthology, 6. 280, and L. Robert, *Collection Froehner*, No. 24 and pl. 14

24. Cf. Plutarch, *Amatorius* 755 A

25. See L. Robert, in *Athenian Studies presented to W. S. Ferguson*, pp. 509–19

26. P. Roussel, *Lettres d'Humanité* Vol. 9 (1950) p. 10

27. Plutarch *Life of Lycurgus* 15. 4–7

28. See above, p. 51

29. Plutarch, *Life of Lycurgus* 15. 12

30. Xenophon, *Oeconomica* 7. 7

31. Euripides, *Medea* 236–7

32. Menander, fr. 546

33. Eg Aristophanes in the *Thesmophoriazusae*

34. Lysias, *On The Murder of Eratosthenes* 7–8, 20

35. Xenophon, *Oeconomica* 3. 12

36. *Ibid.* 7. 35–7

37. Plutarch, *Life of Phocion* 18

38. Homer, *Odyssey* 19. 350–94

39. Theophrastus, *Characters* 18

40. Aristophanes, *Lysistrata* 327

41. Aristophanes, *Wasps* 497; *Thesmophoriazusae* 387

42. Demosthenes, *Against Eubulides* 34, 35

43. See M. Clerc, *Les Métèques athéniens* (1893) p. 395, and G. Glotz, *Le Travail dans la Grèce ancienne*, pp. 218, 221

44. Aristophanes, *Clouds* 41–3 and 60–5

45. P. Roussel, *Lettres d'Humanité* Vol. 9 (1950) p. 20

46. Ps - Demosthenes, *Against Callicles* 23

47. Theocritus, Idyll 15 ('The Syracusan Women') 1–17

48. Plato, *Laws* 658 d

49. Aristotle, *Politics* 4. 17

50. O. Navarre, *Le Théâtre grec* (1925) p. 245

51. Montaigne, *Essays*, Vol. 3 Ch. 5 (Florio's translation)

52. Thucydides, 2. 53

53. Aristotle, *Politics* 6. 15 [p. 1299 a]

54. Aristophanes, *Women in Parliament* 214–28

55. Ps - Demosthenes, *Against Neaera* 122

56. Cf. Xenophon, *Oeconomica* 3. 14, and Plato, *Menexenus*, *passim*, though allowance must be made here for Platonic irony

57. Aristophanes, *Acharnians* 526–7

58. Marie Delcourt, *Périclès* (1939) p. 77

59. Eg, in particular Demosthenes, *Against Boeotus*, I and II, and Isaeus, *On the Succession of Pyrrhus*

60. Plutarch, *Amatorius* 753 D

61. Isaeus, *op. cit.* 28

62. Plutarch, *op. cit. ibid.*

63. See G. Colin's introduction to his edition of Hyperides (Coll. G. Budé) pp. 10–12

64. Plutarch, *On the Pythian Oracles* 401 A

65. Cf. Aristophanes, *Peace* 165

66. Athenaeus, 13. 569 d

67. Isaeus, *On the Succession of Philoctemon* 19–20

68. Ps - Demosthenes, *Against Neaera, passim*

69. Amphis, *ap.* Athenaeus, 13. 559 a

70. Hesiod, *Works and Days* 376–7

71. Plato, *Laws* 11. 930 d

72. Plutarch, *Life of Solon* 20

73. Plutarch, *Amatorius* 769 A

74. Menander, fr. 656

75. Posidippus, fr. 11

76. Aristotle, *Politics* 7. 14. 10–11 [p. 1335 b]

77. Solmsen, *Inscriptiones graecae ad inl. dial. sel.* 39 B, lines 24–7

78. P. Roussel, *op. cit.* p. 26

79. Cf. Aristophanes, *Thesmophoriazusae* 505, 509; *Frogs* 1190

80. Plutarch, *Life of Lycurgus* 16

81. *Ibid.*; cf. P. Roussel in *Rev. des Et. Anc.* Vol. 46 (1943) pp. 5–17

82. Photius, s.v. *rhamnos*; cf. L. Moulinier, *Le Pur et l'Impur dans la Pensée des Grecs, d'Homère à Aristote* (1952) p. 69

83. Aristophanes, *Birds* 493–8

84. Aristophanes, *Clouds* 60–5

85. Moulinier, *op. cit.* pp. 66–71

86. L. Lerat in *Rev. de Philologie* Vol. 17 (1943) pp. 62–86

87. Plutarch, *Life of Solon* 21; cf. the 'Law of Iulis' in *Sylloge Inscriptionum Graecarum,*[3] Vol. 3 No. 1218

88. Aristophanes, *Wasps* 609; *Birds* 503; *Women in Parliament* 818

89. Theophrastus, *Characters* 6

90. Aristophanes, *Clouds* 507

91. *Sylloge Inscr. Graec.,*[3] *ibid.*

92. Ps - Demosthenes, *Against Macartatus* 43

93. Antiphon, *On the Choreutés* 34

94. Ps - Demosthenes, *Against Euergus and Mnesibulus* 69

95. Cf. Moulinier, *op. cit.* pp. 76–82

CHAPTER FOUR, CHILDREN AND EDUCATION

1. See F. Ollier, *Le Mirage Spartiate*, I (1933)

2. Plutarch, *Life of Lycurgus* 23. 2

3. *Ibid.* 14. 4

4. Plato, *Republic* 5. 458 d

5. Plutarch, *Life of Lycurgus*, 16. 4

6. H. I. Marrou, *Histoire de l'Education dans l'Antiquité* (1948) p. 47

7. Marrou, 'Les classes d'âge de

la jeunesse spartiate', in *Rev. des Et. Anc.* Vol. 48 (1946) pp. 216–30

8. Plutarch, *Life of Lycurgus* 16. 10–11

9. P. Roussel, *Sparte* (1939) pp. 61–2

10. Cf. Flacelière in *Rev. des Et. Gr.* Vol. 61 (1948) pp. 398–400

11. See H. Jeanmaire, *Couroï et Courètes*, pp. 540 ff.

12. Cf. P. Girard, *L'éducation athénienne au Ve at au IVe siècle avant Jésus-Christ* (1899) p. 69

13. Plato, *Laws* 7. 790 d–e

14. Lysias, *On the Murder of Eratosthenes* 9

15. Aeschylus, *Choephori* 749–760

16. Homer, *Iliad* 9. 485–95

17. Aristophanes, *Clouds* 1381–4

18. Aesop's *Fables* (ed. Chambry) no. 223

19. Plato *Phaedo* 61 b

20. Aristophanes, *Wasps* 1185. See Aesop's fable about the rats and the weasels (Chambry No. 237): we know that domesticated weasels performed the same functions about the house as cats do today

21. Plato, *Laws* 7. 793 e

22. Aristotle, *Politics* 5. 6. 1

23. Aristophanes, *Clouds* 861–864

24. See, eg, A. Laumonier, *Exploration archéologique de Délos* (Fasc. 23, 1956), 'Les figurines de terre cuite'; Nos. 258, 265, 1340, 1344, 1346

25. Aristophanes, *Clouds* 878–881

26. Plutarch, *Life of Dion* 9

27. Aeschines, *Against Timarchus* 9–12

28. See H. I. Marrou, *Histoire de l'Education dans l'Antiquité*, pp. 496–7, and n. 3

29. *Sylloge Inscr. Gr.*[3] III, 956

30. Plato, *Charmides* 153 a; Plutarch, *Life of Alcibiades* 3

31. Plutarch, *Life of Themistocles* 10

32. Cf. Plato, *Protagoras* 326 c: 'The sons of the wealthy are sent to school later than the others, and stay there longer'

33. Plutarch, *Life of Aristides* 7

34. Aristophanes, *Clouds* 18–24 (Strepsiades keeps his own written account of his debts); cf. *Knights* 188–9

35. Aristophanes, *Clouds* 963–5

36. See, eg, E. Pottier, *Douris et les peintres de vases grecs*, p. 112, fig. 22

37. Plato, *Protagoras* 325 c–e

38. Ie, the *paidagôgeion*, or 'pedagogues' waiting - room', if this is the meaning of the word in Demosthenes *On the Crown* 258; but it may simply be a synonym for *didaskaleion*, or classroom

39. Demosthenes, *ibid.* [see preceding note]

40. Pottier, *op. cit.* p. 112 and fig. 23

41. Theophrastus, *Characters* 30. 14

42. This was the *scripta continua*. When describing it (in the Budé edition of Aristophanes, Vol. I p. vi) V. Coulon asserted, very oddly, that 'it [the text] contained *no words, no phrases*, no accents, no punctuation-marks'

43. These competitions are known to us from inscriptions, and

an epigram in the Greek Anthology, 6. 308: 'As a prize for beating all the other children at handwriting, Connarus has been awarded twenty - four knuckle - bones . . .'

44. See F. Buffière, *Les Mythes d'Homère et la Pensée grecque* (1956) p. 10

45. See Marrou, *op. cit.* p. 219, and the plate facing p. 216

46. See L. Séchan's study, *La Danse grecque* (1930)

47. *Odyssey* 8. 479–81

48. *Iliad* 9. 186–9

49. Plutarch, *Life of Themistocles* 2

50. Plato, *Republic* 4. 424 c; Plutarch, *Life of Agis* 10

51. See P. Boyancé, *Le culte des Muses chez les philosophes grecs* (1936), *passim*

52. See C. Dugas, *Aison et la peinture céramique à Athènes à l'époque de Périclès*, (1930) fig. 2

53. P. Girard, *op. cit.* p. 183

54. See the *Homeric Hymn to Hermes*, 24–61

55. See the opening section of the *Life* of Isocrates, in the Budé edition of Isocrates' works, Vol. 1 p. xxxiii

56. See P. Girard, *op. cit.* illustrations on pp. 103, 105, 109, 111, 165, 171, 173

57. Aristophanes, *Clouds* 966–972

58. Plutarch, *Life of Alcibiades* 2

59. See C. Picard, *La Sculpture antique*, Vol. 2 p. 197, fig. 81

60. Plutarch, *On the E at Delphi*, 394 B–C

61. See, eg, Plutarch, *Amatorius* 753 D

62. Aristotle, *Politics* 1338 b 38

63. Cf. Marrou, *op. cit.* p. 198

64. The *Life* of Sophocles, §3 (Sophocles, ed. G. Budé, Vol. 1 p. xxxiii)

65. *Sylloge Inscr. Gr.* 3 III, 1087

66. Marrou, *op. cit.* p. 504, nn. 1–3

67. See Plato, *Lysis* 206 d

68. Thucydides, 1. 6

69. See above, p. 100

70. See, eg, Girard, *op. cit.* figs. at pp. 193 and 199

71. See, eg, Pierre Louis, *Les Métaphores de Platon*, p. 214

72. Lucian, *Asinus* 8–10

73. Lucian, *Hermotimus* 40; cf. L. Robert, *Hellenica* VII, pp. 106–13

74. See the figures in the article by F. Chamoux, *Bull. de Corr. Hell.* Vol. 81 (1957) pp. 141–59; according to Chamoux, the decorated stele in the famous bas-relief of the 'mourning Athena' is one of these *termata*, and we have to do here with an ex-voto offering by some athlete who had been victorious in the foot-race, at the Panathenaic Games. But this theory has been contested by C. Picard, in *Revue Archéologique* (1958), Fasc. 1, pp. 95–8

75. J. Charbonneaux, *La Sculpture grecque classique* (1943–1945), Vol. 1 pp. 22–4, plates 4, 5, and 6 c

76. Cf. P. Girard, *op. cit.* p. 205, fig. 24

77. Plutarch, *Life of Lycurgus* 19. 9; cf. Flacelière in *Rev. des Et. Gr.* Vol. 61 (1948) pp. 400–1

78. Marrou, *op. cit.* p. 179; cf.

the English translation (*A History of Education in Antiquity*, London, 1956) p. 127

79. Aristotle, *Politics* 8. 3. 3 [p. 1338 b]; cf. *Nichomachean Ethics* 2. 2. 6

80. For ball-games (eg rounders and hockey) see the two archaic bas-reliefs reproduced by C. Picard in *La Vie Privée dans la Grèce classique* (1930) pl. xlvii; and for hoops, the vase-painting 'Ganymede with a cock' in J. Charbonneaux, *op. cit.* Vol. 1 plate 14

81. Plato, *Laws* 689 d

82. Marrou, *op. cit.* p. 168–9

83. Plutarch, *Amatorius* 766 E 768 B; cf. above, Chapter III, pp. 58–9

84. Plutarch, *Amatorius* 760 B–C

85. The whole question is dis-cussed by Marrou, *op. cit.* pp. 55–8

86. Plutarch, *Amatorius* 750 D

87. Plato, *Symposium* 217 a–219 e

88. Plutarch, *Amatorius* 752 A

89. See Marrou, *op. cit.* pp. 64–7

90. See Boyancé, *Le Culte des Muses*, etc., *passim*

91. See on this Plato's *Protagoras*, which deals with the same problem

92. Plato, *Protagoras* 315 a–b

93. On the Academy, see above, Chapter I, pp. 22–3

94. The fundamental source is Plato's *Phaedo*. A useful adjunct is Victor Goldschmidt's *La Religion de Platon* (1949)

95. See above, p. 102

96. Aristotle, *Politics* 8. 2. 3 and 8. 2. 6 [pp. 1337 b, 1338 a]

CHAPTER FIVE, JOBS AND PROFESSIONS

1. Homer, *Odyssey* 11. 487–491: this is the famous reply which Achilles made to Odysseus in Hades

2. See André Aymard, 'L'idée de travail dans la Grèce archaïque', in *Journal de Psychologie* (1948) pp. 29–50

3. Aristotle, *Politics* 3. 3. 2–4 [p. 1278 a] and 8. 2. 1–2 [p. 1337 b]

4. Plato, *Gorgias* 512 c; Xeno-phon, *Oeconomica* 4. 2–3

5. Xenophon, *Memorabilia* 2. 7

6. See the passage from Plu-tarch's *Life of Lycurgus* 24. 3, cited above, Chapter II, p. 53

7. Plutarch, *Life of Solon* 2. 5–7

8. Plutarch, *Life of Pericles* 2. 1

9. In his *Electra* Euripides draws Electra's *autourgos* husband as a highly sympathetic character

10. See the Budé edition of Isocrates, Vol. 1 p. xxxiii

11. Thucydides, 2. 40

12. Herodotus, 2. 167. Here I follow Chantraine's line: see his essay 'Trois noms grecs de l'arti-san' in *Mélanges offerts à Mgr Diès* (1956) pp. 41–7

13. See above, Chapter II, p. 53

14. Plutarch, *Life of Lycurgus* 9

15. Aeschylus, *Persians* 238

16. See J. Labarbe, *La Loi navale de Thémistocle* (1957) pp. 10–51

17. See L. Robert, *Etudes de numismatique grecque* (1951) pp. 105 ff.

18. M. N. Tod, *A Selection of Greek Historical Inscriptions*, I, No. 67; further copies of this decree have been found since. See J. and L. Robert in the *Bulletin Epigraphique* of *Rev. des Et. Gr.* Vol. 64 (1951) pp. 152–3, No. 70

19. Aristophanes, *Birds* 1040–1

20. Aristophanes, *Peace* 169–172; cf. P. Roussel's article, 'L'Amende de Chios', in the *Rev. des Et. Anc.* (1933) pp. 385–6

21. Aristophanes, *Women in Parliament* 815–22

22. For a description of funeral ceremonies, see above, pp. 80 ff.

23. See E. Bourguet's study, *L'Administration financière du sanctuaire pythique au IVe siècle*

24. Aristophanes, *Clouds* 16–18

25. See T. Homolle in *Bull. de Corr. Hell.* Vol. 50 (1926) p. 87

26. Xenophon, *Oeconomica* 5. 4–17

27. See P. Roussel, *Sparte* pp. 71–8

28. See above, Chapter I, p. 26

29. See above, Chapter I, p. 27

30. Cf. Glotz, *Le Travail* etc. p. 303

31. See P. Cloché, *Les Classes, les Métiers, Le Trafic* (1931) plate viii, 1

32. Cloché, *ibid.* pl. ix, 2

33. Cloché, *ibid.* plates xxiii, 2; x, 2

34. Cloché, *ibid.* plates xi and xii

35. Aristophanes, *Peace* 571–9; see above, p. 27

36. Aristophanes, *Peace* 253–4

37. Cloché, *ibid.* pl. xxxvii

38. Plato, *Republic* 2. 373 c

39. Aristophanes, *Peace* 374. See below, Chapter VIII

40. Aristophanes, *Clouds* 71–2

41. See L. Robert, *Hellenica* VII pp. 161–70

42. Cf. the extract from Xenophon's *Memorabilia* quoted above, p. 118

43. Glotz, *Le Travail*, etc. p. 315

44. Aristotle, *Constitution of Athens* 50. 2

45. Plutarch, *Life of Pericles* 12

46. See Cloché, *op. cit.* pl. xxi, 1. Among the apprentice vase-decorators in this painting, on the right-hand side, there is a young girl

47. Aristophanes, *Wasps* 100–2

48. Aristophanes, *Birds* 489–92

49. Aristophanes, *Peace* 13–14; cf. Athenaeus 548 c

50. See E. Ardaillon, *Les Mines du Laurion dans l'Antiquité* (1897), *passim*

51. For a general idea of these types see, eg, C. Dugas, *La Céramique grecque* (1924), the figures on pp. 8, 10, and 15

52. Cloché, *op. cit.* pl. xviii, 1

53. Tod, *op. cit.* II. 162

54. Cloché, *op. cit.* pl. xxiii, 1 and 3; pl. xxiv, 1 and 2

55. Cloché, *ibid.* pl. xxvi; xxvii, 3 and 4; cf. xxvii, 1

56. Cloché, *ibid.* pl. xxx, 2 and xxxi, 1

57. Xenophon, *Cyropaedia* 8. 2. 5

58. Cloché, *op. cit.* pl. xxviii, 1 and 2; xxix, 1, 2, and 5. A comparison with the spinning and weaving techniques employed in modern Greek villages is enlightening: see P. de la Coste-Messelière and G. de Miré, *Delphes* (1943) plates 9 and 11

59. Plato, *Republic* 4. 429 d–430 b

60. Theophrastus, *Characters* 10. 14

61. Cloché, *op. cit.* plates xxxii–xxxiv, xxxvi

62. Aristophanes, *Lysistrata* 457–8

63. Glotz, *Le Travail*, etc. pp. 345–6

64. Aristophanes, *Knights* 217–218

65. Aristophanes, *Acharnians* 870–80

66. On the *diolkos*, see *Bull. de Corr. Hell.* 81 (1957) pp. 526–8, and figs. 1–8; also G. Roux, *Pausanias en Corinthie* (1959) pp. 88–9 and figs. 2 and 3

67. Ps-Xenophon, *Constitution of Athens*, ch. 2

68. Tod, *op. cit.* II, 115 and 167

69. Demosthenes, *Against Leptines* 31–3

70. Plato, *Alcibiades* 131

71. In the *Iliad*, it is the 'sons of Asclepius', Machaon and Podalirius who care for the wounded. Cf. *Iliad* 11. 514, and *Odyssey* 17. 384

72. Herodotus, 3. 125–37

73. Louis Bourgey, *Observation et expérience chez les médecins de la collection hippocratique* (1953) p. 270. Cf. René Dumesnil's article on Hippocrates in *Lettres d'Humanité* III (1944) pp. 33–70; and the Hippocratic treatise *On Ancient Medicine* (trs. W. H. S. Jones and E. T. Withington, Loeb Classical Library)

74. Plato, *Republic* 3. 406 a–b

75. See L. Robert, *Hellenica* IX, pp. 25 ff.

76. Xenophon, *Anabasis* 3. 4. 30; 5. 5. 4; 7. 2. 6

77. Plato, *Phaedrus* 268 c

78. Aristophanes, *Thesmophoriazusae* 504

79. C. D. Buck, *The Greek Dialects* (Chicago, 1955) pp. 210–13

80. Plato, *Gorgias* 455 b

81. Aristophanes, *Women in Parliament* 363–4

82. Plato, *Theaetetus* 149 a ff.

83. Euripides, *Hippolytus* 293–296

CHAPTER SIX, DRESS AND TOILET

1. Xenophon, *Symposium* 2

2. Athenaeus 13. 590 f. Here and in what follows I am much indebted to the forthcoming work by R. Ginouvès entitled *Balneutiké: Recherches sur le bain dans l'Antiquité grecque*. The author was kind enough both to allow me access to his manuscript and to let me utilize his findings: I am most grateful for his generosity

3. See J. Jannoray, *Le gymnase de Delphes* (1953) pp. 61 ff.

4. Aristophanes, *Clouds* 991 and 1045 ff.

5. Athenaeus, 12. 519 E

6. Aristophanes, *Birds* 1282

7. Plutarch, *Life of Phocion* 4

8. Aristophanes, *Plutus* 535; see above, Chapter I, p. 15

9. Aristophanes, *Acharnians* 17–19; *Frogs* 709–12

10. Theocritus, Idyll 15 ('The Syracusan Women') line 30, and P. E. Legrand's note *ad loc.*

11. Plato, *Symposium* 174 a

12. See the quotation from Lysias, *On the Refusal of a Pension to the Invalid* 20, as cited above, Chapter I, p. 8

13. Cf. Aristophanes, *Women in Parliament* 12–13

14. *Ibid.* 65, 68–72; *Thesmophoriazusae* 215–18. Cf. P. Lévêque, *Agathon* (1955) p. 39

15. Thucydides, 1. 6

16. Theophrastus, *Characters* 10

17. Cf. Charbonneaux, *op. cit.* I, pl. 69

18. Cf. *Bull. Corr. Hell.* Vol. 80 (1956) p. 237, fig. 6

19. Xenophon, *Oeconomica* 10

20. Aristotle, *Hist. Anim.* 5. 9. 11

21. Herodotus 3. 47, 106

22. L. Heuzey, *Histoire du Costume antique* ... (1922) p. 5

23. Plutarch, *Life of Cleomenes* 37. 2

24. Cf. Charbonneaux, *op. cit.* I, pl. 62

25. Hesiod, *Works and Days* 344

26. Cf. C. Dugas and R. Flacelière, *Thésée, Images et Récits* (1958) pl. 9; see, too, the young Troilus on another cup by Euphronius, in E. Pottier, *Douris* etc. p. 89, fig. 18

27. F. Chamoux, *L'Aurige de Delphes* (1955) p. 51

28. Cf. Heuzey, *op. cit.* pp. 80–4

29. See Cloché, *op. cit.* plates xxiv B and xxx B

30. Plutarch, *Life of Lycurgus* 16. 12

31. Cf. Ollier, *Le Mirage Spartiate* I, pp. 172–3 and 184–5

32. Xenophon, *Memorabilia* 1. 6

33. Aristophanes, *Birds* 1568–1569; cf. F. Robert in *Rev. des Et. Gr.* Vol. 70 (1957) pp. xvi–xvii

34. Plato, *Theaetetus* 175 e

35. Aeschines, *Against Timarchus* 25

36. Cf. Heuzey, *op. cit.* p. 102, fig. 53; with which we may compare the statue of Demosthenes shown *ibid.*, p. 30, fig. 19

37. Aristophanes, *Women in Parliament* 266–7

38. Lycurgus, *Against Leocrates* 40

39. Cf. Charbonneaux, *op. cit.* I, pl. 64

40. Plutarch, *Alcibiades* 1. 39

41. Aristophanes, *Women in Parliament* 311–32

42. See above, Chapter III, p. 76

43. Plutarch, *Comparison of Lycurgus and Numa* 3. 6–7

44. Heuzey, *op. cit.* p. 156

45. Charbonneaux, *op. cit.* I, pl. 46

46. *Ibid.* pl. 83

47. Herodotus 5. 87–8

48. Charbonneaux, *op. cit.* I, pl. 41

49. See the alabaster vase by Pasiades, reproduced in Heuzey, *op. cit.*, pl. v, opposite p. 220

50. Cf. Charbonneaux, *op. cit.*

II, pl. 104, and E. Pottier, *Diphilos et les modeleurs de terres cuites grecques* (1909), *passim*

51. Plato, *Letter* 13, 363 a

52. Euripides, *Medea* 1156–66: on the final verse, see the note *ad loc.* in Weil's edition

53. See Charbonneaux, *op. cit.* II, pl. 57

54. See, eg, E. Pottier, *Diphilos et les modeleurs de terres cuites grecques*, pl. xii; P. Guillon, *La Béotie antique* (1948), pl. xxi

55. See above, Chapter V, p. 134

56. Xenophon, *Hellenica* 2. 3. 30–1

57. Herodas, *Mimes* 7. 56–85 (with omissions)

58. Herodotus 3. 12

59. See, eg, the funerary stele in Guillon, *op. cit.* pl. xxiv

60. Plato, *Republic* 3. 406 d

61. See Flacelière, 'Le bonnet de Solon', in *Rev. des. Et. anc.* Vol. 49 (1947) pp. 235–47

CHAPTER SEVEN, FOOD, GAMES AND RECREATION

1. Aristophanes, *Women in Parliament*, 651–2

2. Eubulus, ed. Kock, *Comicorum Atticorum Fragmenta*, fr. 119, *ap.* Athenaeus 1. 8 b–c

3. See Guillon, *op. cit.* pp. 79–92

4. Plato, *Republic* 2. 372 b

5. Aristophanes, *Frogs* 62–3

6. Aristophanes, *Peace* 529, 1127–9

7. Aristophanes, *Peace* 374

8. See Flacelière, 'Thémistocle, les Erétriens et le calmar', in *Rev. des Et. anc.* Vol. 50 (1948) pp. 211–17

9. Plato, *Gorgias* 518 b

10. Plutarch, *Life of Lycurgus* 12, 13

11. See A. Delatte, *Le cycéon* (1955) p. 27, citing Aristophanes, *Peace* 712 and 1169, and Theophrastus, *Characters* 4. 2–3

12. Plutarch, *Life of Lycurgus* 9. 8

13. See *Inscr. Gr.* XII, suppl. 347, i, and, most recently, J. Pouilleux, *Recherches sur l'Histoire*

et les cultes de Thasos (1954) pp. 37–45

14. Homer, *Iliad* 9. 202–3

15. See Aristophanes, *Peace* 1136, and P. Mazon's note *ad loc.* in his edition

16. Plato, *Symposium* 201 d–e; see here the introduction to L. Robin's edition, pp. xxii–xxvii

17. Plutarch, *Quaest. Conviv.* 3. 1 (647 E)

18. Athenaeus, 2. 66 c–d

19. Plato, *Symposium* 176 a

20. *Ibid.* 176 d–177 c

21. *Ibid.* 212 c–e

22. On this passage, and the various types of *psyktér*, see G. Daux in *Rev. des Et. Gr.* Vol. 55 (1942) pp. 268–9

23. See the interesting article by P. Boyancé, 'Platon et le vin', in *Lettres d'humanité, Supplément au Bulletin de l'Ass. G. Budé*, Vol. 10 (1951) pp. 3–19

24. Plato, *Symposium* 223 b

25. Xenophon, *Symposium* 1

26. Such *thymiatéria* frequently appear in vase-paintings: see, eg,

H. Metzger *Les représentations dans la céramique attique du IVe siècle*, plates i, 1 and ii, 2. On a somewhat specialized use of perfume see Aristophanes, *Lysistrata* 938–47

27. Xenophon, *Symposium* 7–9
28. See Girard, *L'Education athénienne* p. 182
29. Xenophon, *Hellenica* 2. 3. 56
30. So F. Chapouthier, in *Syria* Vol. 31 (1954) p. 199, citing the Ovidian elegiac poem *Nux*; but this game is attested as early as the Greek classical epoch, and Chapouthier refers to a late fifth century Attic vase (fig. 16, p. 200) on which he claims to have identified a scene with three small children playing it
31. See Jean Taillardat, *Rev. des. Et. anc.* Vol. 58 (1956) p. 191; this game was known as *ostrakinda*
32. See A. Gardner in *Journ. Hell. Stud.* Vol. 43 (1923) pp. 142–3, and Picard, *La vie privée*, etc. pl. lviii
33. Picard, *ibid.* pl. lix, fig. 1
34. See H. Jeanmaire, *Dionysos* p. 42
35. Picard, *op. cit.* pl. xlvii, fig. 3
36. See Picard, *La Sculpture antique* I, p. 397, fig. 119
37. Plato, *Lysis* 206 e
38. See P. Wuilleumier in *Istros*, Vol. 1 (1934) pp. 14–18: 'Dé à jouer de Tarente'
39. Aeschylus, *Agamemnon* 32–33
40. See Taillardat, *ibid.* p. 193
41. See, eg, *Odyssey* 1. 107. On the dubious *naumachia* see H. van

Effenterre in *Bull. Corr. Hell.* Vol. 79 (1955) pp. 541–8
42. Thucydides, 2. 38
43. See E. Delebecque, *Essai sur la vie de Xénophon*, pp. 173–81
44. See Cloché, *op. cit.* p. 24 fig. 9, and pl. xiv, fig. 5
45. P. Chantraine, *Etudes sur le vocabulaire grec* (1956) p. 64
46. Chantraine, *ibid.* p. 84
47. Cloché, *op. cit.* pl. xv and text; cf. Aristotle, *Hist. Nat.* 8. 28. See also Cloché *ibid.* pl. xvi
48. Plato, *Laws* 823 e
49. Plutarch, *De sollertia animalium* 9
50. Cloché, *op. cit.* pl. xvii, fig. 7
51. Louis Robert, *Hellenica* X, p. 272
52. Oppian, *Halieutica* 4. 640–646; cf. F. Vian in *Revue de Philologie* Vol. 28 (1954) pp. 50–1
53. Cf. Stratis Myrivilis' nove! ἡ παναγία ἡ γοργόνα, translated into English as *The Mermaid Madonna*. The present translator can vouch for the accuracy of this statement: at Mytilene or Methymna, about six o'clock in the evening, the night fishing-boats regularly set out, each with its bright lantern, and can be seen far out in the bay or the Turkish channel during the night. Occasionally the lantern-technique is used close inshore for attracting feeding shoals, or lobsters
54. See above, pp. 154–8 and 181
55. See Carl Sittl, *Die Gebärden der Griechen und Römer* (Leipzig, 1890) pp. 78–81
56. See especially Plato, *Laws* 3. 700 c

57. See above, p. 155

58. See Mazon's note to line 549 of his edition of Aristophanes' *Peace*

59. Theophrastus, *Characters* 16. 14

60. See the account of Socrates' last hours in Plato, *Phaedo* 117 c and 118 a

61. Lucian, *On Funerals* 12

62. See above, Chapter III, p. 82

CHAPTER EIGHT, RELIGIOUS LIFE AND THE THEATRE

1. See P. Decharme's work *La critique des traditions religieuses chez les Grecs*, which, despite its age, still retains nearly all its interest and value today

2. A more recent demonstration of the same point has been made by E. R. Dodds, in *The Greeks and the Irrational* (Sather Classical Lectures, Vol. 25, Univ. of California Press, 1951)

3. An excellent analysis of the semantics of *thambos* has been made by A. J. Festugière in *Histoire générale des religions, Grèce-Rome* (1944) pp. 41-2

4. Alfred de Musset, the opening lines of *Rolla*

5. For the Sophists see above, Chapter IV, pp. 112 ff.

6. Plutarch, *Life of Pericles* 38, based on Theophrastus' treatise *On Ethics*

7. See Victor Goldschmidt's study, *La religion de Platon* (1949)

8. Cf. Festugière, *Epicure et ses Dieux* (English translation, *Epicurus and his Gods*, published Oxford 1955)

9. See E. Derenne, *Les Procès d'impiété intentés aux philosophes à Athènes au Vᵉ et au IVᵉ siècle avant Jésus-Christ* (Liège 1930)

10. Martin P. Nilsson, *La religion populaire dans la Grèce antique* (1954) pp. 6-7

11. Homer, *Iliad* 1. 37-42

12. For the *suovetaurilia* see, eg, *Odyssey* 11. 130-1

13. The Fathers of the Church professed astonishment that 'the gods, who had the opportunity to feed off nectar and ambrosia, should be so delighted by the unpleasant stench of burnt bones'. (Theodoretus of Cyrus, *Graecarum Affectionum Curatio* [*Therapeutikē*] 12. 73)

14. See Moulinier, *Le Pur et l'Impur*, etc. *passim*, and for apotropaic spitting in particular, p. 74

15. See above, Chapter III, p. 82

16. For this act of enfranchisement see *Griech. Dial. Inschr.*, Delphi, 1807; cf. L. Lerat, in *Revue de Philologie* (1943) p. 82

17. See above, Chapter VII, pp. 184-5

18. See above, Chapter IV, pp. 105-6

19. The essential study is that by L. Deubner, *Attische Feste* (Berlin 1932)

20. Aristophanes, *Clouds* 615-622

21. This type of race appears to have been extremely popular, and

was also included in the festivals of Hephaestus, Prometheus, and Pan. See Marie Delcourt, *Hephaistos, ou la légende du magicien* (Bibl. Fac. Phil. et Lettres de Liège, Fasc. 146, 1957) pp. 200–3

22. Plutarch, *Life of Theseus* 22

23. Ie, boys whose father and mother were both still alive: see above, Chapter III, p. 63

24. I find it very probable (despite Jeanmaire's reservations in his *Dionysos*, p. 486) that the Oschaphoria was, in fact, a vintage festival

25. See Aristophanes' play the *Thesmophoriazusae*

26. See Theodoretus, *op. cit.* 12. 73

27. See Delcourt, *op. cit.* pp. 195–200

28. C. Michel, *Recueil d'Inscr. gr.* Nos. 1597 (dedicatory) and 1820 (epitaph). The *thiasos* was a religious association which might also bring together members of the same trade or profession

29. Cf. the reproduction of this *peliké* from London in Deubner, *op. cit.* pl. 3, fig. 3

30. See Aristophanes, *Acharnians* 247–62

31. Tod, *op. cit.* I. 44, 1, 11–13

32. See above, Chapter VII, pp. 182–3

33. See Jeanmaire, *op. cit.* pp. 44–7

34. Aristophanes, *Acharnians* 504–8

35. See above, Chapter IV, pp. 90–1

36. See Jeanmaire, *op. cit.* pp. 48–56

37. See J. and G. Roux, *Grèce* (1957) plates at pp. 74–5 and 104–5

38. See E. Canac, 'L'acoustique des théâtres antiques', in *La Revue scientifique* (May 1951) pp. 151–69

39. See above, Chapter III, p. 171

40. See above, Chapter VII, p. 189

41. Plato, *Laws* 3. 701 a

42. See above, Chapter IV, p. 103

43. Plutarch, *Life of Cimon* 10; cf. above, Chapter I, p. 25

44. Plutarch, *Life of Nicias* 3

45. For this use of the *skénai* see L. Robert, *Le sanctuaire de Sinuri*, p. 50, and *Hellenica* X, p. 287, where the resemblance to the Turkish *çardak* is noted: in Arab countries, Egypt in particular, marriages and other such ceremonies furnish an occasion for erecting large marquees, in which the guests are entertained

46. Cf. Andocides 4. 29–30, and Isocrates, *De Bigis, passim*; see also Jean Hatzfeld, *Alcibiade* pp. 130–1 and 139–40

47. See above, Chapter IV, pp. 105–7

48. Plato, *Apologia* 36 d

49. See above, p. 199

50. For the bath of Phryne, see above, Chapter VI, p. 145

51. See Delatte, *Le cycéon* (1955), and above, Chapter VII, p. 171

52. See M. P. Nilsson, *Les croyances religieuses de la Grèce antique* (1955) p. 179

53. Plato, *Republic* 2. 364–5 a

54. Moulinier, *Orphée et l'Orphisme à l'époque classique* (1955) pp. 115–16

55. C. Michel, *Recueil d'Inscriptions grecques*, No. 1330

56. See Plutarch, *Life of Pericles* 6, where we find the birth of a one-horned ram on one of Pericles' farms being interpreted differently by Lampon the seer and the philosopher Anaxagoras–both of them personal friends of the Athenian statesman

57. Homer, *Odyssey* 17. 541–6

58. Xenophon, *Anabasis* 3. 2. 9

59. Plutarch, *De sollertia animalium* 22

60. Euripides, *Electra* 826–33

61. This emphasis on the liver in divination had two important consequences. It brought about an early familiarity with the anatomy of this particular organ, and also had a direct influence on both Plato's and Aristotle's theories concerning divination – besides, in a more general way, modifying their physiological doctrines

62. For further details see, eg, Festugière in *Histoire générale des religions, Grèce-Rome*, pp. 128–36

63. Cf. also Socrates' prediction to his judges after they had condemned him: Plato, *Apologia* 39 c

64. Lucian, *Bis Accusatus* 1

65. See in particular P. Amandry, *La Mantique apollinienne à Delphes* (1950); R. Flacelière, 'Le délire de la Pythie est-il une légende?' in *Rev. des Et. anc.* Vol. 52 (1950) pp. 306–24; Marie Delcourt, *L'Oracle de Delphes*; (1955) and H. W. Parke

and D. E. Wormell, *The Delphic Oracle* (2 vols., Oxford, 1956)

66. This 'goat-test' is referred to only by Plutarch, writing in the second century AD, but was, in all probability, employed from the classical period onwards. If the she-goat remained motionless when douched with cold water, it might prove dangerous – or even fatal – to the Pythia to prophesy in this particular instance. Cf. Plutarch, *De Defectu Oraculorum* 51

67. On the influence exercised by Delphi see especially J. Defradas, *Les thèmes de la propagande delphique* (1954)

68. The Choes, or Feast of Pots, was the second day of the Anthestéria: see above, p. 202. Laurel, like sea-water and garlic, which are subsequently mentioned, was regarded as possessing purificatory qualities

69. A bad omen – like an owl's hoot or some object gnawed by mice, both of which are referred to later

70. A foreign god of Thracian origin, whose cult, like that of Bendis, entered Greece at least as early as the fifth century: the serpent is one of his regular attributes

71. The reference here is to 'betyls', the sacred stones of Apollo Agyieus, which, like the Delphic *omphalos*, were adorned with bunches of woollen ribbons (see above, p. 221), and anointed with oil

72. The *exegétés* was an official diviner who ranked, at Athens, as

a magistrate: see James H. Oliver, *The Athenian Expounders of the Sacred and Ancestral Law* (Baltimore, 1950)

73. Cf. Bion Borysthenites, fr. 45: 'What is surprising about a starving rat gnawing holes in your sack? The really surprising thing, as Arcesilas once said by way of a jest, would be if the sack devoured the rat'

74. Goddess of nocturnal apparitions and every kind of sorcery: see below, pp. 224-5

75. Days regarded as unlucky (*apophrades*)

76. They may be associated with Hermes: the text here is doubtful

77. 'It was customary to leave Hecate food-offerings at crossroads. These would in due course go bad. What we have to do with here, in my opinion, are garbagemen whose task it was to clear away such detritus: a superstitious person would regard himself as defiled if he encountered one of them.' (O. Navarre's note *ad loc.* in his edition of the *Characters*)

78. Theophrastus, *Characters* 16

79. Menander, fr. 109

80. Fustel de Coulanges, *La Cité antique* (15th ed., 1895) p. 264, citing Thucydides, Book VII, and Plutarch, *Life of Nicias* 23

81. Plato, *Gorgias* 513 a

82. Pindar, *Pythian Odes* 4. 213-16

83. Milligen, *Peinture de vases antiques* pl. xlv; cf. de La Genière's article cited in n. 84 below

84. J. de La Genière, 'Une roue à oiseaux du cabinet des médailles', in *Rev. des Et. anc.* vol. 60 (1958) pp. 27-35. [See also the very detailed account by A. S. F. Gow, '*Iynx, Rhombos,* Rhombos and Turbo', in *Journ. Hell. Stud.* vol. 54 (1934) pp. 1 ff., and the same scholar's notes *ad loc.* in his Commentary on Theocritus, Vol. 2, pp. 33 ff. Flacelière's text appears to identify the *iynx* with the *rhombos*, as do most older commentaries; but there can be no doubt, in the light of Gow's note (p. 44) and the references there cited, that the *rhombos* was a *bull-roarer*: cf. Gow's plates IV (A) and V. In the circumstances I have, on this one occasion, taken the liberty of very slightly modifying the text in translation. (Trs.)]

85. See C. Michel, *Recueil d'Inscriptions grecques*, Nos. 1319-25, and L. Robert, *Collection Froehner* I, Nos. 11-12. [For further literature on the curse-tablets see A. Audollent, *Defixionum Tabellae* (Paris 1904); R. Wuensch, *Defixionum Tabellae Atticarum* (Berlin 1897) and the same author's *Antike Fluchtafeln* (2nd ed. 1912)]

CHAPTER NINE, LAW AND JUSTICE

1. Thucydides 1. 130-4

2. Aristophanes, *Wasps* 549 and 620

3. Jérôme Carcopino, *L'Ost-* *racisme athénien* (2nd ed. 1935) p. 5

4. See above, Chapter VIII, pp. 200-3

5. Philochorus, fr. 79 b

6. See Carcopino, *op. cit.* plates i, ii, and iii. More recently discovered *ostraka* have been published in the periodical *Hesperia*. The total number of known *ostraka* in 1952 was 1650: see A. E. Raubitschek, in *Actes du IIᵉ Congrès international d'épigraphie gr. et lat.*, p. 62

7. See the anecdote related by Plutarch on the subject of Aristides' ostracism, referred to above, Chapter IV, p. 93

8. Plutarch, *Life of Aristides* 7. According to Philochorus, the figure of 6000 did not refer to a minimum quorum of voters, but was the minimum number of votes that must be cast against any individual to secure his banishment. Carcopino prefers Philochorus' version to that of Plutarch, but the problem remains undecided

9. Glotz, *La Cité grecque* p. 275 [See also now D. M. MacDowell's admirable monograph *Athenian Homicide Law* (Manchester University Press, 1963)]

10. Xenophon, *Hellenica* 1. 7

11. See above, Chapter II, pp. 38–9

12. See above, Chapter II, p. 38

13. The passage concerned is §§63–5 of the *Constitution of Athens*. The two articles by Ster-

ling Dow to which I refer are: 'Allotment Machines', in *Hesperia*, Suppl. I, (1937) pp. 198–215; and 'Aristotle, the Kléroteria and the Courts', in *Harvard Studies in Classical Philology*, vol. 50 (1939) pp. 1–34

14. See Aristophanes, *Wasps* 219, 248, 257

15. Dareste, *Plaidoyers civils de Démosthène*, p. 17

16. Aristophanes, *Peace* 452

17. Aeschylus, *Eumenides* 185–190

18. The study by Keramopoullos (ὁ ἀποτυμπανισμός) was published in 1923: cf. L. Gernet's article 'Sur l'exécution capitale', in *Rev. des Et. gr.* vol. 37 (1924) pp. 261–93

19. Herodotus, 7. 33

20. Plutarch, *Life of Pericles* 28

21. Aristophanes, *Thesmophoriazusae* 930–1014

22. Aristophanes, *Knights* 1037–49

23. Gernet, *op. cit.* pp. 264–5

24. See Kurt Latte's article in Paully-Wissowa, suppl. VII, under the heading 'Todesstrafe', cols. 1606–8

25. Plato, *Republic* 4. 439 e

26. Herodotus 9. 5

27. See Glotz, *La Solidarité de la famille dans le droit criminel en Grèce* (Paris 1904) pp. 406 ff., and *passim*.

28. Plato, *Phaedo* 118 a

CHAPTER TEN, WARFARE

1. See the remarkable monograph by Jacqueline de Romilly, *Thucydide et l'Impérialisme athén-* *ien* (1947) [now published in English translation (1963) as *Thucydides and Athenian Im-*

perialism]; also Albert Thibaudet's stimulating book *La campagne avec Thucydide* (1922)

2. See above, Chapter V, pp. 139–41

3. See J. Labarbe, *La loi navale de Thémistocle* (1957)

4. See above, Chapter IV, pp. 84 ff.

5. Plutarch, *Life of Lycurgus* 24

6. Xenophon, *Polity of the Lacedaemonians* 11. 5–10; see F. Ollier's edition and commentary, pp. 57–62, illustrated by sketches which clarify the problem remarkably

7. Herodotus, 7. 208. This was undoubtedly a ritual act, which we find in other contexts: cf. the opening of the 'Song of Deborah', *Judges* 5. 2, which means 'the warriors in Israel have undone their hair', ie prepared themselves for the fray. The Beduins still perform this custom before going into battle

8. Herodotus, 9. 28

9. Xenophon, *Hellenica* 6. 4. 15

10. See L. Lacroix, 'Le bouclier, emblème des Béotiens' in *Revue belge de phil. et d'hist.* vol. 36 (1958) pp. 5–30, and plates ii–iv

11. Plutarch, *Amatorius* 761 B. According to Marrou, *op. cit.* p. 57, Greek pederasty was, fundamentally, a comradeship between warriors. See above, Chapter IV, pp. 109–10

12. See above, Chapter IV, pp. 91 ff.

13. Xenophon, *Hellenica* 6. 1. 5

14. Aristotle, *Constitution of Athens* 53. 4, where the forty-two eponyms of the military call-up classes are carefully distinguished from those of the ten tribes

15. Thucydides, 2. 13; cf. Glotz and Cohen, *Histoire grecque*, II, pp. 223 f.

16. Aristophanes, *Wasps* 578, where the heliast Philocleon says: 'When the young men come up for inspection, we get a good chance to look at their private parts'

17. See L. Robert, *Etudes épigr. et phil.* (1938) pp. 296–307

18. Aristotle, *Constitution of Athens* 42. 3

19. See above, Chapter VI, pp. 155–6 and for the colour, P. Roussel, 'Les chlamydes noires des éphèbes athéniens', in *Rev. des Et. anc.* Vol. 43 (1941) pp. 163–5

20. Aristotle, *Constitution of Athens* 42. 3

21. A. Martin, *Les Cavaliers athéniens* (Paris 1887) p. 327

22. Aristotle, *Constitution of Athens* 42. 4

23. See L. Robert, 'Péripolarques', *Hellenica* X, pp. 283–92

24. J. Pouilloux, *La Forteresse de Rhamnonte* (1954) pp. 81–2

25. Eg, the hoplite Aristion, see J. and C. Roux, *Grèce* (1957) pl. 80; the scene of the warrior's departure, see C. Dugas, *Aison* fig. 3; and various illustrations in P. Couissin's *Les Institutions militaires et navales*, plates vii–xxi. For a more remote period it is interesting to compare P. Courbin, *Bull. de Corr. Hell.* Vol. 81 (1957) pp. 322–86, plates i–iii

26. See Aristophanes, *Peace* 303 and 1172–8

27. See above, Chapter IV, p. 107

28. Herodotus, 6. 112

29. A. Plassart, 'Les Archers d'Athènes', in *Rev. des Et. gr.* Vol. 26 (1913) p. 202

30. Plassart, *ibid.* pp. 187–95

31. Glotz and Cohen, *Histoire grecque*, II, pp. 343–4

32. Xenophon, *On Horsemanship* (ed. Delebecque 1950) ch. 12

33. See H. Bengtson, 'Aus der Lebengeschichte eines griechischen Distanzlaüfers', in *Symbolae Osloenses* Vol. 32 (1956) pp. 35–9

34. See Aeschylus, *Agamemnon* 8 ff., and especially Thucydides 2. 94. 1

35. Herodotus, 9. 61–2

36. Plutarch, *Life of Theseus*, 35

37. Cf. G. C. Picard, *Les Trophées romains* (1957), esp. pp. 13–64 on 'Le trophée grec'

38. Plutarch, *On the Pythian Oracles* 15

39. Aristophanes, *Peace* 528–9

40. See the bas-relief referred to by G. Fougère, *Athènes* p. 143, and for inscriptions, Tod, *op. cit.* II, 104 and 105

41. Plato, *Symposium* 221 a–b. The line quoted from Aristophanes, who was himself present at this banquet, is *Clouds* 362

42. See Pouilloux, *op. cit.* pp. 9–66

43. Aeschines, *On the Embassy* 115

44. Aeneas Tacticus has been included in the Loeb Classical Library (ed. and translation by the Illinois Greek Club). For the part played by the dogs in sieges, see P. Roussel in *Rev. des Et. gr.* Vol. 43 (1930) pp. 361–71

45. Plutarch, *Life of Themistocles* 4: Plato and other philosophers regarded the existence of a navy as harmful to the State

46. See above, Chapter V, pp. 122 and 181–2

47. See Labarbe, *La loi navale de Thémistocle* (1957) p. 42

48. On the merchant marine, see above, Chapter V, pp. 37 ff.

49. See plates xxvii–xxix of Couissin's book *Les Institutions militaires et navales*

50. Couissin, *ibid.* pp. 97–8

51. Thucydides, 2. 93

52. See above, Chapter VIII, pp. 209–10

53. Thucydides 6. 30–2. 2

54. It was the 'Paralia' which brought the news of the Aegos-Potami [Goat River] disaster to Athens in 404: see Xenophon, *Hellenica* 2. 2. 3

55. Xenophon, *Hellenica* 6. 2. 27–30

56. Plutarch, *Life of Lycurgus* 27. 2–3; cf. R. Flacelière in *Rev. des Et. gr.* Vol. 61 (1948) pp. 403–5

57. Thucydides 2. 34

58. See Tod, *op. cit.* I, 48 and 59

59. Aeschines, *Against Ctesiphon* 154

60. Plutarch, *Life of Solon* 31

61. Aristotle, *Constitution of Athens* 49. 4

62. Thucydides 5. 84–116

63. Glotz and Cohen, *Histoire grecque* III, p. 42

A SUMMING UP

1. Picard, *La vie privée*, etc. p. 97

2. *Ibid.*

3. Nikos Kazantzakis, *Du Mont Sinaï à l'île de Vénus, Carnets de Voyage* (French translation, Paris 1958), pp. 205–6. [Ideally, this passage should have been translated from the original modern Greek text; but – somewhat paradoxically – I have been unable to locate a copy on the Greek island where I live. (Trs.)]

4. The title of a book by F. Ollier on the romanticization of Sparta.

5. See Defradas, *Les thèmes de la propagande delphique*, pp. 268–283

6. See A. Diès, *Platon* (1930)

7. See R. A. Gauthier, *Mag-*

nanimité, *l'idéal de la grandeur dans la philosophie païenne et dans la théologie chrétienne* (1951)

8. See above, Chapter VIII, pp. 191 ff., 221 ff.

9. A. J. Festugière, 'Sur une épitaphe de Simonide', in *La Vie intellectuelle*, 25th January 1937, p. 302

10. *Iliad* 24. 529 ff. See R. Flacelière, *Homère* (1955) Introduction, pp. 47–50

11. Theognis 425–8

12. This is the implied conclusion to be drawn from the story of the Argive twins, Cleobis and Biton, whose statues have been discovered during excavations at Delphi: see Herodotus 1. 31.

13. Euripides fr. 449

INDEX

abortion, 77–8
Academy, the, 9, 22
Acropolis, the, 3–6, 9, 10, 198–9, 272
Acheloüs, river, 2
Achon, 103
adultery, 65
Aegean Sea, 1–2
Aegina, currency of, 121
Aeschines, 16, 238
Aeschylus, 180, 193, 273; on nurses, 88; on pederasty, 109; on necromancy, 223; on punishment, 240–1
Agathon, 176–7
aged, care of, 80, 119
Agesilaus, 218
Agora, the: as a public centre, 4–5, 35, 184; the buildings, 6–8, 10; the markets, 135–6, 170; the voting place for ostracism, 227
Agoranomoi, 11, 39
agriculture, 3, 26–8, 124–8
Agryle, 5
Alcé, 76
Alcibiades: his house, 19–20; with Socrates, 111; in Plato's *Symposium*, 176–7; his munificence, 210, 211; on Socrates at Delium, 261; as a naval commander, 267
Alexander the Great, 218
aliens, *see* Metics
Alpheus, river, 2
ambassadors, 36–7
Ammon, sanctuary of, 12
Amorgos linen, 160
Amphiarius, sanctuary of, 12
Amphidromia, the, 79
Amphyctionic money, 123
amphorae, 172
Anacreon, 119, 180
Anaxagoras, 44, 193
anklets, 161
Anthestéria, festival of, 202–3

Antimoerus of Mende, 114
Antisthenes, 178
Anytus, 124
Apaturia, festival of, 200
Apelles, 145
Aphrodite, 195
Apodektai, 39
Apollo, 194, 196, 199, 203, 220
Apollo Patröus, temple, 7
Apollo Zôster, sanctuary of, 16
Apothetae, 78
applause, 189–90
apprenticeship, 130
archers, 254–5; *see also* Scythian
Archilocus, 119
architecture, 9–13, 17–19, 272
military, 261–2
archons, 11, 39–40, 227–8, 232–9
King, 40, 205–8, 231
War, 254
Areopagus, council of, 11, 226, 230
Ares, temple of, 7
Ardettus, Mount, 4
areté, 113
Arginusae, battle of, 38, 40
Aristodemus, 176
Aristogiton, 110
Aristophanes: on the Assembly, 33–7; baby-care, 89; the calendar, 198; cavalry, 256; children's games, 90, 91; clothes, 154; country life, 27–8; currency, 122; education, 22, 93; food, 127; housing, 17–18; jurymen, 238–9; justice, 226; the Lenaea, 202; literacy, 93; poverty, 15; punishment, 241; razors, 149; religion, 193; robbery, 24; shopkeepers, 136, 137; singing, 101; slaves, 52; Socrates, 114; timekeeping, 167–8; usury, 123; women, 68–71, 72–3
Aristotle: on abortion, 77; athletics, 108; children's games, 90;

**PHOENIX
PRESS**

GENERAL EDITORS:
SIMON SCHAMA AND ANTONIA FRASER

*Phoenix Press publishes and re-publishes hundreds of the very best new
and out of print books about the past. For a free colour catalogue listing
more than 500 titles please*

telephone: +44 (0) 1903 828 503
fax: +44 (0) 1903 828 802
e-mail: mailorder@lbsltd.co.uk
or visit our website at www.phoenixpress.co.uk

*The Phoenix Press Daily Life Series is a collection of popular social histories which
vividly re-create the manners, morals, and everyday life of peoples living in another
civilization, another age.*

Daily Life in Palestine at the Time of Christ

HENRI DANIEL-ROPS

"The wealth of information in this book about customs, language,
habits, clothes, food and all the other features of everyday life will
make the reading of the New Testament far more real and vivid"
The Times

Paperback
UK: £12.99   512pp + 24pp b/w   1 84212 509 5
USA: $19.95
CAN: $29.95

Daily Life of the Aztecs

JACQUES SOUSTELLE

A vivid account of the fierce, honourable, death-obsessed, profoundly religious Aztecs on the eve of the Spanish conquest. Even
in the darkest symbolism of their blood-drenched worship they
appear as people with whom we can sympathise. "It is, without
question, the most brilliant, the clearest and most readable
portrayal of Aztec life available in any language" *Observer*

Paperback
UK: £12.99   352pp + 24pp b/w   1 84212 508 7
USA: $19.95
CAN: $29.95

Daily Life of the Etruscans

JACQUES HEURGON

On the evidence of their brilliantly evocative wall paintings, terracottas, bronzes and jewellery, the Etruscans appear to have had a tremendous zest for life with a fondness for dancing, horse-racing, every form of musical activity and sooth saying. ". . . the high literary intelligence informing it makes the book a most desirable companion to the more purely archaeological works which have been appearing of late" *Sunday Times*. "The best popular book yet published about those mysterious people" *New Yorker*

Paperback
UK: £12.99   352pp + 24pp b/w   1 84212 592 3
USA: $19.95
CAN: $29.95

Life and Leisure in Ancient Rome

J.P.V.D. BALSDON

What did a Roman citizen do between getting up in the morning and going to bed at night? Dr Balsdon uses a wide variety of sources to answer this and many other questions about what life was like in Ancient Rome. "Precise, detailed, and reliable, and informed throughout with a genuine sense of what it all felt like . . . By far the best single volume on its subject" *Guardian*

Paperback
UK: £12.99   464pp + 16pp b/w   1 84212 593 1
USA: $19.95
CAN: $29.95

Daily Life in Ancient India

JEANNINE AUBOYER

Throughout *Daily Life in Ancient India*, Jeannine Auboyer evokes the fascinating complexities of India's ancient epoch, with its caste system, its endless ritual, and the ceremonial nature of human relations – even in matters of love. Here is the perfect introduction to one of the world's most noble and refined civilizations.

Paperback
UK: £12.99   352pp + 24pp b/w   1 84212 591 5
USA: $19.95
CAN: $29.95